DANISH SETTLEMENTS IN WEST AFRICA
1658-1850

GEORG NØRREGÅRD

Danish Settlements
in West Africa

1658-1850

Translated by Sigurd Mammen

BOSTON UNIVERSITY PRESS • 1966
Boston, Massachusetts

Translated from "De Danske Etablissementer
Paa Guineakysten" in *Vore Gamle Tropekolonier,*

© Copyright 1954 by Hassing Publishers Ltd.

Translation © Copyright 1966 by the
Trustees of Boston University

Library of Congress Catalog Card Number 66-21611
PRINTED IN THE UNITED STATES OF AMERICA

Preface to American Edition

IN THE HISTORIES of overseas countries the enterprise of great European colonial powers often plays an important part. Portuguese, Spanish, French, Dutch, and English sea travels and trading companies are dealt with in numerous books. The contributions to colonial history made by present-day smaller powers is not so well known. Few historians have studied this subject, and their books are not always available in English. Still, the archives of the smaller nations are often as rich as those of the great powers, and their reporters can be as well informed as those from London or Paris.

One of the aims of this book is to compare material from the State Archives of Copenhagen with manuscripts and books from other countries. A colourful series of events can be followed in its pages. Sometimes these events seem to be only of local or special interest, but in many cases they are details in a wider context. Often the fate of Europeans is interwoven with the history of Africans. The mulatto school of Fort Christiansborg, founded in 1722, is one of the sources of literacy and modern culture in Accra. Moravian missionaries were among those who planted the first seeds of Christianity on the Guinea coast. The education of natives for handicrafts or office work in the forts of the Europeans has had an influence upon material and commercial development of the coastal people. Discussions among Danes on the usefulness of plantations in Africa touch general problems in African economy.

Behind the enterprise of the northern nations is the spirit of the Vikings still alive. People went to the tropics in order to get money, but they were also attracted by travel and discovery, by adventure and fame. Quite a few left the home island after an unhappy love affair. Many looked for a new life in a distant country.

While this book relates the suffering of Africans as a result of intercourse with Europeans, it shows that the white people also paid heavily. The percentage of Danes perishing in the African adventure is very high. It is not enough to state that they gained so and so many florins or pjastres—it must be remembered that they paid in health and lives and human happiness.

Georg Nørregård

Contents

Contents

vii

Illustrations

Introduction

How MANY READERS of the various synoptic histories of the country for so long known as the Gold Coast realized that the Danes were in continuous occupation of parts of the coast for a longer period of time than the Portuguese had been? The Portuguese were there for 155 years, from 1482 when they built Elmina castle until 1637 when the Dutch took it from them; whereas the Danes were there for 192 years, from 1658 when they took over Swedish forts until 1850 when they sold their holdings there to the British. Yet the segment of history with which Professor Nørregård deals in this work is known to very few, especially in the English-speaking world. Now that the British occupation also has ended, since 1957, it is time that we try to see all the European settlements in this area with the dispassion that usually comes only with hindsight and in regard to issues that have run their course.

General histories of Denmark briefly mention its tropical colonies only in passing when the pertinent reigns and ministries are discussed. Histories of the Gold Coast (now Ghana) refer to the Danes in a very sketchy fashion, noting their appearance, points of conflict or cooperation with the English, their departure, and usually little else. Studies which concentrate on the Danes in West Africa have been few in number and until the publication of this translation none were available in English.

The present study was first published as part of a larger work devoted to the East and West Indian as well as the Guinea coast possessions of Denmark: *Vore Gamle Tropekolonier,* edited by Johannes Brønsted, is a magnificently bound, profusely illustrated, two-volume work which is accepted as the standard study of the former Danish tropical colonies. Professor Nørregård's account thus supersedes older works such as Kay Larsen's *De Danske in Guinea* (København, 1918), and Sophie Petersen's *Denmarks Gamle Tropekolonier* (København, 1946), and consequently was our choice for translation.

It is unfortunate that the entire work edited by J. Brønsted is not translated for there are naturally some interrelations among the West African, West Indian, and East Indian phases of the Danish activities. However, a good history of the Danish West Indies does exist in English: Waldemar Christian Westergaard's *The Danish West Indies under company rule (1671-1754)* (N.Y., 1917). The relations between the Danish

West Indies and Danish West Africa were far more frequent and important than those between either of them and the Danish East Indies, and so perhaps this will suffice for the present even though Westergaard's study does not cover as extensive a period as that with which we are concerned in this book.

The possibility of an English translation was explored with the author in 1961 during a visit to Copenhagen which I had made for the purpose of surveying the Africa-related papers in the Rigsarkiv and to buy for the Boston University Library some Danish books on the Danish African activities. Professor Nørregård had earlier considered such a translation but had failed to find an interested publisher in Britain. Hassing Forlag, which holds the copyright to the original, agreed to allow the African Studies Center of Boston University to undertake the translation and publication of Professor Nørregård's work. Sigurd Mammen prepared the translation. Svend Holsoe was of invaluable assistance in helping prepare the manuscript for publication. His knowledge of Danish and of American idiom has been useful in checking difficult passages in the text. He has also standardized the endnotes to conform to American practice, after obtaining further information from Professor Nørregård for this purpose; from the amplified notes he has assembled the bibliography and list of cited archival sources. He also prepared the Appendix. Finally, I wish to express my gratitude to Professor Robert Moody for advice in technical details.

Place names (with the exception of Ursu, which has been changed to the more familiar Osu, because it appears so frequently) have been left in the Danish spelling; Aflahu is easily seen as Aflao in the context and no confusion is likely to arise. African personal names have also been left in the form in which they appeared in the Danish original. No changes, additions or deletions, have been made from the original text. It must be remembered that this was written for Danish readers and whereas the introductory background on West Africa may seem to English readers either unnecessary or superficial, on the other hand Americans, Africans, and British may find that in order to understand the background of this history of the Danes in Africa, one must know something of Scandinavian history. Unfortunately the best histories of Denmark have not been translated and only panoramic surveys are available in English.

Those familiar only with the contemporary map of Europe will think of Denmark as a small country, but it was not so in the seventeenth century when the events recounted in this book began; and although it surprises some people to learn that Denmark had colonies in the tropics, it would not be so unexpected if we consider that it was a full millennium since its monarchy was founded, and that during most of this time it has been a redoubtable power.

Written records of this area begin with the emergence of Denmark as a strong and consolidated kingdom. Gorm and his son Harald, early in the tenth century, brought other local kings under a central control. (By this time Danes had already settled in England and elsewhere as a result of successful Viking operations.) Harald's son Sweyn had conquered much of England by 1013, and the latter's son Canute the Great extended his control over Norway in 1028. But this first empire, which encompassed lands on both sides of the North Sea, soon fell apart. A century later a new Danish empire was built up by Valdemar the Great (1131-1182) and Valdemar the Victorious (1170-1241), this time in the Baltic Sea area; it included parts of northern Germany, Estonia, and the island of Gotland. Denmark was thus the first nation to attempt to control the Baltic Sea, which from then on would be, like a kind of northern Mediterranean, the scene of struggles for maritime hegemony.

The Hanseatic League, which developed gradually from the defensive alliance of Lübeck and Hamburg (1241), succeeded to the domination of the Baltic after the 1330's. The league's first headquarters was at Visby, the old Danish stronghold and market on the island of Gotland. Later the leadership was shifted to Lübeck, which had replaced the Danish city of Slesvig as terminus of the transpeninsular land route from the Baltic to the North Sea. This southward shift emphasized not only the Germanic character of the Hanse but also the more strategic position that the German towns and merchants enjoyed in their competition with the Danes. (They had greater exposure to the nourishing influence of the more-advanced southern countries which faced the Mediterranean and the East.) It is not without significance that Cologne, in the old Roman Rhineland, was one of the important Hanseatic towns. Although the league of Hanse towns was primarily a commercial organization, it did have a military aspect and furthermore enjoyed a sort of alliance with the Teutonic Order of Knights, which was then expanding also.

The Scandinavians rallied somewhat in the face of Hanseatic competition. In 1397 by the Union of Kalmar, one of the great rulers, Queen Margaret, united Denmark, Norway, and Sweden. From about this time the merchants were closely associated with the crown. Soon afterward, partially as a result of the growing importance of the merchants in the realm, the capital was changed from Roskilde to København (the merchants' harbor). The union of the three kingdoms was not easy to maintain (some historians claim that it never had reality for more than two of them) and there were disputes and restlessness in Sweden. A Danish king at his accession had some fractious nobles assassinated; this led only to a stiffening of Swedish resistance, and by 1423 Sweden was again independent and now dangerously anti-Danish. One might speculate on what might have been were there no unfortunate "Stockholm bloodbath": would the united Scandinavian power, unweakened by internecine wars, have been able to maintain itself more effectively in European power politics and in tropical commercial and colonial enterprises? Perhaps, though there were also economic factors which might have precluded such a destiny.

At any rate, there were a long series of wars in the north. During the first century after the rupture of the union, the Danes tried vainly to force the Swedes back into the union under the Danish king, only to lose some of the territory they had long held (Skanĕ) in what is today southern Sweden. For another century Denmark fought Sweden to regain the lost provinces. It is this phase of the Scandinavian wars that intrudes into the history of the West African ventures.

It is interesting that during the very period that Denmark was being constricted in Europe, she acquired her tropical colonies. The attrition in the north, which had begun as far back as 1469 when the Shetlands and Orkneys were mortgaged to the king of Scotland and never redeemed, was to continue. The Baltic had become virtually a "Swedish Lake," Sjaelland itself had been invaded by a Swedish army and the existence of the kingdom endangered. Later, as a result of the Napoleonic Wars, Norway was taken from Denmark and given to Sweden. In the mid-nineteenth century Sleswig and Holstein were lost to Prussia. The newer overseas possessions also slipped from her hold. In 1845 Tranquebar was purchased by the British and in 1869 Nicobar was relinquished to them. The Guinea lands were sold, as we shall see, to the British in 1850. The United States bought the Virgin Islands in 1917. All that remain now are Greenland (resettled in 1721, after the earlier settlements had been abandoned), which in 1953 ceased to be a colony and received the status of a county of Denmark, and the Faroes Islands, which since 1948 have had self-government with their own parliament and representation in the Danish parliament in Copenhagen. The Danish king gave up his empty title, king of Iceland, in 1944, the Icelanders having unilaterally declared their independence while Denmark was under Nazi occupation; the Danes had previously agreed to the separation and had granted the islanders home-rule in 1903.

All of this far-flung activity testifies to the strength of a very old maritime tradition. Scandinavian rock engravings of the Bronze Age show armed men in boats. The Viking long boats were known in all European waters and crossed the North Atlantic. If the Normans reached West Africa as sometimes claimed, their voyages would be more in the Scandinavian than in the French tradition. In the seventeenth and eighteenth centuries Denmark still ranked as a substantial maritime power. The destruction of the Danish fleet by the British, under Horatio Nelson, then Vice-Admiral, in 1801 at Copenhagen probably was motivated by commercial as well as military considerations. The Baltic powers, Denmark, Sweden, Prussia, and Russia, had formed the year before an alliance to resist the practice of the British searching their ships at sea (the same grievance over which the United States would soon fight a war with Britain), though the presence of Russia in the alliance was less morally defensible than that of the others since Tsar Paul I was involved with Napoleon in anti-British schemes. Danish naval power never fully recovered from this blow and never regained the relative position it had formerly held.

In the twentieth century, we in the English-speaking world, historians included, have tended to forget the former greatness of Denmark and the role she played in helping to create the conditions of the modern world in which we live. We must not only take a fresh look at Denmark to understand these two centuries of Danish-African relations, but we must also reconsider the social conditions of both Europe and Africa during the period.

The first Danish trading company was chartered in 1625 but no ships were sent out for several years. This is not surprising since Denmark at that time was carrying the brunt of the Protestant side in the Thirty Years War. Christian IV though a valiant soldier was not very fortunate in his wars. The losses which Denmark suffered must have made conditions difficult for the promoters of African trade.

Less obvious than the wars were certain general trends which characterized the seventeenth century. This century saw a transformation in the system of monarchy in many European countries. The kings since early feudal times had attempted, often with little success, to obtain and/or maintain control over the nobles. This struggle of "the State versus the Estates" had usually found the merchants siding with the king, but the struggle took a new turn when the merchants, growing richer from wider overseas trade, could make their support more effective. Thus it was that in 1660 in Denmark, Frederich III was able to make the monarchy absolute and the throne hereditary because he had the support of the merchants (some of them with interests in African trade). The merchants were not afraid of an absolute monarchy then as much as they were of parliamentarianism. The parliamentary institutions were dominated by the landed gentry, who were often selfish and conservative whereas the monarch was responsible for the general welfare and often sympathetic to the development of industries and trade—if only for the pragmatic reason that the revenues from the royal domains and dues were insufficient to meet the rising costs of increasing court and military expenses. Furthermore, taxes obtained from the merchants rose with the growth of manufacturing and foreign trade. Under the mercantile philosophy of the time, the states were, it has been said, a hothouse for the establishment of industries.

Nonetheless, the relation between the crown and the merchants was not always stable. In France, the king overshadowed the commercial classes and the strengthened monarchy made innovations in administration which would be widely copied. In England, the king was for a while completely eliminated and under Cromwell there existed what one English historian has called the "dictatorship of the bourgeoisie"; for a while the commercial class dominated Parliament as well as the executive power. In the Netherlands the royal institutions were kept, but subordinated to the burgers. In the Baltic countries these developments did not go to either extreme.

Another aspect of mercantilism was the concern with the elimination of foreign competition. Commercial treaties constituted an important part of the diplomacy of the time. Colonies were forbidden to trade with nations other than the parent country. This restriction was unenforceable and apparently was evaded everywhere, but it led to conflicts with other commercial and colonizing nations. Chartered companies were in a significant way an extension of the crown. They maintained their own armed forces and administered their territories under their charter from the king. In this way they foreshadowed the later period of direct colonial administration by the crown.

Although the chartered companies proliferated in the early part of the seventeenth century, it was not commercial enterprise which absorbed most of the energy of the people of the time: the first half of the century was dominated by religious war. (The Thirty Years War was the last of Europe's religious wars; since then wars have always been promoted on strictly secular motives.) However, the contest between Protestantism and Catholicism was not without economic considerations. When King Christian III (1503-1559) of Denmark adopted Lutheranism as the state religion, he seized church lands and properties (just as Henry VIII of England did); naturally, this strengthened the monarchy and its alliance with the merchants.

Furthermore, the seventeenth century was the time when scientific societies as well as commercial societies were being founded. The rebirth of science is conventionally dated at 1543 with the publication by Nikolaus Kopernicki (or "Copernicus," 1473-1543, a Pole with an Italian education) of *De revolutionibus orbium coelestium,* which overthrew Ptolemaic astronomy and replaced it with a new system based on observation and the use of (crude) instruments and mathematics. But it was during the seventeenth century that science began to affect the nature of society. The advance of science made possible the improvement of old processes of production and the development of new techniques of manufacture, and thus aided the growth of industry. This systematization of knowledge as well as the discovery of new facts and principles was exemplified by the publication of Newton's *Principia* in 1687, which was based on the previous findings of many other scientists. The telescope and the microscope, the thermometer and barometer, and many other inventions appeared in this period. Improvements in shipbuilding and navigation somewhat facilitated communication with the new worlds of the Americas, Hither Asia, and Sub-Saharan Africa, which Europe had "discovered" in the previous two centuries.

The conjunction of these two tendencies, the encouragement of industry by the state, and the development of new scientific processes, resulted in a great expansion of goods. A significant proportion of these manufactured goods was exported to the new lands. In exchange, exotic products and, more important, precious metals came to the enterprising countries from Guinea, the Caribbean Islands, and the lands of the Indian Ocean. The products might need to be processed, giving rise to new industries. The gold and silver—especially the former—strengthened the national currency and reinforced the money economy which was undermining the older social order based on dealing in kind, fiefs, and privileges. Thus, once embarked on this path, there were always pressures for continuing, despite disappointments: ships lost at sea, or capture of overseas establishments by foreign competitors or local peoples. Nonetheless, not all who began were able to finish. Denmark's role is important because it managed to survive so long in competition with the Netherlands and England.

The greater the development of industries, the better the position of the nation in the struggle for foreign trade, although to some extent it was possible to buy from a manufacturing nation in Europe and sell these goods in the tropics; many nations did buy Dutch goods to supplement their national products so that their ships could go out on the long voyage to Africa with full cargoes.

The Netherlands was, until after the Dutch-English wars (the third ended in 1674), the leading industrial and commercial nation in Europe. Amsterdam was the financial and commercial capital of Europe. The "Burger Culture" of Holland was equally pre-eminent in art and literature, and much of Europe—especially Protestant Europe—looked to the Dutch, and no longer to Italy and Spain, for cultural as well as economic inspiration. The university of Leyden, with such men as Hugo Grotius, J. Scaliger, J. Arminius, and D. Heinsius, was the leading center of learning and until the end of the eighteenth century attracted scholars from everywhere, including Sir Joseph Banks and Linnaeus.

Perhaps our greatest need is for an understanding of the Dutch interests and activities in Guinea. Dutch scholars have tended to center attention on their East Indian connections and to pay less attention to the

West African colony. But even these studies have not been translated into English and no account of any length is available except to readers of Dutch. Sooner or later English-speaking scholars who are interested in this area must have readily accessible a fuller account of the Dutch experience in West Africa.

Even in our present state of knowledge we have long realized that the Dutch were the dominant presence on this coast and that their principal competitors were the English. Professor Nørregård's account shows how important was the Dutch influence on the Scandinavian activities on the Guinea coast. In fact the Dutch influence extended beyond its affect on the Scandinavians; it was the main stimulus to what we might call the seventeenth-century Baltic-African complex. For in addition to the Swedish and Danish companies, the Brandenburg and Kurland ventures into African trade were inspired by the phenomenal Dutch success, which was enriching the country and transforming Amsterdam into a grandiose city. William the Elector of Brandenburg had spent some of his youth in the Netherlands and he married into the Dutch royal House of Orange. He encouraged a company which built forts on the African coast. Duke Jacob of Kurland was related to the British royal House of Stuart and drew some of his stimulus from the British; but he was an even more ardent admirer of the Dutch maritime merchants, and had spent much time on the wharves of Holland as a young man. He founded a fort on St. Andrew's Island (now St. James) in the Gambia River and also settled the West Indian island of Tobago.

It is interesting to consider that the Baltic-African complex might have been even larger, for there was another sovereign in that area who was greatly impressed by the Dutch achievements: Peter the Great, the creator of the Russian navy. However, Peter never chartered an African company. Perhaps he had his hands full with his reforms, wars, and hearty carousing, or perhaps there was no push from local merchants or a paucity of capital to form a company, or maybe Peter was just a little too late. Peter did not reach the Baltic until the opening years of the eighteenth century. St. Petersburg was founded in 1703; but it was not until after the battle of Poltava (1709) that he was really secure there, and then Russia held Rega, Ravel, and Viborg as well as St. Petersburg. By that time Sweden and Kurland had ceased to be involved in African trade and the Brandenburg possessions were in sharp decline. Their failures may have demonstrated to Peter the difficulties and costs of such ventures.

Russia's Slavic neighbor, Poland, the only other independent country on the Baltic was even more indifferent to maritime matters. Undoubtedly two of the main reasons were that Poland was the only European country aside from Hungary where kings failed to achieve some consolidation of power (and both were soon to be unable to resist being overrun by their neighbors): thus Poland under landed aristocracy lacked the encouragement of trade by the state. Secondly, as a Catholic country, the admiration for Protestant Holland, elsewhere so prevalent, was naturally not so strong.

The Baltic was at that time the great supplier of naval materials. Its extensive forests yielded timber and tar, and before American cotton and Asian hemp were available, fibers for cordage and flax for sails were sought in this region. Having these supplies at home, the Baltic powers could easily build their fleets once it had been decided upon as a matter of policy. Gustavus Adolphus realized Sweden's need during his wars to the south and his (and his successor's) minister Axel Oxenstierna was responsible for the establishment of a Swedish naval force. Jacob Kettler, Duke of Kurland, had 44 armed men-of-war and 60 marchantmen, one of the largest navies of his day. But because the man-power of his duchy was so limited, his naval pretensions led to the gibe of the Swedish king, Charles Gustavus, that he was "too poor for a king, too rich for a duke." He built ships for his kinsman also, the Stuart king, and, although an ardent Protestant, offered to supply the Pope. Baltic-built ships were sturdy and in demand.

The Atlantic powers with naval interests intervened in Scandinavian affairs to maintain access to the Baltic naval supplies and other trade. Therefore the Dutch in 1658 came to the aid of Denmark when the Swedes tried to overrun, apparently with intent to occupy, the Danish kingdom. The Dutch did not want to see both sides of the Orosund controlled by Sweden. But helping the Danes in Europe did not prevent the Dutch from attempting to oust them from West Africa.

As navies grew (partly as a result of the Anglo-Dutch wars, partly due to the ambitions of France's Louis XIV, and partly as a consequence of the need to protect merchantmen on the extended waterways being increasingly used by the competing national companies, "interlopers," and pirates), other sources of naval supplies were found and home industries of rope-making and canvas manufacture were started. The Baltic gradually lost some of its strategic importance.

Denmark, as it turned out, was the only Baltic power to persist in West African trade and since Denmark is not only a Baltic power but also an Atlantic power, we may have some doubts about the adequacy of the Baltic position for maintaining a trade which was so intensively competitive, not only commercially but militarily. Did Sweden give up its African establishments so readily because Denmark (to which Norway was then united) could close the Orosund and the Belts (the passages from the Baltic to the Atlantic)? This strategic factor was never put to a test, but it must have contributed to the discouragement of the promoters of African ventures in Baltic countries. (Sweden, it is true, had Bremen and Vreden after 1648 but did not control the intervening land between them and her possessions in western Pomerania.)

Most of the Baltic enterprises in Africa were of brief duration, but they were not the shortest. That distinction undoubtedly belongs to the Scottish African Company which never established a fort on the African coast and sent only one ship to African waters. (See George Pratt Insh, *The Company of Scotland Trading to Africa and the Indies* [London & N.Y., 1932].)

The main reason for failure was an inadequate economic base. The Baltic countries certainly had a lively commercial background, but in the mid-seventeenth century not one of them could exhibit an economic development comparable to the Dutch, English, and French economies. If we look at the smallest of the Baltic states, the Duchy of Kurland, we will see how admirable were the efforts and at the same time how limited were the results. Under Duke Jacob there were established 17 foundries, 18 sawmills, 100 tar refineries, 10 woolen mills, 85 linen mills, 14 saltpeter factories, 5 fodder mills, 10 glassworks, 30 limekilns, 20 brickworks, and 5 paper mills. (See A. Bilmanis, *A History of Latvia* [Princeton, 1951], 188.)

The difficulties of raising capital for the ventures, and especially of making up losses due to enemy depredations and losses at sea, were more than most Baltic economies were capable of sustaining over a long period. Smallness of the economic base is evident in Denmark also, though in contrast to tiny Kurland, Denmark stretched from the mouth of the Elbe to the northern tip of the Scandinavian peninsula. Nevertheless, the ports of Christiana (Oslo), Bergen (an old Hanse town), and Trondheim were not significant to the Danish companies' activities in Africa. The concentration of African trade to such a large extent in Glückstadt and Copenhagen would seem to have reduced Danish maritime strength below its potentials and this is important when we realize the small number (relative to their commitments as well as to their competitors) of ships which Denmark sent out to Africa. In his conclusions, Professor Nørregård does not mention the factor of shipwreck in the Danish experience, and yet the losses were so high that we might apply to Denmark as well as to Portugal the equation of shipwreck and loss of empire. (See James Duffy, *Shipwreck and Empire* [Cambridge, Mass., 1955].) Despite its vicissitudes Denmark held on to its African settlements for virtually two centuries and thereby forces on our attention the need to understand the place of these settlements in the history of West Africa.

Let us turn now to look at the background of conditions in West Africa when the Danes arrived. We should consider the coast and the interior as separate but interrelated areas.

The interior, a grassland belt between the rain forest and the Sahara, had for centuries been tending toward unification. This development reached its apogee under the imperium of Songhai, during the fifteenth and sixteenth centuries, the power of which was felt from the Atlantic to what is, in the present day, Northern Nigeria. But the seventeenth century was for this area a new epoch of changed conditions. A Moroccan invasion in 1592, using firearms for the first time in a Sudanese war, had toppled Songhai though they were unable to establish Moroccan domination. Therefore, the interior of West Africa in the seventeenth century was broken up into the constituent ethnic and political blocks of which the old Sudanic empires had been built. A kind of Sudanic "Dark Ages" ensued and the security of the person and goods of a merchant were no longer guaranteed by the royal protection Arab travelers and chroniclers had found so effective and laudable. By the end of the eighteenth century some kingdoms had stabilized certain regions which made traveling more secure for explorers; for example Mungo Park was the grateful beneficiary of the generosity of the ruler of such a kingdom, the "benevolent prince," Mansong of Segu. The nineteenth century saw new military and politico-religious struggles among the reconstituted kingdoms for regional hegemony. Al-Hadj Omar and Samory were successful against their Sudanese opponents but lost to the greater military might of the French.

The coast had not known large-scale political entities. Yoruba and Benin, at the eastern end of Upper Guinea, were the only states we know to have existed before the arrival of the Europeans. Fetu and Accra, though still small, had become stronger and wealthier as a result of trade with the Portuguese. Conditions on the coast were influenced by contact with Europe. The global war in which the Dutch had ousted the Portuguese from large areas of the East Indies, a lesser area of South America, and all of West Africa resulted in wider European contacts for Africans and consequently more opportunities for Africans to enter into trade. The Dutch attempted to enforce a monopoly as the Portuguese had done, but with even less success. The Dutch claim to exclusive rights was based on conquest, but that in turn depended on the legitimacy of the Portuguese claim, which was based in part on discovery (considered valid) and in part on papal bulls (which of course the Protestant Dutch could not consider valid).

Before the seventeenth century the "interlopers" from the Netherlands, England, and France had come out surreptitiously and generally without royal backing; but in the post-Portuguese period there were chartered companies, and each contested the other's claims. Whereas previously the "interlopers" had traded from their ships and slipped away as quickly as possible to avoid being intercepted by naval patrols, now the various companies built forts and established themselves as permanently as possible.

The two hundred mile stretch known as the Gold Coast had the greatest concentration of forts. Many of them changed hands as a result of military actions by the companies and their African allies; as often as not these minuscule wars were in times of "peace" for their home governments. Allowing for double counting as a consequence of these transfers, the Dutch had fourteen forts and posts (not counting out-forts) in the seventeenth century, and the English had seven such establishments. Brandenburg and Sweden each had three; the Danes entered on the scene by capturing the three Swedish forts during one of their numerous wars with their neighbor. During the eighteenth century the Danes built four new posts while the English built two, and the Dutch retrenched somewhat. In the nineteenth century both Dutch and Danish settlements were quiescent and the British were generally flourishing (at least in the context of the coast)—after 1870, the British, having bought out their two surviving competitors, remained in solitary possession for the next 87 years.

The forest people, farther back from the coast than the Fetu and Accra whom the Danes first met, were also undergoing change. The arrival of the Danes coincided more or less with the emergence of Ashanti although it was some time before there was direct contact between the two. The rise of Ashanti was probably related in some way to the turmoil in the Western Sudan at that period. Perhaps even earlier some of the Mande peoples may have become interested in the forest area and the gold of the Ashanti region. Mande experience and influence seems to have helped mold the new Akan states. (See I. Wilks, "The Northern Factor in Ashanti History," *Jrl. of Af. Hist.*, pt. 1 [1961]; a booklet with the same title, Institute of African Studies, Legon, 1961, has two additional chapters; J. Goody, "The Mande and the Akan Hinterland," *The Historian in Tropical Africa,* ed. J. Vansina et al. [London, 1964].)

While the forms of political organization were derived more from the north, the fortunes of Ashanti were to be made in the south. Trade with Europeans was always important to the Ashanti. Kumasi was an emporium through which European goods passed to the Sudan and Sudanese goods made their way to the coast. (See Caseley Hayford, *Gold Coast Native Institutions* [London, 1903], 95.)

We can see in Professor Nørregård's narrative that Africans played more than a passive role in the trade of the area. K. O. Dike's *Trade and Politics in the Niger Delta 1830-1885* (London, 1956) stands as a watershed in the establishment of the now universally accepted view that African entrepreneurs, as well as Europeans, formulated policies to control the conditions of trade and acted on them when their interests were involved. Professor Harry Rudin in his *Germans in the Cameroons 1884-1914* (New Haven, 1938) was perhaps the first modern historian to point out the importance of the African middleman in the control of trade. The "closing of the paths," which Europeans tended to see merely as obstruction to trade, or as the irresponsible and irrational behavior of savages, was in fact one means used by African states to control trade; it was comparable to the obstacles which different European companies put in each other's way. The inter-African wars were often as trade-related as were the inter-European wars. William Bosman recorded that Dinkira fought Awine and that, as a result of the latter's defeat, there was a shift of the trade pattern; Axim, the Awine outlet, dried up and trade there languished. Soon after, Ashanti destroyed Dinkira and got control of the lion's share of the gold supplies; as a result Elmina, Dinkira's main outlet but also Ashanti's, was more amply supplied with gold than before.

A description of the commercial organization of a West African state is given in K. Polanyi's *Trade and Markets in the Early Empires* (1957) (section on Dahomey). Polanyi's "administered trade" concept has been criticized by some economists, but before the appearance of *Trade and Markets* I had described Ashanti trade in comparable terms:

> The trade in these expensive commodities [gold, ivory, slaves, kola, monkey furs, and kente cloth, and the imported goods from the coast and the north] was in the hands of the men [i.e., in contrast to the later dominance of trade by women]. To prevent the power of wealth from disrupting the kinship, political and military systems of power, trade was strictly controlled by the state. No one could trade without the permission of the king, or as we might say, a royal patent. These chartered merchants were required to trade with the king; but "The king's weights are one-third heavier than the current weights of the country which is a source of emolument to the household." [Wm. Hutton, *A Voyage to Africa* (London, 1821), 326]. Cf. T. Bowdich, *Mission from Cape Coast Castle to Ashantee* (London, 1873), 335-36. The king also had a monopoly on the kola trade; all kola trees no matter on whose land belonged to the king, and he had kola plantations worked by slaves. The king's caravan always started out earlier than those of other merchants who were required to give the royal caravan a head start. The king entrusted his own trading to favorites of the court and gave gold dust to those he wanted to advance so that they could trade and eventually they would make an accounting to him [from my dissertation, "The Effect on Family Structure of Changing Economic Activities of Women in a West African Town" (Columbia University, 1956)].

The African states were thus, in their own way, mercantilist and they competed bitterly with each other, though all Africans agreed that they wanted many European companies on the coast so that they could play one against another in haggling over prices.

The Dutch learned in their first assault on Elmina than the African allies of the Portuguese were more powerful than the European settlement. They thereafter wooed the allies of the Portuguese and then, with their acquiescence, took the fort. The Dutch admiral, De Ruyter, having taken all of the other English forts on the coast, decided not to attack Cape Coast Castle because the African allies of the English were too strong. Africans frequently invited Europeans to settle and trade, though at certain times they did not want particular Europeans to settle at a particular place. The Ga destroyed a Portuguese fort in 1578 and the people of Kommenda destroyed a French fort in 1688.

Africans had occasional experience also in running forts. John Kabes built a fort in 1798 at Kommenda. The Fetu took a fort from the Danes in 1660 and the Akwamu under Asameni took Christiansborg from the same power in 1694. None of these experiments, however, lasted much over a year. Kabes' fort was abandoned and the others returned to the Europeans. Forts did not fit well in the functional role of the African trader.

We need to know more about the African middleman in the Gold Coast area; we recently have had additions to our knowledge of early middlemen in the Niger Delta area (*Efik Traders of Old Calabar,* ed. D. Forde [London, 1956], and G. I. Jones, *Trading States of the Oil Rivers* [London, 1963]) and there are many indications that they were at least as important around the forts as they were in the rivers of the Delta.

The link among them all, the various Europeans, the coastal peoples, and those of the interior, was trade and the outstanding feature of trade became for a considerable time the demand for slaves. The Americas had plantations, Africa had the labor for them, and Europe, with its industries and ships, absorbed their raw products, did the carrying, and found markets in all continents. This imposed some variation of the "triangular trade" on each of the carrying nations, a pattern that was further encouraged by the wind system. The Dutch, English, Danes, and even little Kurland had Caribbean as well as Guinea possessions. Europe, Africa, and America were tied together in a drama that was composed on the one hand of tragedy and greed and on the other of enterprise and development. The lamentable phase of the slave trade is now over and it can be argued that each area has suffered and also benefited from the trade. Europe acquired wealth but also the intellectual reaction of de Gobineau which led into a *herrenvolk* philosophy and mass destruction of life. The Americas got labor and built up their countries but still are faced with the divisions of society because color continues to connote to certain groups of people the inferiority of the former slave status, now redefined in biological rather than social terms. African kings and traders likewise shared in the acquisition of riches through the sale of slaves, but experienced a disturbance in their social fabric and a loss of some of the cultural features of the more peaceful times that had preceded. (The decline of the Yoruba under the raids of the warlike Dahomey is an example.) Slavery has been legally abolished everywhere and relations are on different grounds, but the paths of the three continents have never been wholly separate since, and probably never will be, and this is just as well. In all the American nations the Amerindian, European, and African races and cultures have mixed to some extent, though few individuals can claim to exemplify the high degree of cultural as well as racial synthesis achieved by Central American poet Ruben Dario. Nevertheless, the culture which is so often called Euro-American must be seen as having a component which is Afro-American.

It may be mentioned here that a Danish-speaking African, known as Denmark Vesey, a former seaman on a Danish ship, having come from the Danish West Indies to Charleston, South Carolina, where he resided as a "free Negro," led a slave conspiracy in 1822 to rebel and seize power; he was informed on and executed with the other conspirators. This abortive uprising ranks with Gabriel's (1800, Richmond, Virginia) and Nat Turner's (1831, also Virginia) as one of the three large-scale attempts of Negroes to overthrow the slave owners' power in the United States.

The removal of Africans to the Americas was followed, particularly in the nineteenth century, by a smaller movement of return of Africans (or individuals who were African, or partly African, in descent) to Africa, notably from the United States to Liberia, from Nova Scotia and Jamaica to Sierra Leone, and from Brazil to Nigeria. The Basel Mission was instrumental in bringing some West Indians to Danish Guinea. These migrants were bearers of some variety of Western culture, and their presence reinforced but also modified the cultural impact of the Europeans and the locally born mulattoes on the coast—where the Dutch have bequeathed names such as Vroom and de Graaf, the British, Byrd and Bannerman, and the Danes, Quist and Reindorf.

So interconnected are all of these areas that events in one place affected the other areas. All of the wars of Western European countries naturally had some consequences for the Europeans on the African coast, but somewhat less expectedly the War of Independence of the English colonies on the Atlantic coast of North America provided an opportunity for the growth of Danish shipping in African waters. On the other hand, the realities of the coast could affect decisions of Europeans in contexts which had a wider scope. For example, the English while fighting the Danes at Copenhagen and seizing their Indian Ocean and West Indian settlements did not disturb the Danes in West Africa. For although West Africa may not have had strategic importance in that war, there was also the factor that the English did not wish to weaken the European presence vis-à-vis the Ashanti in the conditions obtaining at that time. Likewise, the Dutch forts on the Gold Coast were unmolested although the Capetown settlement in South Africa was occupied.

We should see this Danish history, on the one hand, as meshing with this international and intercontinental history, but we should see also the particular achievements of the Danes. Several experiments of the Danes are important for the history of the region. The plantations on which the Danes attempted to practice a somewhat extensive tropical agriculture, and the philosophy behind these efforts, anticipated the arguments of Sir Thomas Foxwell Buxton's *The African Slave Trade and its Remedy* (London, 1839) by several decades. The arrival of the Moravian Brethren antedates the visit of Reverend Thomas Thompson, sometimes claimed to be the first Protestant missionary on the Gold Coast. Nørregård's presentation of the early development of castle schools by the Danes adds to what we have known on this topic, mainly until now from the study of F. L. Bartels (dissertation, University of London). The prohibition of the slave trade (1792), the first such promulgation by any slave-trading nation, while influenced by intellectual currents from England and France, was no doubt related also to the abolition of serfdom in Denmark (1788).

Each historical study which is well done suggests further research and permits greater syntheses. It is easy to see a number of directions in which scholars can lead off from Professor Nørregård's work. First, as a study of one European group in West Africa, the assessment of Europeans *in toto* in this region is facilitated. A first step could be the comparison of Nørregård study with: Victor Granlund, *En svensk koloni i Afrika eller Svenska-Afrikanske Kompagniets Historia* (Stokholm, 1879); German Imperial Staff, *Brandenburg-Preussen auf den Westkuste von Afrika 1681-1721* (Leipzig, 1912); S. P. L'Honore Naber, *De Nederlanders in Guineë en Brazilië* ('s-Gravenhage, 1931); Otto Heinz Mattiesen, *Die Kolonial- und Uberseepolitik der Kurländischen herzöge in 17. und 18. Jahrhundert* (Stuttgart & Berlin, 1939); Roussier, *L'éstablissement d'Issiny 1687-1701* (Paris, 1935); and such works in English as those of J. W. Blake, *European Beginnings in West Africa* (London, 1937); E. C. Martin, *British Settlements in West Africa 1750-1821* (London, 1927); and K. G. Davies, *The Royal African Company* (London, 1957).

And in this comparative European study the role of the Jews should also be sought. It was the Portuguese Jew, Pereira, who led Windham into the secrets of West African trade. The Portuguese Jews who settled in the Netherlands and in Danish Glückstadt brought with them the experience of their participation in Portuguese enterprise, and the far older tradition of long distance commercial ventures that goes back at least to the time of Solomon and the Tarshish ships. Jews had been in North Africa since Carthagian times; they were in the Sahara when the Arabs arrived and undoubtedly, farther south as well. (See Raymond Mauny, "Le judaïsme, les juifs, et l'Afrique occidentale," *Bull. I.F.A.N.* [1949], a better guide than J. J. Williams, *Hebrewisms in West Africa*

[New York, 1930].) In the sixteenth century they began to settle at São Thomé and in the Cape Verde Islands. Jewish history, which has been so assiduously cultivated for some other areas, has not yet been sufficiently studied in regard to Jewish participation in early European exploration, trade, and settlement in Africa.

That comparative study could be enriching even for an appreciation of the part played by the Danes in West Africa is indicated by the fact that Danes and Norwegians were hired by the Duke of Kurland for his ventures; furthermore in 1652, Peter Schulte, commander of the Kurlander vessel *Crocodile,* threatened Major Fock, commander of St. Andrew's Isle, during a dispute, that he would go to Denmark and get a force of men to take the Kurland fort and turn it over to the King of Denmark. The threat was no doubt based on a knowledge of the interest of the Danish crown in West Africa as well as on the presence of Danish subjects in the Kurlander settlement. If it had been carried out, Denmark would have been in possession of African territory a few years earlier, but on a different part of the coast. And since Denmark might have been less easy to dislodge than Kurland, the Gambia might have become Danish rather than British! (See John Gray, *History of the Gambia* [Cambridge, 1940], 34.)

Even more important than a comparative study of European activities on the coast would be what some French historians have called "l'histoire bilatérale," e.g., the Danish impact on Ga-Adangme, Akwapim, Akim, and other peoples on the one side, and the impact on Denmark of the African contact. It has not been Professor Nørregård's purpose to deal with this, but his work suggests that it be undertaken. It would be interesting, for example, to see precisely what consequences guinea gold had for Danish currency, and what particular Danish industries were founded on, or made use of, African ivory, hides, wood, spices, etc., and what part these enterprises had in the total Danish economy and what use their products had in the Danish society. Nor should the products of African labor in the Danish West Indies be ignored in this respect. Eventually we should relate all the various European and West African groups in this way. Then perhaps one would have to speak of a multilateral history—indeed we would be approaching the ultimate level of World History.

However, the most urgent task to follow the present assessment of the Danes in Africa is to go back to the same archives, this time with a research focus on the Africans, and see how much we can find out from Danish records about African societies and of individuals who were prominent in leadership and/or trade. When Joseph Reindorf has completed and published his cataloguing of the Africa-related papers in the Rigsarkiv in Copenhagen, scholars will be able to exploit these resources more easily. Already Svend Holsoe and Kofi Finn have made incursions into these papers in African-focused research. The Danish papers should be used in conjunction with the British archives and with the Dutch archives. (The latter have recently been catalogued by R. Carsen, *Materials for West African History in the Archives of Belgium and Holland* [London, 1962]—which incidentally lists several references to the Danes.) A foretaste of what we can expect can be had in Ivor Wilks' excellent study, "The Rise and Fall of the Akwamu Empire" (unpublished except for the short article in *The Transactions of the Historical Society of Ghana*, pt. 2 [1957]), which is based on both Danish and Dutch sources, excerpts of which were collected by J. T. Furley and are now housed at the University of Ghana.

Unfortunately, one cannot give many such instances of research drawing on the less commonly known languages. It is really to our shame that in African research so few scholars from the English-speaking world have made use of the archives where the papers are mainly in other languages. Welmer made some use of the Brandenburg story in his book on Ahanta but in a scarcely adequate way. J. M. Gray (now Sir John) cited above, consulted H. Dietrichs' *Herzog Jacobs von Kurland Kolonien an der Westküste von Afrika* (Mitau, 1890), but does not appear to have visited any one of the five archives listed by Mattiesen in Riga. Actually, Professor Nørregård's work has been occasionally referred to, though not extensively used; it has been cited under the editor's rather than the author's name. (See A. W. Lawrence, *Trade Castles and Forts of the Gold Coast* [London, 1963], and G. Metcalf, *Maclean of the Gold Coast* [London, 1962].) It has been the exception rather than the rule for English-speaking historians in this area to pursue their quest through whatever languages may be required. It is an author's privilege to define the limits of his study as he chooses—or is required by certain limitations—but these limits can be simply stated to guide other scholars as to what further lines of research remain to be followed. However, when misleading statements about sources consulted are made and when there are implications that nothing further exists in a certain category there is a hindrance to additional research in that area. When a phrase such as "the fragmentary Danish records" is used in a preface (Lawrence, *Trade Castles,* p. 19), one can be sure that the writer of such a phrase has never visited the Danish archives. Such an omission is of course his privilege, but it is not granted to him as a privilege in the world of scholarship to divert other searchers, by such a wildly exaggerated description, from realizing the potentialities of an important research source.

The truth is that we did not need a book, such as this, to inform us that the Danish papers exist; the archives are listed and the pertinent collections are described by that remarkable man A. W. Cardinall in *A Bibliography of the Gold Coast* (Accra, 1931). It seems certain that interest is now aroused to further exploit these sources.

Let us hope that an earnest of a trend toward more exhaustive search-ing for documents relevant to a given historical quest can be seen in cer-tain recent works. Even though much is still to be desired in the average performance, linguistically, of African historians, we will probably soon come to recognize that an historian of Africa, even if a European, should know an African language, or more than one, as the focus of his study might indicate. The next generation will expect more of its scholars than the past has, but that should not surprise us.

Finally, it may be noted that the Danish archives hold information on other areas of Africa beside the coast of present-day Ghana. The ships which went out to the Indian Ocean had to round the Cape; they often stopped at Cape Town and may have sometimes stopped elsewhere.

In view of all these possibilities for further elucidations, it seems reasonable to assert that not only is Professor Nørregård's work of enor-mous interest to us now, but that it will become more important the more African historical research progresses.

Daniel F. McCall

Boston, Massachusetts
July 1965

DANISH SETTLEMENTS IN WEST AFRICA

1658-1850

1 / THE GOLD COAST

IT MAY BE SURPRISING to learn that the Kingdom of Denmark ever possessed colonies on the Guinea coast. The Danish venture there is a tale of sun and wealth, adventure and excitement, and abundance and luxury. There was a time when ships left Danish settlements on the coast of Africa, bearing cargoes of gold, ivory, slaves, precious woods, tropical fruits, and innumerable curiosities never before seen in Scandinavia. Those who returned home from a voyage to the Gold Coast would describe for days and nights the wonders of the tropics, all the adventures and dangers they had experienced, and the splendors they had seen. On such an expedition turbulent spirits quenched their thirst for adventure; and for those who remained at home, the stories meant food for their imaginations and sometimes stimulation for action. This colorful chapter of the Danish past seems far distant, almost forgotten; and yet, little more than a century has passed since its conclusion.

An explanation must be found to understand why the Danes should have embarked on such a risky undertaking and why, having started, they later abandoned it. That both practically and economically they should have tried to fly the Danish colors in those distant places may seem incomprehensible to their twentieth-century descendants, but the philosophy of their epoch was different from ours. The forces which for generations kept this adventure going have since found other outlets, and the problems inherent in Denmark's former colonies no longer exist. As the following will show, a particular political point of view was of some importance for the Danes in the acquisition of their first African possessions. In the long run, however, economic considerations, even pure greediness, were the motivating forces. In forming an opinion of the African settlements based upon their own inherent potentialities, we must first find out if they were profitable. In comparison, it is of secondary importance whether Denmark gained political or military glory from the enterprise or whether it made important contributions to the spread of civilization. Of course, by her handling of the slave-trade problem, Denmark won a leading place among civilized nations and thereby won greater fame than by the sum of all her overseas achievements.

The enterprising spirit manifested in the Guinea traffic is justifiably still admired today. Like the Danish possessions in the East and West Indies, the African undertaking involved considerable risks. Dangers lurked on stormy seas and in hot climates. Daring and capital were necessary for the completion of the voyages. The ships on expedition to both the East and West Indies had to be equipped like those going on voyages of exploration. The provisions on board had to last a long time, and men and arms had to be sufficient to ward off attacks by pirates. For centuries participation in European overseas trade and colonization was considered among feats of bravery.

We do not know when the first white men set foot on the Gold Coast, but it may have happened in antiquity. Herodotus writes that the Egyptian pharaoh Necco in about 600 B.C. gave Phoenician seafarers ships and sent them southward along the east coast of Africa, and that three years later they returned by way of the Strait of Gibraltar.[1] The Phoenicians usually kept close to the coasts, so on their circumnavigation of Africa they must have passed the Gold Coast. Whether they landed on the coast remains unknown, but they may have since they had to land occasionally to find fresh water and provisions. Likewise, we know from ancient accounts that Carthaginian navigators frequently sailed south along the west coast of Africa.[2] However, we do not know how far they reached. The most famous of these expeditions was made by Hanno for colonization and trade; but we do not know when it took place, and even with very detailed descriptions we cannot locate all the places mentioned. Judging from the account, however, Hanno's expedition could easily have reached the Cameroons.

It is also possible that a few white men from North Africa may have crossed the deserts of the Sahara and reached the Sudan and the Guinea coast, but we have no account of them. During the Middle Ages powerful states arose in northern Sudan, some ruled by black Africans, others by Berbers. In both cases most of the rulers had accepted Islam. These states had communication in the west with Morocco, through the Fessan with Tripoli, and in the east with Ethiopia and Egypt. Thus to some extent they were able to profit by Mediterranean civilization and are believed to have attained a cultural level which for centuries remained higher than that of contemporary Western Europe. Undoubtedly the African states of the Guinea coast were in communication with these northern states and profited by this to some extent. The communities which could have had influence on the inhabitants of the Guinea coast were most likely the western Sudanic states of Ghana, Mali, and Songhai.[3]

Ghana was the oldest and most famous of these states. Its capital was perhaps Walata, and its territories may have included the region of the upper Niger. However, in the thirteenth century it was conquered by the Negro state of Mali, whose rulers were Mandingo or Wangara. In the fifteenth century the Songhai state succeeded Mali, but in 1591 it was vanquished by Morocco, causing the state's downfall.

The first reliable evidence of Europeans on the Gold Coast is the account of the Portuguese arrival in 1471.[4] Continuing the large-scale explorations begun under the leadership of Prince Henry the Navigator, Portugal sent successive expeditions to these regions. Thus, in 1471 Juan de Santarem and Pedro d'Escobar reached Oro do la Mina, supposedly situated near Elmina or Shama on the Gold Coast. Shortly after its discovery the Portuguese attempted to mine gold there, but no permanent settlement was founded until 1482. Then, having obtained permission from a native chief, they began building Fort Elmina.

While it has been maintained that the Guinea coast was first explored by French sailors from Dieppe as early as the fourteenth century, there are no positive proofs of this.[5] The Portuguese, on the other hand, left numerous traces of their exploration: buildings and monuments, place names and other verbal influences. A kind of African Portuguese even developed along the coast which was spoken for centuries by native traders in their dealings with Europeans. Danish Guinea traders also had to learn this language.

The Portuguese must have profited greatly by their discovery, and they did their best to conceal their knowledge of the newly-discovered lands. Therefore, only bits of information about them reached other European nations. In the long run, however, it proved impossible for them to monopolize such riches. In 1553, the first English expedition to Guinea was launched under the leadership of Thomas Windham and Antonio Anes Pinteado, and this was soon followed by others.[6] During the reign of Queen Elizabeth I, English freebooters made constant inroads into the colonial wealth of both Spain and Portugal. Thus began an epoch in which ships making long trips always had to be prepared to defend themselves, not only against pirates, but also against privateers.

After having shown the way, the English were soon followed by the Dutch.[7] The first Dutch ship to reach the Gold Coast was *de Maagdt van Enkhuisen* during 1593-94. In the next century no other nation was more ambitious in accumulating wealth on the Gold Coast. It was easier for the Dutch, because English enterprise slackened about 1590. Also Portuguese interests were neglected since Portugal was then under Spanish sovereignty. Consequently, the Dutch were able to found permanent establishments on the coast. Having conquered the main Portuguese stronghold of Elmina by a mixture of trickery and violence, they gained a decided advantage over the other European powers on the coast. Gradually, the Portuguese were forced to give up all their forts in Upper Guinea as far as the Volta River. The armistice of 1641 gave the Dutch the forts and territories they had conquered. By the peace treaty of 1642 between the two seafaring nations, the Dutch won the Gold Coast and promised in return not to interfere in Portuguese Brazil. After that in Africa the Portuguese had to content themselves with colonies farther south in Lower Guinea and a few islands in the Gulf of Guinea.

It was during the period of Dutch supremacy that the Scandinavians were drawn into the competition for the African coast. Furthermore, it was under Dutch influence that the Danes ventured into the East Indian traffic, so contact with them was important for the launching of the Danish Guinea expeditions.[8]

The name of Upper Guinea is usually applied to the coast from Gambia or the River Casamance to the Niger. Europeans soon divided up the coast into several sections. The first section to Cape Palmas became the Pepper Coast, in Dutch, the Grain Coast. It was so named because of a special kind of peppercorn or paradise grain (*amomum grana paradisi*) grown there, which was then widely used in Europe. This section today corresponds to the coast of Sierra Leone and Liberia. The next section as far as the Tano River was called the Ivory or Tooth Coast, because on their arrival the Europeans found incredible quantities of elephant tusks there. The eastern part of this stretch, however, the Dutch named the Quaqua Coast; *quaqua* is the native word for goodday and welcome.[9] This part of Guinea, once belonging to the French colonial empire, now is a part of the Republic of the Ivory Coast. The section between the Tano and the Volta rivers was known as the Gold Coast and farther east was the Slave Coast.

The Gold Coast was always the most attractive of these coastal strips to the Europeans, presumably because it yielded the richest harvest. So it was there that they sought to gain a foothold by building forts and trading stations. Most of the Gold Coast as far as Accra was made up of low mountains and hills; there were small rocky knolls near the sea. East of Accra towards the Volta there was a plain which was sandy near the coast but fertile farther inland. Only at a considerable distance from the coast did the land rise into mountains which were high enough to be seen out at sea. The Volta formed a swampy estuary, and the nearest part of the Slave Coast was equally flat with many lagoons. Throughout the first centuries the Europeans rarely tried to interfere with these lowlying, unhealthy parts, but the rocky knolls on the western part of the coast formed excellent sites for their forts. There they were slightly raised above surrounding forests and bush, refreshed by salutary breezes, and had no difficulty in keeping an eye on ships at sea.

In planning forts and trading stations the possibility of keeping the natives at a safe distance was an important consideration. Immediately after building their strongholds, however, the Europeans certainly did not become the masters of the country. True, the Africans had no means of conquering a fort of European construction; but they controlled the garrison's communications with the surrounding country, could cut off the Europeans' landward supplies, and thus could prevent their trade with the inhabitants of the country. The fertile inland soil was covered with dense bush and virgin forest whose tropical luxuriance made it impenetrable. The Africans could travel along narrow paths, which were often made by wild beasts, but the Europeans preferred to travel with an ax in hand. Supplies had to be brought to the forts by sea but to make their venture profitable, in the long run the Europeans could not do without trade with the interior. Therefore, it was necessary for them to remain on good terms with the Africans to obtain the coveted profits. In fact, over a period of many years we see that time and again the Africans were a decisive influence upon the lives of the Europeans and the existence of their forts. A French writer makes it quite clear that the Dutch would never have allowed the English and the Danes to share the coastal trade with them if they had not been compelled to do so by the Africans.[10] The natives were well aware of the advantages of competition.

On their arrival the Europeans found the country split up into a number of petty states. The most important to the Danes were Fetu near Elmina and Accra about forty miles farther east. It is probable that previously there had been more powerful states. The coastal peoples who were most powerful at the time of the Europeans' arrival were immigrants from the north. This, as far as we know, was also true of the dominant tribes in the Elmina district, who seem to have been descendants of the Akan (Accanis). At an earlier stage in their history they are believed to have lived on the plains to the north of the forest belt; but then another wave of people from the north must have moved southward, pushing them into the forests where they were able to defend their independence. Gradually, they recovered and inhabited the forest all the way to the coast along with groups of other tribes. At some point the Akan split into two tribes: Fanti and Ashanti. Of these, the Fanti migrated farthest south, while the Ashanti made their center at some distance in the interior. Traditionally, however, the Elmina people are believed to have been Ashanti and always to have controlled a considerable part of that nation's coastal trade. Proof of the close relationship between the Fanti and Ashanti can be found in the uniformity of their customs and social structure. The Ashanti may have split up into several tribes, some of which spread southwards to the Ivory Coast. They are not known ever to have been under the domination of any of the great powers of western Sudan, but it has been maintained by Muhammadans that Ashanti once formed part of Wangara, which belonged to Mali. The case of the Accra people was different. Their language was in no way similar to that of the Akan, and they are believed to have been the descendants of immigrants from the Slave Coast, possibly Benin.

In the opinion of the earliest Europeans, the Africans on the Gold Coast were wild and many of the tribes quite unruly. Their fetish worship and human sacrifices seemed to the Christians to be the doings of Satan. They saw no reason for humanity toward them; but the Africans were sturdy, good workers, and made desirable slaves. This fact and the rich natural resources of the coastal regions were enough to arouse the greed of the Europeans and attract swarms of them.

2 / THE DANISH-SWEDISH RIVALRY

THE SCANDINAVIANS BEGAN TO participate in the Guinea venture at a rather late date. Of all the nations of Western Europe they lived farthest from this fountain of wealth, and so they were the last to arrive and exert a political influence on the coast. Given the political situation, their arrival was bound to lead to strong rivalry between the two kingdoms of Scandinavia: Denmark-Norway and Sweden-Finland.

It is probable that a few Scandinavian sailors had taken part in the earlier Portuguese expeditions along the west coast of Africa. It seems fairly certain that there were Danes, Norwegians, or Swedes on board some of the ships sent there by the Dutch. Scandinavian filibusters or pirates may soon have found their way to Guinea, too, but we have no reliable information about them. Such ventures were best left unrecorded as long as they had to be kept secret from the Portuguese, the Dutch, and the English.

The first plan for a government-sponsored trading venture seems to have been directly due to Dutch stimulus. The original proposal was, presumably, made by a Dutchman, Willem Usselinx.[1] He was first instrumental in the foundation of the Dutch West India Company in 1621. After being outmaneuvered and dismissed from this company he turned to King Christian IV of Denmark to obtain his support for the launching of a rival company. In 1624, unable to gain the Danish king's ear, he went to King Gustavus Adolphus of Sweden to lay his plans before him and was given a better reception there. On December 21, 1624, the Swedish government authorized him to establish a "General Commercial Company for Asia, Africa, America and Magellanica." The last name signified all the countries discovered by Magellan on the other side of the globe which were believed to form a continent situated approximately in the position of Australia. Usselinx's work led to the foundation of the so-called "South Company" which was granted a charter in

7

Swedish and German on June 14, 1626, but which was far from successful in carrying out the global projects envisioned by Usselinx. It
should be noted, nevertheless, that the expedition which founded the
Swedish colony along the Delaware River on the east coast of America
sailed in "South Company" ships.[2] This colony existed from 1638 to
1655, when it was conquered by the Dutch; it was finally ceded to
England in 1667 along with the Dutch-founded town, Nieuw Amsterdam
(New York).

The reason for Willem Usselinx's failure in Copenhagen seems to have
been due to the local merchants' desire to reserve the profitable undertaking for themselves. At any rate, a consortium headed by Johan de
Willum applied to King Christian IV for the right to sail and trade
in the West Indies, Brazil, Virginia, and Guinea, just as "the subjects of
several Christian potentates and states already possessed." Johan de
Willum was a thrifty Dutchman who had settled in the Danish capital,
where he traded in grain and other merchandise. Among other things he
joined in purchasing the silk-weaving factory which had been established
with King Christian IV's permission. Of course, the king was bound to
prefer Danish initiative to a foreign one, so by letters of patent of
January 25, 1625, he allowed the applicants to start a company.[3] With
an eight-year monopoly this company was to trade with the above-mentioned countries on the express condition that it avoid places where
it might cause the king to be "misunderstood." The king's desire to
plan for the prosperity of Copenhagen was evident, for the partners of
the company were ordered to equip their vessels at the capital on the
Copenhagen Sound and to unload all cargoes there on their return.
Only Danish shareholders, or participants as they were called, were
allowed.

As far as we know, this fine project was abortive, and several years
went by before another Danish effort was made. By letters of patent of
May 15, 1636, the king authorized Johan and Gödert Braem "with their
partners" to found a Guinea and Africa Company.[4] These two men, the
sons of a Hamburg bailiff, carried on extensive business in Copenhagen.
Johan Braem was one of the king's chief contractors, and he was especially active in whaling in the Arctic Sea. This time the conditions
under which the new company was to start its trade to Guinea were
far more favorable. Either the king must have thought that he had
been too strict the first time, or the two gentlemen were in his good
graces. The new company was granted an exemption from duty for
twelve years as well as permission to accept foreign participants. If it
proved workable, the king promised "further and greater privileges."
However, with the severe financial depression of the last years of Christian
IV's reign, these concessions seem to have been insufficient. The second
attempt was as abortive as the first.

Perhaps it was the Swedes who arrived there first.[5] In any case, they were the first Scandinavians to send official ships to Guinea. The great leader of this venture was Louis de Geer. This commercial genius, the son of a Liege banker, had been trained in France and lived in Amsterdam. In 1627 he moved to Sweden to make use of the Swedish iron-works and made such a considerable fortune as a contractor for war materials that he became a financier throughout Europe. Out of his own funds he equipped a naval squadron for the Torstensson War with Denmark, 1643-1645, and soon after this war he began to trade privately with Africa. It was Samuel Blommaert, a merchant of Amsterdam, who had inspired him to do so; although as a director of the Dutch West India Company, it might have seemed against de Geer's own interests to create foreign competition. De Geer's first expedition proved very prof-itable. On August 1, 1647, a ship commanded by Captain Arent Gab-besen returned to Gothenburg with a cargo of tobacco, sugar, indigo, calico, and ivory plus "a goodly store of gold." Some of the goods had been obtained in Lisbon, while the tobacco and sugar seem to indicate that the ship had also visited the West Indies.

These treasures inspired new ventures, and a sea pass issued on January 15, 1648, for the *Christina* bound for "Africa, Guinea, America, and other parts" shows that de Geer had founded a company. In the spring of 1648 the *Christina* together with the *Stockholm* sailed from Stade, a town in Sweden's newly acquired Archbishopric of Bremen. The *Christina* returned to the same port in July 1649 and the *Stockholm* somewhat later. Both brought good cargoes, the *Stockholm* having visited both Africa and the West Indies. The reason for the success of these first ex-peditions may have been that in these years the Dutch were badly har-assed by the Portuguese. For some time they may not have sent ships to the Gold Coast, and so Arent Gabbesen may have met with no competi-tion on the coast.

Gabbesen possibly found a valuable helper in Hendrik Carlof, a "clerk and fiscal" in the service of the Dutch West India Company, who helped him obtain the permission of the African chiefs to trade on the coast. Carlof was to become the central figure in the first chapter of the history of Scandinavian ventures on the Gold Coast. He is said to have been a native of Rostock and must have been twenty-six or twenty-seven years old when he first met Gabbesen. As far as is known, he seems to have returned to Europe on the *Christina* and then left the Dutch service to join the Swedes.

The Swedish company was now fully developed. De Geer succeeded in silencing the voices raised against admission of foreigners and on December 15, 1649, was granted a charter and monopoly for the par-ticipants in the newly established African, Asiatic, and American Trad-ing Company. To safeguard national interests it was stated that as far as possible the company was to use Swedish ships, built in Sweden, and manned by Swedish crews. Imported goods were to enter Sweden duty-free, and the company was granted the right to enter into contracts and sign treaties with the natives, found colonies, and build forts, for which it could call up Swedish soldiers. This charter was an almost verbatim copy of the Dutch West India Company charter of June 10, 1621.

In regard to the company's 150,000 rixdollars of capital share, de Geer had invested 127,000, and Carlof had contracted for 10,000. In fact, however, the company was de Geer's private business, controlled by himself and his relatives in Amsterdam. The ships they used were Dutch and manned mostly by Dutch sailors. The leader of the first expedition, which sailed from Stade in December 1649, was Carlof, who had been appointed director and general by Queen Christina. In actuality, the company was a thinly disguised rival of the Dutch West India Company; thus one of its two ships was captured by a Dutch privateer, but de Geer was fortunate enough to have it returned.[6]

On April 22, 1650, Carlof arrived at the Gold Coast. Here he called at Cabo Corso, where Portuguese, Dutch, and English had had trading stations ("lodges," "factories") which at that point were unoccupied. At once he renewed the agreement which years ago Gabbesen had made with King Bredeva of Fetu. Then, in spite of the protests of the other native states, he began building a fort, Carlsborg or Carolusborg, later known as Cape Coast Castle.[7] The cornerstone is believed to have been laid by a Swiss named Isaac Melville.

Carlof maintained that the Swedish Crown had obtained territorial rights by the agreement with the Atvian king. For the time being the Africans put up with this, because the Swedes sold their goods more cheaply than the Dutch; but it was an open question whether the Africans were aware of the import of the document they had signed.

Thus, while the Africans were content with the new state of affairs, the European powers who traded on the coast did not like to see a new rival. The Swedish establishment on the coast later gave rise to demands for indemnification and protracted negotiations. The Dutch attempted a siege of Carlsborg to drive out the Swedes, but it was in vain. Several ships arrived with building materials for Carlof. Besides the main fort he built fortified trading stations at Anamabe (Annamobu) in 1652 and Takoradi (Tokorari) in 1653, as well as smaller ones at Butri (Boutri) in 1650, Osu (Orsaki, Orsu, Ozzou, Ursu) in 1652, Gemoree (Jumoree), whose location is not known for certain, and Cape Apollonia in 1655. In the subsequent years the English and Dutch were at war with each other, so Swedish trade on the coast flourished. The Communications with the home country suffered, however, from the privateering of the belligerents. On the whole, the company's balance sheet seemed promising and its business sound.

After the death of de Geer, the company was reorganized, and the capital invested was more genuinely Swedish. The management was moved from Amsterdam to Stockholm, and in July 1655 a new charter was granted.

Of course the subjects of the Danish King could not ignore all this. They had to try to compete with the Swedish company. However, for some time to come it was not Copenhagen but rather Glückstadt which became the center of Danish interest in Guinea.[8]

Glückstadt was a fortified town on the Elbe which had been built by Christian IV after 1615 to serve as an open door for the trade of the king's realms with Western Europe and the world. Foreign businessmen were received in this town with great courtesy, invited to settle there, and favored with privileges. Two separate groups of foreigners were of importance for the prosperity of the town: the Portuguese Jews and the Dutch. Best known among the Portuguese Jews was Albert Dionis, assay-master to the Royal Mint, who opened trade to Spain and was instrumental in the signing of an Hispano-Danish trade agreement.[9] He also persuaded the king to grant special privileges to Portuguese Jews. It may be of interest to note that with these privileges, which received the royal signature on June 19, 1630, Portuguese Jews were allowed to receive among them "other Hebrews coming from the Levant, Italy, Africa or any other parts, but no German Jews." In the following year the Dutch were given similar privileges.

Through the Jewish and Dutch immigrants it was easy to contact business circles in the nations whose trade with tropical countries was most important. So it would seem to be a foregone conclusion that Glückstadt, too, would send expeditions to overseas countries. It may be noted in this connection that the said privileges included shipbuilding rights. In 1640 the possibility was discussed that Gabriel Marselis, Danish resident commissioner at Hamburg, along with his partners might form an East India company at Glückstadt, but as far as we know nothing came of these plans. It is possible, however, to document that some years later trade to Africa and the West Indies was established. On February 18, 1641, captains of German and Dutch nationality in Glückstadt organized themselves into a Captain's Company. During 1642 and 1643 their company was given sea-passes for twenty-nine ships which included the *Martin* of 170 commercial lasts* and the *Patriarch Jacob* of 160 commercial lasts. It remains unknown if any of these ships reached the Gold Coast. However, in 1646 Arend Ghorriedsen, skipper and burgher of Glückstadt, handed to the patron of the town, Ditlev Reventlow, an application for a sea-pass for Africa which stated that he had both wealthy partners for his project and the recommendation of the town council.

* 1 commercial last = 5200 Danish lbs., or 2 tons (F. Mayers *Fremdordbog*, [København], 163).

Next we see that on November 20, 1647, sea-passes and letters of recommendation were issued for two Portuguese Jews, Simon and Henrik de Casseres which enabled them to go and trade at Barbados.[10] The first reliable evidence that an expedition to Africa really was made is found in two letters from a merchant and factor in Glückstadt named Wilhelm Coppin.[11] They are dated 1649 and tell us that his ship, the *Fadtura*, had been on a long voyage, had taken on a cargo for the island of St. Thomas, and had been captured by the Dutch West India Company while homeward bound. The St. Thomas mentioned in this case did not mean the later Danish island in the Caribbean, but rather the Portuguese island of São Thomé on the west coast of Africa which was an important sugar island.

Most interesting, however, is a draft of a charter for an East and West India Company in Glückstadt presumably written in the winter of 1649-50.[12] It mentions that on the seventh day of September in the previous year, i.e., 1649, a ship was sent to Guinea (another source gives the date of departure as December 7 of that year); and now an effort was being made to start a company, since Glückstadt was most favorably situated for trade both by land and by sea. To please the newly chosen king, Frederik III, the town was designated as "erb- und eigenthumliche königliche Stadt." The king must have felt especially linked with Glückstadt before this, for his marriage with Sophie Amalie had been celebrated there in 1642; and it also must have been particularly pleasant for him, at a time when the hereditary monarchy had not yet been established in Denmark, to be told that the town regarded itself as his hereditary property. The company was to trade with Asia, Africa, America, and "Magellanica oder Terram Australi." It also sought a monopoly on passports to these countries, especially the Barbary Coast (North Africa), Guinea, and Angola, as well as in America to (St.) Christopher, Barbados, and Virginia. The charter was to be valid for fifty years beginning either at Easter 1650 or from the departure of the first ship. They also applied for an exemption from customs duty and other dues. On the whole these were all the same privileges that Copenhagen and the East India companies in Holland and England had obtained—including rights to make treaties, build forts, appoint governors, hire troops, mint money, and to fly the royal flag on which was sewn "Fortuna von Glückstadt," the town's coat of arms. Ships were to leave in March and October with the first one going to India in the autumn of 1650.

It may have been due to this application or perhaps to the happy return of the ship sent off in 1649 that on May 16, 1651, Glückstadt was granted privileges for the African trade.[13] The king promised his assistance by means of sea-passes and letters of recommendation, once the trade had been more firmly established and continued by citizens who were really residents of the localities in question, and once the earlier trade carried on by "unterlauffene lourdendreyere" had been stopped. "Lourdendreyere" was the term then used for captains not officially sponsored by the government. Therefore, it seems that the ship sent out in 1649 must have been a "lourdendreyere" venture. The moot question is whether other ships of a similar kind had sailed from the king's realms. The information here stated is all that is available in the Danish material, and evidence from other sources regarding Danish trade to Africa at the time seems quite unreliable.[14] There are thus grounds for questioning whether any Danish ship at all left for Africa before 1649. It seems likely, however, that unofficial traffic was continued from 1650 on. Dutch sources mention the arrival of several Danish vessels on the Gold Coast in 1656.[15] There is nothing to prove that these ships came from Glückstadt, but it is a fact that on December 2, 1656, a sea-pass to Africa was issued for the sloop Die blinde Fortuna to three citizens of Glückstadt, namely Henry and Martin Baers and Gerhard Bremer.[16]

In the meantime Copenhagen, too, had become active. During these years several privileges were granted for trade to the Caribbean Islands.[17] One was issued on October 19, 1653, to Jens Lassen and his partners, which granted them the right to trade to some places in the North Sea, "along with the Caribdiske Insuler." Jens Lassen was an energetic young man, who was not yet thirty years old and who had already risen to the post of Secretary to the Exchequer in Copenhagen. He was one of the few Danes of his day to show any large-scale commercial enterprise at all. What he understood as "some places in the North Sea" turned out to include the west coast of Africa, for he had hit upon the idea of obtaining a share in the slave trade from Guinea and Angola to America. Influenced by the Spanish minister to Copenhagen, de Rebolledo, he even went to the trouble of applying to his Spanish Majesty for permission to enter upon this trade.[18] The minister, however, remarked to his government regarding the application that the trade was bound to start even if permission was not given. Respect for Spain as a significant colonial power had long since ceased.

What Johan de Willum and the Braem brothers had been unable to do was accomplished by Jens Lassen, perhaps because among his helpers he counted the king's private secretary, influential Christopher Gabel whose father, moreover, had been town clerk and master of the king's provisions at Glückstadt. This time a ship was dispatched. On the day the privilege was granted, the Admiral of the Realm, Ove Gedde, was ordered to provide a captain, and on February 8, 1654, Admiral Christopher Lindenow was ordered to fit out the ship Neldebladet for the voyage. Later the rent payable for the ship was fixed at 12,000 rixdollars. It was left to the participants to provision the ship and provide a crew. They could hire whomever they pleased including the sailors of the

Royal Navy, provided only that upon their arrival home they would return all those who survived. Since it is stated that a participant who signed up for one-thirtysecond of the expenses contributed 718 rixdollars, one can conclude that the equipping of the ship cost the participants 22,976 rixdollars.[19]

The voyage was successful. The ship returned to Copenhagen with a rich cargo of sugar, ivory, palm oil, and a quantity of gold. Though it was allowed to pass through the Sound duty-free, most of the profits went to pay expenses and rent for the ship. In any case, there were no dividends paid to those who had shared the cost of preparing the voyage. One of them afterwards complained that all he had received was three loaves of sugar "as a sample and present," and yet, on the whole this expedition proved a stimulus to fresh enterprise. The cargo of sugar led to the foundation of the sugar refinery behind the Royal Exchange in Copenhagen. When an application was made to prevent foreigners from obtaining shares in the refinery, the king granted the African Company, as it was now called, twenty years' sole right to sugar refining. It may also be worth mentioning that during 1657-58 ducats were minted in Copenhagen from the Guinea gold.[20]

If the *Neldebladet* was the first ship to return from the Guinea coast to Copenhagen, it must have caused a considerable sensation in that city. From then on the tales of the returned sailors about Africans, elephants, and the wealth of the tropics must have stimulated the Copenhageners' imaginations. At any rate, there was an evident interest in the continuation of the company; and above all, the idea was discussed that on the next or following voyage a fort should be built on the Guinea coast "for the more profitable continuation of the trade." The company promised to pay the costs with its own capital. The participants agreed to double the company's capital and afterward asked for various privileges which were granted to them by the king. On June 19, Vincent Klingenberg of Hamburg and two others were appointed directors, and the king promised that no seizure should ever be made of the company's capital and lawful profit.[21] Similarly, on June 28 twenty-year privileges were granted to the participants.[22] In these the king promised sea-passes, allowed their ships to fly the royal standard, and exempted them from visitations by Danish men-of-war. They were, however, to pay 1 per cent duty on exports and, curiously enough, the king reserved his right to change the privileges "according to the times, occasions, and nature of the trade."

After that not another word is heard about the African Company in Copenhagen, presumably because of the war declared by Denmark against Sweden in 1657. As early as May of that year Jens Lassen was given a freebooter's pass with the names of ships and captains left blank.

His ships no longer needed to go as far as Africa in search of good prizes. Thus for many years Glückstadt rather than Copenhagen became the starting point for the Danes' African ventures.

In the spring of 1657 a sea-pass was issued to Gabriel Marselis for four ships to go from Glückstadt or Norway to Africa.[23] Gabriel Marselis belonged to a Netherlands family who had founded an important business in Denmark. He now held the post of Danish resident commissioner in Amsterdam. Two of the mentioned ships of 150 commercial lasts each had Dutch names (*Der Oranienbaum, Der bonte Krijgemandz*) and Dutch captains. The third, which was only 50 lasts, was called *St. Oloff,* or *Olaus,* and its captain was Peder Vibe. The fourth *Den norske Lowe,* also only 50 lasts, had a Dutch captain like the first two. It is a moot point whether from the start all of this activity was not actually, like de Geer's Swedish African Company, the result of a Dutch group or family of merchants wanting to compete with the official Dutch West India Company by allowing their ships to sail under the flag of a foreign country.

The name and flag of the Danish king were, however, soon to be put to still stranger uses. This was due partly to the war with Sweden and due partly to the previously mentioned Carlof. He had now fallen out with the Swedes in spite of the fact that they had granted him a patent of nobility, which thus enabled him to style himself a knight. The Swedes accused him of having carried on trade on his own account. Carlof complained that it was impossible for him to earn his pay and cover his expenses. It may have proved more difficult for him to remain friends with the Swedes after Louis de Geer died, and Swedish nobles flocked to the Swedish African Company in increasing numbers. Be that as it may, on his arrival at Stockholm in 1656 he resigned, moved first to Hamburg, and thence to Emden. In his anger against the Swedes he applied for a Danish letter of marque when the war broke out, and on August 1, 1657, an agreement was signed whereby Carlof was commissioned to capture the Swedish fort on the Guinea coast.[24] He was himself to defray the costs of arming and provisioning the necessary ships. If he took any prizes, they were to be sailed to Glückstadt. Nevertheless, he could sell them to foreigners, if he thought fit to do so; but the loading and unloading of cargoes must take place at Glückstadt. In case he succeeded in capturing the fort, he was to hold it until he had informed the king, after which they were to negotiate about the development of the Danish company. He would then be entitled to invest in this company, be appointed one of its directors, and draw a certain percentage of the profits. If at that time the king no longer desired to have the company, Carlof would be entitled to buy the fort and dispose of it to others provided they were not enemies of Denmark. If he did not capture the fort but only captured ships and merchandise, he was to pay one tenth of it to the king. He was given express orders to confiscate all Swedish ships but to leave neutral and allied vessels in peace.

By virtue of this strange contract the knight Carlof was placed in a position of sovereign independence similar to the part sometimes played by the Danish ministers Corfitz Ulfeldt and Hannibal Sehested. It appears strange that while entering the Danish service, Carlof was secretly negotiating with the Swedes and the de Geer family in the hope of bringing about a reconciliation.

On December 1, 1657, armed with the agreement with the Danish king, Carlof sailed from Glückstadt harbor.[25] His ship, the *Glückstadt*, carried eighteen guns and a crew of forty-eight. On January 25, 1658, he arrived at Gemoree, which is situated to the west of Cabo Tres Puntas on the Gold Coast. Afterward, it was said that he showed the Swedish colors and the local Swedish agent at once sent a man out to him. Carlof detained him in order to get the necessary information about conditions at Carlsborg. Then he sailed on to the Dutch Fort Axim (Atchin) near the promontory of the same name to ask for assistance. Obviously it was impossible to accomplish anything with only his own forces. The Dutch gave him four boats and fifty-six slaves; and with these and twenty-two well-armed sailors he sailed that evening to Elmina, which was only about ten kilometers from Carlsborg. During the night he marched this last stretch, and on the way he sent messages requesting aid from the neighboring African chiefs. The most important of them was a brother of Hennique, King of Fetu.[26] His name was Acrosan, but he was called Johan Classen by the Europeans. He held the office of *Tay* or *Day,* that is, vice-regent, royal treasurer, and protector of the Christians in the country, and evidently he was a man who understood his work. Before his departure Carlof had entered into a solemn agreement with him that he, Carlof, was to be given the Swedish possessions whenever he claimed them. Carlof now reminded him of the terms of this agreement and added that the directors of the Swedish company had mortally affronted him. To add weight to his requests he promised Johan Classen the remission of all his debts to the Swedes. Convinced by these arguments, the African chief promised to do his best to give aid. Under the cover of night he let Carlof into Ogua (Ugua, Qvagva), the African town situated close to Carlsborg. Then he called together the slaves of the Swedish company and promised them rich presents in return for their assistance.

In the morning a dense fog covered the area. As usual the company slaves came to the fort to fetch their tools which were iron bars used for quarrying stones. A large and a small gate led into the fort. At night everything was closed, but in the morning the slaves were let in at the small gate. No sooner had they picked up the iron bars than they knocked down the unsuspecting sentry and then proclaimed that those who offered no resistance would receive their pay. The entire garrison consisted of a mere sixteen men. Resistance was, therefore, hopeless. The Swedish commander and governor, J. Ph. von Krusenstierna, was taken prisoner. There was, at the time, a richly laden ship, the *Stockholm Slott,* lying off the fort. In the name of Krusenstierna a message was sent to the captain ordering him to come to the fort, and without sensing any danger he came through the fog and was also taken prisoner. The Dutch then persuaded the Dutch sailors who made up the majority on board to leave the ship. As the Swedish sailors were too few to sail her, the ship could be made a prize. Krusenstierna and the captain were taken on board the *Glückstadt* as prisoners. Those in the garrison of the fort and the crew of the ship who were willing to enter Carlof's service were allowed to do so. Carlof gathered them in the hall of the fort, and made them swear an oath of personal allegiance to him and give a written confirmation of it. The Danish flag was hoisted over the fort, the Danish signal was fired, and thus was the curious beginning of the Danish king's African dominions.

Among the other Swedish stations, Takoradi, Anamabo, Gemoree, and Accra were afterward taken. The rest of the Swedish places were, presumably, no longer occupied. The agreement between Carlof and Johan Classen was renewed, and the African chief promised not to give the fort to anyone except Carlof. Finally, a Dutchman named Samuel Smidt was designated as commandant, a force of about forty men was left behind, and at the end of February Carlof set sail with both ships for Europe.

On June 8, 1658, his arrival at Glückstadt caused excitement. He reported to the Danish Field-Marshal Eberstein and was well received. The next day, however, the Swedish minister resident at Hamburg complained and demanded that the Swedish ship with prisoners and cargo be returned to Sweden in accordance with an article in the Roskilde Peace Treaty of February 26, 1658. By this treaty the Danes had promised the return of all prizes which had not entered Danish ports before the Taastrup Agreement of the previous February 18. Furthermore, the Swedes demanded that Carlof be arrested as a pirate. Eberstein did not think that he could run this risk, for Carlof had acted in the name of the Danish king; and so, while Carlof was his guest that evening, the Swedish demands were revealed to him. During the night Carlof escaped on board a small ship, carrying with him his precious spoils, which included eight hundred pounds of gold taken from the Swedish company.

This, of course, infuriated the Swedes who accused the Danes of having aided the flight. The Danish government tried to base its argument on a section of the Taastrup Agreement which stipulated that forts and territories conquered by the Danes were to be returned, but that the

Stockholm Slott could not be included under this. Instead it was argued that the ship had anchored at Carlsborg before the Taastrup Agreement, and the fort then had to be regarded as Danish. This kind of reasoning aroused the anger of Carolus Gustavus. He demanded an enormous compensation in cash or territories in exchange for it. In fact, the Guinea dispute became one of the chief reasons why he decided to renew his war with Denmark immediately and to march his army against Copenhagen, an action which for the time being prevented Denmark from handing back to the Swedes both Carlsborg and the *Stockholm Slott*.[27]

It was impossible to settle the matter until the war was over, when, by the Copenhagen Peace Treaty of May 27, 1660, and after very difficult negotiations, the Swedes waived the demand put forward by Carolus Gustavus in 1659.[28] Their claim was fixed at 400,000 rixdollars or four barrels of gold. Formal cession of the territories by Sweden to Denmark was never contemplated, and the Swedes certainly did not intend to allow the Danes to acquire rights in Africa in the future.

In the meantime, events in Africa had followed lines quite different from those planned in Europe. Shortly after Carlof left the Gold Coast with his rich spoils, two Swedish ships, the *Thisbe* and the *Johannesburg*, arrived under command of the brothers der Vos.[29] They attempted, with the help of money and arms and with the support of the Africans, to enter Carlsborg. However, there were already three English ships lying at anchor; and when they threatened to seize the *Johannesburg*, the Swedes sailed on to Anamabo where they tried to land. This time, however, the Danish guns hit some of their landing craft. So they retreated and tried a third place, the nearby Adja (Agga) where the Danes had had a lodge for a while.[30] This third attempt met with no more success, so after being on the coast from March 15 to April 22, 1658, they set sail. This Danish success was due partly to the support of the natives of Fetu and to the Dutch governor, Valkenburgh, who placed 800 pounds of gunpowder and 100 cannon balls at their disposal. This he did, he said, to avoid a revolt among the natives.

There were, however, other reasons for the Dutch helpfulness. Presumably, they regarded the Danes as weaker than the Swedes and preferred to have them on the coast, since they would be less difficult to dislodge. At any rate, the Dutch were planning to rid themselves of both rivals at the earliest opportunity, and they did not have to wait long. During the nights of April 15 and 16, 1659, the Danish commander Samuel Smidt abandoned Carlsborg and handed over the fort to the Dutch West India Company for a sum of money. Anamabo, Takoradi, and Osu were also abandoned. Afterward it was maintained that Masper van Heussen, the Dutch commander, had made Smidt believe that Denmark had been conquered by Sweden and that it no longer existed.[31] Similarly, the Dutch West India Company insisted that in March 1659 they had bought Carlsborg and the other forts from Carlof. The Danish king, of course, refused to acknowledge this agreement, and Carlof flatly denied it. When one learns that the Dutchman Samuel Smidt later became a merchant at Moree to the east,[32] one must again ask whose interests Carlof and his partners actually served.

At least the King of Fetu realized that the Dutch had made a fool of Smidt. So he ordered Johan Classen to attack the fort, and after a six weeks' siege the Dutch had to surrender to the natives who then temporarily occupied the fort. Soon after the capture Johan Classen assured Johan Nyman, a commissioner from the Swedish Africa Company who was staying with the English on the coast, of the friendship of the King of Fetu and offered to hand the fort over to the Swedes if they arrived within a year. The important thing for the Africans was to establish contacts with as many nations as possible in order to enjoy the benefits of competition.

So the Swedes hastened to reopen trade. They succeeded in equipping the ship *King David* in Hamburg, so that by September 1660 it was able to leave for the Gold Coast. On December 10 of that year the Africans handed over Carlsborg to the Swedes. This act of loyalty on the part of the Africans has ever since moved Swedish hearts. The Swedes, however, bought it dearly, for they had to pay Johan Classen 27,000 "species-dollars" * in gold, and afterward they had to hire forty to fifty Africans at high monthly salaries. In order to reap the full benefits of its possessions the Swedish company had Lidbert Wolters, a Hamburg merchant, equip the ship *Christina,* which set sail under the command of Johan Nyman late in 1661. This, the Dutch could not tolerate; so as the *Christina* neared Carlsborg, she was attacked by four of the Dutch company's ships, captured, and taken to Elmina where Nyman was thrown into prison, tortured, and put to death. In order to end all Swedish ventures in Guinea, the Dutch next launched an attack on Carlsborg on March 31, 1662. At first they did not make much headway, for the Africans supported the Swedes; but later, after Johan Classen was dead and his countrymen tired of waiting for the Swedes to come to their relief, the Dutch succeeded in bribing them to take the fort by surprise and then to hand it over to them. This occurred on April 22, 1663, after the Dutch had waited patiently for thirteen months. The English and the Danes also had tried to persuade the Fetus to give them the fort. They succeeded only in making the Africans extract from the Dutch the promise to remain at peace with their European rivals. To punish the Swedish commander, Tonnies Voss, for his perseverance in defending the fort the Dutch placed him under a gallows with a rope round his neck.[33] There he was left for three hours and then sentenced to imprisonment. While in prison he was sometimes fetched from his cell and made to dance

* A Danish-monetary term; a double dollar.

naked before the natives. He escaped, however, and managed to return home to Sweden. There seems to have been good reasons for the dislike with which other nations looked upon Dutch colonial rule during the seventeenth century.

Thus the Swedes ended their story, but in Europe their participation in the Guinea traffic led to protracted legal action for compensations and diplomatic negotiations. The Danes, on the other hand, did not give up after the loss of Carlsborg in 1659 but continued their activities, although they, too, were made to suffer from Dutch persecution. Swedish attempts to wrest the Guinea trade from the hands of de Geer's Dutch clique for the Swedes themselves was a complete failure. From the start, however, the Danes took better care not to fall into the hands of foreigners. The cosmopolitan citizenry of Glückstadt was fortunate and found support in Hamburg, which was still formally under Danish sovereignty. At any rate, the Danish king's subjects proved more successful than the Swedes in getting something out of their African ventures.

3 / THE GLÜCKSTADT COMPANY

AFTER CARLOF'S EXPLOIT OF 1657-58, Glückstadt rather than Copenhagen had become the most likely starting point for the Danish Guinea trade. Good opportunities which now seemed to present themselves were not to be neglected, and the desire to take advantage of the situation was strong.

Nothing more was heard from Carlof for a while after his nocturnal escape with the rich spoils. He first had gone to Holland; but as the Swedes tried also to seize him there through diplomatic negotiations, he was obliged to retire to Antwerp in the Spanish Netherlands. Of course, he was in no hurry to throw himself into the arms of the Danes who could claim part of his booty. Eberstein vainly tried to persuade him to come to Glückstadt. It was impossible to do without him, for the fort in Guinea was held at his disposal. So a citizen of Hamburg, Poul Klingenberg, who was Danish Postmaster General, Councillor of the Admiralty and himself a great speculator, was authorized to issue a passport and commission for the knight.[1] Klingenberg, too, had considerable difficulty in contacting the runaway, but because of the persecution of the Swedes Carlof needed whatever support he could get. So, on March 28, 1659, negotiations between him and Klingenberg were started in Hamburg. An agreement was drawn up and confirmed by the king on May 20. It was thereby recognized that Carlof had acted on the orders of the Danish king. He was allowed to keep the captured Swedish ship and merchandise, and the king would protect him from the Swedes. In return for this, in the future the conquered fort and outposts with arms and ammunition were to be the property of the king of Denmark. Carlof and his coparticipants were, nevertheless, to have the privilege of trading there. The commanders of the fort and outposts were to obey the king but also to assist Carlof and his men in the trade.

In the agreement "Carlof and coparticipants" meant the new African

21

company which could be established under the previous agreement with Carlof in 1657.[2] This company was now beginning to take shape. It was founded on March 29, 1659; its charter was signed by the king the same day as the agreement with Carlof, May 20. Shortly afterward the Danish resident minister at The Hague, Peter Charisius, received orders to support the company instead of the Dutch West India Company.[3] We do not know to what extent the shareholders of the Copenhagen African Company were admitted to the Glückstadt company. However, in 1660 Jacob de Boys (Delbos, Delboger) and Vincent Klingenberg are mentioned as its directors. The latter had been one of the directors of the Copenhagen company, so in all probability there was a connection between the two companies. On application from the directors, the privileges of the company were extended by a patent of September 8, 1660, which allowed it to trade not only at the African places belonging to the king of Denmark but also along the entire coast of Africa. Only after the first year were the privileges of the company finally agreed upon, and on July 24 the king renewed its charter for a period of twenty-four years. The privileges were reconfirmed for the same period, after the death of Frederik III, by King Christian V in June 1671.[4]

In contrast to the Glückstadt company, earlier Danish companies had had strong capital support.[5] However, the starting investment was considerable for that period, amounting to 392,700 marks. On October 31, 1660, another 69,200 marks out of the first year's profit were added to the capital; and in 1661, when the two merchants, Martin Baers and Gerhard Bremer, with partners, who had been granted sea-passes to Sierra Leone among other places for their ship *Fortuna,* were allowed to join, an additional 36,000 marks were added to the investment.[6] Thus the total share capital amounted to nearly half a million marks, and the company was able to carry on a brisk trade with Guinea. It is impossible to say how many ships left the Danish king's ports annually for Guinea, but there seems to have been at least two or three.[7] The first two which sailed were the *St. Martin* and the *Die Liebe,* which reached the Gold Coast in October 1659. On board was Jost Cramer, a native of Lindau in Schwaben, whom the company had designated as Commandant of Carlsborg. On his arrival, however, he found that six months earlier the Dutch had tricked Samuel Smidt out of the fort, and thus the Danish company was without a stronghold. Negotiations with van Heusen, the Dutch commandant, of course, proved fruitless. The Fetu, on the other hand, showed interest in the newcomers. They were quite willing to allow them a permanent foothold in the country and gave them the choice of three locations. So after some weeks, on December 20, 1659, Cramer made a contract with Hennique, king of Fetu, cousin and successor of King Bredeva, and with whom on behalf of the Swedish company Carlof had a few years before entered into an agreement.[8] By this contract the king of Denmark acquired lawful rights on the coast, for the first time by peaceful means. The contract was made not only with the king of Fetu himself, but also with four other prominent Africans including Johan Classen. Three copies of the contract were made, one for the company, one for Cramer, and one for Johan Classen. Evidently, the latter was the principal representative of the Fetu in arranging the agreement. He must have been a clever man with a talent for making the Europeans pay up. The contract was to remain in force "for all eternity." It was confirmed by an oath and fetish was eaten. This was the natives' custom when they wanted to give to a legal act the highest and most sacred force. It was a declaration that they wished a calamity might strike them if they broke their promise. After this, by way of confirmation, they ate something which had been placed on a fetish.

In this way the Fetu "sold and transferred" to the Glückstadt company the Castle of Amanfro, "which the Germans call Frederiksberg," with its coast and harbor. It became their free property for the sum of fifty benda gold which was distributed among the native participants in the contract. Included in the purchase was a free lodge near Cabo Corso, with permission to build a stone house there, "the better to free them from fire and other misfortune."

What the sale meant in terms of modern juridical thinking is difficult to say. The Africans probably regarded it as something in the nature of a sale of land for private ownership. The contract did not say that the Danes were to pay a monthly rent, the so-called "custom" to the Fetu king, as Europeans usually had to when they built forts or trading stations in their countries. Thus, one might conclude that the purchase included sovereign rights, and, consequently, that on this occasion the Danish king had acquired a colony. If we look at the way in which the terms of the contract worked in practice, however, this view is untenable. In fact, the Danes, like the other Europeans on the coast, paid a monthly tribute of three or four ounces of gold to the "Day" and always had to be prepared to give offerings and presents to the natives. Similarly, they paid customs duties on what they imported from Europe, the Africans getting the first sample of each imported good. The monthly tribute was later to be called "ground rent," and its payment must be regarded as conclusive proof that the Fetu king kept his sovereignty over the district purchased by the Glückstadt company. Further proof of the Fetu king's retaining formal sovereignty can be deduced from the fact that on several occasions when a Danish commandant died, the Fetu were given a vote in the election of his temporary successor.[9]

Frederiksberg, sometimes called Frederiksborg, was situated within artillery range (1130 yards) east of Cabo Corso. Since it was impossible to build a harbor there which a cargo boat could enter, the contract gave

the Danes free entrance to the harbor of Cabo Corso and the right to
load and unload there. There was no place on the entire Guinea coast
where sea vessels could come close to the coast. They had to anchor at
some distance and make contact with land by means of boats, but the
ocean's breakers along the coast were so violent that, as a rule, even the
ships' boats were unable to land, especially where dangerous rocks lined
the beach. Even the best landing places necessitated the use of specially
built boats and very skillful crews to get through the surf. In practice,
therefore, the Europeans preferred to anchor their boats at some distance
from the coast and there await the arrival of the natives. Their canoes
were more suitable for the difficult transport to the beach where goods
and passengers were carried ashore by the Africans. To this day there are
very few real harbors on the Guinea coast. In the great majority of
places embarkation and disembarkation is still carried out in the old-
fashioned way with the assistance of the natives.

Most remarkable of all, in case the Swedes should come back to Cabo
Corso, the Fetu also undertook to see that they kept peace with the
Danes. They even guaranteed the Danes freedom from all attacks whether
from Europeans or Africans. The contract further promised that in case
the Swedes did not arrive at the promised time, they would not give
Cabo Corso, where Carlsborg was situated, to any other nation than the
Danes. However, as we have already seen, the Swedes were in time and
installed themselves in the fort. Finally, the Fetu allowed Cramer to apply to the king of Sabo (Sabu), a neighboring state to the east, to obtain
possession of the Cong Height and certain other localities including some
harbors.[10] These places were just on the other side of the boundary between the two African states, only a couple of kilometers from Frederiksberg. Cong had been occupied by the Dutch until the spring of 1659;
but when Johan Classen besieged Cabo Corso, they evacuated Cong, and
the guns they left behind were removed by Johan Classen. The Danes
succeeded also in obtaining a contract with the king of Sabo for the hill,
and so they installed themselves there. Later, however, the Dutch maintained that the Danes had driven them out by force, insulted the Dutch
flag by dragging it on the ground, and finally fired on Dutch ships from
the lodge. In any case, on April 24, 1661, they attacked the Danish lodge,
pillaged and burnt it, and dragged the garrison in chains to Fort Nassau,
a possession of theirs farther east in Sabo.

This is only one of many similar events which shows how willingly
the Dutch would have driven the Danes away from the coast by using
the methods which had already proved successful against the Swedes.
True, after Charisius' *démarche*, the States General had given orders
that the Glückstadt company was to be respected, but the Dutch on the
Gold Coast took no notice of this order. Similarly, in 1659 they tried to
drive away from Frederiksberg's road the above-mentioned two ships,

the *St. Martin* and *Die Liebe*. Only after three hours' fighting did the Glückstadt ships succeed in forcing the Dutch to leave them in peace. They attacked also the *Fredericus Tertius* in 1660 and the *St. Martin* and the *Fortuna* in 1661. In February 1661 they captured the *Kurier von Venetien* on the open sea and then brought it into Elmina, where the crew was put in prison.[11] The Dutch maintained that, since in reality the ship had been sent by Dutch shipowners who did not belong to the Dutch West India Company, it had infringed this company's privileges. Carlof, who was in Amsterdam at the time, is said to have given evidence to the effect that the real head of the Glückstadt company was Jan de Swan, its factor at Amsterdam. The Danes defended themselves vigorously against the accusation, but the Dutch authorities, in 1662, confirmed the legality of the ship's confiscation. Similarly, in January 1662 the *Wapen von Glückstadt* was taken "fine warm" with a considerable cargo. On all such occasions, the Dutch respected neither flags nor papers issued either by Danish or by Dutch authorities. When, in November 1662, two ships, the *Fredericus Tertius* and the *Prins Christianus* (formerly *Die Liebe*) arrived at Frederiksberg's road, they were attacked by three Dutch ships: the *Den Gouden Keeuw*, the *Christina* (a former Swedish ship), and the *De Faem*. Out of respect for the flag of his king, as it was said, the Danish captain could not avoid returning the attack. Thus began a fight which ended in the Danes being routed. Shortly afterward, in December 1662, the Dutch commander, Valckenburg, with two ships attacked the Danish lodge, Bagos, on the Sierra Leone River. Years before the Danes had established a lodge there, but it had later been abandoned. It was in a state of complete decay when in 1661 it was reoccupied. The reoccupation was accomplished by the above-mentioned merchant, Gerhard Bremer, who arrived in the *St. Martin*. With a few men he rebuilt and fortified the lodge and began trading there. Valckenburg found a goodly store there, including many elephant tusks, which he sacked before destroying the buildings. Gerhard Bremer was taken to Elmina in irons and thence sent to prison in Amsterdam.

The losses caused to the Danish king's subjects by these Dutch acts of violence gave rise to many complaints and diplomatic demands from the Danish Crown to the Netherlands States General.[12] The Dutch company, on the other hand, held to its view that in reality the Glückstadt company was made up of Dutchmen who were thus able to evade the Dutch company's privileges. A number of letters of complaint concerning the quarrel between the two companies were printed and used in mutual agitation campaigns. Also, in England and France complaints were lodged by the Danes against the Dutch West India Company. Among these the representations of Hannibal Sehested proved especially efficacious. Almost certainly his arguments helped to induce the English in 1664 to send a fleet to Guinea under Admiral Robert Holmes to conquer the Dutch possessions there. At that time the English were the outstanding rivals of the Dutch for control of the seas. A new English company, the Royal Adventurers of England Trading to Africa, had been founded in 1662, and tension between this new company and the Dutch West India Company was growing.[13] The English were just as inclined as the Danes to oppose the claims which the Dutch thought they could make for the sovereignty over territories in certain African states. They maintained that the Europeans possessed only the property rights to the forts, while sovereignty still belonged to the African kings.

This was the background for the course of events which were to follow when, in 1664, the Dutch made an attempt to rid themselves entirely of the Danes in Guinea. First, on March 23, 1664, they attacked the Danish lodge at Cabo Corso, sacked it, smashed doors and windows, and put the Danish official in prison in Elmina. Next, on the following days they kept Frederiksberg under fire from the sea. Thanks to the good assistance of the natives, the garrison was able to put up quite a gallant defense; but the result would probably not have been very happy for the Danes, if they had not been relieved just in time. On April 14, Robert Holmes arrived with a fleet of six or seven ships.[14] Because of the English attitude, the Danes had no difficulty in entering into an alliance with the admiral.[15] Under its terms the Danish commander gave written promise, with the reservation of the Danish king's rights, to assist the English in the conquest of Carlsborg. With expensive presents they obtained the Fetu's sanction of their plans. Having landed artillery, ammunition, and provisions, the combined Danish and English forces launched the attack upon the fort by land as well as by sea. Day and night the fort was kept under fire, "but greatest, and most faithfully" from Frederiksberg. After eight days the Dutch sub-commandant, a Frenchman named Thomas Pensade, had to send his standard-bearer, a Hungarian, to the Danish fort to be informed of the terms of surrender. So, on May 3, 1664, the fort of Cabo Corso fell into the hands of the English. They named it Cape Coast Castle and have kept it ever since then. In return for their assistance, the English allowed the Danes to keep the lodge near the fort which the Dutch had recently disturbed. The Danes had worked in close cooperation with the English for the expulsion of the Dutch from this principal fort, and from that time forward they kept very close ties. This, presumably, was the real reason why it was possible to preserve the possessions on the coast of Africa for so many generations and with such slender resources.

From then on, the Danish possessions on the Guinea coast were no longer at the mercy of the Dutch. It is true, however, that in the following year the States General sent their famous Admiral de Ruyter to Africa with a considerable fleet.[16] He captured several English strongholds such as the former Danish possession of Anamabo. Fort Witzen at

Takoradi was blown up and destroyed forever, but he gave up trying to capture Cape Coast Castle.

Danish friendship with the English at Cape Coast Castle was soon to be put to the test. In 1665 Anglo-Dutch rivalry developed into open war. The Copenhagen government did not know which party to turn to for support, and so, for a long time its policy was one of vacillation. When it was informed in 1666 that the French would support the Dutch, it decided on war against England. However, this quarrel did not spread to the Gold Coast. The commandants of the English and Danish forts agreed not to molest each other; the garrisons of the two forts fraternized, ate and drank together.[17]

In Europe, Denmark's entrance into the war led to the formal conclusion of the dispute between the Dutch West India Company and the Glückstadt company. On February 1, 1666, a treaty of alliance was signed by the States General and Denmark to which was added an accompanying document containing some conditions which Poul Klingenberg had drawn up and made the Dutch agree to.[18] The Danish king thereby gave up his claims to Cabo Corso, Takoradi, and Anamabo. On the other hand, he was allowed to keep Frederiksberg, Osu, and the lodge near Cape Coast Castle until the expiration of the Glückstadt company's charter in 1679, after which these places were to be handed over to the Dutch company subject to compensation. The Danish king had to promise that no Dutchmen would be admitted to the Glückstadt company, and that negotiations about the two companies' mutual claims against each other would be carried on peacefully. The war between Holland and England ended with the Peace of Breda on July 21, 1667, by which England and Holland each kept the Gold Coast forts they had had at the outbreak of the war. Denmark, too, was a signatory to this peace treaty, and afterward the Glückstadt company and the Dutch West India Company agreed on a compromise. However, that was not the end of the matter, and for many years to come it remained a recurring subject of diplomatic negotiations.

The section imposing cession of the Danish places in 1679 does not seem to have been carried out. Presumably, the Dutch were too weakened by the French invasion in 1672 and the war that followed to press for its fulfillment. So the Glückstadt shipowners could go on exploiting the Guinea trade for the benefit of His Danish Majesty's rightful subjects. If their ventures had really been backed by Dutchmen they probably had to withdraw or cover their participation. They apparently were freed from Carlof at some time before 1665. The last that was heard of him was when, in 1665 as captain of a trading vessel, he called at la Rochelle and Sweden demanded his arrest.[19] After that there is no further trace of him.

The compensation for the damage the Dutch had done was far from sufficient.[20] The lodge at Sierra Leone was valued at 35,174 marks, the ship *Wapen von Glückstadt* at 35,215 marks, and the ship *Kurier von Venetien* at 27,932 marks. The loss of 5,859 marks caused by the Dutch confiscation of some goods in London was added to this. Thus the sum total of these losses was estimated at 105,180 marks. In 1672 a compensation of 40,093 marks was paid, but there remained a deficit of 65,187 marks. To this must be added the loss in 1659 of Carlsborg, Takoradi, Anamabo, and Osu, for which we have no proper estimate. Later, however, the company maintained that the Dutch company's raids had cost them 549,252 marks. This total would include the costs of acquiring new forts and lodges, heavy arms for the ships to enable them to fight on equal terms, and the losses incurred due to the Dutch inroads which prevented Danish trade projects. It would be difficult to make a correct estimate, especially for the last item; so, in taking into account the fact that the sum mentioned was put forward to appeal to the king's pity, it can safely be taken for granted that the estimate is far too high.

Nevertheless, the losses inflicted on the company in its early years by the Dutch seem to have proven fatal in the long run. True, the company succeeded in keeping its right to several advantageous sites in Africa where trade seems to have flourished, but the loss of capital had been so great that it was deprived of the reserves which would have enabled it to meet adversity.

4 / FORT FREDERIKSBERG

FOR THE TIME BEING, however, Fort Frederiksberg prospered. The place had been quickly built. After its purchase by the Danes, the Fetu sent 300 slaves who cleared the hilltop of brush, leveled it, and obtained timbers for the buildings. Next they erected a number of houses in the usual native style "of wooden frames covered with clay, and thatched with straw" into which the company's men moved.[1] After the death of Jost Cramer on June 6, 1662, the chief trader of the fort, a citizen of Hamburg named Henning Albrecht, assumed command. He began to fortify half of the hill by building a wall of rough-hewn stone and clay. He had a somewhat larger house built of stone and clay facing the sea. In addition he built three bastions: one facing the sea, one toward Cabo Corso, and one toward Sabo and Fort Nassau. All of these were solid enough, at least, for the garrison to hold its own against the Fetu. After the completion of these fortifications, "the Danish Hill" was described as 300 feet high and rather steep.[2] At the foot of the hill the company's slaves built a village, and Henning Albrecht persuaded some Akan traders to settle in the neighborhood.[3] They were useful to have near by for they could act as agents for wealthy merchants in their own country farther inland. Similarly, Albrecht induced some native fishermen to build a village to the east of Frederiksberg Hill which they named Hittacqui (because its inhabitants came from Hittacqui) or Komenda, a state on the western border of Fetu. Saltmakers, too, settled close to the Danish fort.

Evidently Henning Albrecht was a capable and enterprising man with the knack for making useful contacts. Villault, a French traveler who visited Frederiksberg in March and April 1667, gives the following description of him: "a small, proud, courteous, intelligent, accommodating man, who spoke Latin fluently, but did not understand French." [4] Long before Villault had reached Fetu, he had received a letter from

Albrecht with offers of trade, and his reception at the fort was most cordial. The company, too, acknowledged Albrecht's excellent service and, on September 10, 1664, appointed him as Cramer's successor.[5]

Fortunately, we are fairly well informed about conditions at Fort Frederiksberg in those days. Two of the men who went out in the Glückstadt company's ships published books on what they saw and heard in Guinea. One writer was Hans Jacob zur-Eich, a Zürich locksmith, who went out in 1659 on the *St. Martin* and so witnessed the building of the Danish settlement right from the start. Bitter experience enabled him to describe Dutch villainy. Not only did he survive the three-hour battle on their arrival at Cabo Corso, but also later, when traveling along the coast in a canoe to Osu, he was captured by the Dutch, thrown into a dark cell, and fed only bread and water. Attempts were made to persuade him to enter the Dutch service, but he refused, knowing that the Dutch treated their employees badly unless they were natives of Holland. After some months he was taken on board a Dutch ship and thence liberated by the English in 1664, so that he could return to Fort Frederiksberg. After nine years of service on the coast he sailed for home in the ship *Patriarch Jacob* by way of the Portuguese island of São Thomé, where a cargo of 200 slaves was sold and a cargo of sugar taken on board. On arriving at Hamburg, his salary was duly paid, and before Christmas of that same year he was back in his native city. There in 1677 he published his *Afrikanische Reiszbeschreibung in die Landschaft Fetu,* in which he deals primarily with the life of the natives. The same subject interested the other writer, a clergyman from Hamburg named Johan Müller. He was engaged by the company in 1661 and remained on the coast for eight years. Apparently he was the first clergyman to be sent there under the Danish flag. His book came out in Hamburg in 1676 under the title *Die Afrikanische auf der Guineischen Gold-Cust gelegene Landschafft Fetu.* It was published a year before zur-Eich's book, and it is quite obvious that the latter made extensive use of Müller's. As a curiosity it may be worth mentioning that Müller gives a list of Fetu words in an appendix.

Henning Albrecht held the post of commandant until 1669 when, like zur-Eich, he sailed for home in the *Patriarch Jacob*. His successor, Bartholomaeus von Gronestein (Gravenstein), had already been appointed on September 13, 1667.[6] His sphere of activity was specified as the traditional Danish places and St. Thomas. This latter must be taken to mean São Thomé, and therefore, we are led to suppose that for a time Denmark may have possessed a lodge there. Along with Captain Cornelis Janssen, who since 1664 was the commander of the *Sophia Amalia* (formerly the *St. Martin*), Gronestein was ordered to assume responsibility for finances.[7] The company may have been dissatisfied with accounts rendered or thought Albrecht's building operations too expensive. On the other hand, no legal action seems to have been brought against him. Gronestein came out in June 1668 and took over command directly from Henning Albrecht.

Things were no longer going well for the company. The *Sophia Amalia* with its cargo for Guinea was wrecked, and there was not sufficient capital to continue.[8] So, the directors demanded a 25 per cent additional payment from the shareholders—but they refused to pay. The board of directors then obtained a royal order whereby the shareholders were to pay or lose their investments in the company. There is nothing, however, to show that payment ever took place, and three years elapsed before a ship again was sent out.

In the meantime, Gronestein and his men in Africa were having a difficult time. The Gkana were at war and were neglecting the trade. It was they who had procured the gold. What little trade there was gradually fell into the hands of the English and the Dutch, while at the Danish fort they had to use their capital. Later the Danes on the coast often were neglected for long periods of time by those at home, and in their loneliness they would see one after the other of their little circle succumb to the tropical climate.

It was not until January 26, 1672, with David Beck as captain, that the *Patriarch Jacob* returned, loaded with a good cargo.[9] The ship further brought promises of a new commandant to succeed Gronestein; but no money was sent out, and an order was delivered stating that everything in the fort was to be sent home with Beck. Worst of all, the ship brought the rumor that the company was ruined, and so the stations were to be given up. Consequently, their neighbors became more and more insolent, and the few remaining Danes were in imminent danger. There were only eight men at Fort Frederiksberg, two at Cabo Corso, and three at Osu. Gronestein sent home a written complaint, but no one arrived to relieve him. In 1674 their faithful servant died at his post.

First of all, it was the English who gradually became dangerous rivals. By 1679 their trade was conducted mostly by means of privately owned ships; but in 1672 their African company had been reorganized and renamed the Royal African Company, and afterward it proved even more aggressive.[10] In 1675 its men attempted to destroy the Danish lodge at Cabo Corso. The man who after Gronestein's death had taken over the command of Fort Frederiksberg, Conrad Crul, protested, but the perpetrators simply answered that they were prepared to defend their doings to the company in London.[11] Crul proposed to the government in Copenhagen that it send a diplomatic protest to London, but nothing was done because of the war with Sweden which broke out in 1675.

With Danish trade at a standstill, the buildings of the fort decayed. The mud and stone walls of the fort were continually crumbling. The thatched huts inside the walls were on the point of collapse. There was no longer even any protection against native attacks. The guns, of which there were fifteen or sixteen, were poorly kept but were, nevertheless, used to salute forigners or to toast guests. The custom of giving visitors a grand reception seems to have been kept up from Albrecht's time. Barbot, a French traveler who visited Fort Frederiksberg in 1679 and again in 1682, says that the Danes lived more recklessly than the English and often spoiled their digestion by heavy drinking.[12] Although the situation of their fort was more elevated and cooler than most others on the coast, they had, relatively speaking, the highest mortality rate. In particular, it was impossible for Danish women to endure the hot climate. The only thing about the Danish possession that Barbot praised was the garden, which was situated one kilometer to the northeast of the fort and included various trees and plants, such as orange and lemon trees. In the middle of the garden was a fine summer house, before which one afternoon the natives carried on a mock battle for Barbot's amusement.

Apart from such pleasures, the pictures painted by his descriptions are most depressing. He must have written them under the impression of conditions at the fort, as they changed in about 1680 after the death of Crul. The cause for all the problems, Barbot tried to show, was due to the men's unreliability. Here he touches upon something which, at least periodically, was to remain characteristic of the Danish venture in Guinea until the end. No commandant who was loyal to the company managed to live long on the coast. If the climate did not finish him off, he was put to death by his subordinates, who occasionally had the assistance of the natives. So, often persons of quite inferior rank advanced to the position of commandant, even though they were devoid of the necessary qualifications. Perhaps they took the post just to enrich themselves as much and as quickly as possible, for they must have known that they would be discharged as soon as the company was able to send out a man with better qualifications.

Admittedly, Barbot was speaking of the period of decline at Fort Frederiksberg. However, as late as 1836 a Dane named W. J. Wulff in private and confidential letters to his family tells how easily a European might be poisoned out there if he incurred the ill-feelings of those around him.[13] Everybody sent out there to take over one of the higher posts had to realize this and act accordingly.

It is not surprising that after a period of neglect by the officials at home and with these defects spreading through the garrisons along the coast, Fort Frederiksberg was lost forever. In order to cope with daily expenses, the commandants had to borrow money from the English at Cape Coast. By 1679 Fort Frederiksberg owed them 8500 florins. At last, Hans Lykke, who had become commandant at a very early age, on July 11,

1684, went so far as to pawn Fort Frederiksberg for a sum in gold to Captain Henry Nurse, the English commandant of Cape Coast Castle. So, presumably on April 16, 1685, the English took over, and the Danish flag was struck from the decaying buildings.[14] After that, the Danes had only one possession left at Osu in the Accra territory. That too had been lost for a while, but this will be discussed later.

Frederiksberg was renamed Fort Royal by the English, but they did nothing to repair its buildings either.[15] It was decided to rebuild the fort in 1699, but nothing came of it. In the course of time, the fort sank into total decay, nay disintegration; so today there are hardly even ruins to be found on the former "Danish Hill." In 1933 seven ancient guns were found under the bushes. One of them was mounted and provided with a metal plaque recounting these historic events.

It seems ironic that at about the time when news of the loss of the fort reached Copenhagen, Brandenburg offered to buy it.[16] Since 1680 the Great Elector, too, had been trying to obtain a share of the Guinea trade. For a while Brandenburg possessed some forts on the African coast, but in 1717 she sold her rights to the Dutch West India Company. Although the English had already installed themselves at Fort Frederiksberg, in December 1685 the West India Company in Copenhagen decided to keep negotiations open with Berlin. Owing to the agreement later reached with the English, however, nothing came of these negotiations.

By the acquisition of Fort Frederiksberg the English had fulfilled an old wish of theirs. The guns of the fort, in fact, dominated Cape Coast Castle as events in 1664 had proved, and as early as 1679 the English had informed the Danish government of their desire to purchase the fort.[17] After the English takeover, Copenhagen tried to get it back. Diplomatic negotiations were opened, but Denmark could not afford to pay the £3,000 which was the English price for giving up the mortgage.[18] So the Danes had to be content with ceding all claims to Frederiksberg against the payment of £900 (3768 rixdollars, 72 skillings). An agreement to this effect was reached between the Royal African Company in London and Councillor of the Chancery, Jens Rosenheim, the Danish envoy, on April 1, 1688, and ratified by the king on June 30 of that year.

Thus the first important chapter of the history of the Danish possessions on the Guinea coast came to an end. The results of the daring and enterprise of merchants and skippers, the Danish king's subjects, had been lost. It was not without sorrow that at home on the shores of the Elbe and the Sound it was learned in what a wanton and humiliating manner the key point of the Danish possessions had been surrendered. Certainly, with its thatched huts and crumbling walls the fort had not been a sparkling jewel among the ornaments of the Danish Crown. Nor had the African company of Glückstadt succeeded in making the Guinea gold pour into its coffers. Nevertheless, some of the cargoes brought home must have given rich profits to whomever it was that received them; and it was encouraging to think that out there on that distant coast fortune was waiting for whomever was willing and able to take it.

5 / THE FETU

After their arrival on the Gold Coast the Scandinavians first came into contact with the Fetu.[1] They were a tribe of the Fanti who inhabited the coastal strip nearly all the way to Accra. They were powerful, well built people with broad noses, thick lips, white teeth, and small ears. Their skin was very dark, "the blacker, the more beautiful." [2] Elderly men wore beards; and when their hair turned grey, they would often obtain a venerable appearance. They were clever, not to say cunning, intelligent, with very retentive memories, clean, hospitable, and mutually helpful. On the other hand, they were hot tempered and vindictive. They would often use derisive nicknames, swore easily, resorted to lies, committed certain kinds of theft, and murdered without remorse.

Their king's residence was some distance inland. His court was housed in extensive but simple buildings. The royal household was rather large, consisting of advisers, wives, slaves, and soldiers. Usually the king's life was given up to indolence, good food, and the pleasures of family life. Whenever he emptied his cup, the sound of drums and flourishes from horns made of elephants' tusks were heard, female slaves beat their bells, and often guns were fired. The king and his closest relatives wore colorful clothes and rich gold ornaments. Color and music were the Africans' delight. The most important member of the domestic staff was the speaker, who was also Keeper of the Key of the Royal Gold Coffer and in charge of the royal kitchen. The people paid their taxes in corn, fruit, fish, meat, oil, and palm wine, and the king had further revenue from customs duties and fines. Part of the money was spent on fine clothes and silks, guns, gunpowder, and knives, which the Fetu merchants purchased from the Europeans. When a king died, he was not succeeded by his son but always by a matrilinial relative such as a brother, uncle, or sister's son. By limiting the royal succession to the maternal side, they could be sure that the king was always of the true blood.

The king was treated with great respect because of the veneration his subjects had for his fetish, but he was far from possessing absolute power. Great power was vested in the council whose members were: the chancellor, the treasurer, and the general. It was the treasurer (the *Day*) who dealt with all matters concerning the Europeans. Under these important personages was a kind of nobility of chiefs, the so-called *cabuceers,* who had votes in important matters which concerned the realm as a whole. Nor were the "young warriors" without influence. Other distinct classes were the *mercadors* or merchants and *remidors* or fishermen and boatmen. The artisans were few: goldsmiths, blacksmiths, carpenters, potters, hatters, matmakers, and lastly, cutters of ivory trumpets, bracelets, and combs. The rest of the population made a living without excessive hard work by farming and a little hunting.

Every town had its marketplace where the women made their daily purchases of fish, poultry, millet, bananas, pineapple, and such other fruits as happened to be offered for sale, as well as tobacco. Their currency was small grains of gold or *taku,* a kind of pod whose beans might have a variety of colors. The fishermen plied their trade in canoes in which they would venture as far as twenty kilometers out to sea. They used bast nets, hooks, a kind of harpoon, and flares at night. Farms were on burnt land. When the bush had been burnt off, the soil was loosened superficially with hoes; and a short time before the rains were expected the millet was planted, grain by grain. In three months it was ripe and ready for harvest. For this work they used large knives which they purchased from the Europeans. Twice a year it was possible to garner a crop of several hundredfold. "So abundantly," said the Rev. Wilh. Müller, "does the Almighty and Merciful God fill the bellies of these heathen and yet they bring him no offerings of thanksgiving but on the contrary, to the devil called Kuku and to their fetish." The Fetu knew how to brew beer and tap palm wine which, when fresh, was a delicious refreshment. Palm oil was used both as a nutrient and a skin lotion.

Hunting was not, as in Europe, the pastime of the rich but the trade of the poor. Deer, roe, boars, and civets were plentiful. Leopards were more difficult to capture; they had to be trapped, and so the natives would sometimes ask sixty guilders for the skin of a leopard. The wild buffaloes were no less difficult to kill. Numerous other species were represented, but hunting does not seem to have been as important as might have been expected in such an uncultivated country. The main staple in their diet was millet bread. The day before baking the grain was soaked and ground between two stones. Before baking, the bread was kneaded with water and wrapped in palm leaves. The round loaf was put into a pot of water and boiled for some time, and it was laid out to cool on a wooden platter. When palm oil had been poured on it, the loaf was ready to be served. It was regarded as a delicacy and sometimes eaten with a little fish or chicken. For that matter, the Africans were excellent cooks. Villault tells us that the native cook at the Danish Fort Frederiksberg was able to vie with many a Parisian cook in the preparation of soups and ragouts.

Fetu clothing was extremely simple. Nobody was ashamed to show his nakedness. The common people, both men and women, were all naked above the waist. The most important garment of the men was the loincloth or *pantjes*, a longish piece of material which hung round the hips and between the legs with its ends hanging down to the knees in front and behind. For this the poor used coarse linen. Rich and aristocratic persons used fine linen and covered it with an outer garment which they sometimes threw across their shoulders so it hung down to their feet. Most of them wore hats of straw or fur. For ornaments they had bracelets, corals, and gewgaws made up of fetishes. Hair and beards were plaited with gold and precious stones. When out walking, they carried long canes which they had received as presents from European traders. Native leaders in the neighborhood of the European forts liked to dress completely, or at least partly, in European clothes. Poor women wore only a piece of linen which was held round their waists by a belt and too short to reach their knees. And they, like the men, rubbed themselves with palm oil which gave their bodies a glossy sheen all through the day. Ladies of rank wore underclothing of *say* covering them from waists to feet. The upper part of their bodies was covered with East Indian silks. On their foreheads, cheeks, shoulders, arms, and breasts they placed stars or crescent-shaped patches of red or white. With coral necklaces, abundant ornaments, carefully dressed hair, and their bodies rubbed in perfumed lotions they must have been very attractive.

The ordinary African houses were similar to the Danish peasants' cottages of the day with mud-and-wattle walls and thatched roofs. The doors were low, and there were no windows, but holes in the walls instead to let in sunlight and fresh air. Their protruding eaves of thatch provided needed shade from the scorching noonday sun. Washing and cooking were usually done in the neat little courtyard. The interior of the house was divided into many rooms but was very scantily furnished. A copper kettle, a washbasin, a chair, a pot, a couple of calabashes to drink from, and a dish for the food made up the necessary household utensils. In the daytime the mats on which the inhabitants slept and the skins with which they covered themselves when sleeping were rolled up and hung on the wall. The female slaves kept everything tidy and maintained absolute cleanliness throughout the house. Members of the ruling class had picked up some ideas of interior decoration from the

Europeans. They built larger houses with pillars in front and bought furniture. In their bedrooms they had chests for their best clothes as well as for their gold, jewels, and precious mats imported from afar. Dinner sets, spoons, knives, and forks of silver were seen with fine towels and napkins, and for their daily ablutions they used richly decorated copper tubs which were bought in the interior at great expense.

The esteem in which a man was held corresponded to the number of his wives and slaves. Marriages were often arranged by parents, and when a man acquired his first and most important wife, there were celebrations with dancing and drinking. His later wives were brought to him without public celebration. The marital fidelity of the wife was guaranteed by her husband eating fetish with her relatives beforehand. If she broke her word, he had the right to repudiate her. A man also could bind slave concubines to himself by oath. The right to sleep with the husband belonged to the legitimate wives by turns, and some had a right to more connubial nights than others. For the peace and order of the home, the husband was very loath to change the usual succession. His visits to his concubines were not regulated by this arrangement. The fertility of the family was believed to be entirely at the mercy of its fetish, so a pregnant woman would sacrifice to this deity. Deformed children were disposed of immediately. The mother tied healthy children round her waist with cloth. Later they were carried on her back or on her hip, even when she was dancing. When they were a fortnight old, they were given names, and this was the occasion for a feast.

From the age of eight or nine the boys would follow their father to learn some trade and be initiated into the customs and traditions. As the Fetu knew no alphabet, the young had to seek information about the past by listening to their elders. The young men, especially, had to attend sessions of the law courts to become acquainted with tribal law. Murder, theft, and marital infidelity were severely punished. If a man of high rank killed one of inferior rank, it was possible for him to escape execution by paying a fine. Otherwise murderers were put to death. Moreover, if an inferior had killed a superior, not only he but some of his relatives, too, paid for it with their lives. The death penalty was inflicted for theft, too, even if the stolen goods were only a hen or some firewood. The infidelity of a slave concubine was likewise punished with death, while lawful wives born of free parents were cast out as unfaithful. If the husband got the chance, he would wreak his vengeance on the seducer and force him to pay a large compensation. It was said that some natives kept many wives and ordered them to commit adultery in order to get a good income from the subsequent compensations. The usual procedure at executions was that the criminal's arms were tied behind his back, and then he was carried out of the town and flung face down on the ground. There, while his head and legs were being held down, some gallant fellow would cut off his head with a cutlass. Afterward, the head was carried about the town in triumph.

With some justification the natives were described as bloodthirsty. They were extremely warlike. The least cause would serve as pretext for a campaign. They preferred the seasons when the crops were ripe in the fields and the trees were laden with fruit, so that provisions for the army presented no problems. Their arms were muskets, which, like the gunpowder, they bought from Europeans, bows and poisoned arrows, swords, spears, and javelins. Other war instruments were square, plaited shields, a broad leather belt, and a helmet of leather or crocodile skin, which was sometimes decorated with feathers, gilt horns, and horsetails from the interior. They carried ropes with which to tie up their prisoners, and from their belts they hung sacks for the heads of fallen enemies. Last and most important, the family fetish was carried in a basket. Each chief brought his own orchestra of drums and elephant tusks and had his own distinguishing signal. The armies chose to clash with each other in the dense forests with narrow paths through which the contenders necessarily had to pass to advance. Battles would continue until one of the parties retreated. The victors would take up the pursuit and reap a harvest of prisoners and heads. For prisoners of high rank large ransoms would be paid, but ordinary prisoners would be sold as slaves in distant parts from which it would be impossible for them to escape to their own country. Most wars were decided by a single battle; depredation of the conquered country was rare. Afterward the victors celebrated their triumph with processions, salvos from their muskets, dancing, and drinking. When they arrived at a town, the conquered enemy heads were thrown on the ground, and everybody would run out to trample on them. Sometimes the head would be flung into the air and caught again; each warrior would demonstrate how he had felled his enemy. When the triumphal processions reached the European places, one had to treat the gallant warriors to great quantities of gin and reward them with gifts. After their homecoming the enemy heads were boiled to remove the flesh, and the skulls were kept as trophies. They were often hung on the drums, since it was believed that the deceased would be tormented by the noise. The relatives of the fallen were never allowed to ransom them. Peace negotiations were carried on with the eating of fetish and celebrated with great feasts, often with the harmonious participation of both parties.

It is extremely difficult to form an opinion of their religion. They preferred to leave unanswered questions about it. Wilh. Müller came to the conclusion that they worshipped a good god and an evil one. The god Kuku was feared throughout the land, but regarded as a protector. The moon was sacred, as were certain stones, rocks, trees, animals, and the most peculiar objects which the native priests declared to be fetish.

Below Fort Frederiksberg a sacred giant snake lived to which daily sacrifices were made. The Europeans dared not kill it. The traveler would often see numerous fetish sticks, colored with red clay and stuck into the ground in front of the houses in Fetu. There would also be a bigger stick to which the inhabitants tied rags, bones, goats' heads, etc., which were all sprinkled with sacrificial blood. An African trader living near the fort received a leather strap from his fetish priest, and he was advised to hang it up and pull on it several times during the day and night to make the fetish send a Danish ship with a cargo of merchandise. Each family had its own household fetish, which was carried along when the head of the family departed on important business. Every morning this idol was worshipped, and on occasion it was thanked for its favors. Mighty household deities could be bought at exorbitant prices. At critical times the Fetu would ask the advice of sanctuaries possessing powerful fetishes which were used as oracles. There were also certain itinerant priests and witch doctors who, benefiting by the superstition rampant among the people, offered their services as soothsayers. The Fetu kept Tuesday holy, but in addition each householder had his own special holy day in the course of the week. Every year in September they had a great harvest festival with feasting, drinking, and dancing. To these celebrations, the Europeans would send representatives, who were escorted by native troops, to the accompaniment of music, and with banners flying. Only on the most solemn occasions, such as the conclusion of peace treaties, did the Fetu resort to human sacrifices. In certain other African states, however, streams of human blood were sacrificed. Sacrifices of domestic animals, eggs, and calabashes of wine were customary everywhere, and Kuku received his daily offering of fruit. These offerings were placed along the roads. When the Dutch commanded Fort Frederiksberg, an African trader at Cabo Corso sacrificed twenty goats to avert danger from the Danes.

Deaths and funerals, also, occasioned feasts and ceremonies. As soon as a man had died, loud howls went up. Neighbors would come and join in the lamentations. The wives and concubines of the deceased would strew dust on their heads and rub their naked breasts with it too. The greatest possible noise would be made to drive away the evil spirit who was responsible for the man's death. Before burial the corpse was washed and the body, arms, and legs wrapped in linen. When the body had been tied to a board, two men carried it away on their heads, now running, now walking quite slowly. Beside them walked the women whose task it was to chase the flies away from the body. The funeral procession followed, headed by the deceased's favorite wives howling loudly. The funerals of the noble would be to the constant accompaniment of discharging guns, drums, and trumpets. Usually the grave was outside the town, and as soon as it had been filled with earth, a table was set up on it. On it the dead man's tools and implements were laid, as well as jars of palm wine and palm oil so that the deceased should not lack anything. Because of their belief that he was going to a life of honor and wealth in happy regions, at a rich man's funeral they would kill several of his concubines and slaves, so that they should be ready to serve him in the afterlife. Afterward a statue in clay of the deceased was erected near the grave. Following the death of beloved relatives, the mourners would fast for many days until they were quite emaciated. The women would have their hair cut off or would neglect to plait it. Wives and children had every reason for sorrow. The inheritance would not come to them but to the dead man's matrilineal relatives. It would be entirely up to these relatives, if they would give anything to the children. Consequently, widows and fatherless children often lived in extreme misery.

Thus, hardly influenced by the presence of the Europeans on the coast, the African nations kept up the customs and traditions which had for generations regulated their lives. In a rich and beautiful country, because of their superstition and bellicosity, they became their own tormentors. Constantly exposed to dangers, their lives were quite insecure, but normally this hardly bothered them. On the contrary, they would give themselves up to dancing and feasting whenever they could find a pretext to do so. If they were unfortunate enough to be reduced to slavery, they would bear misfortune without a murmur. European attempts to become acquainted with their innermost feelings or religious secrets usually remained unsuccessful.

6 / ACCRA AND FORT CHRISTIANSBORG

AFTER THE LOSS of the fort and stations in Fetu, Hans Lykke and his remaining European assistants had to take refuge at the last Danish possession on the Guinea coast, which was situated close to the African town of Osu in Accra country. From then on this place was to be the center of Danish activities on the Gold Coast.

The French may possibly have had a lodge there as early as the fourteenth century. The Portuguese probably held a trading station in the district around the year 1500. We know also that about 1565 the Portuguese built a fort in the Accra area. They did this in spite of the opposition of natives. So, when the opportunity presented itself, the natives took the garrison by surprise and slaughtered them. This was said to have taken place in 1578. Afterward, the Africans are said to have offered the fort to the French. The offer was accepted; but because of the constant attacks of the Portuguese, the French soon departed. After the Dutch had made themselves masters of the sea, they signed a contract with the king of Accra on August 30, 1641, whereby they received permission to establish a fort. On August 4, 1649, they persuaded him to grant them sole rights to trade in his territory. This contract, however, was not respected by the natives, for, as we have seen, the Swedes built a lodge near Osu in 1653. It was seized in 1658 by the Danes, who in turn lost it to the Dutch in 1659.[1]

Later the Dutch maintained that on April 14, 1661, the Danes had taken repossession of the lodge.[2] They said that Jost Cramer had sent one Joan Jacob Rajot who, with the assistance of several hundred natives, drove away the employees of the Dutch West India Company and stole their merchandise. The Danish version was entirely different. When the king of Accra found out how the Dutch had fooled Samuel Smidt at Carlsborg fort and tricked him out of the Danish possessions, he advised the Dutch to depart. They took his advice and so managed to escape with all their belongings without being robbed. With the lodge vacant, the Danes entered and occupied it. In their opinion they had every right to do this, for the fort had been built by the Swedes and in 1658, thanks to Carlof's exploit, had by conquest become Danish property.

After the lodge was occupied, Jost Cramer, by a contract of August 18, 1661, bought a piece of land on which he could build a fort from King Kankoy of Great Accra.[3] The price he had to pay was 50 benda gold (3,200 florins). Christian Cornelissøn was appointed chief trader for the area.[4] Having formerly served the Swedes in Guinea for seven years, he now became a loyal and "thrifty" servant of the Danish company. At the same time he knew how to make the Africans love him, so that they protected him against poisoning and other dangers. Numerous babies were named after him and when after six years' activity he departed, he was sincerely and profoundly missed by the natives. The king of Accra even ordered all his wives and his entire court to escort him to his boat; the king himself could not, without breach of the fetish rules, go anywhere near the coast. In return for all these honors, the Danes had to hand out large donations.

Under the leadership of Cornelissøn, Fort Christiansberg (or Christiansborg as it was usually called) was built on the purchased land. Solid foundations were laid on a rock cliff right on the beach, and its buildings were comparatively tall and spacious. A tower rose above the residence, and a salient with a full view of the African town of Osu was built by the gate. Three bastions were built at once, the fourth was added later. The landing facilities were even worse at Christiansborg than at Cape Coast. Ships could anchor only to the east of the fort. However, here the sea bottom was strewn with sharp rocks which could easily cut through the anchor lines. So, every day the anchor had to be raised, if one did not want to lose it. "And there is at that place a most vile harbor for landing, so that thereby many Christians have suffered injuries both of their persons and their goods when trying to land." [5]

During this period both the English and the Dutch acquired forts at Accra.[6] In 1641 the Dutch obtained a contract with the king of Accra, and the following year they built a lodge near Little Accra, which in 1652 they enlarged and called Fort Crèvecoeur. It was within artillery range of Osu to the west. In 1673 the English company, having been reorganized in 1672, built a fort near the African village of Soko (Sioco) and within artillery range to the west of Crèvecoeur. They named the place Fort James after the most prominent shareholder of the Royal African Company, viz., the Duke of York, the later King James II. Both the Dutch fort and the English forts were on a smaller scale than Fort Christiansborg, though the Dutch fort was situated on a more healthful spot and had better landing facilities than the two others. The Dutch, as the first comers, had chosen the best location.

There was bound to be rivalry when three European nations had forts so close to each other—from Fort Crèvecoeur it was possible to hit either of the other two. The kingdom of Accra was still at that time the largest and most powerful of the native states along this part of the coast. It had a brisk inland traffic; abundant supplies, gold, and especially slaves arrived there. For a time there seems to have been sufficient trade for both the Dutch and the Danes, and thus the parties got on peacefully together. They supported each other against the natives, and their garrisons often fraternized. Christiansborg had a special advantage. It was the easternmost and last fort on the Gold Coast at which many European captains called. So, when they got there, they were often willing to sell what remained of their cargoes at reduced prices, thus enabling the officials of the fort to do some profitable business on their own.

As far as we know, those years in the 1660's, when Christen Cornelissøn was in charge of the Christiansborg trade, were among the best, while at the same time, the Frederiksberg trade was most flourishing under the leadership of Henning Albrecht. Soon, however, relations with the natives became difficult. The political situation among the native states was very unstable. Wars among them were frequent, territories and dependencies constantly changed hands, and as a consequence of this instability there were long interruptions of traffic and trade. In 1667 when Villault visited Henning Albrecht at Fort Frederiksberg their conversation turned upon the damage done to the trade of the European forts by the constant wars of the natives. At that time provisions for Fort Christiansborg could be obtained only by sending them in canoe from Fort Frederiksberg, for the Accra people had become involved in dangerous quarrels which lasted many years. These wars ravaged the country far and wide.

The population in the Accra districts was very mixed.[7] A series of immigrations had taken place in the course of time. After the stone age peoples, the first arrivals seem to have been the Guan (Cyerepons). They are believed to have been related to the Akan but to have come down to the coast from the north somewhat earlier than they. The Guan are believed to have founded a kingdom stretching from the coast northwards and situated to the west of the Volta River, where they still inhabit the hills some distance inland. Next, presumably in more recent times, the Ga people, to whom the Accra belonged, came from the east. Their leader when they immigrated was Ayi Kushi. His successor, Ayite, built his capital, Great Accra, near the Pocoase Hills about twenty kilometers inland. In this town a market developed to which traders from the inland states brought their merchandise and exchanged it with European goods purchased by the Accra from the Europeans on the coast. The Accra did not allow the traders coming from the interior to enter into direct trade with foreign ships; thus they were assured of a substantial profit, often of 100 per cent or more.

During the seventeenth century in a new wave of migration from the north, the Akan Akwamu, or Aquambu, flooded the plains to the west of the Volta River. The Accra said that the Akwamu had originally been a band of robbers who had run away from Accra. What may have been true was that malcontents from Accra deserted and joined the Akwamu in the hills. In any case the Akwamu increased in numbers and strength until at length there followed a number of battles between them and the Accra. Under most dramatic circumstances Okai Koi, the last powerful king of Accra, took his own life after the defeat of Ayawaso on June 20, 1660. Ashangmo, his successor, strove for many years to regain the Accra's former power; but he never managed to get the better of the Akwamu, and at length they conquered Great Accra, his capital, and destroyed it.

Driven to despair by the lack of unity among his followers and ridiculed on all sides, in 1680 Ashangmo led part of his people eastward back to the country from which they had come. They settled at Little Popo, some distance east of Volta. There, under the protection of the king of Whydah, the Accra regained so much strength that later they were able to wage new wars against the Akwamu and support Whydah against Dahomey. Immediately after the departure of their kinsmen in 1680 those Accra who still remained to the west of the Volta were forced to submit to the sovereignty of the Akwamu. So ended the mighty kingdom of the Accra which, because of the trade, between the Europeans and the Africans, to the interior, had reached such a high level of prosperity.

As long as one nation after the other was pressed toward the coast, where further migrations were impossible, violent quarrels were unavoidable. The Europeans were fully justified in regarding the Accra people as one of the most savage and warlike of African nations.

Every time a new campaign was being prepared, the African kings called up all able-bodied men. The paths leading through bush and forests to the interior were blocked and trade came to a standstill. Consequently, there were long periods when the Danes at Christiansborg were unable to do any business at all. When, at the same time, the ships from home failed to arrive, their position must have become extremely precarious. It is no wonder, then, that Christiansborg was lost for a while. This happened in 1679 when the fort's able commander, Johan Ulrich, a merchant and a native of Glückstadt, was murdered by the natives under the instigation of one of his own subordinates, a Greek. The next commandant was another merchant, Peiter Bolt, who shortly afterward treacherously sold the entire fort for 36 pounds of gold to a

Portuguese named Julian de Campo Barreto. Barreto had formerly been a governor of the Portuguese island of São Thomé, but at Christiansborg he could not keep his own men under control. Later they rose against him and imprisoned him in a room at the top of the tower. There Barbot saw him during his second visit to the coast. The Portuguese rechristened the fort, calling it Fort St. Francis Xavier after the great Catholic missionary. Not wishing to allow Africans inside its walls, they manned the fort with a European garrison. The fortifications were strengthened at considerable expense, the bastions were made a yard higher, and a chapel was erected. A lake situated at some distance from the fort, which had formerly been one of the holy places of the natives, was divided up and used for the manufacture of salt. Nevertheless, the trade can hardly have been profitable; and when, as mentioned, Barbot visited the place in 1682 he found the Portuguese at the fort in depressing poverty and almost without merchandise.

On the loss of Fort Christiansborg, Peter With, the Danish commandant of Frederiksberg, of course, protested to the Portuguese, but in vain.[8] He was hardly able to act with authority, for he was a simple gunner who had assumed command after the death of Conrad Crul. Apart from protesting, all he could do was to report the loss to the home country. Nor was his successor, Magnus Prang, able to do more.[9] At long last the Copenhagen government passed on the protest to the Portuguese king who, curiously enough, did something about the matter. The order went out to Guinea to give the fort back to the Danes, after which the Portuguese garrison quietly disappeared. After an interval when the fort was occupied by the natives, the Danes of Fort Frederiksberg were able to reoccupy it on February 26, 1683. Shortly afterward Peder Hoffmann was installed as merchant of the fort. When Hans Lykke pawned Fort Frederiksberg to the English in 1685, all Danes on the coast were to take refuge at Fort Christiansborg.

Even if the natives at Accra were more warlike than the Fetu and often disturbed trade considerably, the situation of Christiansborg had certain advantages which Frederiksberg could not offer. Trade seems to have been considerably better at Accra than at Cape Coast. Gold flowed in more abundantly, and above all, the many wars provided large numbers of prisoners who were sold mostly to the Europeans as slaves. The prospects of Accra were far better. Frederiksberg was very tightly squeezed between the English at Cape Coast Castle on the one side and the Dutch close by at Fort Nassau on the other side. True, at Christiansborg the Europeans were near at hand on the western side, but to the east there was a long stretch of coast without a European fort. This meant more freedom for trade and expansion; the question was, how great an effort those at home would make to exploit these advantages.

7 / THE WEST INDIA AND GUINEA COMPANY

WITH THE GLÜCKSTADT COMPANY reduced to the verge of ruin by 1669, it was quite natural for the Danish government to be concerned about the future of the Guinea trade.[1] On November 26, 1670, the new king, Christian V, ordered the deputies of the company to report on condition of Danish possessions in Africa and to state whether they wished to continue the use of them. In January 1671 an emphatic repetition of this order followed.

The company finally was sufficiently roused from its lethargy to apply for a reconfirmation of its charter. This was customary at the accession of a new king, but now the company also asked that a committee be set up to deal with the matter. Its privileges were duly confirmed on June 17, 1671, though this cannot have been because the state of the company gave grounds for optimism. According to the accounts kept by its bookkeeper, up to New Year's 1672 the shareholders had received only 47,264 marks, barely 10 per cent of the share capital.[2] As we have already seen, great losses had been caused by the inroads of the Dutch. Two of the company's ships, *Prinz Christianus* and *Fredericus (Tertius)*, had been sold, and the *Sophia Amalia* had been wrecked. The equipping of these ships had cost more than 300,000 marks. A similar amount had been spent on the building and maintenance of the forts on the Gold Coast, and expenses incurred at home for the operation of the company amounted to more than 50,000 marks. To this various loans and claims must be added. So, the bookkeeper calculated that total investments amounted to 1,188,279 marks. What the company's capital investment amounted to and how much money its employees had made privately and undercover remains unknown, but it seems very probable that the balance was such that the Glückstadt company had no chance of making a profit out of its possessions.

The results of the Guinea expedition of the *Patriarch Jacob*, 1671-72, remain unknown. Presumably, nothing very useful came of it. In the meantime, Henning Albrecht quarreled with Jacob de Boys and Johan Backmann, the directors of the company, about the payment of Albrecht's salary.[3] So, on May 25 the king appointed a committee of two, Poul Klingenberg and Councillor to the Chancery, Conrad Wasmer, to examine the condition of the company.[4] The memorandum which these two gentlemen handed to the government after a month's investigation made it clear that the company was incapable of continuing the Guinea trade; thus the king's forts and lodges were in danger and might easily fall into foreign hands, "which would be both injurious and contemptible." Next the matter was sent to the Commerce Collegium (Board of Trade), which proposed that twenty soldiers be sent to Guinea and that a Copenhagen-African company be started. This proposal met with the approval of the State Collegium, the equivalent of the state council of the times, on November 23, 1672. Some councilors apparently were inclined to support the Glückstadt company, but the vice-president of the Commerce Collegium, Jens Juel, who was the brother of the naval hero Neils Juel, dealt the finishing blow to the old company. He reasoned that it would be a good thing if the Guinea trade could be reduced "so as thereby to help both the East Indian Companies."

Jens Juel was himself director of these two companies, which were founded in 1670 and 1671 respectively. He evidently wished to reduce the Guinea trade to a second-class position which would be tolerated only for the sake of the two other Danish colonies. Juel also worked very energetically for the development of trade in accordance with mercantilist principles, but he did not want to see it centered in the king's duchies in Holstein. He agreed with the nationalistic attitude of Christian V and with the general tendency of Danish absolute monarchy to concentrate as much as possible in Copenhagen, and so he wanted to have a company located in the duchies rather than in the kingdom itself. The Glückstadt company usually bought equipment and cargoes in Holland. However, from this point on an effort was made to create a new market for the Kingdom of Denmark through sales to the ships. For the period of transition and until a new company could be started, the State Collegium agreed that all should be given a charter and sea-pass whenever they wished to trade at the Danish places in Africa, on the condition that they paid a "recognition" for the upkeep of the garrisons in the forts. The Glückstadt company was allowed only to recover its stores of merchandise from the forts. They had to surrender the buildings and ammunition. However, by an act of God the Glückstadt shareholders were allowed to join the new company.

On the basis of these decisions a royal patent was issued on December 10, 1672, for the foundation of a Guinea company in Copenhagen.[5] Applications for membership could be sent to the Commerce Collegium, and the king promised that once the company had been established, he would grant a charter and sea-passes. It seems doubtful that there were any applicants. On April 22, 1672, the king advised the West India Company to consider the continuation of the Guinea trade. Most likely this was Jens Juel's idea, for in his opinion the best way to put the Guinea trade into its proper place would be to put it into the hands of the West India Company. From a business point of view it seemed most advantageous first to send ships with European cargoes to Guinea, then to send them with slaves to the West Indies, and from there to have them return home with West Indian goods. As far as we know, the Glückstadt company traded only directly to and from Guinea and Portuguese São Thomé, and presumably it never carried out any large-scale slave shipments. The necessity of providing slave labor for the island of St. Thomas in the West Indies, of which the Copenhagen West India Company had obtained possession, weighed heavily in favor of adopting the triangular route and making the slave trade the company's chief business. At this early stage participation in the slave trade caused no scruples of conscience.

The more business-minded directors of the West India Company, such as Peder Pedersen Lerche and Hans Nansen, made certain stipulations before they were willing to take up the Guinea traffic. First of all, they thought a settlement should be made on the claims of the Glückstadt company. Probably, they did not want to offend their colleagues in Glückstadt and Hamburg. At any rate, the company temporarily left the Guinea question open.[6] Then, on August 15, 1673, the Glückstadt company made obvious its disinterest in equipping any further ships to Guinea and at the same time gave up all its privileges. In the course of the winter new initiative was taken; the owners of a ship, the *Spes,* offered to join the West India Company. The directors of that company immediately took up the matter. First, they applied to the king for permission to increase the share capital. They referred to a clause in the company's charter of March 11, 1671. It stated that in case the Glückstadt company did not wish to continue, the West India Company could then take over its privileges as well as obtain possession of the African forts, if it paid the old company the value of its goods, guns, and ammunition which were left behind. The increase of the company's share capital was approved by the king on March 6, 1674, and on the next day by the shareholders.[7] Thus at length it was decided that the company should take up the Guinea traffic. A few days later a royal letter was issued inviting subscriptions. It seems to have been a little difficult to persuade good people to risk their savings.[8] After some time, however, it became possible to equip a ship which had been bought in Amsterdam and given the sterling name *Charlotte Amalia, Regina Dania.* On November 13, 1674, the king granted an exemption from customs duties for all goods exported to Guinea, but as in the case of the Glückstadt company, some of the cargo had to be purchased in Amsterdam. Finally, on November 28 of that year a royal patent was granted permitting the company to trade to Guinea under the same conditions as the Glückstadt company had had formerly. It now was possible to send out orders to the commandant of Fort Frederiksberg.[9]

However, the *Charlotte Amalia*'s expedition went very badly. The ship left Copenhagen too late in the season, partly we are told, because the shareholders dragged their feet in contributing the necessary capital. It was not until New Year's 1674 that the ship sailed from Copenhagen. In the Kattegat it ran into continual storms and so for a time returned to the Sound. However, on January 18, 1675, it was wrecked off Vinga near Gothenburg, Sweden. Little of the cargo was saved; there was no insurance, and at the same time another of the company's ships, a sloop named *St. Vincent,* went down off the coast of Norway. The company's total losses amounted to 40,000 rixdollars, and thus its very existence was endangered. For the time being further Guinea investments were out of the question. The directors had to content themselves with demands for new capital. The king issued a proclamation on May 20, 1675, which permitted his subjects, with the agreement of the directors, even if they were shareholders of the company, to sail to the West Indies. Thus the participants were allowed to carry on trade to St. Thomas, if they paid a "recognition" of 10 per cent of the outgoing cargo's value. The company, however, did not send a single ship to Guinea during the war against Sweden (1675-79).

Under these circumstances, the Guinea trade was left to private enterprise.[10] As permitted by the decisions of the State Collegium, a few sea-passes had already been granted. On August 6, 1673, a prosperous Bergen merchant, Jørgen Thormöhlen, and his partners obtained a sea-pass to Guinea for their ship, the *Cornelia,* whose captain was Jørgen Thiessen Mölmer. Similarly, on October 11 of that year Admiral-General Cort Adeler and Colonel Markor Rodsteen of the Arsenal were given a sea-pass for their ship, *Den Forgyldte Ørn,* which was captained by Joris Bacher. The *Cornelia* carried 103 slaves to St. Thomas. It was given a new sea-pass on July 11, 1674, but afterward was captured by the Dutch West India Company.

The loss of the *Charlotte Amalia* did not discourage other ships from sailing for Africa. The ship *Den Forgyldte Ørn* was issued a new sea-pass on February 10, 1675. A month later Ulrich Frederik Gyldenløve, governor-general of Norway and president of the Commerce Collegium, was given a sea-pass for his ship, the *Frederich,* which was captained by Børge Andersen of Oslo. Sea-passes were also issued to Cornelis Bermann in 1677 and Captain Johannes Hauschild of Altona in 1678, the latter for the *Junge Tobia.* Finally, Admiral Rodsteen and Admiral of the

Realm, Henrik Bielke, with other inhabitants of Copenhagen, received a pass in 1679 for a ship, which was captained by Gerhard de Tetz. We do not know if all the ships mentioned reached the forts in Guinea. It seems that after the arrival of the Glückstadt company's last ship in 1672, the number of ships sailing to Guinea from Danish ports throughout the rest of the 1670's averaged one per year. It was in this period that the forts fell into decay, and that, as we have seen, Fort Christiansborg was lost to the Portuguese.

Not until 1679 did the West India Company think of sending a ship to Guinea again, and even then they did not think they possessed the necessary capital.[11] On March 3, 1680, however, the king issued a decree concerning the trade of the West India and Guinea Company.[12] He promised to send a ship to Guinea at his own expense to carry garrisons to the forts and slaves to the West Indies. Shareholders were ordered to pay their share capital arrears immediately. Furthermore, they were all to pay 10 per cent over and above the capital subscribed. The government even forced people to become shareholders. It was decreed that all officials in the king's territories receiving salaries of at least 300 rixdollars should be invited to subscribe 10 per cent of their annual income to the company. If they did not volunteer, the king would withhold 10 per cent of their salaries and pay it to the company. Finally, those who had coaches but had not subscribed at least 500 sletdoler were to subscribe 60 sletdoler; this last clause was not immediately enforced.[13]

This decree set things going again. A committee was set up to take charge of loading the ships, and a frigate, the *Havmanden,* was fitted out for the Guinea expedition. On August 31, 1680, Magnus Prang (or Pranger), a citizen and merchant of Copenhagen, was appointed *Opperhoved* (chief head) of Fort Frederiksberg, and on September 30 of that year a new royal charter was issued whereby only the company, a subject of the Danish king, received a confirmation of its right to trade to the north coast of Africa, Guinea, and the Danish forts there. At the same time the king ordered that all forts and lodges, guns and ammunition, letters, goods, and chattels be handed over to Magnus Prang. He was provided with written instructions, copies of all necessary documents, and a secret code to be used in reports sent home to the government. On October 23, 1680, the *Havmanden* sailed under Captain Ove Ovesen (Aage Aagesen) with the assistance of Jacob van Tetz, who was placed in charge of trading along the coast. Among the forty passengers in addition to Magnus Prang, there was a clergyman, the Rev. Hans Jensen Grum of Ringkøbing.[14]

In contrast to earlier events, historic sources provide adequate information about the *Havmanden's* expedition. We have the ship's logbook, which among other things tells us how, off Assini their first call on the Gold Coast, they observed a ship lying at anchor. It set sail, however, and was about to make off, but they fired at it and thus persuaded it to stay. On board they found Thomas Thorsen, a captain from Glückstadt, whose name was later to be mentioned frequently in connection with the Guinea trade. He was the first to inform the men on the *Havmanden* that Fort Christiansborg had been surrendered to the Portuguese. On their arrival at Fort Frederiksberg on February 2, 1681, they found two Danes alive. The garrison had quarreled with the Fetu, their king had put Peter Valck, the Danish commandant, in prison for bad conduct, and Andreas Jacobsen had taken over the command. The situation was about as bad as it could be for the new arrivals, and yet it was to become still worse. During the voyage Ovesen and Prang had quarreled, so the captain with a pistol in hand forced Prang to remain ashore. Yet in the meantime business had to continue. The first few slaves were taken on board. A few ivory tusks had been purchased on the coast before they reached Assini. After landing several cannons, the ship sailed on to the easternmost part of the coast, but they met with little success. Much time was lost, and when they returned to Frederiksberg at the end of April, many Danes had already died, including the clergyman and the commandant. Other casualties at Frederiksberg were the bookkeeper, Captain Ovesen, and the captain's mate. The previous commandant was succeeded by Johan Conrad Busch, but he lasted only eleven days.[15] In that short term of office he behaved like a madman, was never sober, kept up continual feasting, and with great pomp celebrated his marriage to a mulatto girl. The king of Fetu refused to do business with him, and at last he was replaced by the earlier-mentioned Hans Lykke, who gave up the fort to the English.

There were a number of other ships on the coast, and so the *Havmanden* did not succeed in buying more than a small number of slaves. Because of this failure and the many casualties, the voyage to the West Indies was given up. The slaves were put ashore, and the ship returned to Europe with Peder Pedersen Stud as captain. On the way, many of the crew and passengers died, including Johan Conrad Busch, who was being taken home as a prisoner. On September 18, 1681, the *Havmanden* with a mere handful on board called at Stavanger in Norway, and on October 21 it reached the road of Copenhagen. The most curious item in the cargo was a leopard (then called a tiger); as for merchandise there was only "the merest trifle," that is, 1,498 pounds of ivory which sold for 678 rixdollars, and some gold, which the Royal Assay Master minted into ducats bearing the royal profile on one side and a picture of Fort Frederiksberg on the other.[16]

The king's generosity to the company had been practically useless, and the forts had received no substantial support either. All those who had been engaged to carry on the company's trade in Africa had already died. Under these circumstances, the company was forced to seek outside assistance. In January 1682 an agreement was made with some citizens of Glückstadt who were allowed to trade with Guinea in return for the transportation of a little capital, merchandise, and garrisons for the forts. On this occasion sea-passes were issued for the *Charlotte Amalia* and the *Printz Friedrich* of Glückstadt, the former captained by Thomas Thors. Among the merchandise sent out in these ships were chests of East Indian goods for the Gold Coast.[17]

Shortly afterward, the king granted the company the right to allow outside participation in the Guinea traffic in return for the payment of a "recognition." Also, the king promised to contribute 1,500 rixdollars annually for the upkeep of the forts in Guinea. Finally, the company obtained permission to borrow the *Havmanden* for another expedition. With great difficulty fresh equipment was procured, and this time, as a praiseworthy precaution, the cargo was insured. The crew was sworn to ship's articles of law borrowed from the East India Company. By a special clause the crew was forbidden to take on board privately owned goods and offer them for sale at the various ports of call without special permission from the directors. A Dutchman named Bronckhorst accompanied them as chief trader and was permitted to take along 4,000 rixdollars' worth of goods in return for the payment of a 30 per cent "recognition." The ship's captain was Jan Bloom. The expedition was to have gone to both Guinea and the West Indies, but almost from the start everything went wrong. After a series of dramatic events the ship was wrecked off Marstrand, Sweden, and the sailors responsible for these misfortunes were most severely punished. Iron discipline was required to control the heterogeneous crowd that made up the crew of a ship bound for unhealthy places like Guinea.[18]

So far, the West India Company of Copenhagen had been unable to develop its African possessions or make them yield a profit. The Glückstadt ships were more successful. With their help Hans Lykke received the minimum of assistance necessary to maintain the Danish possessions in Africa for a little longer. The leading person behind this new enterprise was Moses Josua Henriques, a Portuguese Jew from Glückstadt. He is mentioned in 1675 as being active in the transportation of slaves to the West Indies. It was probably he who backed Thomas Thorsen. He seems to have had an understanding with the company's bookkeeper in Copenhagen, Oliger Pauli (Holger Pauli, who later became a well-known religious fanatic), for on April 8, 1683, immediately after the loss of the *Havmanden,* he was given a royal license for private trading voyages to the Guinea and African coasts. On June 23 of the same year he obtained a sea-pass to send the *Charlotte Amalia,* captained by Thomas Thors, to Guinea. About the same time, two other Glückstadt captains got sea-passes for the *Princessin af Danmark* and the *Printz Friedrich*. In the period immediately following, Henriques or Pauli sent one or more ships annually to Guinea. Among the ships mentioned were the *Københavns Børs, Holger Danske, Christian V, Spera Mundi, Det. kgl. danske vestindiske Compagnies Vaaben, Jomfru Margrethe, Nordstjernen,* and a sloop, the *Fortuna.* Among the captains were David Beck, Jan Wagener, and again Thomas Thors, whose son Johannes Thors also became a Guinea captain. In 1684 Pauli obtained an agreement with the West India Company which allowed his ships to trade without paying a "recognition" if they carried 1000 rixdollars' worth of the company goods to the forts. Thus, connection with the forts was kept up by private enterprise, and in 1686 Henriques was appointed royal factor for the Glückstadt trade to Africa. According to the instructions then evolved, each ship was to pay the company 100 rixdollars and promise to carry certain goods and personnel necessary for the maintenance of the forts and trading stations. Later it became the rule for the Glückstadt ships to pay some "recognition" to the company.[19]

By agreement of March 6, 1685, some Portuguese Jews in Holland, too, were allowed to trade at the Danish places in Africa in return for the unusually small payment of 2 per cent "recognition"; and they were allowed to sail under the Danish flag. We find that a Danish sea-pass was sent to Amsterdam for a ship to take part in that trade, although in Copenhagen some anxiety was voiced that it might be misused.

All this proved insufficient. It was in 1685 that Fort Frederiksberg was lost, and not long afterward the Guinea trade suffered new losses. In 1686 the frigate *Det kgl. danske vestindiske Compagnies Vaaben* was captured by Moslem pirates from North Africa. It had been sent from Flushing, Holland by Oliger Pauli to procure eighty slaves which he had agreed to supply to the West Indies. Afterward, in order to successfully fulfill his contract, he had to send another ship. The loss incurred in this transaction does not seem to have been too excessive, for he was later able to provide the company with merchandise on credit.

Henriques, too, suffered losses. His sloop, the *Fortuna,* was captured by the Dutch off Elmina, and in 1688 they took his *Nordstjernen,* also. Even if he, as well as Pauli, was strong enough to overcome these disasters, they reflected upon the Copenhagen company and weakened it. It had as yet never paid a dividend, and the shareholders were discontented.

In 1689 it was stated that more than 25,000 rixdollars had been spent on the Guinea venture, and yet the company was still powerless. Admittedly, the purpose of these lamentations was to persuade the king to hand over the 1,555 rixdollars per annum which he had promised but never paid. There must, however, have been very good grounds for their complaint. Before the end of the year the company gave up, relinquishing its privileges to the Guinea trade for many years to come.

8 / NIKOLAJ JANSEN ARF

FRESH INITIATIVE WAS TAKEN when one of the most important shipowners in the capital, Nikolaj Jansen Arf, became interested in the Guinea trade. In the course of the previous years he had built himself warehouses in Overgaden and Wildersgade, in Christianshavn.[1] He now applied to the king for the privileges to the African trade hitherto possessed by the West India and Guinea Company and the king was graciously inclined to listen to him.

By a charter of July 27, 1689,[2] Arf, to the exclusion of all other subjects of the Danish king, was granted the right to trade in Guinea for himself and his heirs.[3] For this he was to pay the company a "recognition" which amounted to 2 per cent of the value of the slaves he carried to the West Indies. If other subjects of the king violated Arf's privilege, Arf might capture and confiscate their ships and merchandise. At the same time, to promote Copenhagen's trade, all foreign trade to the Danish stations was prohibited. Arf, like the company before him, obtained the right personally to hire garrisons for the forts. All that he exported to Guinea was to be free of duty, but on all imports from there he was to pay 2 per cent if the goods were not re-exported. The capital necessary for the trade could be borrowed from the king at 12 per cent interest. Arf was given permission to use the royal seal. If at some future date he or his heirs wished to give up the privileges, they were to return the African possessions in the same state in which they had received them. If they were lost in a war or by an act of violence, Arf would not be held responsible. The following year the company in the same manner surrendered its West Indian trade to the Bergen merchant and commerce director for Norway, Jørgen Thormøhlen. Arf also had ships' articles of conduct issued for the Guinea trade, probably to prevent quarrels and rivalries on board his ships.

As soon as the documents were ready, this energetic merchant sent off to the Gold Coast no less than three men-of-war: the *Gyldenløves Vaaben,* the *Københavns Vaaben,* and the *Laurvigen,* respectively. The ships brought the king's order for the transfer of Fort Christiansborg to Arf's men. Since the death of Hans Lykke in 1687, the commandant of the fort had been Nikolaj Fensman, who had first been "medicine master" and afterward the merchant for the fort.[4] In the latter capacity he had carried on a flourishing private trade with the Portuguese and the interlopers. Thus, he had been able to hold the fort though the Copenhagen company failed to send necessary supplies. After he became commandant, he even repaired the crumbling fortifications and purchased some cannons.

When Arf obtained the charter, Oliger Pauli turned to the Mediterranean trade. The Glückstadt merchants, however, were less willing to give up the Guinea trade.[5] For more than a generation it had been one of the town's sources of revenue. More than anything else the Guinea trade was in keeping with the maritime-commercial interests which had led to the foundation of the town, and it had surrounded the town with an aura of gold and adventure. Probably Thomas Thors felt most injured.[6] For fourteen years he had been a citizen of the town; and, in his own words, he sailed to Guinea with a royal sea-pass, paid his taxes, and equipped his ships. Now, in the autumn of 1689, he was once more ready to sail. His ship was well stocked with the articles which were in demand at Fort Christiansborg. His first thought was to enter the service of another country, but he decided against this and instead set sail. However, at Dunkerque he was captured. Because his cargo included guns and gunpowder, that is, war contraband, Henriques had to ask the king to use diplomatic channels to have him freed.[7] In the autumn of 1690 he again lay in the road of Glückstadt ready to sail. This time Arf got the authorities to place an embargo on the ship, because Thor's expedition was a violation of his privilege. In the end since the king was unwilling to support the citizens of Glückstadt, Thors and his son had to pay Arf a sum of money for permission to sail to Guinea.

Fate was against him, however. Leaving on December 26, 1690, this was to be the last time Thomas Thors set sail. In 1693 the blow fell. He had sailed up the Sierra Leone River in the frigate *Charlotte Amalia,* a large, well-equipped ship with thirty-six guns; but he was careless. A small English pirate ship, carrying only four guns, attacked his ship—presumably at a moment when nobody was on the look-out—and captured it with ease. Afterward the pirates did much damage along the Guinea Coast by using this large, good ship. In the end an English naval squadron chased it from Guinea to the West Indies, where, as far as we know, it was burnt with other pirate ships. For Glückstadt this event proved fatal. The town's Death Register states that after this blow "the Guinea traffic left the town"; and from then on Glückstadt declined. As it was, the privileges granted to Altona in 1664 created a dangerous rival. Altona also had tried to capture the Guinea trade. Joseph Fidanque, a Portuguese Jewish resident of Hamburg, had applied for permission to send two ships annually from Altona to Guinea. Soon Glückstadt was totally eclipsed. True, Henriques continued to work for the revival of the Guinea trade, and as late as 1703 he complained about the developments and applied to the king for the renewal of his privilege for the trade. But due to the interference of the West India and Guinea Company his application was unsuccessful. As long as the town of Glückstadt remained part of the Danish king's territories, however, it continued sending ships on whaling and sealing expeditions to the Polar seas. And so, Christian IV's town on the flat bank of the Elbe never sank into total inactivity.

Nikolaj Jansen Arf's business was not always as successful as its promising beginning.[8] The three above-mentioned ships which he sent to the Gold Coast left Copenhagen on July 22, 1690, and reached Fort Christiansborg on the last day of the year. On board was Jørgan Meyer, Arf's trusted agent who on January 5 took over command from Nikolaj Fensman. After some time he also made a new alliance with the king of the Akwamu, and gave him presents. Christiansborg had had bastions facing only the sea, and east and west; now Meyer built a forth bastion facing north. Thus, at length the fort was completed as originally planned. All the materials for the last bastion had been brought out from Denmark, in three ships which then returned home safe and sound. In 1692 Nikolaj Arf made another expedition in the frigate *Gyldenløves Vaaben,* while the ship *Københavns Vaaben* successfully completed a voyage from Glückstadt.

Fensman brought out a new commandant, Harding Petersen, who was to succeed Meyer. He was not a happy choice, for his "lax control and management" are said to have brought about a disaster. For some time the Africans had again been exerting a fateful influence upon the history of the Danish possessions, and now they gave rise to a picturesque interlude.

After the Danes again took possession of Fort Christiansborg in 1683, it was the Akwamu who controlled the environs of the fort.[9] Compared with the other natives of the coastal strip they were "nothing but rough peasants and stupid people" but "well trained in villainy and violence." All their sayings and doings bore the stamp of arrogance and rampant bellicosity, and the unfortunate peoples whom they subjugated were incessantly exposed to the robberies of the Akwamu kings. In the 1690's their total armed force, when all twenty-two towns sent their contingents, amounted to 7,000 men. Their capital, Nyanawase (which the Danes called Quambu) consisted of one straight street ten kilometers long with the royal residence halfway along it. At the time of the war against the

Accra, the king, according to Danish accounts, was a tall, heavy-set man named Rensang Sasaru. He died shortly after the war leaving as his heir a small son, Ado. Until Ado reached maturity, the country was ruled by its general, Bansiar (or Abinsam), who is said to have been Rensang's brother. According to a statement made by Wilhelm Bosman, the Dutch chief merchant at Elmina, who, in a series of letters gave an excellent description of Guinea, this regent was a jealous and malicious man and hated the Europeans. From each of the three European forts near Accra he was paid one ounce of gold per month as a "custom." Nevertheless, he did not always respect the peace of the forts. If one of the foreign nations had offended him, he might decide to block the roads to all the forts to bring their trade to a standstill.

It was with his permission that the episode occurred which, in the view of other Europeans on the coast, was most shameful for the Danes. Because of a number of deaths the garrison of Fort Christiansborg was very small at the time. One June day in 1693 the fort was tricked by a band of warriors from the Akwamu capital.[10] Pretending to have come for trade, they were admitted to the fort where they at once attacked the guard and beat down all resistance. Their chief was Assemeni (Assemone), who was later said to have been one of the company's runaway slaves at Christiansborg; he was, therefore, familiar with the field of operations. The garrison was treated with great cruelty. The merchant was quartered limb by limb. Several others were killed. Harding Petersen, the commandant, received four or five knife wounds in the neck; the tendons of his thighs were almost cut through to prevent his escape. Afterward he was thrown into the latrine, but in the night he succeeded in getting out and over the wall. After having dragged himself along for two nights, he safely reached the Dutch fort.

The value of fort and merchandise, according to Nikolaj Jansen Arf's estimate, amounted to 71,315 rixdollars which did not include Nikolaj Fensman's loss of 4,000 rixdollars and the loss of 4,164 rixdollars' worth of gold.

Having mastered the fort, Assemeni and his men made themselves comfortable. As far as possible everything was to be carried on in the same way as under Danish rule. Assemeni donned the commandant's uniform and made the others salute him as if he were the governor. The commandants of the Dutch and English forts were invited to formal dinners, and the food was excellent, for Assemeni, a former cook at an English fort, kept an eye on the kitchen. To reach the dining room the guests had to clamber up a ladder through a hole in the floor. During the dinner the warrior drank to the health of His Britannic Majesty, after having taken up a formidable position flanked on either side by a young bodyguard carrying a pistol. Throughout this the guns fired salutes as if the supply of gunpowder could never be exhausted. Above the fort flew a "blue banner with a blackamoor and a dagger in his hand." Interlopers (privately-owned English and Dutch ships trading without permission from the companies) also were well received by this commandant and some trade was carried on.

However, these splendors did not last very long. In December of that year, armed with twenty-six guns apiece, Arf's two ships, the *Christiansborg* and the *Gyldenløves Vaaben,* left Glückstadt for the Gold Coast. On board were two merchants, Hartvig Meyer and Johan Trane. When, after their arrival on the coast, they became aware of the situation, they hurried to Accra. There they anchored off the Dutch fort, Crèvecoeur. Fortunately they won the support of the Dutch, and thereafter Meyer initiated negotiations, and they obtained the surrender of the fort in June 1694 in return for a compensation fixed at 3,000 rixdollars' worth of merchandise. Afterward Thomas Jacobsen was installed as commandant, a volunteer crew of thirty sailors was left behind, and then the ships sailed. The ships' crew, in the meantime, were so reduced that they were now unable to defend themselves. Thus, in August while the ships were at anchor off the Portuguese island of Principe, in the Gulf of Guinea, they were attacked and captured by a pirate named Avery (also called Long Ben). The *Christiansborg,* in particular, had many dead and wounded, and among the casualties was Harding Petersen. The Dutch afterward maintained that the Danes had shown ingratitude for the support they received for the reoccupation of their fort; so it was probably with malicious satisfaction that they learned about the pirate's success.

This was a fatal blow to Arf's business. Beside this he had trouble with the dishonesty of the assistants he had sent out. In the autumn of 1693 he asked for the arrest of both his chief and assistant merchants at Christiansborg who had returned home on board the *Københavns Vaaben* and rendered no accounts of any kind.[11] In the following years, he does not seem to have sent out any ships at all.

Of course, in the long run neither the West India and Guinea Company nor the government could rest satisfied with this state of affairs. Both parties were interested in the preservation of the Danish trading stations. The demand of the West Indian planters for more African slaves could not be neglected—during this same time the planters began to clamor for a greater supply of Negro labor. As early as 1695 Henriques' applications gave rise to discussions of the matter, and in the spring of 1696 Jens Juel and Privy Councillor Mathias Moth persuaded the company to decide upon a reopening of the traffic to both Guinea and the West Indies.[12] For this purpose the shareholders were to make an investment of 10 per cent of the share capital. Next they bought the *Gyldenløve* and sent her off on the triangular route to both Africa and America. It returned in March 1697 with a cargo "so good that the like of it had never before reached Denmark from St. Thomas." This success further stimulated the desire to reopen the Guinea traffic. Arf had given up his rights on August 8, 1696, and on August 15 the king ordered the directors of the company, Jens Juel, Mathias Moth, and Jens Harboe, to demand the surrender of Fort Christiansborg.[13] Since neither the king nor the company was in a position to take over the fort at once, Arf had promised, in return for the payment of 1,500 rixdollars, to maintain it and pay the "custom" until the end of March 1698. So in October 1696 he sent out two ships, the *Københavns Vaaben* and the *Castellet,* with supplies. In the spring of 1697 Juel and Moth proposed to the king that the West India Company would reopen the Guinea trade if they could receive His Majesty's support to start the operation. Shortly afterward the company entered into a contract with Jacob Lerche, a merchant, for cooperation in sending a ship first to Guinea, and then to the West Indies. On July 10, 1697, Arf and his deputies in Guinea, Thomas Jacobsen, Hans Petersen, and Georg Andreas Taxter, were ordered to hand over the fort. Jens Juel and Mathias Moth were to take over on behalf of the company, to which the king promised rich privileges.

In the course of the following weeks, instructions were drawn up for the captain and trader as well as for the commandant of Christiansborg. On September 28, 1697, a new charter was granted to the company.[14] By this charter they were granted, in addition to their West Indian possessions, permission to retain Fort Christiansborg free of charge along with such territories and forts in Africa as they could acquire without infringing upon the rights of other European nations. Similarly, they were given permission to enter into contracts and alliances with the African states. All other subjects of the king were barred from the African traffic. In addition, the company was to remain exempt from customs and excise, with the exception that henceforward a 2½ per cent duty was payable on goods imported from overseas territories into Denmark. However, if the goods were re-exported, only 1 per cent would be payable. Whoever could offer irrefutable proof of loans to the company was given the right to claim compensation from its property. Commandants and chaplains for the forts were to be appointed by the board of directors of the company, but appointments were to be subject to royal confirmation. The directors were given juridical powers over the company personnel except in cases concerning their lives and honor. The board was to be made up of at least six members, one-third His Majesty's Ministers, and the rest Copenhagen merchants "of sufficient means." It was later resolved that after two years' unpaid service they were to receive 10 per cent of the dividend in return for their services, and the larger shareholders were to receive 5 per cent. On the other hand, they were duty bound to provide the company with capital. To obtain one vote a shareholder would have to invest at least 1,000 rixdollars. Nobody was allowed more than one vote no matter how large his investment. To regulate conditions on board the company's ships, ships' articles of conduct were issued on March 26, as had been the case earlier with the ships of the East India Company.[15]

Arf still had time to send out a Dutch-type flight ship (*fluitschip*) *Mynten* or *Nye Kфbenhavns Mynt* from Copenhagen to get his possessions back from Africa.[16] It arrived at Christiansborg on December 6, took on board its cargo, and sailed on to the Slave Coast. Thomas Jacobsen, the former commandant, sold as much of the goods stored in the fort as he could for cash, and installed one Erik Losen Lygaard, who had formerly taken part in four Gold Coast expeditions, as temporary commandant.

At the same time the company was planning to send out a ship to take over the fort, but they met with great difficulties due to the lack of capital. At first a temporary arrangement was made which enabled Mathias Moth to use the credit open to him personally. In Amsterdam he bought a cargo which, according to his own later statement, cost him no less than 60,000 rixdollars. It was sent from Amsterdam in the *Kфbenhavns Bфrs* on November 3, 1697. The company, however, owned only a half of this ship. The other half belonged to Jacob Lerche who, as of New Year's 1698, became the business manager of the company. Its captain was Jens Petersen (Imme Pieters); the special agent of the company on this expedition was one Erik Tillemand who had formerly served as a lieutenant at Fort Christiansborg. He had just published *En liden enfoldig Beretning om det Landskab Guinea* ("A Short Simple Account of the Province of Guinea"), the first book on this subject written in Danish. He now acted as the merchant and was given full powers to bring about law and order at Fort Christiansborg. This was no easy task. On his arrival at Accra on February 8, 1698, the building was found to have been repaired with new beams and newly built vaults, but nothing remained of the inventory. At the fort, beside Lygaard, there were only a Jewish clerk and nine soldiers, several of whom were ill and all of whom were on the point of starving to death, because they had been left with such meagre supplies. Everything had to be started anew. Lygaard, whom Tillemand knew to be an honest man, was sworn in as the temporary commandant. The garrison was increased and new agreements were made with Bansiar, the Akwamu regent, and with the chief of the Osu people.[17]

In the meantime, the company in Copenhagen was not totally inactive after sending out the *Kфbenhavns Bфrs*. Mathias Moth persuaded some of his friends to join him in making new investments to enable them to send another ship. The investors were to get 12 per cent interest on their money. In addition, they were appointed directors or chief participants, and were thereby guaranteed priority rights to part of the dividend as

introduced by the regulations mentioned above. Recently the *Victoria*
had been bought from Jacob Lerche. Presumably, this was the ship now
renamed the *Christianus Quintus* and sent to Guinea in the summer of
1698. It carried a cargo worth 30,000 rixdollars to properly stock the fort
with merchandise. It also carried enough soldiers to provide the fort
with a fairly large garrison. On its arrival at Fort Christiansborg, the
post of commandant was passed on to Johan Trane on December 23. He
had received royal confirmation of his appointment on September 9.
Frederik Snell was installed as chaplain of the fort, and in addition there
were twenty-five civilian and military servants. Lygaard handed over a
sum of gold worth 2,350 rixdollars as well as some merchandise. On the
last day of the year Jan de With, a mulatto born at Fort Frederiksberg,
was enlisted as drummer, messenger, and soldier. Soon after New Year's
a cane was sent to Bansiar as a present from the Copenhagen authorities.
He and Ado, who now jointly ruled the kingdom of Akwamu, were given
further presents valued at 60 rixdollars. These presents were accompanied
by an invitation to trade with the Danish fort. Everything, in short, was
done to stimulate trade.

Fort Christiansborg was now stronger than the two other forts in the
vicinity of Accra. With its four bastions facing all four directions, it
looked quite imposing; it was armed with twenty or thirty cannons, and
its vaults were so solid that it was possible to place the guns anywhere on
the flat roof. Pictures seem to indicate that in front of the gate there was a
kind of outwork, and above the height of the other buildings there was
the tower with flagstaff and flag. The walls were of uneven thickness on
the four sides; the thickest part faced the sea. In the vaults below was
stored the valuable stock of merchandise.

That it had been possible, against all odds, to maintain a trading
station in Africa for so many years, was due to the citizens of Glückstadt
and Nikolaj Jansen Arf. How profitable their ventures were, we do not
know. The Glückstadt citizens probably made a profit, since it was the
same persons who continued to invest. On the other hand, Arf is not
likely to have gained anything. On the contrary, the Guinea trade seems
to have put an end to his business career. The first attempt of the West
India and Guinea Company to take part in this trade had been no more
successful. While the fact that ministers, merchants, and shipowners in
Copenhagen were willing to continue the African adventure may have
been due partly to patriotic vanity, the decisive factor was the needs of
the West Indies. If, after Arf's failure, the company was to risk continuation of the Guinea trade, such trade had to be reduced to the level
of an appendix to the West Indian trade—according to Jens Juel's plan.

9 / ADO AND AQUANDO

CONDITIONS UNDER WHICH THE West India and Guinea Company renewed its activities on the Gold Coast were better than might have been expected. The situation was relatively peaceful. The supremacy of the Akwamu was a firmly established fact, and trade with them continued. True, Bansiar, the regent, hated the Europeans; but he died on March 23, 1699, shortly after the company had regarrisoned the fort and laid in a good stock of merchandise. His nephew, young Prince Ado, was more civilized, friendlier to the Europeans, and more inclined to work for peace among the African tribes.

The traditional enmity between Akwamu and Akim, however, was a serious hindrance to large-scale trade. The latter tribe was often called the Akenists by the Danes. Like Akwamu, the Akim belonged to the Akan tribes, and they lived to the northwest of Akwamu. The gold came from them at this time. Akim claimed sovereign rights over Akwamu and tried, with varying success, to levy taxes there. The chiefs of Akim were constantly quarreling among themselves. In fact, the people consisted of three tribes: Akim Abuakwa, Akim Bosome, and Akim Kotoku. It was the first of these three sections that invaded Akwamu and settled between the Pra and Birrim rivers. Instead of becoming master of other tribes, Akim was in danger of becoming a subject nation of Ashanti. This kingdom, which was later to become the most important of all the African states on the Gold Coast, was organized around 1700. The alliance of tribes was brought about by King Osei Tutu with the assistance of a priest named Okomfo Anokye. About 1740, the latter died at a very old age; he has always been regarded as one of Africa's great statesmen. Under the rule of these two men a number of excellent laws were introduced or codified. Okomfo Anokye also provided the Ashanti kings with the golden stool in which it was believed the people's power

63

was concentrated and symbolized, and around which, in the course of time, legends wove a series of strange events.

As we have seen, the political situation within the country was rather complicated. It must further be borne in mind that several other African tribes were constantly trying to change the course of events. Although it is impossible to disentangle all the threads of this pattern and trace the causes and effects of every incident, it is evident that the quarrels of the native peoples profoundly influenced the trade of the Europeans on the coast and interfered with the existence of their forts.

This was also true of the Danes at Fort Christiansborg.[1] During the reign of King Ado, things went fairly well though not without grievous complaints from the commandant, Johan Trane.[2] After Bansiar's death it was rumored that Akwamu was to pay 3,000 benda gold to Akim, and then trade was to be reopened. But, as far as we know, this did not happen. So, in his reports to the company directors in Copenhagen, Trane continually bemoaned the everlasting wars; and finally he passionately excused himself for not being able to make the trade more profitable. Besides the wars another cause for complaint was the very large number of European ships which came to the coast, so many "that they could have rained from the clouds." From December 1695 to February 1701 he counted 200 ships. He asserted that the English alone sent 300 ships a year to the Guinea coast and that Dutch ships were also numerous. Thus, none of them could obtain a full cargo. Even if the wars produced large numbers of slaves to be offered for sale, the constant demand for them made prices soar, and the millet used for their provisions on the voyage to America became difficult to procure. In spite of these difficulties, Trane's efforts bore visible fruits. On April 25, 1699, the *Christianus Quintus* sailed for the West Indies with a cargo of 549 slaves (of whom 295 were men and 254 women), 61 elephant tusks (whose total weight was 2,371 pounds), and a store of gold valued at 2,488 rixdollars. The next company ship to arrive at Fort Christiansborg, the *Fridericus Quartus*, left on July 29, 1700, after having taken on board 542 slaves and 7,195 pounds of ivory. After that a long time elapsed before the next ship came out; and because of the grain shortage at the fort, the slaves which Trane had bought began to die while still in his custody. Still, when the *Christianus Quintus* finally anchored off the fort on September 11, 1703, Trane was able to hand over to his successor, Hartvig Meyer, the colleague who took part in the negotiations with Assemeni, 228 gold marks (each worth 160 rixdollars) and 8,510 pounds of ivory.[3] Then, fever-ridden and physically exhausted, Trane boarded a Dutch interloper and sailed for home. He did not want to embark on the Danish ship, because the captain, one Willem Resen, was a coarse and ill-mannered man who quarreled with everybody. Unfortunately, his homeward journey was not peaceful. In the Atlantic the interloper became engaged in a fight with French men-of-war. Later the ship caught fire, so that he had to count himself lucky when he was put ashore almost empty handed at Plymouth. His traveling companion throughout these vicissitudes was Frederik Snell, the chaplain of Fort Christiansborg, who was succeeded by Jørgen Bagge.

Before Trane left the Gold Coast, however, the situation had badly deteriorated. Ado had died in 1702, and his successor, Aquando (Akonno, Akwanno) was an intelligent, but harsh and warlike, ruler. At once he attacked the Accra, perhaps because he was envious of their profits from the slave trade. When he was six or seven kilometers from Christiansborg, with his entire force, he began to drive the Accra away from the whole length of the coast and pursued them far beyond the Volta River. The native town of Accra was completely emptied of its population, and trade at the forts was brought to a standstill. Not until the following year, after the Danes and the Dutch had brought about a cessation of hostilities, did the exiled people venture to return. Nevertheless, Aquando showed no great respect for the Europeans. Every time he had some reason for complaint about them or wanted to blackmail them, he blocked the roads to the forts. Then, as a rule, they would have to pay before being permitted to trade again with the natives. Thus, in the autumn of 1703 Aquando had blocked the roads to the Dutch and English forts near Accra. Hartvig Meyer, the newly arrived Danish commandant, tried to win favor with the African ruler by means of presents larger than the company had authorized him to give. Now Meyer's commercial talents were put to the test. Aquando accused him of having plotted with the English to kill him and demanded five benda gold. As was usual in the case of such blackmail by the Africans, these demands were not completely met; but Meyer still had to pay two benda. Some days later the king returned and demanded a reduction of prices on all goods at the fort. Again Meyer had to compromise. He also had to pay for hospitality and banquets every time the king made an appearance.

Another disagreeable consequence of Aquando's expedition against the Accras was that it became difficult to obtain a cargo for the *Christianus Quintus*. In order to supplement the cargo obtainable at Christiansborg, the ship continued to the Slave Coast and found that the whole western part of it had been laid waste. Thus, it became necessary to sail on to Wida (Fida, Whydah). Even there trade was slow, although a contract was made with a native slave trader. In the meantime, mortality on board among the sailors and cargo had risen to dangerous heights. They were forced to depart with a cargo of only 249 slaves.

Commandant Hartvig Meyer died on April 23, 1704, and the trader Peder Sverdrup[4] was chosen as vice-commandant. Shortly afterward some of the garrison, headed by sergeant Christopher Gottschalk, plotted to attack him and usurp his power. But some Africans who understood

Danish betrayed the plot. Thus, one day when the sergeant was drunk, Sverdrup baited Gottschalk into insubordination, and thereby obtained a pretext for his arrest. However, Sverdrup lived only until May 5, 1705. At that time the *Cron-Printzen* was on its way from Copenhagen and was already at anchor off one of the forts on the coast. On May 25 it arrived in the road off Fort Christiansborg. In the short interval before the arrival of the ship, Peder Pedersen (Töyberg or Todbjerg, sometimes also called Aarhus) served as vice-commandant; thereafter Erik Olsen Lygaard took command.[5] He had come out in the ship and received royal confirmation of his appointment as commandant on November 3, 1704.

In the following months the fort became the center of hectic activity in order to provide slaves for the large ship. Before September 1, 466 male and 382 female slaves had been purchased. Prior to their embarkation an epidemic of smallpox had broken out among the slaves. Nevertheless, 460 men and 360 women were taken on board for a total of 820 slaves. This was the largest cargo of slaves ever to leave Guinea under Danish flag; but they were not to reach their destination. From the Gold Coast they sailed to the Portuguese island of Principe in the Gulf of Guinea for supplies. Here the ship was struck by disaster. The powder magazine caught fire, the whole ship exploded, and only five men were saved. Thus the company got nothing from the enormously rich cargo, nor was there anything left for those who sat at home and waited for their legacies from the dead company personnel. More than 2,500 rix-dollars' worth of inheritable goods had been on board.[6]

Apparently, the Akwamu had supplied the great number of slaves and sold them at low prices to the traders. The war between Akwamu and Akim continued sporadically; meanwhile Lygaard succeeded in making friends with King Aquando. True, the king accused him of keeping part of his present from the company directors in Copenhagen, which had consisted of four barrels of ardent spirits plus tobacco and pipes. The king believed that there must also have been some curio for him. Lygaard satisfied him, however, out of his own pocket by presenting him with some gold and a hunting knife with which he was very pleased.

Full of optimism about the future of the slave trade, Lygaard had a building large enough to house 300 or 400 slaves erected outside Fort Christiansborg. Inside the castle walls there was room for only a couple of hundred. He also collected a store of millet to feed a large stock of living merchandise. But his great expectations were not fulfilled. For some time hardly any "interlopers" came to this part of the coast. The few who ventured out finished their trade at Assini and Axim on the western part of the Gold Coast. At times the sale of guns to the warlike Africans went briskly enough, but otherwise trade remained rather slow. So when the *Christianus Quintus* came out again after waiting off Fort Christiansborg from February to April 1707, it had to leave with only

238 slaves on board. On the other hand, it carried no less than 11,439 rixdollars and 241 elephant tusks; and on the Slave Coast off Popo and Wida it got no less than 211 slaves. It was on this expedition that Peder Wessel, the great naval hero who was later to be ennobled as Torden-skjold, took part as the youngest apprentice.[7] He thought the voyage so hazardous that "no peril or difficulty could be enumerated which did not, on that same voyage, happen to us."

In the spring of 1707 Aquando launched another large-scale campaign. The trade routes were closed in April, and all the native traders of the coast followed his army. First, he marched to the Volta where he de-stroyed a native town, then, in July he crossed the river and continued inland. After a visit to the country of the Krepi, he marched far into the interior and attacked the Kwahue (Akwahue), whom he drove before him all the way to Ashanti. There, at last, the fleeing forces reorganized and defeated him. So, early in 1708 he returned home to plan his revenge. For the Danes at Fort Christiansborg this meant a brisk trade in gun-powder and hand weapons, for the flintlock muskets then in stock were of a quality inferior to those usually sent out from Denmark. In the late summer Aquando attempted another expedition but was defeated again. Consequently, the Europeans on the coast began to secretly hope that the Akwamu would be so weakened that direct trade relations with the rich gold-producing peoples of the interior would be possible. How-ever, this did not happen. Some months later Aquando gathered suf-ficient strength to settle his account with the Accra, who must have shown signs of betraying him. From November 28, 1708, until April 1, 1709, he camped with his forces near Accra and destroyed four villages: Osu near Christiansborg, Labadi, Tessing (Teshi), and Ningo (Nungo, Nungwa) farther east.

Faced with this feud, Lygaard chose to declare himself neutral. Though that was easiest at the moment, it proved a real advantage to Aquando. The Accra flocked to Fort Christiansborg and begged for protection, but Lygaard and his men remained inside the fort and watched them being massacred or taken as prisoners below its walls. Understandably, they never forgave Lygaard for this heartless passivity. To his way of thinking he was stationed on the coast to carry on trade not to become involved in feuds, but this utilitarian inclination to handle the situation only with a view to gain made him hated by both the Africans and Europeans. After that day he had great difficulty in getting along with others. When he realized how impossible his position had become, he wrote to Copenhagen asking to be relieved.

In the midst of these circumstances the company's two large ships, the *Christianus Quintus* and the *Fridericus Quartus*, arrived off Fort Chris-tiansborg on the 16th and 25th of April 1709 respectively.[8] Soon a quar-rel broke out among the new arrivals about Lygaard's treatment of the

Accra, and some tried to have him discharged. Nevertheless, he kept the post; but to remain on friendly terms with the African king, he had to deliver goods worth 12 benda to Aquando. After this he seems to have relied on a sort of alliance with the native king for support. Other difficulties arose also. Afterward the company was blamed for sending two ships at the same time, since, normally, it was difficult to provide enough cargo for one. Due to Lygaard's energy large supplies, such as 100 gold marks and 8,000 pounds of ivory, were stored at the fort. It was, however, next to impossible to obtain sufficient supplies of slaves. The trade routes to Christiansborg were blocked, so the *Christianus Quintus* had to be sent to the Slave Coast. Here, on June 14, off Whyda, an accident took place. A canoe was smashed by the surf, causing the drowning of Captain Hans Hansen Maas, Peder Pedersen (Todberg), the trader, and the chaplain, Anders Vinter. Though there were then many ships off the coast, after prolonged efforts they succeeded in scraping together a decent cargo. At their departure on October 2, the *Fridericus Quartus* had 435 slaves on board and the *Christianus Quintus* had 334. The large gold cargo on both these ships was about equal. The voyage, however, took a most unfortunate turn. At first the wind was contrary. Later they lost their course and so sailed past St. Thomas straying into the western part of the Caribbean Sea. Thence it was impossible to turn back, for the current carried the ships southward. Their provisions were almost exhausted. The slaves were put ashore on the coast of Nicaragua, and after a mutiny the crews plundered the gold chest. Then, on March 7, 1710, they took to the boats and left the ships to their fate. The *Fridericus Quartus* burned on the following night, and the *Christianus Quintus* drifted ashore and was splintered by the breakers. The crews tried to reach Portobelo on the Isthmus of Panama. On the way some of them were taken by a Spanish privateer; all were robbed to their very shirts, and only their lives were spared. Most of them were later sent to Jamaica. Only one of the captains, Anders Pedersen Wærøe, remained behind and tried to get the Spaniards to return the company's gold. After fantastic judicial proceedings, sentence was passed to the effect that the case was to be tried at Seville. Unable to obtain support from Copenhagen, Wærøe could not, however, pursue the case in Europe and had to return empty-handed.

With the company's loss of three large ships in the course of a few years, the Guinea traffic was bound to suffer, and for a long time the number of sailings from Denmark was very limited. Usually no more than one ship came out every third year. This again made the situation for the Danes on the Gold Coast much more difficult, while at the same time the profits of their labors were reduced.

As we have seen, Lygaard tried to maintain his position by means of support from Aquando. Under the circumstances this was probably the wisest thing to do, for Aquando's supremacy was undisputed. From February 11 to July 1, 1710, he conducted another victorious campaign against Kwahu. Even if on his return he made demands on the Danes which Lygaard thought exorbitant, it paid to satisfy him to keep the trade going with the Akwamu. Lygaard was, however, considerably weakened by the climate, and the animosity which had grown up against him made his situation still worse. On one occasion, he was even assaulted and wounded, while at the same time an attempt was being made to get him discharged. The leader of the opposition against him was Johannes Rask, the chaplain who had come out in the *Fridericus Quartus* to relieve Anders Vinter, who was drowned at Wyda. Lygaard maintained that the chaplain had begun to trade and stored his merchandise in the native town outside Christiansborg. This, Lygaard thought, was unworthy of a clergyman, so he confiscated part of his property and perhaps even dismissed him from his office. The chaplain could not forgive this and in his indignation hit upon the idea of writing an order for the arrest of the commandant. Johannes Rask remained as chaplain of the fort until September 1712 when, with shattered health, he sailed home in an English man-of-war. Later he became a parish priest in Nordland (northern Norway) where, using his diary from the journey, he wrote "A Short and Truthful Account of a Journey to Guinea and Back." After his death it was printed in 1754 by the Bishop of Trondhjem, Fr. Nannestad. In this book, the practical parson gives a graphic description of life on the Gold Coast.

Lygaard's doom was sealed with the choice of his successor, a merchant named Bfanz Boye,[9] who had already been to Christiansborg in 1709 and at that time was one of Lygaard's most fanatic opponents. He was granted royal confirmation of his appointment on March 30, 1711, and arrived in a foreign ship at Christiansborg on August 17. Delivered into the hands of his enemy, the sick Lygaard shut himself up and died shortly thereafter. On this occasion a tradition began, which was afterward to be revived on the arrival of nearly every new commandant. The work of the retiring commandant was torn to pieces by his successor and his management of the company's funds found fraudulent. The books were discovered to have been kept incorrectly, goods to be missing from the storehouse, loans to have been granted rashly to the Africans, goods purchased to have been entered at higher prices than they had cost, and goods sold at lower prices than had been paid for them. To set the state of affairs in the proper light, a description was given of the large profit that the culprit had been able to make for himself by private trade. This last item in particular was apt to make a strong impression on the company's directors back home in Copenhagen. Earlier, after Trane's departure from Guinea, his business methods had been carefully looked into. For the company it was all to the good if a commandant could be proven by his private transactions to have robbed them of their dividends. Afterward the company would be strictly within its rights to demand compensation from him and relieve him of any money he returned home with. These actions led the commandants to send money home to their relatives through secret channels, as Boye thought he had found proof of in Lygaard's case.

The description of all this villainy would be followed in the report from the new commandant by a vivid picture either of his own energy and skill or how he would send home revised accounts, recover debts, remain on friendly terms with Africans and Europeans alike, and think up new openings for trade. He would also point out that he always kept in mind the company's profit and prosperity. Of course, all such promises afterward proved difficult or impossible to keep. Boye makes special mention of his good reception when visiting the other European forts and of all his efforts to make friends with their commandants. Evidently, he was trying to secure reliable backing through his intimacy with the foreigners.

At any rate, he did not intend, like Lygaard, to make himself dependent on Aquando. At the beginning, the native potentate made fairly heavy demands on him. Among his claims was a large compensation for one of his women. He maintained that he had entrusted her to Lygaard during one of his campaigns, but Lygaard had betrayed his trust and slept with her. So Aquando threatened to close the roads to the fort. Boye, however, was not impressed. When, at the same time, Aquando's men came to buy muskets, he refused and added that they were to be kept in readiness for the punishment of those who came to close the roads. Afterward one of Aquando's chiefs came to say that no one had been thinking of closing the roads, but that, on the contrary, there had never been anything but close friendship—"which is not to be relied on" Boye adds. Subsequently, he sent presents to Aquando. These included a flintlock musket, a brace of pistols, a hat with gold lace, a beautifully embroidered cap, and a barrel of ardent spirits. Not content with this, however, the king demanded (in accordance with the old, customary regulations) a specimen of every kind of merchandise that came out from Denmark and a large collection of goods for his "custom." Boye would agree to this only if he were refunded the usual monthly custom. So the result seems to have been that Aquando withdrew his trade from the Danes and sent his men directly to the "interlopers."

It was not long before Boye had to change his attitudes, and he began to complain loudly of all the hindrances thrown in the way of trade. There were the continual wars between Akwamu and Akim, the poor quality of the goods supplied from home, the long waits between arrivals of ships and stores from Denmark, the constant lack of suitable staff, the annoying rivalry from the other forts, and so on and so forth. As far as Boye was concerned, it is safe to say that many of his complaints were groundless.[10] Before very long he entered into a traffic at least as dangerous as the one of which he accused Lygaard. Even during his own term of office several of his subordinates, led by one Peder Østrup, secretly sent home stray accusations about his cheating the company and carrying on an extensive private trade. Every profitable deal was made in his own name, all the unprofitable ones in the company's. His friendship with the English and the Dutch led to his buying, in the name of the company and at high prices, all their unsalable goods. The English could come unmolested and trade outside Fort Christiansborg, for Boye had given the Danish company's slaves orders to work for them gratis. In the company's books slaves were written off as dead, although they were in perfect health. In short, the instructions given to the commandant were violated in every possible way. "Whoring, gambling, and swilling are his favorite diversions, and [he] turns the company's fort into a brothel, and himself into a pimp, in order to also provide whores for foreign English captains, whereby the gates of the fortress are often kept open until 11, 12, or even 1 a.m., which might lead to its being taken by surprise."

This much is certain: Boye's business management brought the company no greater profits than Lygaard's. The latter left, as the result of his last two years' work, 3,885 rixdollars and 14,705 pounds of ivory in the company's possession. Boye found a deficit of 8,560 rixdollars in his accounts. Lygaard's private fortune amounted to 6,272 rixdollars, while he had secretly sent 76 gold marks to relatives in London and Copenhagen. As for Boye, after a little more than two years' work he was able to send home 31,889 pounds of ivory by the *Cron-Printzen Christian,* which had brought a cargo from Amsterdam to Fort Christiansborg early in 1714.[11] Of this quantity, it will be remembered that Lygaard had left behind about half. The rest of Boye's cargo was made up of 178 slaves worth 8,200 rixdollars. Later, in August 1717 he sent home 80 gold marks with two English captains, while 45 remained in the cash box at the fort. At the same time he had in stock 50 slaves and probably about 8,000 pounds of ivory, but these were the results of three or four years' business.

Shortly afterward he was relieved. Østrup's accusations were felt to be sufficient grounds. However, it took a long time for the reply to reach the fort. On November 25, 1717, the *Cron-Printzen Christian* arrived at Fort Christiansborg bringing orders for an investigation of Boye's management. Knud Rost, a merchant who had spent many years on the coast, was appointed as the next commandant.[12] (In the meantime, Østrup had caused Boye so much vexation, that the latter thought it best to sack him and accused him of lechery and drunkenness.) Boye was sent home at once but his books were in such great disorder that accounts were long delayed. Later he became chief merchant of the English Cape Coast Castle, but he was recalled from there also.

Mismanagement and the long intervals between the arrivals of ships made the situation at Christiansborg precarious, especially as the numbers of the garrison gradually decreased. The mother country's resources all went to her participation in the Great Scandinavian War, so no help was to be expected from her. Aquando's blackmail was a constant source of expense. Once, for example, while he was spending New Year's at Fort Christiansborg, he pressed 50 rixdollars' worth of presents out of the commandant as well as 100 rixdollars to be spent on colorful loincloths (*pantjes*) for his numerous wives and attendants. Gradually, the war between Aquando and Akim brought the gold trade to a near standstill. On the other hand, it provided abundant supplies of slaves. For these, however, the numerous English "interlopers" made prices soar, so there is not likely to have been a large turnover at Fort Christiansborg. In 1719 things came to such a pass that the only Dane with any knowledge of the trade was Peder Østrup, and in 1720 he and Rost were the only ones who could write. When Rost died on August 6, 1720, orderly management came to an end. It was impossible for Peder Østrup, who succeeded him as commandant, both to keep the accounts and to preserve order in the warehouse. Possibly he took his duties lightly. At any rate, when the next ship arrived from Copenhagen, everything was found to be in a hopeless state of confusion.

This occurred when a frigate named *Haabet Galley* reached the fort shortly after New Year's 1722. David Herrn was installed as commandant on January 25[13] while Peder Østrup was taken on board the ship where he died before it reached the West Indies. Herrn was entirely new on the coast and at first felt very uncertain among "such numbers of strange and unknown Africans." Due to his natural arrogance, however, he soon began to feel master of the situation. Though his term of office was short, more than any other Danish commandant he was to exaggerate and suffer great losses. He must have been the best penman of all the people sent out to the Danish stations in Africa; he also possessed a sense of the larger political patterns. But he was a great self-advertiser, always full of schemes and never successful in their realization. In criticizing Østrup's management, he found an easy prey. He accused him of having given presents and loans to friends and acquaintances "and having lived lecherously and shamefully with drinking and shooting day and night." The gentlemen of the company were probably less pleased with reading Herrn's eloquent account of the insufficiency of his own salary —he was paid no less than 1,000 rixdollars per annum. In his opinion, he had to spend half of the amount on banquets when heads of neighboring forts and when captains called because they had to be received courteously. Large sums had to be spent on New Year's presents for the local chiefs and other such expenses. "So what am I to receive for making my body sweat in this dry and unhealthy country in the service of the company?"

Herrn seems to have been dreaming of fortifying and expanding Danish power on the coast far beyond what it had ever been. For this purpose he made plans for the permanent supply of manpower necessary for such a regime. In cooperation with the chaplain, Elias Svane, he founded a school for the mulatto children of Danes and native women. A soldier was made schoolmaster for 12 boys and 8 girls. Svane and Herrn bought skirts and caps for them and paid contributions for their food. Next, Herrn tried to make friends with the Africans. He tried to win Aquando's friendship by valuable presents, but in the end he found that the African king was most troublesome with his constant feasting and carousing. Some African merchants who had been driven out of Osu were brought back by Herrn. He persuaded the inhabitants of Labadi, who because they had been dissatisfied with Østrup had kept aloof, to come and trade again at Christiansborg. He wished to add the villages farther east to the Danish area of trade. So, after the English had already occupied several places and were preparing further expansion, Herrn established lodges at Great Ningo and Lay. He even made a journey to Lay, 90 kilometers east of the fort. He cannot have been very pleased with the result of all these labors. His successors maintained that he had quarreled violently with the natives, but it is difficult for us to ascertain the truth of this. During the natives' New Year's celebrations in Dutch Accra on August 9, 1722, he was attacked by the natives and robbed of his hat, wig, and sword. The hammock in which he was carried was beaten and dragged in the dust, and the Danish flag which was carried before him torn to shreds. The reason given for the attack was that Herrn had robbed the natives of some slaves off Labadi's road. It is a moot point, however, whether the attack was not instigated by the Dutch themselves, since they made no attempt to prevent it. Afterward he was said to have revenged himself for the disgrace he had suffered at the Dutch fort by applying to Aquando for help, though there is no proof of this accusation. This much is certain: the king attacked and sacked the towns on the coast, and throughout this campaign Herrn accompanied him everywhere. On this occasion the lodge at Lay was destroyed, while the local Danish factor barely escaped.

Herrn seems, at first, to have carried on trade energetically, for the *Haabet Galley* was able to leave by February 11, 1722, with over 200 slaves. He never managed, however, to get Østrup's bookkeeping tidied up, and he neglected his own. Soon he was himself broken by the climate, and when he died on January 22, 1723, he left behind the same inextricable mess as many of his predecessors. His successor, Niels Jensen

Østrup, maintained that he had taken from the company's warehouse goods which he sold, pocketing the profit.

Niels Jensen Østrup seems to have tried to make order out of chaos, but by October 30 of that year he was dead. A week later the *Christiansborg*, captained by Anders Pedersen Wærøe, arrived from Copenhagen with fresh supplies. On November 7, 1723, an assistant named Chr. A. Syndermann was elected commandant.[14] The ship arrived unexpectedly and most of the slaves which the fort held had been sold shortly before. Niels Jensen Østrup, however, had left 32 gold marks at his death. Part of this sum was now spent to buy slaves for the ship's cargo. Nevertheless, when the *Christiansborg* sailed in March 1724, after having taken on board 412 slaves, there were still 20 marks left. Though, Syndermann's management was very prudent, by April 27 of that year he was relieved of duties when, after an exceptionally fast voyage, the *Haabet Galley* arrived and brought a new commandant. This was Captain Henrik Suhm, whose appointment had been confirmed by the king on December 17, 1723.[15] The ship remained at Christiansborg till August 16, when it left for the West Indies with a cargo of 250 slaves.

Suhm was a strict and dignified commandant, and his stay on the coast was of sufficient length to produce visible results. Among these were new buildings and repairs at the fort. However, throughout his entire term of office the local political situation remained extremely depressing. Aquando's campaign had destroyed the native towns at the coast, and most of their populations had fled. Therefore, it was impossible to purchase even the simplest provisions in the neighborhood of the forts, and the stay at Accra proved very expensive for the Europeans. True to his lifelong habits, Aquando continued his feuds with his neighbors. In 1724 he entered into an alliance with his neighbors to the west, the Fanti. Together they launched an attack upon Agona, which was situated between their territories. The Fanti attacked first, causing the Agona to flee to Akwamu, where every one of them was taken prisoner. Thus, having secured a great number of slaves Aquando promised to pay his debt to the Danes. He never kept this promise. On the contrary, he invented new pretexts for extortions of cash.

Shortly after, in the summer of 1725, warlike King Aquando passed away. For 23 years he had vigorously led his Akwamu peasant warriors on to numerous victories and rare defeats. To his neighbors, African and European, he had been a scourge, harassing them with trickery and violence, and reducing many of them to the position of tributaries. Only the Akim had proved too strong for him, but they, too, raised terrible accusations against him. During one of their wars with Ashanti, they sent their women and children for safety to Akwamu. Afterward, Aquando refused to return the refugees. Instead, he gave them to his men, so that many were sold into slavery. He kept the sister of the king

of Akim for himself and treated her as a slave; and in spite of promises
of great gifts, she had not been returned to her relatives when Aquando
died. No wonder Akim's hatred was bitter and unquenchable. To the
frequently changing and often morally frail Danish commandants of
Fort Christiansborg, Aquando's supremacy was a constant threat. They
did not have the courage not to enter into alliance with him, even
though by so doing they were exposed to constant extortions. Thus
Lygaard and Herrn were compelled to treat the Accra most abominably
and thereby bring the Danes into disrepute. Some commandants, such as
Boye, sought the support of the other Europeans on the coast against
Aquando, and in so doing risked betraying Danish interests to their European rivals. Wretchedly powerless, most of them sat in their fort making a modest living by trade with "interlopers," Portuguese, and French-
men. Thus the period of Akwamu supremacy brought neither wealth nor
glory to the Danes.

THE DEATH OF THE great warlike Akwamu leader did not bring happier days. During his lifetime there was at least some political stability in the Accra district, and the king had been an individual with whom the Europeans could deal. Soon after his death everything changed for the worse. His successors did their best to maintain the supremacy he had won but they were unsuccessful.

In the meantime several ships appeared on the coast. The *Christiansborg* sailed for the West Indies in September 1726 with 281 slaves, and the frigate *Haabet Galley* sailed in March 1727 with 238 slaves and again in May 1729 with 20 gold marks and 120 slaves. In January 1726 the galiot *Vergo Juvenis* or *Unge Jomfru* arrived to be used for the coastal trade. In September 1727 this boat also was sent to the West Indies with a cargo of slaves (it could hold only 47), but from St. Thomas it returned directly to Guinea. In 1727 Henrik Suhm sailed on board the *Haabet Galley,* and on his arrival in the West Indies he took over as vice-governor of St. Thomas. On March 4, 1727, Suhm had turned over command of Fort Christiansborg to a trader named Frederik Pahl, but Pahl died on September 18 of that year and was succeeded by Andreas Willemsen. The latter remained in Guinea until Christmas Eve 1728, when ship captain Anders Pedersen Wærøe took over. Willemsen's management was later investigated by a commission, after he had been taken prisoner on board the *Haabet Galley*. Nevertheless, he was subsequently appointed town judge on the island of St. Thomas.[1]

Gradually the power of the Akwamu kings seems to have crumbled. It started when a prince of Akwamu, Amaga, independently began to pillage the native towns on the coast. Their inhabitants ate fetish as an oath of revenge. So Amaga had to appeal to Ensangqvau, king of Akwamu, for help. He was refused, however, because Ofori, king of Akim, has just died, and the intentions of his successor were still un-

76

known. So Amaga turned to his own father, a powerful caboceer, who in spite of the king's resistance helped him. After that, everybody feared him and sent him presents.

This seems to indicate a decline of the king's power. Ensangqvau was said to rely on youthful advisers. Altogether his rule appears to have been rather despotic. Since the Danes sold some gold which he had given them as a pawn, he wheedled no less than 47 benda from them. Discontent with the rule of Akwamu was spreading like fire, and the neighboring native states were planning a collective attack upon them. Among the Europeans the Dutch especially came into conflict with them. The king of Akwamu had a cousin whom the Dutch kept in confinement for him at Fort Crèvecoeur. When this cousin was murdered by a slave, Amaga took the case into court, where the king claimed damages amounting to 1,000 benda. The Dutch flatly refused. War seemed imminent, and the native population of Accra began to flee.

At the same time the Dutch harbored ill will against the Danes.[2] This rancor dated from Peder Østrup's days, when he and the Dutch trader of Fort Crèvecoeur marched their natives out into a pitched battle, one against the other. There was also, it must be remembered, the assault at Dutch Accra upon the Danish commandant Herrn. Later the Danes maintained that Jacob de la Planque, the Dutch trader at Fort Crèvecoeur, was stirring up the natives against the Danes, and that he was being helped by Amoe, the cunning caboceer of Dutch Accra. The reason given for Planque's jealousy was that the Danes had succeeded in getting slaves for the *Haabet Galley*. At any rate, Amoe went to the hill tribes of the interior and inflamed or bribed them to rise against their masters, the Akwamu. In March 1729 the hill people came down to the coast and ate fetish with the Accra. The Dutch and English forts received them with salutes and military honors. When they came to Fort Christiansborg to invite Danes to join their alliance, Commander Wærøe declined the invitation and would not allow his guns to salute the native visitors. His reasoning was the same as Lygaard's and Herrn's had been; he had come to the Gold Coast to trade not to fight. After that the alliance between the coast tribes and the hill tribes was confirmed outside the Dutch fort. Then, about midsummer, all the allies marched into the hills, where Amoe acted as general of the combined forces. The caboceer Tette from Osu near Christiansborg set off with his people on June 22. The Dutch provided arms and equipment on credit against promises of all prisoners of war as slaves. At the same time, Planque set a high price on the head of the king of Akwamu.

This plan came to nothing, however. The Akwamu burnt the coast towns of Tessing and Labodi. Their ambassador to Fort Christiansborg was given a favorable reply. Unfortunately, on his way back the messenger was intercepted by the Dutch and at once put on board a Dutch slaver. Early in September the army of Akwamu fell upon the Accra and put them to flight. "Most of them threw away both flintlocks and cartridge bags, and came straggling home. They were ashamed because they did not return as victors, as they had boastfully said they would, six months earlier." Nevertheless, when, shortly afterward, ambassadors came from Akwamu to Accra to announce this victory, the Accra intercepted most of these messengers, after which the inhabitants of Osu, including women and children, fled to Dutch Accra. Now the Danes were placed in an awkward position, because they were faced with starvation and every kind of shortage. Fortunately, the sloop *Printz Friderich*, which had been sent out to serve the coastal traffic, arrived from Denmark on September 25, 1729. With the assistance of this ship the Danes were able thereafter to procure the needed millet from the more westerly parts of the Gold Coast. For six months the fort was actually in a state of siege, and during all that time the commandant never set foot outside its gate. Beyond the walls there was complete anarchy. In October it so happened that the Accra made a raid eastwards on the town of Ponny, captured its inhabitants, and sold the unhappy victims to the Dutch trader.

That was the state of affairs when, on December 28, 1729, the *Haabet Galley* came directly from the West Indies without first going to Denmark. This ship brought the fort a most welcome supply of gunpowder and bullets. After having lured the Danish company's slaves away from the fort and stolen the cattle belonging to the fort whenever possible, on January 8, 1730, the Accra hid among the huts of Osu and began firing at Fort Christiansborg. For more than a fortnight there were continual exchanges of fire between the Danes and the Africans; it was a state of war. Wærøe, however, bore up very well. He got sailors from the ship to help him and sent messengers to ask for reinforcements from Amaga and the king of Akwamu. One day he thought of a good joke. He set up a stuffed figure dressed in a Danish uniform on which the besiegers spent hundreds of shots. Although several Danes were wounded and one died in these critical days, the morale of the Danish garrison was excellent. All attacks were beaten back, and Wærøe wrote "We brushed them Bravely."

So the morale was still high on the morning of January 23 when five Akwamu caboceers appeared before the fort. They were followed by their forces and flew the silken Danish banner which Wærøe had sent to the king of Akwamu. Thus began a *bataille* which raged the whole morning. At noon—and this was typical of native warfare—there was a pause, because of the stifling heat. During this break the Akwamu were supplied with better gunpowder from the Danish fort. So when hostilities were resumed around three o'clock in the afternoon, they were able to give the Accra a thorough thrashing. In the evening they drove them back to the Dutch fort, and the Akwamu camped in Osu. The next few days passed in much the same way; then fighting came to a temporary standstill. On the afternoon of February 14, the king arrived with a great force, and the natives now pressed bravely forward to the very walls of Fort Crèvecoeur. This they dared in spite of the fact that they were being fired at by both the Dutch and English forts. They even were able to sack and burn the native towns outside both forts. After that the English asked for peace and acted as mediators. After peace had been settled between them and Akwamu, the king departed with his army on March 22, 1730.

In the meantime, a new director general of the Dutch Gold Coast territories arrived, and Planque was transferred to Elmina where he was made chief merchant. At Wærøe's complaint the director general promised to work for peace. Later, efforts toward peace developed into a lengthy correspondence between the parties. To the end Wærøe maintained that the whole trouble resulted from Planque's schemes and plots, and that the real purpose of the Dutch had been to possess Fort Christiansborg for themselves.

The hasty disappearance of the Akwamu from the scene of action was, however, due to the fact that they were faced with a danger far greater than the Dutch and the Accra. A number of neighboring tribes were still plotting against them. Mention was made of Ashanti, Akim, Wassaw (Wasa), Fanti, Agona, and Assini. The most dangerous was Akim. Twice the Akwamu defeated their enemies, but then they became foolhardy. While in pursuit of their retreating enemies they waded across a river. Afterward it rained in the upper regions, and the river swelled enormously. This was the moment Akim chose to attack, and now Akwamu was put to flight. In their retreat they tried to recross the river, but four times as many were drowned as had been killed in the battle. Akim pressed the attack home, and in three days destroyed Akwamu. Ensangqvau was killed, and only scattered remnants of his army were able to escape eastward along the coast to the other side of the Volta. The former rulers of the Accra district had either been killed off or driven into exile. For many kilometers north and east of Fort Christiansborg the country had become a no man's land. The news of this crushing defeat reached the Danish fort on September 17, 1730.

Now that the nation to whom the Danish settlements on the Gold Coast had paid tribute for so many years and on whose support they had relied had collapsed, the days of the Danes would seem to have been numbered. They had supported the losing side. That they were let off cheaply considering the circumstances was no doubt largely due to the presence of the *Haabet Galley* in the road. Under the stress of these shattering revolutions, the like of which had not been seen for fifty years, the Danish garrison kept the ship for a whole year, and the frigate was not allowed to leave until December 12, 1730. There was a certain element of luck too, in the way in which contacts were made with the new masters of Akim. Messengers had at once been despatched with presents and congratulations to the victors. On September 25 a "lieutenant" arrived at Accra. He had been sent by one of the three most important Akim caboceers, called Frempung Nansung by the Danes. Although the Dutch seem to have tried to deprecate the Danes in the eyes of the new rulers, Wærøe succeeded in winning over the lieutenant. A contributing factor may have been that the lieutenant's men quarreled with the people of Dutch Accra. Shortly afterward, on October 6, he returned to say that in the future Frempung would be willing to accept from the Danes the monthly tribute formerly paid to the king of Akwamu. In return, he would favor the Danes with a monopoly on Akim's trade. After that he returned several times, but there were intervals of months and years between Akim's trade expeditions to the Accra coast. Wærøe reported that, in his opinion, Akim was a very touchy nation, not as malicious as Akwamu but very self-willed.

Later the lack of stability in Akim became a constant source of trouble.[3] Frempung was regarded as an enemy of Ashanti, while the other two powerful Akim caboceers befriended that nation. The Danes got into trouble for not having had any contact with Frempung for a long time. In 1732 one of the two other important caboceers, Bang Qvantin, sent messengers demanding a "custom" from Fort Christiansborg. At first Wærøe sent only an assistant to him with presents. Later, however, he had to pay, since otherwise the Dutch offered to do so. After that he took the safe course of paying for the friendship of both Frempung and Bang.

The war period had been hard on the Danes at the fort. Beside the Danes and some of their slaves, many of the women and children of Osu had taken refuge behind the walls of Fort Christiansborg. For a short time they had nothing to live on but cheese, millet, and water. Scurvy and fever were rampant. Wærøe's wife went mad. The protracted incarceration depressed their minds. Only very gradually did the inhabitants of Osu and the company slaves come slinking back either one by one or in small bands to offer their services. Many Osu people fled again, however, in November 1730 when Amoe started an expedition against the scattered remnants of Akwamu in the Volta district. There they wandered up and down for two years until after Amoe's death. Then his son, Dakoe, won a victory and was able to lead the Accra home. Nevertheless, Osu lost more than half its male population in the course of these years, and the armed forces of the town dwindled from 88 to 40 muskets. Akim reinstated the former caboceer of the town. He had, it seems, not really been against the Danes but had been forced to join the alliance against Akwamu.

Even after the decisive battle, conditions at Fort Christiansborg were not very satisfactory. Although an agreement was made with the Akim victors, relations with the natives of Dutch Accra were still strained. The new trader at Fort Crèvecoeur, Eleth, went on making trouble for the Danes. Three Europeans from Fort Christiansborg had been *panjared* at Ningo, that is, imprisoned for debt by some natives from Dutch Accra, and the Danes had to incur a large debt to free them. The garrison of the Danish fort gradually sank into a poverty so wretched that even the natives spoke pityingly of the poor Osu Danes. It did not improve matters that the sloop *Printz Friderich* did not return after September 1731, because it was wrecked to the east near Popo. After that they had great difficulty in obtaining the vital supplies of millet. Trade had almost come to a standstill at Christiansborg. Worms and rats spoilt the store of goods, and a large quantity of ardent spirits which they had hoped to sell to the Akwamu was now almost unsaleable. Three months after the departure of the *Haabet Galley*, the *Grevinden af Laurvigen* anchored in the road on March 28, 1831. With the circumstances then prevailing, it was next to impossible to provide a cargo for the large vessel. So it remained for many months and finally sailed on April 1, 1732, with 17 gold marks and only 116 slaves. In addition it carried Wærøe's reproaches addressed to the company directors in Copenhagen for not sending a much smaller vessel. Trade with Akim had one advantage. They always brought good gold, and this was some consolation for the shortage of slaves. Early in 1733, while the *Laarburg Galley* was anchored for a month in the road, it took on board 4 or 5 gold marks from the Danish fort but only 52 slaves. Even the supply of gold was smaller than formerly.

Possibly, Wærøe's administration degenerated under the stress of circumstances. Cornelius Bagge, captain of the *Grevinden af Laurvigen*, spoke ill of him, but he was none too reliable himself.[4] We have evidence from several sources about his rough manners, and Wærøe himself calls him "a coarse ox" and "an ignorant rogue." In the course of one of their quarrels, Wærøe had struck him on the mouth. So, the skipper had no reason to have friendly feelings toward the commandant of the fort. Of course, Bagge saw to it that the directors were informed of his view of the matter. So when the *Grevinden of Laurvigen* was again sent out captained by Bagge, it brought a new commandant, Andreas Jørgensen. It brought also an order that a commission with Bagge as chairman look into Wærøe's administration. Off the Canaries, however, Andreas Jørgensen died, so there was nothing to do but let Wærøe remain in command until the arrival of the next ship. Wærøe was fully justified in complaining that the company was making his enemy pass sentence on him. He regarded it as ingratitude on the part of the company to treat him like a criminal, since by his courage, he had steered the company's possessions safely through the most dangerous situations they had ever run up against. The fifty-year-old man reminded the directors that he had been a sailor since the age of ten and had served the company for thirty years.

It was not yet possible for Wærøe to attract much trade. When, after a stay of nearly six months, the *Grevinden af Laurvigen* sailed for the West Indies in February 1734, there were only 10 or 11 gold marks on board, and of its 224 slaves only 74 had come from Christiansborg. Little by little trade began to improve. The Akims came down to the coast and brought more gold; so when at last Wærøe was relieved on August 12, 1735, he left 28 marks in the company's money box at the fort. The snow *Jomfruen* had brought a new commandant, Søren Schiellerup (Schieldrup).[5] This official, who deserves praise for his own work on the coast, conscientiously followed the best traditions in his treatment of his predecessor by mercilessly abusing Wærøe for his "bad husbandry and lecherous comportment." His worst accusation was that Wærøe had reserved the slave trade to himself by allowing the company to take over the worthless slaves and keeping the healthy ones himself. Many of the company slaves had died at the fort, and the rest were so miserable "that they were better likened to skeletons than fine slaves." The male slaves were greyhaired and the female slaves old and toothless, but Wærøe's own slaves were young women with firm breasts whom he either reserved for his own needs or for whom he found a ready market. Schiellerup listed, without compunction, on Wærøe's account 3,320 rixdollars, the value for 41 slaves who had died. Schiellerup estimated the sum total of goods missing from the warehouses and Wærøe's debt at more than 18,000 rixdollars while Wærøe himself stated the amount was only 7,300 rixdollars. Schiellerup estimated that Wærøe had put his private gold into the hands of the Dutch, and that he was the cause of the enmity of de Bordes, the Dutch trader at Fort Crèvecoeur, toward him. That Wærøe had lived a drunken and licentious life, we know from other sources, too. Above all, Schiellerup found that Wærøe's two daughters had a bad reputation. Unlike all other Europeans they spoke "the African language" to perfection, and so there was no possibility of controlling their doings. When Schiellerup discussed all these matters and especially the deficit with Wærøe, the old man burst into tears. Schiellerup sent both him and his daughters home under arrest in the snow *Jomfruen*. When the documents of the case finally arrived home, legal proceedings against him were opened but were not concluded before Wærøe's death in 1742.

By and large, the treatment of Wærøe was very rough. The abuses which Schiellerup emphasized were mostly common practice on the Gold Coast. That commandants carried on their own private trade and pocketed the best profits themselves was no novelty. Wærøe may have been hard on the slaves, but even apart from that many slaves normally died. It would have spelt ruin for most commandants if they had been ordered to pay compensation for the slaves who died at their fort. Whether the sexual excesses at Fort Christiansborg were worse in Wærøe's day than under many of his predecessors will forever remain an open question. As far as we can see, as long as he remained, the other officials were well satisfied with him even if he did have a sharp tongue. This is not to say that he was a respectable man if measured by the standards of other ages and different places. In fairness, however, it must be borne in mind that he steered his ship resourcefully, courageously, and tenaciously through a stormy period. It was not he who created the difficulties. Both the Dutch intrigues and the African wars were in full swing when he arrived. The slackness of trade in his day was hardly his fault and the transition from the supremacy of Akwamu to that of Akim was negotiated by him with almost miraculous success. In no way were his efforts appreciated by the West India and Guinea Company in Copenhagen. They thought only of the blameworthy aspects of his activities and thereby gave him less posthumous honor than he deserved.

11 / THE SLAVE TRADE

SLAVERY AND THE SLAVE TRADE are as old as history, but the African trade and African slavery have usually been regarded as their most abominable manifestations.[1] As early as the epoch of the great geographical discoveries the Portuguese used black slaves. The great boom in the African trade, however, did not come until the seventeenth century, when the cultivation of the West Indies and of the Virginia plantations was started. The Indians of America were ill suited for hard labor on the plantations, so the white planters chose the Negroes as a race that could endure hot climate. Beside the Portuguese it was especially the Dutch, the English, and the French who profited by the slave trade. Enormous fortunes were being amassed in Western Europe, and the trade in human beings was one of its main sources.

As we have seen, on several occasions the Danes, too, demonstrated their desire for a share in these profits. However, as long as the Glückstadt shipowners and Nikolaj Jansen Arf controlled the Danish-Guinea traffic, Danish ships do not generally appear to have taken part in the transportation of slaves. It was only after 1697, when the West India and Guinea Company really started trade to Africa, that the transportation of slaves seems to have become a regular part of Danish trade. Those inclined to take up this trade must have been greatly encouraged by a report in 1696 from Governor Lorenz of St. Thomas in the West Indies.[2] He described the excellent profits recently made by the Brandenburgers when two of their ships had transported 1,100 Africans across the sea. "All other trade is as nothing compared with this slave trade," he wrote. So the company directors in Copenhagen must have anticipated great dividends when they sent off their first ship, the *Købenbavns Børs*, on the long Atlantic voyage to Guinea and thence to the West Indies.

Slave cargoes for European ships were secured in two ways. One way was to sail along the coast and buy up small numbers of slaves here and there, doing business both with European forts and with the African towns. This was the method preferred by the "interlopers." The other was for European traders at the forts or lodges gradually to collect whatever slaves they could obtain from their district, so they would have a full cargo ready for shipment when a ship appeared off shore. This was the method usually adopted by company ships. Only very exceptionally did the ships steal or kidnap anybody belonging to the peoples of the coast. It is hardly possible to give an example of such doings on the part of the Danes. If it were to happen near the forts, it would result in nothing but endless trouble with neighboring tribes.

The Danes always tried to buy slaves at their forts or lodges, but they rarely, if ever, had a full cargo ready when the ships called at Fort Christiansborg. Either the ships had to wait until the cargo was complete, or they would have to supplement their cargoes at other places along the coast. The former meant a waste of time, money, and human lives, for in the meantime, the climate would take its toll of the crews.

Accra was one of the towns where slaves were easiest to obtain. Continual wars among neighboring tribes provided the African kings with a steady flow of prisoners of war. Furthermore, a nation like the Akwamu unscrupulously carried on large-scale robberies of human beings from conquered or simply neighboring tribes. Some became slaves because they were unable to pay their debts or fine. In America the Accra were regarded as the best workers because of their endurance, but they were looked upon also as the most savage and unruly.[3] The forts had to be prepared to buy and house slaves whenever the natives decided to bring them. They would sometimes turn up in the middle of the night, especially if they brought stolen goods. In such cases it was necessary to get the slaves off their hands without attracting attention. Sometimes even the traders stipulated that slaves be embarked in the night. This was the case, for instance, during the war between Osu and Dutch Accra in Wærøe's days.[4] After a great battle, the victors would bring crowds of first-class "goods," but usually they would bring just one or a small number of slaves to pay for their purchases. Normally it would not be possible to place orders for specified numbers of slaves with the native kings or slave traders.

Before the deal was closed, the "article" was carefully examined. If there happened to be a physician or surgeon at the fort, he would look carefully into the state of "its" health. Usually the purchasers were interested only in vigorous and able-bodied wares. The least deformity would lead to rejection or a considerable reduction of the price. Such cases apart, there were usually fixed tariffs, and slaves were bought up "in categories." Men fetched higher prices than women; there were lower rates for boys and girls. Sometimes reckonings were made for three-fourths of a slave or two-thirds of a slave. Native traders liked to receive presents with the bargain such as a stone mug, a hat, or a tawdry kerchief. Payment was made usually in goods.

Fort Christiansborg was too small to house a full cargo of slaves within its walls, but visitors are still shown the door to the room where the slaves were often locked up. When there were large quantities in stock, they had to be housed outside the fort in the forework or the native town. The male slaves were frequently put in irons. Rings of iron were placed round their necks and ankles and connected by iron chains; and they were often provided with heavy blocks of wood or iron which hindered their movements. Sometimes they were chained in pairs, and during transportation long lines would be made by chains connecting the rings round their necks. At Accra, which was liable to periodic food shortages, it was expensive to keep the slaves for any length of time. Food would run short, and the rate of mortality would then soar. The greatest sufferers would be babies and invalids. It was difficult for the slaves to escape, unless they happened to have their homes and relatives in the neighborhood. The native kings or chiefs who received monthly tribute from the fort often undertook to return runaway slaves or else pay compensation for them. A solitary African fleeing through the impassable country did not have much of a chance. A few times the slaves at Fort Christiansborg tried to mutiny. One night in August 1727 some slaves fell upon the *bomba* or slave overseer, killed him, and escaped.[5] Half of them were caught; the ringleader was broken on the wheel and afterward beheaded. When, in 1736, a slave plot for an attack on the garrison was discovered, it was thought inadvisable to send too many of them by the first ship, because it was short of crew.[6] A slave mutiny in August 1738 cost the life of one soldier, but it was immediately put down.

Because of the irregular intervals between the arrivals of company ships at Accra, it was natural for Fort Christiansborg to sell continually to foreign purchasers when there were numerous slaves in stock. On one occasion a French captain in four days bought more than 500 slaves from the fort.[7] In the bargain he received large quantities of refreshments, which were sent on board his ships. The first decades brought many Portuguese ships to Fort Christiansborg. Later the Dutch succeeded in driving them farther east. In the second quarter of the eighteenth century it was mainly French ships which helped Danish trade. From the start Dutch "interlopers" played an important part, too. In the latter half of the century, English trade flourished. Of the total number of slaves transported from Africa to America, only an infinitesimal fraction sailed in Danish bottoms. At times when the Danes would have at the very most three or four ships engaged in the slave trade, Holland and England would have several hundred. When the Danes were able to send only one ship to the coast at long intervals, ten or even twenty English ships might be lying off Anamabo or Accra at the same time.

Scarcely 1 per cent of the total slave traffic can safely be said to have been carried out by Danish shipowners.

The prices of slaves on the Gold Coast fluctuated with the state of the market.[8] A successful native campaign might produce an incredible slump, while if there were a great many European ships lying waiting for cargoes at a fort, prices would soar. There was a noticeable increase of prices in the decade 1710-1720, when extensive wars were being waged in Europe. Then followed a period of stagnation until the 1740's, when prices rose again. Shortly after the year 1700 a male slave is said to have cost 32 rixdollars and a woman 28-32 rixdollars. In 1705 prices had risen to 40-48 rixdollars for men. Still, at that time the king of Akwamu received only 36 rixdollars for men and 28 for women. Other slave traders were sometimes paid still less. It was all a question of being on the lookout for the right moment and buying when the slump set in. Boye is reported once to have bought slaves at 8 rixdollars per head and sold them at 64 rixdollars. In 1714 prices had risen to 64 rixdollars for men and 40 for women, but to the Portuguese from Brazil they were sold at 80-88 rixdollars for men and 56-64 rixdollars for women. So, it was possible to make a nice profit. The English, too, paid these high prices. In 1720 English interlopers are said to have paid even 100-120 rixdollars for men and 80 rixdollars for women.

This was a temporary peak. In 1727 the Fanti bought slaves from Akwamu, paying 88-96 rixdollars for men and 64-72 rixdollars for women. In 1732 it was stated that a man cost 88 rixdollars and a woman 56 rixdollars. As late as 1744 it was possible to buy from the native slave traders at 64 and 48 rixdollars respectively, but from the French, who were the best customers, it was possible to obtain one and a half times or even twice as much. In the following period, the usual prices were about 112 rixdollars for men and 80 for women. In those days prices were given in ounces of gold at 16 rixdollars per ounce.

During embarkation canoes full of slaves were sometimes dashed to pieces by the breakers. In 1756 a sloop capsized after having taken its native goods on board from the canoes, and fourteen slaves were lost.[9] The greatest danger to the lives of the slaves, however, was the living conditions on board. As a rule these ships were only of slightly more than 100 commercial lasts (about two tons), so they were often terribly crowded. This is not to say that the slaves were willfully tortured. On the contrary, it was in everybody's best interest that the slaves crossed the Atlantic as safely as possible. If any of them were injured or died, so much investment was lost. So they were properly fed. The bread ration included, among other items, the millet bought on the coast. The slaves were divided up into groups and allowed daily visits on deck. Dances and music were arranged for them; tobacco, spirits, and other stimulants were distributed to them. When the ships called at the Portuguese islands in the Gulf of Guinea, they would be given fresh fruit. However, it was of no avail. The slaves would have to spend much of the time below deck. Often they would be packed as close as possible, lying side by side, with the men usually in irons. The smells on such a crowded deck would be unbearable. Some were suffocated for want of air.[10] The risk of epidemics was very high. Every ship had one or two surgeons on board, but how could they possibly cope with smallpox and dysentery. The worst that could befall was a dead calm which would prolong the voyage and finish the provisions. In such cases, they might have to suffer rationing, starvation, and thirst. If worst came to the worst, some would have to be thrown overboard, so that there would be sufficient food for the rest.

To this must be added depression, which weighed upon the minds of the African people when they realized that they were being carried off from their native land. They did not have the faintest idea what fate would have in store for them. They imagined all kinds of horrors. The majority of them had never been to sea before. Some feared that the white men would fatten, kill, and eat them. Some preferred suicide to an uncertain future. It was a strict rule that under no circumstances should a slave be allowed to lay hands on a knife as long as he was on board ship. Many things might produce a fit of depression: a kick from an extraordinary brutish sailor or a harsh word from one of the ship's officers. It was not unusual for the members of the crew to select pretty young women from the cargo to serve their own pleasures.

Only one case of a ship having been insufficiently provisioned has come down to us. On board the *Cron-Printzens Ønske,* captained by Abraham Jensen Sejerø, we are told that they were allotted only a pint of water per person per day. True, heavy showers might blow up which would enable the ship to collect some fresh water in mid-ocean, but nevertheless, there could be no excuse for taking such a chance. In spite of everything the ship reached the West Indies with 195 of the 250 slaves it had taken on board in Guinea. Far worse things happened in 1748 on board the *Jaegersborg,* captained by Ole Eriksen. One hundred seventy-four died out of a cargo of 334 slaves. In this case the surgeon concluded that the slaves had been given too much water. An investigation of mortality on board the Danish slavers in the days of the West India and Guinea Company shows that, of the more than 10,000 slaves carried in the Danish company's ships from Guinea during the period 1698-1754, no more than 7,500 were landed in St. Thomas. Some slaves from the cargoes of the *Christianus Quintus* and the *Fridericus Quartus* may have survived on the coast of Central America. Nevertheless, it is safe to say that about 20 per cent of the slaves died during the passage.[11] This would be a somewhat larger loss than suffered by other slavers. The estimated loss from a normal slave cargo in a ship from Western

Europe was expected usually to be about 15 per cent. An important item in our record of losses was the *Cron-Printzen,* which was lost in 1706 with its enormous cargo of 820 slaves. Exclusive of this extraordinary catastrophe, mortality on board Danish ships seems no higher and even a little lower than in other slavers.

If we consider how many other deaths among the Africans were caused by the slave trade, the sum total is, nevertheless, very depressing. Many lives were lost in the battles or surprise attacks whereby native kings and traders procured their slaves. Some fell by the wayside during the endless marches along the narrow paths through forest and bush down to the coast. Next, some died at the forts, and many died on board the ships. Finally, after landing in America quite a few died from exhaustion due to the sufferings they had undergone. It seems fairly safe to say that, for every able-bodied slave put to work in the New World, at least one African life had been sacrificed on the way.

From the point of view of the whites, the gravest danger connected with the transportation of slaves was the risk of slave mutinies on board the ships. A crew of 25-50 men had to keep order among several hundred slaves. If an incipient mutiny were discovered in time, the crew had, of course, means for calling the slaves to order. It was a question of not killing too many of the valuable culprits and so spoiling the chances of making the expedition pay. If some of the slaves had broken loose and armed themselves, the situation was extremely critical, especially if they had had time to free their fellow-sufferers from their chains. If, in such a situation, the crew failed to act ruthlessly and courageously, it was lost. Fortunately, slave mutinies were rare in Danish ships. On the night of September 14, 1709, a revolt broke out on board the *Fridericus Quartus* while it was at anchor off the Slave Coast.[12] Some of the slaves had managed to break their fetters and free themselves. Unfortunately for themselves, they tumbled on deck amid shouting and noise and thus warned the crew. Two whites were seriously injured, but after prolonged and bitter fighting the crew defeated the slaves. The next morning, in accordance with sentences passed by the ship's council, the ringleader was punished as an example to others. His right hand was cut off and shown to every single slave "with the additional grave threat that now the hotheads would do well to regard themselves in this mirror." Next the left hand was cut off and finally the head. Then the body was hoisted onto the mainsail yard, where it remained suspended before the eyes of all the slaves for two days. The rest of those who had taken part in the mutiny were lashed and afterward rubbed with malaguetta pepper, salt, and ashes. Still worse things happened during the mutiny on the brigantine *Patientia,* the morning of August 5, 1753.[13] The ship was somewhere between Elmina and Cape Coast Castle westward bound. At first only three slaves had broken loose, but they took the crew by surprise, killed three men, and wounded Captain Ole Eriksen. After this the rest of the crew, 19 men in all, fled like cowards in the ship's boat. They got safely ashore and were taken on board an English ship, the *Triton*. With the assistance of the English sailors, the captain succeeded in regaining his ship on August 8. In addition, the crew was able to recapture a great many of the slaves; but while the slaves had been masters of the vessel, they carried off its store of gold worth 1,001 rixdollars and 62 elephants' tusks. Thus the company suffered a considerable loss.

By and large the West India and Guinea Company of Copenhagen made no money by its participation in the slave trade. At an early date discussions were begun as to whether it was worthwhile to continue it. Frederik Holmsted, who was the company's bookkeeper from 1708 and later its director, opposed the trade. From 1727 onward he proved again and again that the company had only suffered harm because of the trade. The profits made in the West Indies and elsewhere were swallowed up by the calamities caused by the Guinea traffic. Consequently, the company sank more and more deeply into debt. Through an examination of all the company's activities to date which he made with P. Mariager who had succeeded him as bookkeeper, he found that, to be sure, the slaves had brought in more money in the West Indies than had been paid for them in Africa.[14] When, however, the cost of maintaining forts and lodges was taken into consideration, there was a considerable deficit. Up to 1733 losses had amounted to 456,021 rixdollars, and property amounting to only 116,883 rixdollars had been preserved. Thus, for example, the losses incurred in connection with the expedition of the *Københavns Børs* in 1697 amounted to 4,941 rixdollars. On its first expedition, the *Christianus Quintus* lost 24,189 rixdollars and on its second, 32,684 rixdollars. Up to 1708 the total losses amounted to 167,125 rixdollars. Now it is quite possible to criticize Holmsted's accounts for he painted a grim picture of the company's affairs. Nevertheless, it was a fact that the Danish slave trade was not paying its way. The least encouraging factor was the depressing state of affairs in Guinea around 1730, when the slave trade seemed about to come to a complete standstill. Therefore, Holmsted was of the opinion that the company should send only small ships to Guinea now and then in order to maintain its possessions on the coast, while the slave trade should be left to whomever of the company's shareholders felt inclined to equip ships for this purpose.

The directors of the company would not agree to such a reduction. Slaves were needed for the plantations on the West Indian islands, and in some way or other these slaves had to be procured. When informed of the situation in 1730, the directors resolved, on November 9, 1731, that ships should no longer sail directly to Fort Christiansborg and take on board most of their cargoes there. Instead, in the future ships were ordered to trade all along the Guinea coast. In this way it was hoped they could obtain full cargoes of slaves faster than when the ships lay waiting in the road off Fort Christiansborg. In order to carry out such a trade, ships would in future have on board a man who knew how to trade with the Africans. To safeguard the company against the dishonesty of the crews, new regulations were issued expressly with a view to preventing them from appropriating the trade to themselves. On the other hand, captains and their mates were given better pay.

The need for fresh supplies of slaves for the Danish islands in the West Indies became particularly urgent after the purchase of St. Croix by the company in 1733. Holmsted had, by the way, been very much involved in this purchase. The acquisition necessitated a complete reorganization of the company including the revision of its charter, ships' articles, written instructions, etc.[15] By a "convention" of September 26, 1733, rules were agreed upon for the future management and business methods of the company.[16] The order forbidding the sailors in the future to take on board their own private goods against the regulations of the directors was restated. Also, the directors reserved their rights to put up for sale at auction whatever the captains brought in their ships. (By the proclamation of October 10, 1730, the company had tried to make rules for the scope of the sailors' private trade.[17]) For the West Indian traffic the company no longer thought it necessary to have their own ships, but the Guinea traffic was a different proposition. It was thought necessary only to keep it going "as best they could" as long as there was a demand for slaves for St. Croix. The order went out that ships leaving directly for Fort Christiansborg should sail from the beginning of March until the end of September, so they would be off the Gold Coast in the good season between September and February. Similarly, a clause was introduced which forbid persons "of ill repute for licentiousness and villainy" to go out to Africa. This certainly proved their most praiseworthy intentions, but it was hardly of any practical significance. In spite of the contemplated curtailment of the slave trade, by the charter of February 5, 1734, the company retained "as long as they need, desire, are able and willing to make use thereof" their right to Fort Christiansborg in return for the payment of tribute to the local African authorities.[18] If the slave trade did not pay, the company was to be under no obligation to keep the fort in repair. It was open to the company to offer their African possessions to the king, in which case he was to pay a fair price for guns, munitions, and furnishings. The company kept its monopoly on the traffic from Danish territories to Africa as well as the right to carry on negotiations or even make war with the native kings. Also, the company remained exempt from certain dues. There was still to be a 2½ per cent duty payable on all goods imported into Denmark, or if they were re-exported, only 1 per cent. Gold was to be duty-free. It will be seen that the company was able to retain all the privileges obtained by the charter of 1697.

Not all the directors, however, wanted a curtailment of the slave trade. In the course of a thorough debate within the company, in February 1734 the demand for slaves was most vigorously pressed by the councillor of conferences, Severin de Junge. He stressed especially that it was not to be expected that any Africans would be transported to the West Indies in times of war, unless the company itself took the matter in hand. He thought that Fort Christiansborg was too expensive to keep up, unless it was utilized for the slave trade and that, consequently, giving up the slave trade ought to mean giving up the permanent holdings in Africa, too. On the other hand, trade with the Guinea coast would hardly pay without such permanent stations. In de Junge's view, the liquidation of Danish slave trade would be the end of the entire Danish investment in Africa.

Although the royal court seems to have shared this opinion, the shareholders were not convinced. They were influenced more by Holmsted. They were deeply impressed by the deficit of 4,697 rixdollars produced by the *Laarburg Galley's* most recent voyage. At a general meeting on February 25 they went so far as to decide by 85 votes to 22, that "the slave trade, until better information and a better state of the market be obtainable, be discontinued." Some days later it was decided, on these grounds, to postpone the departure of a ship for Guinea and to sell the slaves collected at Fort Christiansborg to the Portuguese. They decided also to give up the production of ardent spirits at the company's distillery, since there was no likelihood of this being needed for exportation to Africa within the near future. Before long, however, Holmsted sent a memorandum reminding the directors of the necessity of sending a small ship to Africa. Consequently, the company purchased *La Conquerante,* renamed her *Jomfruen,* and sent her off to Guinea in 1735.

At the same general meeting on February 25, it was decided that the inhabitants of the Danish West Indies should be allowed to organize expeditions themselves for the purpose of obtaining slaves from the Guinea coast and afterward selling them in the Danish islands. In return for this privilege, they were to pay the company a "recognition" of 8 rixdollars per head in St. Thomas and 4 rixdollars in St. Croix. Foreigners were also allowed to put their slaves up for sale in the islands and were subject to payment of the same amount. To put the finishing touch to the work of reorganization, a royal proclamation was issued on April 25, 1735, which permitted all and sundry of His Majesty's trading subjects to call both at Fort Christiansborg and at the Danish colonies in America. They might start from any port they liked within the king's realms and return to both foreign and Danish ports with the sole exception of Copenhagen. In return for these privileges, they were to pay to the company a modest fee of 2 rixdollars per commercial last of the ship's weight. After this, the company retained its monopoly only for the passage from the Guinea coast to Copenhagen. In this city it now set up its own sugar refinery to deal with the return cargoes from the West Indies.

As will be seen later, the company was forced to give up even this privilege for a short period (1743-1747), but then it regained its monopoly. The decisive factor for the rules regulating Danish traffic to Guinea was the connection with the West Indies. Many still shared Jens Juel's view that the Guinea holdings were kept up only for the sake of the islands in the Caribbean. In the long run the company's trade in gold and ivory proved of secondary importance; the slave trade was the main thing. If that failed the Guinea traffic would be of even less importance.

The following period shows, therefore, how the company tried to get along by fitting out only the smallest ships and the most limited number for Guinea. The permission given to private individuals to try their luck did not produce any important results for some time. The period before the acquisition of the island of St. Croix had been disappointing as far as the Guinea traffic was concerned. The first years after the purchase of this island brought no improvement. Only in the last decades of the century did the Danish slave trade flourish for a short time.

Even apart from the moral issue, there can be no glorious place for the slave trade in the history of Danish trade. When the accounts were tallied, they showed a losing trade. To this must be added that it cost quite a few Danish lives. It was not the Africans alone who risked death in the closely-packed ships. Sailors and ships' officers might equally well be struck down by epidemics and scurvy. The fever ridden air of the tropical climes was even more dangerous to them than to the Africans. If the West Indian planters had bought the slaves they required from Dutch or English traders, they would, surely, have bought them more cheaply. The *raison d'être* for a Danish slave traffic was the supply of slave labor it secured for the islands of St. Thomas, St. John, and St. Croix.

THE EASTERN DISTRICTS AND FORT FREDENSBORG

FROM THE VERY EARLIEST DAYS trading stations, or lodges as they were called, were important for the Guinea traffic. Beside Carlsborg, the knight Carlof's activities in Guinea in 1658 secured a number of these branch settlements for the Danes. Most of them were soon lost and only one, the Osu station, became the center of a permanent holding. Later the Danes themselves began to establish new lodges, which in the course of time led to considerable expansion of their sphere of interest.

The earliest reports of these activities date only from the early years of the eighteenth century. In 1700 the king of Acron (Akrong) sent a caboceer to Commandant Johan Trane to ask him to set up a lodge near Apam, about 50 kilometers west of the Danish fort. Acron was a kingdom bordering on Agona to the west. It was later described as part of Fanti. The invitation was declined. However, since the king of Acron asked for a "custom" of only 3 rixdollars a month, it was felt that it might pay to open a lodge there. The Danes responded by only stationing an assistant, a corporal, and a native for a very short period of time in 1701 at the African town of Mangfroe near Dyvelsberg on the border of Acron and Agona. The experiment was not profitable, and a renewed attempt by Branz Boye in 1706 met with no better success. These seem to have been the only attempts to establish lodges on the western part of the coast, though later on Mangfroe was one of the places regularly visited on trips to the so-called Upper Coast or the land to the west of the fort to buy millet. Apart from these trips the Danes' only interest in the Upper Coast was the desire expressed by commandants Lygaard and Rost to purchase Fort Gross Friedrichsburg near Cape Three Points after the Brandenburgers evacuated it. When the Dutch came to occupy the fort, they quarreled with Jan Conny, the local caboceer who had repeatedly offered the fort to the Danes. As late as 1730 Wærøe again expressed a desire for this purchase; to him it seemed suitable compensation for all the wrongs inflicted upon him by the Dutch. However, the permanent Dutch occupation of the fort put an end to such projects.[1]

All practical plans for new lodges concerned the Lower Coast or the land to the east.[2] Here the European settlements were few and far between, and other European nations were slow to take an interest in this part of the coast. Early Danish initiative was taken by Lygaard, who in 1710 placed an assistant at Keta (Qvitta) on the nearest part of the Slave Coast to sell strong liquor. By doing this he hoped to get some compensation for the cessation of trade at Fort Christiansborg caused by Aquando's campaigns. Boye, too, sent a man there with goods. Later Boye settled the man at Ponny in the country of the Adampi people, which was a little more than 40 kilometers east of Fort Christiansborg. In 1716 he had an assistant clerk at Ponny and a constable at Keta, until, fearing war, he recalled them both. Soon he again detailed a man to each of these places; both died at their posts in 1717. For some time after that there was a shortage of qualified staff with a knowledge of the language to run these branches. In March 1718 a couple of men along with some slaves were again placed at Keta, chiefly to maintain the right to the place. For, by this time, the Dutch had cast an eye on it and were making preparations for lodges there. The Danes tried to obtain favor with the local authorities by means of presents, but they did not succeed in ridding themselves of the Dutch. "Seeing that we were the first to seek out and, at great expense, to have established and maintained the said place, it seemed to us equitable that we be left peacefully alone there," wrote Knud Rost, who seems to have been the activating force behind this venture. Altogether, he was very energetic. He sent traders even as far as Wida (Whydah, Fida), about 300 kilometers east of Fort Christiansborg, in the hope of buying gold there. Shortly before his death, however, he had to give up Keta. There was no trade, and in 1720 the men stationed there were withdrawn.

One hindrance to the Keta trade was the difficulty of getting there, for one had to either cross the Volta River or make the trip by sea past its mouth where the current was so strong that only large boats could be used for the trip.[3] So, while there was a lack of staff, the Danes preferred to keep to the west of the Volta. At the time a reliable mulatto was stationed at Ponny once again, and one of Rost's last acts was to send Peder Østrup to Tubreku (Tuberku), a small Adampi town on a minor tributary of the Volta seven or eight kilometers inland. This place was in the lands of Aquando; Østrup made an agreement with the local caboceer and built a storehouse.

Such was the state of affairs when Commandant Herrn arrived in November 1721 full of projects.[4] He did not care about Tubreku, but he wanted to maintain Ponny and Keta.[5] An assistant was at once despatched to Keta, where shortly afterward he died. As we have seen, Herrn tried also to make an alliance with the neighboring African towns to the east of Fort Christiansborg and to persuade them to promise their trade to the Danes. Johan Trane had already proposed the building of a lodge at the African town of Labadi, a couple of kilometers east of Fort Christiansborg. The inhabitants of Labadi were very well disposed toward the Danes. Herrn writes that the town had accepted the gift of a Danish flag a few years before his arrival, and that the inhabitants were now renewing their promises. Furthermore, he boasts that he made the inhabitants of Little Ningo, 15 kilometers east of Fort Christiansborg, promise him their trade. In return for all this, he promised the caboceers of Labadi and Little Ningo a New Year's present of 20 rixdollars each. He was spurred on to further action by the fact that about this time the English occupied the three towns of Tessing, Temma, and Prampram farther east and were also planning lodges at Great Ningo and Lya. In order to forestall the English, Herrn occupied these two towns himself. However, his two assistants at Ponny and Great Ningo died before him, and after his death it was impossible to continue any of his projects. There simply were not, at the time, sufficient stores of goods to supply branch settlements. It is known that the lodges at Ponny were operated later from 1726-1729 with one interruption. On the whole, therefore, the results of the first twenty years' attempts to gain a footing for Danish trade on the Lower Coast were very meagre.

After the fall of Akwamu it was necessary to start from scratch. In the autumn of 1731, at the request of the Tubreku people, a sloop, the *Printz Friedrich,* anchored off the island of Ada in the Volta.[6] The natives had promised ample trade there, so an attempt was made. A factory was set up on the island, but there was the serious drawback that for three months every year, when the inland rains swelled the river, the island was under water. The situation was made still more dangerous by the wars waged in the following years by the Adas against their neighbors in Awuna. This tribe, whom the Danes called Augna or sometimes Agona, lived on the east bank of the Volta and is not to be confused with the kingdom situated to the west of Accra. In April 1732 the lodge on the island of Ada had to be given up temporarily, because the surviving Akwamu, who also made their homes in this area, attacked it.

When he saw that the attempt to build a lodge on the island of Ada was doomed to failure in spite of the support of the local natives, Commander Wærøe advocated building a fort rather than a lodge at Great Ningo in the country of the Adampis. It would be 75 kilometers east of Fort Christiansborg and about halfway between Fort Christiansborg and the Volta estuary.[7] The locality offered fine landing facilities and good trade. The Danes are believed to have already had a lodge there in the days of Nikolaj Jansen Arf. After the situation had deteriorated so badly at Accra, Wærøe thought the Danes had better look out for a new and

Ga women, eighteenth-century sketch.

A ship arrives at a Gold Coast fort, seventeenth-century sketch.

Guinea coast scene, from Frederik V's atlas, eighteenth century.

Fredensborg, eighteenth-century sketch.

Christiansborg, eighteenth-century sketch.

better stronghold. At any rate, the possession of two forts would be advantageous, because in dangerous situations one fort would be able to support the other, especially if there were a suitable ship to carry on the coastal traffic between them.

It would be logical that the new fort be made the main stronghold of the Danes, for Fort Christiansborg would always suffer from the disadvantage of the close proximity of the other Accra forts. For the time being, however, Wærøe only opened negotiations with Akim, the rulers, for the establishment of a lodge. He succeeded in obtaining promises of support from Orsu, nicknamed the "Field-Colonel." In fact, this nephew (a sister's son) of Bang, the great caboceer, promised that, if need be, he would even protect, with his army, the fort during its construction, until such time as it would be able to defend itself.

The realization of these plans was, however, left to Schiellerup, Wærøe's successor who set to work with both intelligence and skill. At once he very wisely sent an assistant to Ada. Next, he came to an agreement with Orsu about Great Ningo. Thus, by paying Orsu 20 benda of gold, he obtained permission to build a fort. A low, fixed price for slaves was agreed upon, and Orsu guaranteed the value of runaway slaves. In April 1736, when the *Jomfruen* had sailed with 150 slaves, the work of building the fort was begun, and before the end of the year a small triangular fort had been erected. Each side measured just over twenty yards and had room for ten cannons and a garrison of three or four soldiers. The total cost for the building amounted to 1,300 rixdollars. Orsu was paid 16 rixdollars per month "custom"; and on the whole he is said to have been quite reasonable, because he was very proud of having a fort paying him a monthly tribute. Peter Nikolaj Jørgensen, the assistant, was appointed its first commandant and merchant and the fort was named Fredensborg.

Before these results had been obtained, however, Schiellerup died on June 14, 1736, of a calculous disease, after he had held office for about ten months only. In that short period he not only reopened the lodge on the island of Ada and started building operations at Ningo, but also he straightened out the accounts at Fort Christiansborg and began repairs on the buildings there. Also, he was favored by increased trade, because the people of the caboceer Frempung found a shorter path to Accra. Posterity has, in addition, praised Schiellerup for his humanity to his inferiors, especially the Africans. He may have been given greater praise than was due to him. Certainly he died without becoming fully accustomed to Guinean ways and so without having been demoralized by them.[8]

Schiellerup did not have time to achieve friendly relations with the Dutch. He reported that the black slave-traders brought far more slaves for sale to him than to de Bordes, the Dutch trader at Fort Crèvecoeur.

Several slave traders even moved from Dutch Accra to the village of Osu outside Fort Christiansborg. This gave rise to considerable irritation among the Dutch. As a consequence they incited Dacon, one of the caboceers of Dutch Accra, to attack Osu by night. Fortunately, Schiellerup had been informed of the plan. He armed the Osu people with the necessary firearms. Dacon and his men were given a warm reception and were forced to retreat with casualties. It is small wonder then that Schiellerup thought it necessary to keep the Dutch in the dark when he opened negotiations with Akim about Great Ningo. Officially, the negotiators were to demand a settlement of the dispute with Dacon, while the order to make arrangements for the erection of the fort remained secret. In retaliation, the Dutch tried to prevent the construction of the fort, and when Schiellerup himself arrived on the spot to get the work started, the Dutch trader is said to have offered a price of 100 benda for his head. Afterward the Dutch did all they could to persuade the natives to destroy the fort. However, the caboceer of Dutch Accra, Okanie son of Ajkuma, refused, and so the Dutch took his sons and daughters as slaves. Next, they tried in vain to get the caboceer Orsu to destroy the fort, by offering him twice the amount he had received from the Danes. Later they succeeded in persuading the local caboceer of Ningo to tolerate the building of a Dutch lodge outside the town; but Orsu prevented this building, and the local caboceers were fined seven slaves for having accepted the gift of a Dutch flag. The Dutch even had to suffer the humiliation of seeing Okanie temporarily make his home at the village of Orsu with his household and slaves. (This was a total of 200 men armed with muskets, beside women and children.) So the Danish African village flourished and soon recovered from the depression of Wærøe's day. Including the garrisons of Labadi and Tessing, the "Danish" natives force now numbered 600 or 700 men. However, the Dutch natives were not easily frightened. On the night of December 31, 1737, and on January 1, 1738, they tried to take Orsu by surprise, because they thought that all its inhabitants would be drunk with the strong liquor which the Danes had distributed for their New Year's celebrations. The Dutch natives were driven back with many casualties. A few days later when it was rumored that Dutch Accra had been reinforced by 200 Fanti, it was the Danish Africans who attacked, advancing until they were fired at from Fort Crèvecoeur. In the end the caboceer Orsu turned up with 6,000 or 8,000 men to maintain order. He was disposed to attack Crèvecoeur but could not get the Danes to sell him gunpowder for this purpose. Due to the shortage of water, which his men had to fetch from a distance of 20 or 30 kilometers inland, Orsu had to break camp and march off a few days later. Now the Danes reaped the benefit of having the Africans on their side, for the situation was almost exactly the reverse of what it had been in 1729-30. Then it had been the Dutch who had been assisted by the natives and who had persuaded them to besiege Fort Christiansborg. Now the Dutch quarreled with the Africans all along the coast, and the director-general, whose residence was Fort Elmina, even had the native town outside this fort razed to the ground. Only after the arrival of a new director-general was it possible for the Dutch to make peace with the Africans.

Schiellerup's successor, a former chief assistant named Enevold Nielsen Boris, skillfully tried to carry on, but several serious obstacles were thrown in his way. To the previously mentioned trouble with the Dutch and their Africans[9] was now added a quarrel which had broken out between the two important Akim caboceers, Bang and Frempung. Unavoidably, too, the aftereffects of the battles taking place to the east of the Volta, where the kingdom of Dahomey was gradually gaining supremacy, were felt. As an offshoot of these wars, a small Dutch fort near Keta was conquered by the natives. The commandant of this fort, a Dane named From, was captured, and the rest of the garrison was massacred. Afterward, the local caboceer offered the place to the Danes, and an assistant was sent down there to trade. But the experiment proved unsuccessful, and he was soon withdrawn.

At the beginning of Boris' time trade at Fort Christiansborg was still fairly good. In the autumn of 1737 he was able to send home by an English ship 13,000 rixdollars or a little over 100 gold marks. Of this amount, Wærøe had, as mentioned, procured 29 marks, Schiellerup's trade had yielded no less than 55, and Boris obtained the rest. But in May 1738 when, after more than a month's stay on the coast, the *Laarburg Galley* was about to leave, all that Boris was able to send was 382 rixdollars and eleven slaves beside Schiellerup's private fortune amounting to 1,188 rixdollars in gold. Provided Bang and Frempung were both given presents, people came periodically from Akim, and they paid well. A single visit from them might yield 1,300 or 1,400 rixdollars. An added advantage was expected when, in the autumn of 1738, Akim made war on Fanti, and destroyed a market place in Agona where goods had been cheap. One real result of the war was that the Fanti lay in ambush along the trade routes from the interior and intercepted all the messengers sent by Akim to the forts on the coast. Nevertheless, when the *Laarburg Galley* returned in the autumn of 1739, it took on board 76 gold marks (9,800 rixdollars) and 45 slaves. And next spring Boris again had gold amounting to 28 marks. In this period slaves were often sold by the Danes to French ships, which for some time were most successful in the slave traffic. The Portuguese, on the other hand, were treated with such severity by the Dutch that they hardly ever came to Accra; however, they might have turned up at Ningo. The "interlopers" were no longer important, since the Dutch company now allowed private trade in return for payment of duty.

Although Boris' health had gradually been broken by fever and dysentery, "which," he reports, "have reduced me to a perfect skeleton," he still found the means in 1740 for beginning an important enlargement of Fort Fredensborg to enable it to endure a siege. After the death of Boris on June 20, 1740, the work on the fort continued for a couple of years. Under the command of Simon Henrik Klein, a trader, a third bastion was built. Thus the fort lacked only a fourth side to have it surrounded by a rectangular fortification with a gate opening toward the sea. That was the extent of the building in 1742. Afterward, Thomas Brock had a fine water reservoir built in the courtyard. The fourth bastion was not completed until later.

Fort Fredensborg was praised as one of the best constructed and best situated of the smaller forts on the Gold Coast.[10] Thus, the Danes had been provided with an excellent starting point for an expansion of their influence on the Lower Coast. The Dutch, on the other hand, had only a thorn in their side. For the time being, however, these improvements did not bring increased profits. Conditions on the coast did not remain tolerable for trade for long, and the Danes hindered their own enterprise on the coast by quarrels among themselves. "Justice had died with Schiellerup . . . her sister with Boris." [11] To these internal squabbles were soon added, as in Wærøe's days, overwhelming external difficulties. Only by acting on the inspiration of the moment and by giving way as the situations required were the Danish settlements steered safely through the turmoil.

13 / THE RISE OF ASHANTI

THE SUPREMACY BUILT UP by Akim after the fall of Akwamu was threatened from the start by Ashanti. This kingdom, founded by Osei Tutu with the support of the priest Okomfo Anokye, was steadily becoming more powerful. It is, however, impossible to extract from existing records a detailed description of these developments.

The Danish Commandant Boris got into great trouble because of an African who deserted from Dutch Accra to the Danes and thence to Akim.[1] There he said that the Dutch paid Ashanti to attack Akim. This, after some time, caused the caboceer Orsu to forbid his people to trade at Accra. Of course the Dutch may have been scheming to provoke hostilities, but even without such provocation there seems to have been sufficient ill will between Akim and Ashanti to cause a war. In 1739 Akim hoped to be able to end hostilities, because they had succeeded in killing Osei Tutu while he was crossing the river Pra, and at the very moment when he was launching an attack upon them with his army. Osei Tutu was succeeded by his brother, Okopu Ware. He, though physically weak, was a great general who transformed Ashanti into a warrior-state, a kind of local Prussia, and soon launched the attack upon Akim. By 1740 it was rumored that Ashanti was preparing a campaign, but on the coast it still seemed doubtful whether Akim or Fanti was to be the victim. At the same time, on the Upper Coast everything was in a state of flux. The Wassaw (or Wasa) were besieging the English and Dutch forts, and Fanti had 30,000 or 40,000 men in arms. All roads leading from Accra into the interior were blocked, and Akim wanted to buy only flint-lock muskets, gunpowder, and ardent spirits. In the hills the caboceer Orsu was training a powerful army, and late that year Akim opened hostilities against the natives of the Lower Coast. In spite of the dangers of the situation the Akim caboceers could not, or would not, shelve their mutual rivalries. So the Danes had to be very careful when distributing their presents among them—if one received more than the other, there were instant complaints. A fresh attempt by the Dutch to persuade them to destroy Fort Fredensborg even induced Bang to ask 100 benda for the place.

With war being waged on all sides, Accra remained peaceful for a while longer; but there was no trade. So Boris' successor, Peter Nikolaj Jørgensen, the former merchant at Fort Fredensborg, was unable to collect as large amounts of gold as his predecessor.[2] He was far too mild, kindhearted to his inferiors and politically cautious. During the troubled time he did not dare keep up the lodge on the island of Ada. When, early in 1742, the *Grevinden af Laurvigen* anchored off the coast, all that he was able to send on board was a little less than 24 gold marks and 53 slaves. Even the gold reserves had dwindled after Boris' death. At the same time there were complaints of the poor quality of the cargo, which was, however, all that the company could afford to send. First, the *Laarburg Galley* had been loaded up for another voyage. While outward bound, however, she had gone down on August 18, 1741, after a collision in the Kattegat with the East India Company's *Kongen af Danmark*. It was a total loss, and there were not sufficient funds available to again purchase an equally rich and varied cargo.

While the *Grevinden af Laurvigen* was lying in the road at Fort Christiansborg, news was received of the decisive battle between Akim and Ashanti. The postscript to a letter of March 19, 1742, gives the following description of this important event: "At this very moment our messengers, who had left for Akim with the presents [from Copenhagen], have returned without being able to deliver them, and declare that the Akims have been vanquished by the Ashanti, whereby our messengers have been in the greatest peril for their lives." They had been robbed of all the presents except some valuable gifts from the directors of the company, which they had been prudent enough to hide in the bush before they dared to present themselves.

The Akim were completely expelled from their territory and almost wiped out. Frempung died, and Apau, his sister's son, succeeded him. The consequences were immense. Shortly after the *Grevinden af Laurvigen* had sailed, the Ashanti reached the coast. First they attacked the town of Great Ningo. Next they blockaded Fort Fredensborg. Though they did not molest it, they made great demands. The commandant, Christian Glob Dorph, who had succeeded Jørgensen when the latter took over at Fort Christiansborg, had no alternative but to pay, because they were short of millet to feed the defenders.[3] Next, the Ashanti marched westward, and after sacking an English fort at Prampram and a Dutch one at Temma, they arrived at Accra. All the inhabitants of Osu, Labadi, and Tessing, beside some from Dutch Accra, sought shelter in Fort Christiansborg. They brought their women and children, and the fort was so packed with refugees that they would have made its defense almost impossible. The decisive factor, here too, was the shortage of millet. After a few days the fort ran out of food, so the commandant of Christiansborg, also, had to submit to the demands of the Ashanti. He paid 110 benda (3,520 rixdollars), and he lent the inhabitants of the coastal towns 30 bendas' worth of the best goods stored in the fort. The Dutch were forced to pay a still higher price for Fort Crèvecoeur; no less than 200 benda. In addition they had to hand over a great number of slaves and all the friends of the caboceer Dacon, who had sided with Akim in the war against Ashanti.

The outcome of these events at the Accra forts could not but strengthen the power of the Ashanti. The coast had been conquered by a people who were to dominate it for almost a century. The Danes later regretted that the fort had not laid in a store of millet sufficient to sustain a siege. It seems undeniable that, if Ashanti had suffered a defeat in front of the Danish fort, the history of the Gold Coast would have taken a different turn.

Peter Nikolaj Jørgensen seems either to have been ashamed of the result or to have feared the company's anger. He did not even dare write home asking for help. Instead, he neglected his office, allowed discipline to slacken, and took to drink. Most serious of all, he allowed the book-keeper, one Hans Hansen Blas, to do as he pleased. Once in a fit of drunkenness Blas, sword in hand, ran upstairs into the commandant's apartment and challenged Jørgensen to a fight by calling him both a coward and a dirty wretch. In the same way, when Cornelius Petersen, the constable, one day in an excessively festive mood, cut down all the trees in a garden which Boris had planted, Jørgensen allowed him to go unpunished. The chaplain, Peder Meyer, was the worst of all: he would sit and drink with the private soldiers and afterward sleep it off on the floor. In the end Blas drank so much that he could not write and Meyer drank so much that he could not perform divine services.

In the end Jørgensen had to hand over command to Christian Glob Dorph, the merchant at Fort Fredensborg. This was on May 26, 1743. At the same time Jørgensen persuaded Dorph to assume responsibilities for the deficiencies caused in the accounts and supplies by his loans to the Africans and by his bad management. The loss of stock alone was estimated at several thousand rixdollars. Dorph, though well liked by the garrison, had a firmer hand. He tried to reestablish order and discipline. He decided to send Blas home at the earliest opportunity. New men were installed in various posts. Meyer mended his ways, so that at his departure he could be given a tolerable recommendation. However, it was impossible for Dorph to increase trade. Jørgensen had sold off the stores of the fort at ridiculous prices; thus though the warehouse was now empty, there was little cash. Millet could be bought only at the highest prices. The slave trade had passed again into the hands of the Dutch, for the Dutch company had recently allowed its traders to buy and sell slaves on their own, if they paid a "recognition" to the company. At the same time a war broke out between Ashanti and Fanti, which might have produced a brisk trade. There were, however, neither muskets nor gunpowder to spare at Fort Christiansborg, so Opoku Ware, king of Ashanti, refused to send his traders to the fort, until a ship had called with a cargo from Denmark. Dorph thought it advisable to inform the gentlemen of the company in Copenhagen that a further reduction of prices would be necessary.

Alarmed by reports from the Gold Coast, the directors of the company realized that extraordinary steps would have to be taken. Since none of the company's ships were available, a contract was made with a merchant named Andreas Bjørn. The company hired his frigate, the *Williamina Galley*, at 500 rixdollars per month. In the autumn of 1743 it sailed from Copenhagen. On board was a new commandant, Jørgen Billsen. It was only after a long and hazardous voyage that the ship arrived at Accra on February 3, 1744. After two months' stay it was able to leave for the West Indies; it had taken on board 100 slaves from the Danish fort. Billsen found that the situation at the fort was the worst possible. There was only one good point as far as he could see: the fort still had a Danish garrison, though they were so poor that they had to borrow gunpowder at Fort Crèvecoeur to salute the arrival of the frigate. In the course of Dorph's period of command, the fort's coffer had lost about 8,600 rixdollars, and in the warehouse goods worth 6,960 rixdollars were missing. So Dorph was sent home under arrest and was held responsible for both his own and Jørgensen's embezzlements. To make doubly sure, Billsen decided to send Jørgensen home, too. His conduct had been so disgraceful that the Danes on the coast risked being considered no better than the Portuguese.[4]

On their arrival in Copenhagen, the company had both Dorph and Jørgensen put in prison. Later Jørgensen returned to the coast privately, but he was unwanted there and so was sent on to the West Indies.

Among the natives, it was now Akim's turn to help Ashanti in their war against Fanti.[5] The presents which had not reached the Akim leaders were now sent to the king of Ashanti. Further gifts were ordered for him from Copenhagen, for he was "a greater King than had, for many centuries, existed on this coast." Shortly afterward it became necessary to begin payments of the monthly tribute for Fort Christiansborg to Ashanti. These had been due since the fall of Akim. The great king at once began demanding presents, and Billsen sent a snuffbox—in addition he was forced to sacrifice his watch. Akim had not quite given up, however. After the departure of the *Williamina Galley*, messengers arrived at Accra from the three Akim leaders. They approached the Dutch, first maintaining that since their defeat the Danes had been but lukewarm friends and had not even sent condolences to them. Under the circumstances, Billsen chose to send presents to the three Akim leaders. Some trade might still come from those quarters, and Akim might later be able even to throw off the yoke of Ashanti.

That Akim's supremacy was a thing of the past was clearly proved when the Akwamu again began to turn up individually at Fort Christiansborg. These old friends of the Danes now brought them slaves.

Billsen still had time to accept the invitation from the king of Popo to build a lodge near Keta and to send two assistants there. Later, however, quarrels with his assistants prevented further activity.[6] He was too strict, would use abusive language and box their ears, reduce their salaries, and was constantly suspicious. The military especially were dissatisfied with him. It was said afterward that Billsen suspected them of preparing a mutiny and therefore planned legal action against them. He could not, however, get others to support him. So he had to be contented with suspending two assistants from their offices: Simon Henrik Klein and Ludvig Ferdinand Rømer. On October 19, 1744, while he was attempting to arrest Klein for carousing with the soldiers, a mutiny was triggered. The garrison forced Billsen to hand over the keys of the fort, and then they tried to persuade an elderly man named Joost Platfuss to take command. He refused, so Klein was made temporary commandant. Nevertheless, since Klein was nervous at the thought of having broken his oaths and having been guilty of insubordination, he came to terms with Billsen. The latter resumed command on October 28. The soldiers, however, were still discontented. Billsen did not give them as large advances on their pay as they wanted and as they had, presumably, been promised by the terms of the agreement. Scared by rumors that a mutiny was again brewing, Billsen one night opened the gate of the fort to 50 natives armed with muskets. At the next morning's parade, his manner was most inquisitorial. He wanted to arrest some of the soldiers. When they tried to defend themselves, they were all overpowered and arrested by the natives, except for two who escaped to Fort Crèvecoeur. Afterward Billsen very zealously proceeded with his legal action against his prisoners. This went on until January 13, 1745, when the chief assistant, Thomas Brock, went mad for two days. From then on everything was neglected until Billsen's death on March 11.

He was succeeded by Thomas Brock, who was dead by March 23. The next was Johan Wilder, who also died quickly on April 23. Several others died during the same period. According to later explanations, all three commandants were poisoned on the instigation of constable Cornelius Petersen's wife, who was working to get her husband out of prison. Brock was said to have been a courteous and sensible man, while Wilder was unaccustomed to the conditions on the coast and was addicted to liquor and women.

The next commandant was August Friderich Hackenburg, a young man who had been a trader at Fort Fredensborg.[7] He had the advantage of not having been a party to all the quarrels at Fort Christiansborg. No sooner had he been installed than a messenger arrived from the English fort, so we are told, informing him that unless Cornelius Petersen were set free, the new commandant would suffer the same fate as his predecessors. Be that as it may, Hackenburg set all the prisoners free, even Klein, and reinstated them in their former offices. The Keta lodge was given up, because it brought nothing but expenses. He remained passive even when the English set up a lodge at Lay a short distance west of the Volta estuary to the detriment of trade at Fredensborg. Billsen had left only 200 rixdollars in the money box and seven or eight slaves. His bookkeeping had been neglected since New Year's, so it was not easy to put the house in order. The directors in Copenhagen thought it inadvisable to have the reins in the hands of one so young as Hackenburg, so they resolved that old Joost Platfuss was to assume command. At first, however, he had the title only of temporary commandant. This order did not reach Fort Christiansborg until June 1746.

Klein had made his departure from Fort Christiansborg and so risked being arrested. L. F. Rømer, on the contrary, had sought safety at the English fort, where he stayed till the danger had blown over. Afterward he went back to Denmark with letters of recommendation from the English so laudatory that the directors of the company were eager to secure his services. Later he returned to the coast, where he served as a merchant at Fort Christiansborg from June 1746. In 1756 he published his "Reliable Information about the Trade on the Coast of Guinea" (*Tilforladelig Efterretning om Negotien paa Kysten Guinea*), and in 1760 he published "Reliable Information about the Guinea Coast" (*Tilforladelig Efterretning om Kysten Guinea*).[8] He claims to have acquired much of his knowledge from the old records and registers at Fort Christiansborg, which he studied in his leisure hours. But he seems to have taken more from the tales of the Africans, particularly from an old, comparatively truthful caboceer in Labadi named Putti. Rømer had married an Akwamu princess, was evidently very well versed in every aspect of fetishism, and so, was highly respected by the natives. However, his second book, especially, is so absolutely unreliable that it serves mostly as an instance of luxuriant African imagination at work on historical records. The book was not enhanced by the fine preface which Erik Pontoppidan, the learned theologian, went to the trouble of writing for it.

About 1745 after many years of limited activity, the Danish Guinea traffic was somewhat revived.[9] This was due partly to a proclamation of June 18, 1743. It went one step further than the mandate of April 25, 1735, by allowing private cargoes from the Danish islands in America as well as those from the Danish forts in Africa to be landed in Copenhagen —but only if the sugar cargoes were sold to the West India and Guinea Company. Above all, the company itself became more active. It was stimulated by an application of August 4, 1744, from citizens and planters of the island of St. Thomas for annual sailings of so-called "slave-haulers." These were ships that bought slaves along the coast of Africa for delivery in America. At first, the company could only point out that slaves might be imported into the Danish West Indies from sources other than the Danish forts in Africa. The company was most willing to meet the planters' demand for more slaves. Since there was not a company ship in readiness at the moment, Andreas Bjørn's *Williamina Galley* was again hired, this time for 550 rixdollars per month. Similarly, on December 3, 1745, an agreement was reached with individual shipowners, who when carrying slaves from Guinea to the West Indies were to put them up for sale by auction immediately after their arrival. On the other hand, the company was to either provide them with return cargoes for Copenhagen or allow them to purchase goods against deferred payment. Goods shipped to the West Indies would be liable for a 5 per cent "recognition"; goods shipped from the West Indies to Denmark, for 6 per cent. In every case the private shipowners would have to obtain the company's permission to trade in its territories. Shortly after, when the shipowners applied for a reduction of the "recognition," the company refused to grant it. On the contrary they asserted that there was a very good market for slaves at the moment and that return cargoes from the West Indies would have to be accepted on the conditions laid down in the Royal Mandate of 1735.

A long time elapsed before the *Williamina Galley* at last set sail. In the meantime a privately owned ship, the *Postillonen,* a brigantine, arrived on the coast and in March 1745 sailed from Fort Christiansborg with 31 slaves. Business was carried on with this ship in the same way as with ships of foreign nationality; but in order to be able to provide a cargo at all, the commandant and merchant of the fort had to borrow money from the captain. The *Williamina Galley* did not arrive until June 21; it was sent at once to Fanti to pick up a cargo of millet. When it weighed anchor after a couple of months, it carried a cargo of 160 slaves. Of these Fort Christiansborg had supplied 46. However, this time, too, it had been necessary to borrow money from the captain. On his return to Copenhagen, the captain had to pay a large sum to the company for having broken the contract by including 77 slaves on his own account.[10]

A third ship, the *Cron-Printzens Ønske,* which was privately owned like the brigantine, was sent off at about the same time as the *Williamina Galley*. However, it was first driven by the current into the Bight of Benin, and afterward it had some difficulty returning against the wind. It did not reach Fort Christiansborg until November 17, 1746, its crew suffering from scurvy. The ship weighed anchor again on February 13, 1747, with 250 slaves, of which the fort had supplied 187. In addition, they were able to send 6 gold marks. Although in debt, the fort, for the first time in years, ventured to ask for a large ship with a full cargo, so that they would have supplies to trade.

Trade was still suffering from the unsettled political situation. At one time even the Dutch and English at Accra had quarreled. A pitched battle was fought and many natives and six or seven Europeans were killed on both sides. The Akim were again trying to assert old influence. Now and again they would turn up outside the forts with a force of several thousand men. They made the Dutch promise them a "custom" for Fort Crèvecoeur, but the English and the Danes gave them only small presents or "ships' custom." After Orsu had been killed in battle, Pobbi, his successor, demanded full tributes from Fort Fredensborg. He was given, if not all that he demanded, at least a round sum of 20 ounces of gold, to stop him from destroying the native towns outside the fort. Once more Akim was strong enough to attack Akwamu and kill or capture a great number of them. The defeated Akwamu were still hiding in the bush to the east and blocking the roads or making them unsafe. This brought the trade of the coastal towns to a standstill, and their inhabitants were beginning to die of starvation. Akim was able also to force the Dutch to pay up when it was found that they had sold some women and children who had come as refugees to their factories at Ponny and Temma.

Very slowly, the supremacy of Ashanti was stabilized. By May 1747 it could be reported that messengers were beginning to arrive unhindered at Fort Christiansborg, and that trade was slowly improving. A couple of months later the situation began also to improve farther east. The Dutch were still so disliked there that they had to give up a lodge at Okko, a somewhat desolate and exposed location between the English lodge at Lay and the mouth of the Volta River. When the *Sorgenfrey* anchored in the road off Fort Christiansborg on July 2, 1747, it was still difficult to secure 120 slaves to complete its cargo. The ship had already bought 170 on the Upper Coast by paying for them with the best part of its cargo. But when the frigate *Princesse Sophia Magdalena* left in May 1748, the fort was able to supply 212 out of the cargo of 300 slaves. This meant delivering "goods" worth far larger amounts than the cargo received from home.

Thus, there was an unmistakable improvement in Danish trade and accounts were in the best order. Platfuss reopened the Keta factory, and this time it was profitable. Considerable numbers of the slaves bought were brought to Fort Fredensborg. At Fort Christiansborg it was not always possible to buy them. In addition it was impossible to continue supplying large numbers of slaves to the ships when they followed closely upon one another. In November 1748 the frigate *Vesuvius* sailed with 300 slaves, of which the fort had supplied 80. In March 1749 it was possible to supply the *Sorgenfrey* with 100 slaves, but in March 1750 the frigate *Princesse Sophia Magdalena* was supplied with only 75. And then again in December 1750, 279 slaves were supplied to the frigate *Jaegersborg.* After that, again only the company sent out ships. The frigate *Grevinden af Laurvigen,* a privately owned ship which left Copenhagen for Guinea in March 1747, was wrecked on the outward voyage near the Dutch island of Ameland. Of 45 passengers and crew there were only 28 survivors. By a convention of February 6, 1747, the company's shareholders agreed to a considerable increase in the capital shares to make room within the company for those individual shipowners who were interested in the Guinea and West Indian trade.[11] Afterward the royal mandates of 1735 and 1743 which permitted private trade with the West Indies and the Guinean forts were repeated by the decree of March 27, 1747.[12] As the hope of ever putting a stop to the sailors' private trade gradually faded, on October 14, 1747, the company issued new regulations about the quantities of private goods they would be allowed to trade along the coast. Now, with the *Jaegersborg* in 1750, the company again adopted the system of ordering some of their ships to sail directly to the forts, so that their stocks should not run too low.

Ashanti was still thought of as a distant power from which news rarely transpired. The Danes on the coast still thought it necessary to make special efforts to placate the powers in the immediate vicinity of the forts. In 1748 the Danes agreed to pay to Abonna, one of the Fanti caboceers, a monthly salary of 8 rixdollars. They did this in the hope of securing permission to buy up millet cheaply on the Upper Coast. Afterward an unsuccessful attempt was made to deduct this amount from the tribute paid to Ashanti. Since the company directors in Copenhagen did not approve of Abonna's salary, it was discontinued after a few years when Abonna found it impossible to procure the millet. Something like a shock was produced by the news of the death of Opoku Ware, the great warrior-king in 1750. His successor was peace-loving old Kwasi (or Kusi) Obodum, who soon became blind. After some time Akim tried to regain power and the hill people took courage, too. Consequently, trade fell into stagnation, and the forts on the coast again had a period of starvation. It was, also, a period of unusually high mortality among the Europeans. But the trouble was soon over. Two Ashanti lieutenants marched into Akim, and soon the roads were again open. If Fort Christiansborg had had a better stock of goods when the Ashanti came to Accra to trade, the Danes might have earned much gold. Ashanti supremacy was now undisputed, and their wealth marveled at.

By and large, Platfuss's administration was good for trade. The sober-minded old man could, with a clear conscience, look forward to the day when he would be relieved. As early as March 20, 1750, the directors chose Major Magnus Christopher Lützow as his successor.[13] It was not until the following winter, however, that he sailed on the frigate *Sorgenfrey*. In order to reach his destination as soon as possible, he changed en route to an English ship, which put him ashore at Cape Coast Castle; he was brought from there by boat to Christiansborg. His health was already broken, and he died on March 8, 1751, two days after his arrival. Since Lützow had been brought ashore alive, Platfuss felt that command had been passed on to him. So he was free to leave for home, and in his place Magnus Hacksen was elected temporary commandant.[14]

His administration was troubled by his quarrels with Marcus Svane, the temporary bookkeeper. Hacksen thought that Svane had been planning for years to secure the post of commandant for himself. Because Carl Engman, a merchant, ranked above him in seniority, he was said to have done all he could to make this man go home. For this purpose, he had even bribed the natives of Osu, Labadi, and Tessing so that they complained about the bookkeeper and asked for his recall. On that occasion an investigation was made. The natives were unable to prove their complaints "wherefore they were punished as an example for others." After this scheme failed, Svane tried to sow the seeds of discord between Hacksen and Engman, as well as to stir the Dutch trader at Ford Crèvecoeur into action against Hacksen. His supporter was Andreas Miltz, the barber, and the chaplain, Jochum Borchenhoffer Klein. Svane attempted to secure the support of the natives by taking into his house a daughter of Patti, the above-mentioned, universally respected Labadi caboceer. Hacksen maintained that he even planned an attack by the natives on the weakest point of the fort. Fortunately, Hacksen had been informed of all this. One day when an African who was generally thought to have poisoned Billsen arrived at the fort, he was driven out by means of whips. Afterward Hacksen ordered all his personal slaves to eat fetish to prove that they would not poison him. He dared not arrest Svane immediately, because of his "family" connections with prominent natives. Instead, as a means of eliminating the influence of the Africans, he made plans for an expedition to the Volta under the pretext of protecting the lodge on the island of Ada. At this point, Svane tried to get the natives to refuse to participate in the expedition. So Hacksen took courage and arrested him. Following a lawsuit, Svane was sent home. Later he entered His Majesty's service in the West Indies.

Hacksen died on July 21, 1752. In spite of the fact that he had made up his mind to go home and even had had his goods and possessions carried on board, Carl Engman was elected commandant.[15] Originally he had come to the coast in the capacity of a surgeon, but he was an astute businessman. So under his command, the Danish forts were able to carry on quite a flourishing trade. But even in this period, the West India and Guinea Company suffered grievous losses at sea. The frigate *Sorgenfrey* sailed from Guinea in May 1751 with a cargo of 82 slaves from the fort. It left the West Indies in September of that year and then disappeared without a trace. The frigate *Princesse Wilhelmina Carolina* sailed from Fort Christiansborg in April 1752 with 203 slaves, 175 of whom had been supplied by the fort. When homeward bound from the West Indies, it was wrecked on the west coast of Jutland in November 1752. Then, in 1753 there was the already mentioned mutiny of the slaves on board the *Patientia* whereby 175 slaves as well as other commodities were lost. The successful voyages of other ships were hardly sufficient compensation for the damage done to the company by these losses. A frigate named *Cron-Printzens Ønske* set out in January 1752 with 338 slaves, of whom only 90 came from the fort. The ship *Princesse Sophia Magdalena* departed in July 1752 with 307 slaves. The *Jaegersborg* sailed in May 1753 with 312 slaves. The *Patientia* sailed a second time in September 1753 with 75 new slaves, beside 100 they had succeeded in recovering from the first cargo. In 1754 two ships, the *Cron-Printz Christian* and the *Cron-Printzens Ønske*, came out almost at the same time. The former left in October with 323 slaves, of whom 255 came from the fort. The latter did not leave until April 5, 1755, and then carried only 125 slaves from Fort Christiansborg. The *Princesse Wilhelmina Carolina* was accompanied by a sloop, the *Mercurius*, which was to be used for the coast traffic.

In the meantime English competition had been increasing. In 1750 the Royal African Company was dissolved, and its property was handed over to the new African Company of Merchants. Any English merchant could become a member of this company by paying £2 sterling, an amount that all could afford. The change meant the virtual abolition of privileged trade, and in the following years there were swarms of English vessels along the Gold Coast.

At this time the authorities at Fort Christiansborg were faced with the difficult problem of what to do about the sums of money lent to the natives. In troubled times the ever-changing governors had been soft hearted and had hoped to buy the support of the natives with their liberality. Now the directors of the company began pressing for recovery of these debts. It was, however, impossible to recover without having recourse to coercive measures, such as taking debtors or their fellow-villagers as pawns. On the other hand, it was the directors' express wish that the native population of the coast be treated with gentleness and humanity. This was to demand the impossible, and Engman repeatedly called upon the directors to make up their minds as to whether he was to prefer humanity or efficiency in his efforts to recover these debts. Under any circumstances it was difficult to make the natives acknowledge and pay a debt. If one of the European nations was too strict with them, they lost no time in seeking the support of another who would be more than willing to win prospective customers.

There were constant rumors of a reconciliation of Akim and Ashanti, when, if effected, the Akim people would soon return to their country. At Fort Christiansborg the Danes were already dreaming of a new influx of Akim's gold and ordering presents sent out from Copenhagen for their caboceers. But for a while longer it was impossible to make peace, since it was impossible to come to an agreement about the amount of tribute Akim should pay the king of Ashanti. Thus the political situation on the coast was to remain unstable for many years.

Ashanti's supremacy did not by any means bring peace to the country. The conquered peoples were still trying to shape their own destinies. They would still at intervals wage war against each other. But the king of Ashanti was always strongest. Wherever he appeared, all the other native states would gradually have to surrender. They feared him, and nobody ventured to dispute his pre-eminence as their ruler. His might was distant but inescapable. From then on, the Europeans too would have to deal with it, and many years passed before they tried to free themselves from it.

14 / THE CROWN TAKES OVER

THE REQUIREMENTS OF THE West Indies often gave rise to changes in the Guinea trade. This was the case when the West India and Guinea Company was dissolved in 1754, and all its assets were taken over by the Danish Crown. The civic council of the island of St. Croix had earlier asked the king to take over the company's islands in the West Indies and to permit free trade. Such a proposal had been aired several times before, only to be opposed by the Commerce Collegium.

Now new evaluations of the company's properties were made, and at last on May 9, 1754, the collegium declared that His Majesty was prepared to buy them. He would pay a sum large enough to cover the company's debts and to refund to the shareholders the full value of their shares.[1] The company was, in fact, in a hopeless economic plight. Since news had been received about one of the latest misfortunes, the revolt of the slaves on board the *Patientia,* the offer was accepted with alacrity. The Crown issued bonds for a total of 2,339,446 rixdollars, of which the share capital took 1,250,000 rixdollars as agreed to in the convention of 1747.

The calculations do not reveal the estimated value of the Guinea forts. The total estimate of the company's property in Guinea and the West Indies was 848,755 rixdollars. Arrears due to a permanent fund were 349,236 rixdollars, and to a circulating fund, 641,662 rixdollars. Presumably, the value of the Guinea property made up a small fraction of this amount. The permanent fund in Guinea was stated to amount to 33,771 rixdollars. Annual expenses for salaries and "customs" in Guinea amounted to 5,148 rixdollars. To this must be added the cost of repairing forts and lodges, and the enormous sums spent to keep the traffic going. Therefore, it was a safe conclusion that the company's total expenses for maintenance of the Danish property in Guinea were far too large to be compensated for by its trade on the African coast. True, after 1733 no calculations of the company's total losses on its Guinea property are available. Remembering the difficulties which its trade had had to face in the last twenty years of the company's existence, it seems highly improbable, however, that it should have been more profitable than during the period covered by Burgomaster Holmsted's calculations.

After the company had accepted the royal offer and decided on the cession of its properties to the Crown, a temporary mandate concerning the Guinea and West India trade was issued on August 30, 1754.[2] This mandate was to remain in force until the end of the year. By this the company's privileges were abolished, and trade was opened to all the king's subjects except the Holsteiners. A decree of April 22, 1755, confirmed the regulations, and at the same time it granted the participants certain preferences for customs duties and other dues.[3] The administration of the company's property was handed over to the Exchequer. P. Mariager, for many years the company's bookkeeper, was transferred also and appointed secretary to the Exchequer. In 1760 a separate West Indian and Guinea General Finance and Customs Office[4] was established, and the government of Guinea was assigned to it. It remained under the supervision of Mariager.[5]

As far as the Guinea trade was concerned, His Majesty's government proved no more energetic than the late company. Indeed, it was even less active. Several of the company's ships were either sold or given away.[6] During a ten-year period only three voyages were made at the government's expense with supplies for the forts: the *Cron-Printzens Ønske's* in 1756, in 1761, and in 1764. This ship carried a total of 768 slaves to the West Indies and sold them there for a total of 152,082 rixdollars.[7] On the whole, the exploitation of the overseas holdings was left to private enterprise. Among the firms sending ships to Guinea was the Almindelige Handels-Compagnie (General Trading Company), established by royal order in 1747.[8] Its share capital amounted to half a million rixdollars, and its purpose was to trade with both the Baltic ports and in the western seas. The first plan for this company had been made by Admiral Ulrik Frederik Suhm, an uncle of Henrik Suhm the former commandant, in cooperation with Andreas Bjørn and Frederik Holmsted. Its semiofficial character was revealed by the fact that its president was Count C. A. von Berckentin, the head of the Commerce Collegium. The General Trading Company seems to have been most active in Greenland, Iceland, and Finmark.[9] For some years after the loss of its forts the West India and Guinea Company's ships continued to ply the triangular route to Guinea and the Danish West Indies. The frigate *Haabet,* captained by Ole Erichsen who was the former captain of the *Jaegersborg* and the *Patientia,* arrived at Fort Christiansborg as early as June 6, 1755.[10] It was he who brought the news to the Danes in Guinea that they had been taken over by His Majesty—a fact which was not to change their way of life noticeably. The Danes at the fort bought goods worth 12,492 rixdollars from the cargo of the *Haabet,* and in return they supplied the ship with 87 slaves. After a two or three months' stay, the ship sailed for the West Indies. This had been the method used for generations when doing business with "interlopers" and other ships which did not belong to the company. And, in subsequent years, this was to be the normal way of doing business with other private ships which arrived.

The official transfer of forts and lodges to the Crown took place on January 17, 1757, with the arrival at Fort Christiansborg of the *Cron-Printzens Ønske,* captained by Johan Friderich Knotzen. The ship brought orders from the government that Commander Carl Engman should hand over command to the merchant Christian Linkholm Schmidt.[11] As the latter, however, had embezzled certain sums at Fort Fredensborg, Engman had him arrested. In his place the bookkeeper, Christian Jessen, was elected Commandant and assumed office on March 11.[12] At the same time Johan Frederick Reindorph was appointed merchant at Fort Fredensborg. After a short visit to the home country, Esau Christensen Quist was again named as factor at the Ada lodge, in spite of the fact that when he had formerly served in this capacity his accounts were found incorrect. No special instructions were issued for the newly appointed royal officials; they had to follow the old ones from the company's days. Thus having put the house in order, the royal ship sailed on to the West Indies in April carrying 238 slaves from Fort Christiansborg and a quantity of ivory. This ship had brought out a supply of goods equal in quantity and quality to that of the *Haabet.* Since then, there had been other ships. The frigate *Mercurius* had come out in 1755,[13] the *Eben Etzer* and the *Landets Ønske* in 1756, and for some time trade had remained quite brisk. A few months after the departure of the *Cron-Printzens Ønske,* Fort Christiansborg was able to supply two privately owned ships, the *St. Croix* and the *St. Thomas,* which had good cargoes and were under the command of two brothers, Nicolay and Christian Höyer. For a while Fort Christiansborg's sales were quite good.

After Christian Jessen had taken over command, he began to have considerable trouble with the Africans, the English having been very lavish in their promises to them. The caboceers from Osu and Labadi appeared, claimed that Engman had promised them fine presents from the Danish king, and maintained that the officials of the fort had kept these presents for themselves. So Jessen had to think of something to give them. The Copenhagen government had, in fact, sent presents for only the most important native princes: the kings of Akim, Ashanti, Akwamu, and Popo. However, the king of Akwamu was not satisfied, even though the present must have meant some degree of recognition of his power.

He maintained that Engman had promised him 8 rixdollars as a monthly salary or "custom," and that the Danish king owed him this money for three years. Jessen would not honor such a claim. The trade brought by Akwamu was far too unstable, so Jessen invited the king of Akwamu to try to get the money out of Engman, who had left the coast by that time. In return, the king threatened to block the roads to Ashanti, though he did not venture to do so. The Ashanti always traveled in large troops, and besides at this time they had begun to use a new route. This route did not take them through the territory of the Akwamu, but instead it took them through the towns of the hill people. From then on the Akwamu themselves had to climb the hills to these towns, if they wanted to trade with them.

Worst of all, however, was the fact that Engman had lost the Danish hold on Tessing. Afterward, it was said that he had never forgiven the Africans for having demanded his recall to Denmark. When he rose to power, he laid plans for revenge. Among other misdeeds, he was said to have lured some of the inhabitants of Tessing into the fort and tortured them. Later, he made the sloop *Mercurius* prevent the fishermen of that town from going out to sea. He also stopped landward supplies, so that the town was reduced to starvation. He meant to collect the town's debts by force. When he caught an important Tessing man named Tette as a pawn, he sold him to America. In the end, the Dutch paid the debt, and in 1757 Tessing placed itself under their protection. If Jessen's portrait is reliable, Engman must have been a most authoritarian master, who was always overruling the decisions of others and assuming responsibility for everything himself. It was also said that Engman, who had originally been a doctor, had stooped to the practises of fetishism and had often called in a "wise woman" from Labadi. When rain was needed or good fishing or good trade, he was said to have had a hen or a goat killed and the doorposts smeared with its blood. In any case, after his departure a good deal of "devilry" was found under his bed by the natives who cleaned his rooms. They brought the abominable things to Osu, where they were hung on poles. The English and the Dutch are said to have had a great time teasing the Danes on this occasion.

Christian Jessen now tried to re-establish the good name of the Danes. He does not seem to have fallen into bad ways himself but merely to have lacked personal authority. The prosperity of Danish trade did not last. A couple of privately owned ships did come out from Denmark annually: the *Emmanuel* and the *Jaegersborg* in 1758, the *Jomfru Catharina* and the *St. Birgitte* in 1759,[14] the *Debora,* the *Friderichs Haab,* and again the *Jaegersborg* in 1760. The private firms may have profited by these trips, but the royal officials of the forts had no cause for jubilations. The supplies of goods brought by these privately owned ships proved very inferior both in quality and quantity. As a rule they bartered away the better part of the cargoes on the Upper Coast and brought only their unsaleable remainders to Fort Christiansborg. This did not give sufficient trade. Vainly the Danes sought by means of letters to attract ships newly arrived on the coast. They almost had recourse to advertising. The commandants of the forts repeatedly complained because the privately owned ships were not given orders to go directly to the Danish fort. The Danes of Fort Christiansborg complained especially, since they had been given orders to sell only to Danish vessels, orders which could be contravened only in times of emergency. Not that it was more profitable to sell to foreigners, for they seldom came there.[15] The colonial war between England and France was now nearing its climax. There were hardly any French ships, and the few English ships that arrived could easily get full cargoes from the English forts. Only the Dutch carried on a steady traffic, but relations between Dutch and Danes on the coast were anything but cordial. The Dutch were still inclined to use force to drive the Portuguese away from Fort Christiansborg.[16] The long intervals between ship arrivals lessened the demand for slaves, so that, at times, male slaves could be bought for 112-128 rixdollars apiece.[17] Danish enterprise was reduced further in 1757 when the sloop *Mercurius* had to be broken up,[18] and when a couple of boats purchased for the coastal traffic were lost in the following years.

Conditions for the interior trade were equally unfavorable. Relations between Ashanti and Akim remained unstable. Akim hid away in the unpopulated country north of Fanti and appeared only after intervals of several years, so, there was no gold. Ashanti rarely sent trading expeditions to Fort Christiansborg. Normally the Danes had to make do with the trade of the neighboring coastal people and the purchase of a few slaves from Akwamu. To make up for the loss of Tessing, the Danes tried to establish a lodge at the native town of Way, east of the Volta River and ten or fifteen kilometers west of Keta.[19] Like the Keta lodge, the one at Way was to be controlled from Ada, but the attempt was given up after a short time.

For a while in 1760 the situation seemed to be improving.[20] The inland roads were open, and the English were trading profitably with Fanti. By November of that year, however, the flames of war were blazing again. The Danish explanation was that the Dutch caused the trouble by bribing Akim to punish the native town of Berku (Bercoe, Beraku), 40 kilometers west of Christiansborg; and when the inhabitants of this town took refuge with the Dutch, they were sold as slaves. Now the war spread along the entire coast and caused extortions, robbery, and pillage as far as Ningo. Akim made a treaty with Krobbo, a nation of hill people living in the neighborhood of the Volta River. Together these two peoples tried to block the road against the Ashanti. All this was occurring while fugitive Berku and natives protected by the Dutch were taking each other prisoner. Consequently, the natives could not do the peaceful work of tending the millet fields, and food prices increased enormously. Matters were not improved when the native mediator, Adovi, tried to drive out Soya from Osu, for Soya was the messenger of the Christiansborg commandant. This gave rise to a protracted quarrel among the Osu. The commandant asserted that it had been caused by J. F. Reindorph, who had taken a daughter of Adovi into his house. After he left the coast on board the *Jaegersborg* in 1760, life became rather more peaceful.

No wonder the spirits of many Danes sank, and many asked to be allowed to return to the mother country. After a period of high mortality in the early 1750's, a time of shorter sick lists followed. Several had served their time; a few had spent many years on the Gold Coast, and so they had every right to ask to be relieved. It was only when the *Cron-Printzens Ønske* arrived in 1762 that a change of commandants took place.[21] After nearly a decade of temporary commandants, the Crown at last appointed a permanent commandant, Carl Gottleb Resch.[22] Christian Lindholm Schmidt had been to Copenhagen to clear himself for his failure in Engman's days. While at home, he had made proposals for the better management of the African property and in the process was restored to favor. He was now appointed chief merchant of Christiansborg. Reindorph's successor at Fort Fredensborg, Gerhard Friderich Wrisberg, and Esau Christensen Quist of the Ada lodge received royal confirmation of their appointments. Quist was not, however, allowed to enjoy his new status very long. He was found guilty of the "underhanded practice of smuggling goods out of the gates" and was sent home by the royal ship. The king did not appoint a new factor for the Keta lodge until 1763.

Resch at once took steps to make peace with all the hostile native towns of the district. At considerable expense he managed to reconcile Adovi and Soya, so that Osu could again thrive. When looking over the stores, he found several irregularities, which he punished. As far as we know, he was a somewhat critical official. As well as having a restless turn of mind, he wanted to see results for his work. However, he was powerless to do anything about the African wars. He had to wait long for a decisive battle, and the inland roads remained blocked for years. So he had to be content with repairing the forts and building a forework around the small Fort Prøvestenen. It had been erected (at an unknown date) at the outskirts of Osu, and now he made it an outpost against Dutch Fort Crèvecoeur. Similarly, he re-established the lodge at Way, for the natives threatened to call in the English, unless he did. In the long run, his energetic efforts were opposed by his inferiors. They thought him too harsh. He drank and treated them roughly. The mulatto children complained that he treated them like slaves. On the other hand, he regarded his entourage as useless and was always asking to have new staff sent out. His demands do not seem to have been unreasonable—Schmidt, who again embezzled a large amount, was arrested a second time and sent home.

When his term of office was nearly at an end, Resch was at last to see Ashanti, after long preparations, launch a fresh attack upon Akim. Akim sought the support of Fanti and all the other coastal peoples to no avail, for they were completely vanquished. This happened either late in 1765 or early in 1766. Afterward the king of Ashanti tried to make Fanti deliver him the severed head of the king of Akim and all his gold. The most serious attempt by the Africans to oppose the supremacy of Ashanti ended with the fall of Akim. The natives around the Danish forts could no longer hope to free themselves from the yoke of Ashanti.

As far as we can see, one or two Danish ships still came to the coast every year. So it seems likely that the shipowners were able to gain some little profit from the traffic. However, the small-scale trade carried on from the Danish forts paid no dividends into the Royal Exchequer, but, at least it did not produce a deficit, either. According to accounts established afterward for the years 1755-1765, the average annual expenditure was 29,900 rixdollars for goods, 7,000 rixdollars for salaries, and 8,600 rixdollars for voyages and freight.[23] On the other hand, slaves worth 45,000 rixdollars were sold, so that there was almost a balance. Expenses connected with the voyages were probably put too low, but that matters were no worse was due, no doubt, to the decided business acumen of Engman, to the honest efforts of Jessen, and the strict and orderly husbandry of Resch. They were, however, powerless to provide any argument in favor of the government's continued management of the Guinea business. On the contrary, the opinion was still generally held that a trading company would be able to run the business more profitably. Consequently, the government seized the earliest opportunity to return again the Guinea trade to private enterprise.

15 / BARGUM'S TRADING SOCIETY

THE TRANSFER OF THE Guinea trade to a private company was preceded by a royal decree of February 24, 1764, whereby the West Indian and Guinea General Finance and Customs Office was ordered "earnestly and energetically to work for a gradual reduction by 100,000 rixdollars annually of expenses for the trade and traffic to the West Indian Islands and the African forts." [1] The underlying reason was the low ebb in government finances caused by purchases of armament during the Seven Years' War, by the government's mercantilistic policy, and by its lavish expenses for the royal court. As matters stood, it was not difficult to get a hearing for a suggestion that the government relinquish the Guinea trade.

Such a project was put forward on August 9, 1764, by a merchant named Henning Frederik Bargum.[2] He was the son of a sister of Madame Gustmeyer, a widow who owned one of the most important business firms in Copenhagen. At an early age he had been made a partner in his aunt's business and had traveled extensively. In 1760 he shocked business circles by obtaining a monopoly for the tobacco trade in Denmark. He was also granted privileges for a hat factory and a fishbone factory. In Western Europe he had seen what profits could be made on the slave trade and West Indian sugar, and he had returned to Copenhagen brimful of new ideas. There, experts on Guinea affairs had to dampen his enthusiasm considerably before his projects became at all realizable. Then, on March 18, 1765, he obtained the necessary charter for a business company, whose official name was Royal Chartered Danish Guinea Trading Company (in Danish: *Kongelige Octroyerede Danske Guineiske Handels-Compagnie*), but which was commonly known as the "Slave Trade Society." [3] It is most frequently remembered as Bargum's Trading Society. Among its members were both Engman and Reindorph. The generous privileges granted by the charter reveal how anxious the government was to get rid of the Guinea trade. The trading society was allowed to accept any number of foreign shareholders. It was exempt from taxation of its profits; it was freely allowed to order foreign goods to supply its ships; and it was exempt from customs and excise on goods for Guinea. It obtained permission even to have its ships fitted with supplies in foreign ports and to use ships belonging to other Danish subjects. Further, it could freely export slaves to the West Indies and import coal, paper, etc., for a sugar refinery which it acquired in Copenhagen. Finally, it was granted an export premium of 5 rixdollars on every 500 pounds of loaf sugar exported by it. In fact, it was given all imaginable privileges which would not involve too large government investments.

Next, on November 8 that year the government, on application, granted to the society a twenty-year concession of the forts and lodges in Guinea. At first the society had tried to persuade the government to pay the cost of keeping the forts in repair.[4] When the government proved unwilling to do so, the society agreed to defray the total expenses. Free access to the traffic was preserved for His Majesty's other subjects, even the Holsteiners, who had already, by the decree of April 9, 1764, concerning the trade to His Majesty's American isles, been granted permission to share in the slave traffic.[5] It was expressly laid down that the society was to use "all compliance and good will" to supply others with the slaves they needed. It was further stipulated that the society's staff should be treated justly and their rights protected. The society was to be responsible for the maintenance of forts, guns, and supplies. It was to defend His Majesty's rights on the coast, especially "our proprietary rights on the banks of the Rio Volta." Quarrels and troubles with the European nations were to be avoided, but in case of emergency the society could appeal to the Danish Foreign Office for help. The Africans who were dependent on the Danish forts were to be protected and kept from interfering with the wars of other tribes. The right enjoyed by the late company of entering into alliances with the African states was granted also to its successor. The society must, however, beware of promises to the native princes of annual tributes, which might prove burdensome, if at a later date the settlements were to revert to the Crown. Officials on the coast were still to swear an oath of allegiance to the Danish king, and "the Commandant or Governor appointed to the coast" was to apply for royal confirmation. This was the first time that the title of "Governor" was officially used to designate the commandant of Fort Christiansborg. Unofficially it had been commonly used since late in the 1740's. After a period of six years, the society would be allowed to withdraw, after giving one year's notice, and hand everything back to the king in the same state in which it had been received.

In spite of all these privileges, it was not easy for Bargum to persuade businessmen who knew the coast to buy shares. They were willing to do so only on certain conditions. On February 19, 1766, the general assembly of the society drew up a convention and thereafter appointed three codirectors to keep an eye on Bargum; they were Engman, Reindorph, and Captain Jesper With.[6] After the accession of the new king, the society's charter was reconfirmed by Christian VII on August 4, 1766, and on September 9 that year the convention of February 19 received a royal confirmation.

Finally, on October 20, 1767, the king granted a prolongation of the concession for thirty years.[7] At the same time, the society was exempted from still more dues: extra tonnage dues and extra slave tonnage dues, plus the so-called *rancon* dues on the crews' wages. (All these burdens had been imposed on shipping by the royal decree of April 9, 1764.) The total capital of the society was 176,500 rixdollars; in addition Bargum was able to obtain considerable loans.

Simultaneously with the granting of the concession, Resch, the commandant, was recalled, and the society was allowed to appoint the necessary officials at the forts. Christian Tychsen was chosen as governor, and his commission was confirmed by the king on April 15, 1766.[8] He sailed out on the society's frigate *Christiansborg,* arriving at the most important Danish fort in Guinea on October 18 that year, after a slow and difficult voyage. He found the fort in an absolutely wretched state. The buildings were in decay; the tower had collapsed. The stock of goods was inadequate and unsaleable; and together with all the supplies at the Danish trading stations, it was valued at only 4,770 rixdollars. Resch's staff threw all the blame for this state of affairs on him, while he, who was ill and upset, kept aloof from the settlement of accounts. The new governor had the greatest difficulty in persuading the garrison to remain in the service. The soldiers protested that they were starved; they did not want to be left to rot in that hole. They were unwilling to stay on, and so, they demanded their discharge. Tychsen had to use much persuasion. He explained that now there was an entirely new regime, that every man would receive his pay, and that they could freely voice their complaints of Resch. It was a long time before they agreed to swear the oath of allegiance, first to the new king, and then to the society. Afterward, as many as possible were replaced, and only one European was left in the Christiansborg garrison. The rest were mulattoes, some of them mere boys, who were soon to prove unruly. Those who had been discharged sailed for home on the frigate which left for the West Indies in February 1767 with a cargo of 216 slaves worth 24,687 rixdollars.

As soon as possible, repairs were started on the fort, and the government of the settlements was reorganized along the lines laid down by the society. This work was ably assisted by the bookkeeper, Niels Urban Aarestrup, an excellent man. Nevertheless, Governor Tychsen was unable to accomplish anything. He died after little more than a year on January 11, 1768, leaving his own accounts in chaos—mere jottings on loose scraps of paper. Indeed, he had caused such confusion that, even before his death, the directors of the society had appointed a committee to investigate his management, which was to be utterly condemned.[9] It was said that, during the short period that he had held office, slaves worth 9,220 rixdollars died. It was understandable that there was surprise when he was found to have left behind six keys to the society's gold chest, though by the regulations there should have been only three. Among those sentenced for their complicity in Tychsen's misrule was Jessen, the former commandant. He died, however, before sentence could be passed on him.

As stipulated in the regulations of the society, Frantz Joachim Kuhberg became acting governor after Tychsen's death.[10] Like Engman, he had first been sent out as surgeon. Later he had proved very useful in the trade and had become chief assistant and factor at Keta lodge. But as governor, he was no more successful than his predecessor. He became involved in the examination of Tychsen's management and was made to pay a considerable fine. In addition, he met with opposition from several of the officials of the society on the coast, such as Aarestrup. In 1768 mortality among the staff of the fort was high, and Kuhberg himself succumbed on July 2, 1769. Gerhard Friderich Wrisberg, the former factor of Fort Fredensborg, was then chosen as his successor.[11] His rule soon gave rise to complaints. He quarreled with Aarestrup and had him arrested. Within a year he was succeeded by an infantry captain named Joachim Christian Otto, whose appointment as governor of Guinea had received royal confirmation on October 11, 1769. This governor arrived at Fort Christiansborg on June 11, 1770, and just managed to get Aarestrup out of prison before he died on June 13. Following the regulations, he was succeeded by Johan Daniel Frölich, who had come out with him to take up the post of chief merchant.

The constant change of governors did not prove as harmful as might have been expected. The erection of Fort Fredensborg and the lodges meant that in future there would always be a somewhat larger number of Danes on the Gold Coast. So continuity could more easily be preserved, and decay never became so widespread as in earlier periods of continual change of leadership. By and large, trade was fairly good in the first years of the Trading Society. Ashanti now and again sent trading expeditions to the coast, and the other native peoples left them alone. So conditions were better for trade at Fort Christiansborg than in most of its previous history. For some time, first-class male slaves could be bought for 128-144 rixdollars and female slaves for 96-112 rixdollars. Thus, it was possible to supply quite good cargoes of slaves which in turn filled the coffers of the fort.

Conditions were less stable around the Volta River.[12] The natives on the river banks could not be kept from robbing the interior trade expeditions, even if Dadecon, the king of Akwamu, did his best to punish them. The worst hindrance was the constant quarrels with the Akwamu east of the river. At Keta lodge conditions were tolerable, partly because Assiambo, king of Popo, acted as peacemaker. He was, in fact, king of the descendants of those Accra who, about 1680, had fled before the increasing might of the Akwamu. The Ada lodge suffered the worst fate. On February 14, 1769, Awuna, which was in league with the natives of Way and Keta, attacked the town of the Ada people on the island in the river. They burnt down the houses and stole the women and children. The Danish lodge was not interfered with, except that the company slaves stationed there were carried off. The apparent cause of this disaster was the killing of a caboceer-elect of Awuna by a man from Ada. During the fighting there was a tragic episode. While the Awuna were still fighting the Ada forces, the Way people ran to the part of the island where the women and children of the burning town were gathered and carried them off. They did not want to be bothered with the babies, and so they struck off their heads and threw them into the river. While many Ada women drowned themselves, the men, in their desperate fury, wanted to fight on. It was of no avail, however, for shortly afterward Awuna called up still greater forces and beat them in several successive battles.

At first the Danish government at Christiansborg was not worried by this train of events. They found consolation in the thought that "these circumstances can result in nothing else but a plentiful supply of slaves." The only regret was that there was no ship at anchor in the road, ready to take the great number of Ada on board as slaves. The Danes did not dare to keep them ashore, and so the English pocketed most of the profits from the battle. For that matter, the Awuna took great care that the Ada were not sold to the Danish fort at Keta for fear that they should be ransomed by their runaway compatriots. The few survivors from Ada were saved because Jens Adolph Kiøge, who in July 1770 had been made factor of the Ada factory, persuaded them to eat fetish with their enemies. This was done in December 1770; afterward the ceremony was repeated.

Another fact which helped to improve Danish trade was the somewhat greater regularity with which ships arrived from Europe.[13] Even before the frigate *Christiansborg* had left the coast, the society's snow *Eleonora* arrived which, as in 1767, left with 160 slaves. In the course of the following years, there were two new company ships loading, the frigate *Fredens-*

borg and the snow *Ada.* In 1769 the *Christiansborg* returned, and in 1770 the *Eleonora* and the *Ada* took on cargoes. All these ships reached the West Indies with a fair number of slaves still alive, but the *Fredensborg* was wrecked when homeward bound. In 1770 the sloop *Qvitta,* commanded by Captain Ferentz, was also sent. It plied among the Danish settlements on the coast, until 1772 when it was sent eastward to Gabon in search of ivory, after which it left for Copenhagen. Beside slaves, most of the ships carried small quantities of gold and ivory home from Guinea. The subsequent years did not bring quite so many ships from Copenhagen. The *Christiansborg* sailed from the coast in 1772 and 1775; the *Ada,* in 1772, 1774, and 1776; the *Eleonora,* in 1773; a packet-boat named *Fortuna* in 1774. In the coast traffic the *Qvitta* was replaced, first by the schooner *Ada,* and after its loss, by the sloop *Way.*

Even though the number of Danish sailings decreased, trade at Christiansborg did not slacken all at once. The Copenhagen company made an arrangement with David and Dubucq, shipowners of Paris, who sent ships to pick up slave cargoes at Christiansborg at least seven times.[14] The terms were that the company was to deliver 3,600 slaves in three years, three or four hundred slaves per ship. Only on one occasion was the stipulated number reached, and frequently the ships were delayed longer on the coast than agreed upon under the terms of the contract. Consequently, the Danes had to pay for these partial breaches of the contract, and this swallowed up part of the profit. The first two ships to arrive at Fort Christiansborg under the terms of this contract were the *St. André* and *L'heureux* in 1770, both from La Rochelle. On board the former was Governor Otto. Later mention is made of *Le Pacifique, L'Experience,* the *Comte de Colbert,* and *L'Americain,* the last-mentioned in 1773. The French firm constantly and energetically protested against unsatisfactory treatment, but the Danes had their complaints to make, too, and in the end, the Danish society withdrew from the contract. In the meantime, the Danish government accused the society of allowing the French firm to take the best slaves and of putting only the inferior ones up for sale in the Danish West Indies. The society's total sale of slaves to the French ships amounted to 1,873, a fairly large number considering that the number carried in its own ships in the decade 1767-1777 totaled little more than 3,000 slaves.

Right from the start the Guinea government protested against the French contract, flatly denying the possibility of scraping together so many slaves. To supply a cargo for the first French ship, a Danish ship had to be detained, and in the meantime a considerable number of the slaves in stock died. Afterward, it was a constant complaint that the settlements did not get sufficient goods with which to purchase so many slaves. Several of the French ships arrived at Fort Christiansborg without any cargo.

The chief reason for the failure of this French experiment was, however, the fresh outbreak of the native wars.[15] The fighting was very bitter, the trade routes were blocked, and the supply of slaves for the forts dwindled. The prelude to this new war was written by King Obrincoran of Akim in connection with the Krobbo. Arriving at Accra early in 1770, he squeezed loans out of the European forts, 50 bendas' worth of goods from each of them. He swore by the king of Ashanti and his mother, the strongest oath imaginable, to keep the paths open, but a few months later Akim and Krobbo began intercepting the Ashanti traders in the mountains. Still worse, in 1771 disputes broke out between Fanti and Ashanti, and the Fanti occupied the paths. The king of Ashanti made all his men swear that they would not bring slaves to the forts till the war was over. Then he marched against Akim. King Obrincoran retreated to Fanti, but afterward he marched into the Volta district to support Krobbo and Ada against their enemies east of the river. A further complication was the hostilities opened by Krobbo against the Accra and Ningos. At first it was only Fort Christiansborg's trade which suffered. From September 1772 the paths to the fort were completely blocked. Later the situation in the eastern districts deteriorated, too, because the people of Awuna, Way, and Keta organized an attack on Aflahu, a town on the Slave Coast, 40 or 50 kilometers east of Keta.

In 1772 at Little Popo, in these outlying parts of the land occupied by the former Accra, J. A. Kiøge set up a Danish lodge.[16] It was situated about a hundred kilometers east of Keta, near what was to become the border between the German colony of Togo and the French colony of Dahomey. This became the most easterly of all the known Danish trading stations on the Guinea coast. Though by 1774 some wanted to give it up, it was kept going for a number of years. The warlike habits of the natives, however, laid the same hindrances in the way of trade here as at Christiansborg, Fredensborg, Ada, and Keta. By New Year's 1775 the areas surrounding all the Danish trading posts were in a state of war.

That, in spite of all difficulties, the Danes were able to manage as well as they did was due to the leadership of the ablest man ever sent to the Guinea coast from Denmark. When the acting governor, J. D. Frölich, died on June 15, 1772, energetic Niels Urban Aarestrup was elected to replace him.[17] This choice was later confirmed by royal appointment on May 2, 1774. After serving as a bookkeeper, he had risen to the post of commandant of Fort Fredensborg. In this capacity he had very ably supported J. A. Kiøge in his difficult dealings with the natives in the neighborhood of the Ada lodge. A high mortality rate among the Danes in 1772 and a period of starvation in 1774 had hindered his activities. Nevertheless, Aarestrup kept everything in good order, and on the whole he succeeded in weathering the storm. Splendid service was rendered also by J. A. Kiøge, now acting as chief merchant of Fort Christiansborg, who in the long run was to prove the most enterprising of all Danes in Guinea. An instance of the energy of Aarestrup and Kiøge in their conduct of the Danish Guinea trade might be mentioned: when, because of the war between Britain and her North American Colonies, the American rum ships failed to arrive, the two traders at once asked the Copenhagen society to see that Danish West Indian rum was sent to Guinea.

Nevertheless, the coast trade was not sufficient to keep Bargum's Copenhagen Trading Society afloat.[18] Before long Bargum was burdened with codirectors who had no personal knowledge of the coast, and his business separated from that of Madame Gustmeyer. The Trading Society seems gradually to have plunged deeper and deeper into complicated financial transactions. The regular correspondence with permanent business friends in Hamburg, Amsterdam, London, Paris, and other cities reveals ever-increasing numbers of ever larger accommodation bills. Gradually the situation became very difficult. The market may have deteriorated. In the spring of 1774 the Trading Society had to press for payment of outstanding debts, as some of its own large debts were due. Nevertheless, the general assembly of July that year decided to invest large sums in the trade; but then the crash came. Bargum disappeared; his private business was bankrupt in 1790. Still later he was traced to Alsace, and he is said to have died as a merchant in Nantes.

His disappearance seems to have dealt the *coup de grâce* to the Guinea society.[19] It was immediately forced to give up its offices in Bargum's private house, the *gule Palae* (yellow mansion) in Amaliegade, Copenhagen. Now the society had to make do with a narrow room in its sugar refinery in the former Iceland and Finmark warehouse behind the Royal Stock Exchange. At the moment, the Trading Society's poverty prevented it from sending out a ship, and in the long run there was nothing for it to do but to appeal to the king's mercy. A general assembly on April 6, 1775, decided that it was time to appeal to His Majesty. It was pointed out that the Trading Society had supplied the Danish West Indies with slaves and had earned 150,000 rixdollars for Denmark by means of the slaves sold to the French. Similarly, the society had used for the Guinea trade goods worth 400,000 rixdollars. Most of these goods had been Danish, and thus employment was provided for large numbers of His Majesty's subjects. Also the building of the company's ships had been of importance for employment. It would be a great pity to allow such a useful business to collapse. In spite of the good results, it must be admitted, though, that until New Year's 1773, 127,600 rixdollars of capital had been lost. Two main reasons were given for this: first, that the king had been unwilling to pay expenses for repairing the Guinea forts, which had amounted to 25,000 rixdollars annually; second, that by his contract with the shareholders, which had been approved by the king,

Bargum had secured for himself enormous emoluments. He got 2 per cent on everything bought or sold in Europe in the name of the company. "It is not just that so many shall suffer loss for the benefit of one single man." In other words, it was all His Majesty's fault for imposing on the Trading Society such hard terms.

Now the society asked to be rid of Bargum as director-general, begging the king to take possession of all their assets, pay their debts, and cover the shares "according to the books." The term was drawing near, and the society would have to pay out 50,000 rixdollars, which they did not know where to find. Evidently, it was hoped that the Trading Society would be let off as cheaply as the shareholders of the late West India and Guinea Company had been 20 years earlier. They, it will be remembered, were paid the full value of their shares.

It remains, in fact, an open question whether, judging from the information obtainable, the society was as badly off as it asserted. According to enclosed accounts: its ships, the *Christiansborg, Fortuna, Ada,* and *Eleonora* were valued at 40,819 rixdollars; the sugar refinery at 113,089 rixdollars; the stock of goods in Guinea at 69,056 rixdollars; and a cargo of slaves en route for the West Indies at 23,627 rixdollars. Even if there were considerable debts, the society was not without resources. So it must have been with a fairly good conscience that the government let His Majesty sign an order of May 15, 1775, which was a flat refusal of everything the Trading Society had applied for. His Majesty's government would neither pay an annual contribution to the maintenance of the forts nor buy the Trading Society.

In the meantime, a series of misfortunes struck the company's ships, which fully justified the pessimism of the directors.[20] While homeward bound from the West Indies in 1774, the packet-boat *Fortuna* was damaged and had to seek port at Dover. The *Ada* was struck that year by an exceptionally high mortality, evidently due to the fact that, owing to the food shortage at the forts, they had begun to put the slaves on board the ships many months before the ship was due to leave. The ship was kept a full year on the Guinea coast. Of the 221 slaves taken on board only 121 reached the West Indies, where some died immediately on landing. The *Christiansborg* was equally unfortunate. On the morning of February 26, 1775, shortly after its departure from the Danish stronghold, this ship became the scene of a dangerous slave revolt. On that occasion the male slaves made themselves masters of the 'tween-deck. They broke into the gunner's storeroom and provided themselves with muskets and gunpowder. They cut the rudder pintles, so that it became impossible to steer the ship, and it drifted eastward along the coast. When the garrison of the Danish forts realized that disaster had befallen the ship, they were able to send help; and after a couple of days the Danes were again masters of the ship. It had then drifted as far as Fort

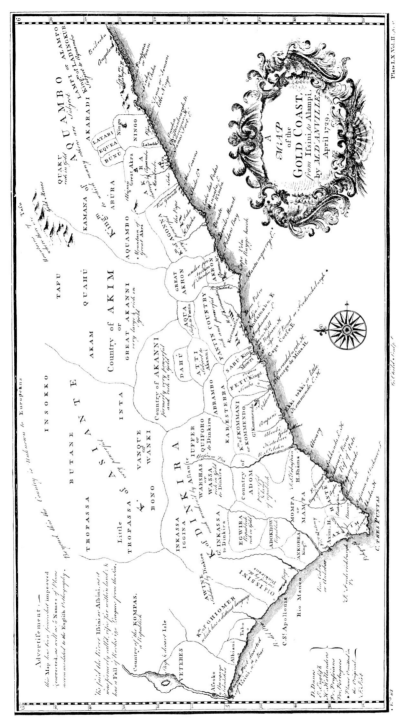

A map of the Gold Coast.

Ships off Christiansborg, painting by Webster, eighteenth century.

Ashanti homestead, early nineteenth century.

Frederiksted plantation, nineteenth century.

Fredensborg, and the company suffered the loss of 45 slaves. By March 16 the ship was fully repaired and able to depart again. However, though it had carried 393 slaves with its first departure, it sailed the second time with only 332. Of these no less than 79 died during the crossing.

So while the work of the Trading Society was still carried on, its position was being considered. Evidently, the shareholders had not given up all hope, but wished to await the outcome of various expeditions which had not yet been completed. On July 24, 1775, the general assembly decided on a renewed appeal to the king for annual contributions to the forts.[21] If these were not granted, they requested that, in consequence of the terms of the concession, the king take back the forts and trading stations. As a reply to this request there followed a royal order of August 25, 1775, whereby all settlements were to revert to the king on September 1, 1776. Not a word was mentioned about any kind of relief or compensation for the Trading Society. The shareholders were still unwilling to accept these terms. However, on November 22 the general assembly decided to sell its most valuable asset, the sugar refinery. This spelt the liquidation of the Trading Society.

Nevertheless, as the year was drawing toward its close, they still sent the snow *Ada* to the Gold Coast; and it returned safely in 1777. On May 22, 1776, the king issued orders that from then on the Guinea trade was to continue at his expense.[22] It was to be controlled by the *Konjelige Guineiske Handels-Direction* (the Royal Guinean Trade Department). Count J. G. Moltke was appointed president. In August 1776 the snow *Eleonora,* now in His Majesty's service, brought out the new royal governor, Major Hohan Conrad von Hemsen, whose appointment was dated July 27, 1776.[23] However, the *Eleonora* met with all kinds of adversity. It had to repair at Marstrand, Sweden, and again at Hull, from which port it was not able to leave until May 1777. In the meantime, a newly built royal frigate, the *Christiansborg,* was fitted out. Sailing from Copenhagen in April 1777, this ship picked up Hemsen, so that he arrived at the Christiansborg road on June 12, 1777. At once Aarestrup, on behalf of the Trading Society, handed over the settlements on June 24 and sailed for home.

The society's sugar refinery was sold to Hinrich Ladiges in 1776.[24] Gradually, its ships were disposed of, and by 1777 most of its debts had been paid. There remained only the settlement of accounts with His Majesty's government after the transfer of the stores of goods in Guinea. To take charge of the final distribution of the Trading Society's assets, the Danish chancellery appointed a committee on September 10, 1777. The members of this committee were the two last directors, Councilor Justice Michael Bredal and Agent Carl Henrich Thalbitzer, and two jurists, Friderich Christian Sevel and Frederich Wilhelm Wiwet. Bredal resigned in 1779. The committee worked very slowly, but in 1788 it handed in accounts showing that, after payment of all debts, there still remained capital worth 57,774 rixdollars.

Bargum's Trading Society had been no more successful than the preceding West India and Guinea Company. Nevertheless, it deserves praise for its daring enterprise. In spite of very moderate financial support from the government, it was the first company in the history of the Danish Guinea traffic to maintain almost regular sailings to and from the Danish forts. The contract with the French shipowners was daring, even if badly prepared. Had conditions on the coast been more favorable, this contract might have earned a considerable sum of money.

Most remarkable it seems that, beside all this, the Trading Society was thinking of starting plantations and bringing the African soil under cultivation.[25] With reference to the good results of the mission in Greenland, missionaries were called in.[26] It was hoped that they would both know how to run plantations and be able to convert some natives to honesty and industry. In 1765 three Moravian brethren actually arrived on the coast; they were Jakob Meder, the leader, a tailor named Schultz, and Lemmicke, a shoemaker. The death of all three of them within a short time was much lamented by the Danes on the coast. Meder was given the posthumous praise that his death causes "no inconsiderable loss to us in respect to many things, not only of company, science, and moral matters, but even in being of assistance to us in the prescription of medicines, tending the sick, nay, he was agreeable and serviceable to all men." The next year a new leader, Johan Westman, with two other brethren followed. They were given permission by the king of Akim to build, dwell, and cultivate the land, as long as they would refrain from building forts. They made an attempt in the neighborhood of Fort Fredensborg. After Westman left, however, the remaining two died within a year. So every good and useful endeavor on the part of the Trading Society came to nothing because of the rampant bellicosity of the natives or the deadly climate. In this, Bargum's endeavors shared the fate of numerous other Danish attempts to improve trade and civilization on the coast of Guinea.

16 / AT WAR WITH THE DUTCH

IN THE LONG INTERVAL between Bargum's bankruptcy and Governor Hemsen's arrival at Christiansborg, the Danish settlements were almost entirely left to their own resources. Only once did a ship come out from the home country. It was a snow, the *Ada,* in 1776. The stock of goods dwindled almost to nothing, and Danish trade gradually suffered badly. This, of course, meant a general weakening of their situation, and their neighbors were well aware of it.

This was the state of affairs when the Dutch made an attempt to usurp the influence over the neighborhood of the Volta River which had hitherto belonged exclusively to the Danes.[1] In December 1775 the Dutch governor at Fort Crèvecoeur, Jacobus van der Penÿe, sent messengers with presents to the natives living round the Danish lodge at Ada, inviting them to send representatives to him at the Dutch fort.[2] Won over by these presents, they accepted the invitation, after which the Dutchman is said to have made them swear an oath of fidelity to himself. The Danes, however, demanded that the Ada people recall their representatives, which they promised to do. In the meantime the Danes received a letter from van der Penÿe which stated that he was negotiating with the Ada for the opening of a lodge near Okko, a short distance west of the Volta estuary. There had probably been a Dutch lodge there earlier, but at the time this spot was uninhabited and overgrown with bush. The Danes, therefore, could have no objection to a Dutch trading station there, provided it did not disturb Ada and the other native towns along the Volta River. The representatives of the Ada did not come back, however. Aarestrup, the Danish governor, demanded their surrender, but in vain.

Instead, on April 17, 1776, van der Penÿe sent a corporal named Hendrick Vitlaar with 100 fully armed Africans eastward from Dutch Accra, marching close by the Danish forts. They did not march to Okko, but to Tubreku. This, in Aarestrup's words was "the first African town within Our Most Gracious King's exclusive property rights on the Rio Volta." When this news was received at Christiansborg, the garrison solemnly vowed to defend the rights of the Danish king.

The charter given to Bargum's society imposed upon this company the duty of defending the king's property rights on the Volta River. Now the phrase was made more emphatic by speaking of "exclusive property rights." What was meant by that? Did the Danish king have property rights to any native town? Did the phrase imply private ownership or sovereign rights? As we have already seen, the contracts which the Danes had earlier made with Fetu or Accra hardly gave grounds for claiming sovereign rights. If now, a century later, the Danish Guinea government used the expression "property rights" in relation to Ada, there might be better reason to believe that it was meant to imply sovereign rights. If so, the Danish settlements in Guinea were to be regarded as colonies.[3] In the following years, this word was now and again used about them, even if the official designation for them usually was the more neutral word "settlements." Of course, the fact that the territories were regarded as colonies was of paramount importance for relations with both the native states and the other European nations on the coast. The sovereignty which the African princes had formerly assumed was thereby abolished, and it became necessary for the Europeans to come to an agreement on how far the rights of each white nation extended.

It is possible to find slight allusions in previous years to the idea that Denmark possessed sovereign rights in Guinea.[4] It will hardly do, however, to attach too much importance to the fact that, on January 7, 1700, Commandant Trane summoned the most important natives from Osu and Labadi and made them swear an oath of allegiance to the Danes and confirm it by eating fetish. The reason for this was that Assemoni, who won notoriety by the coup of 1693, had again been troublesome, which, by the way, afterward caused the king of Akwamu to send his apologies. It is rather more difficult to explain the oaths which the African leaders of Osu, Labadi, Tessing, and, somewhat later Ningo, too, were made to swear to Danish commandants far into the eighteenth century, and which for instance are mentioned at Billsen's installment in office in 1744. Other features difficult to explain were the Danish flags and silver-handled walking sticks with the royal initials,[5] which were now and then granted to African princes. There is also the phrase "Our Africans," which is often used not only about slaves, but also about the free people of the towns near the Danish forts. In all these cases relations between Danes and Africans may equally well be said to have been based on alliances; they can hardly be adduced as juridical grounds for claims of sovereignty.

The fact on which the Danes based their claim for the Volta district was that, on December 4, 1731, the Ada had sworn allegiance to them. This was done in return for a loan from Christiansborg of 45 ounces of gold which they used to settle their quarrel with Akwamu. This agreement was brought about by the trader, H. H. Sparre. By it, the island of Ada "was to belong to us Danes exclusively" for the purpose of erecting a lodge there. No other nation was to be allowed to trade there, as long as the Danish lodge was maintained. The Danes stipulated that they should have the right to close the lodge in case of war. The treaty was clumsily worded, but it could not reasonably be understood to include sovereign rights. Later, the Danes had helped the Ada on several occasions. Above all, in 1769, when Awuna made war on the Ada, the Danes had helped them to return to their island. Nevertheless, as late as 1793, the jurist J. Schlegel speaks of the African nations on the banks of the Volta as "our allies." [6] What the government at Christiansborg, in the 1760's and 1770's, called the Danish king's property rights, certainly implied no more than that Ada should refrain from trade with other nations.

As a practical defense measure caused by Vitlaar's mission, the Danish Christiansborg government sent off chief merchant Biørn and factor Erasmi to Tubreku, where they caught the Dutchman and some of his native attendants. This was on April 26, 1776. An intercepted letter revealed that he was to have begun building a Dutch lodge at Tubreku on that very day. Vitlaar was taken to Christiansborg and questioned. He told the Danes that he had been given verbal orders to march to Okko; but if the Ada called him to Tubreku, he was to go there instead. On May 4, just as the examination of Vitlaar was over, the garrison of the fort saw a large number of armed natives from Dutch Accra with a Dutch flag storm Osu and Christiansborg from the landward side. The Osu people hastily took up arms, and guns were fired to call the Labadi to the assistance. A battle was fought which lasted until nightfall, and although the attackers far outnumbered the defenders, they were beaten back with considerable losses. The Danish Africans had only one killed and thirteen wounded. Most of the casualties were Labadi: they had rallied bravely, and given proof of great valor. The good result was due partly to the Prøvesten Tower on the western outskirts of Osu, even though the tower had not yet been completed. In it was stationed J. A. Kiøge, and from it small guns were fired on the enemy. Van der Penÿe used this firing as a pretext to hoist the Dutch flag over Fort Crèvecoeur and aim some shots on the tower. Afterward the Danes exhibited a cannon ball which had almost grazed Kiøge.

On the morning of May 8 the Dutch Africans returned, this time in far greater numbers. The Danes estimated their total forces at 3,000. The Danes had obtained 50 Ningo as auxiliaries, and themselves had 300 men. At 8 o'clock the battle was renewed. The enemy would probably have conquered Prøvesten, but in the meantime the tower had been armed with heavier cannons. They were loaded with "coarse quid," that is, leaden bars which had been cut into fragments. Their effect was considerable. Fort Christiansborg fired a few shots, too, and at about noon the attackers retreated inland and took cover in the bush for their usual midday siesta. Meanwhile Fort Christiansborg was kept under fire from Fort Crèvecoeur. The Danes did not answer the fire, probably because their heavy guns were rusty. Late in the afternoon the Dutch natives attacked again, but this time Collins, the governor of the English fort, preceded by the British flag and a white flag, stepped in between the belligerents to try to bring about an armistice. The Danes were quite willing to cease hostilities, but the Dutch demanded freedom for the prisoners taken by the Danes as well as a considerable compensation for their costs. While this was going on, 300 enemy natives marched on Labadi and burnt down the whole town except the houses of the fetish priests. The following days were taken up with negotiations. The Danes had no objection to the Dutch settling at desolate Okko, but now it was their turn to demand either compensation or that the dispute be settled in Europe. Stadlander, the head of Fort Berku, was sent from Elmina to take part in the negotiations, and from Cape Coast Castle, Richard Miles, head of Fort Anamabo, was dispatched to support Collins in his efforts to open negotiations. They were able to obtain an armistice out of the negotiations, and on July 1 the prisoners were handed over; but, of course, they failed to bring about a real settlement of the dispute, or even a lasting armistice.

If we are to believe the native tradition, the Africans called the war the Kotoku-Twerebo war or the war between the flintlock and the powder horn—that is a fratricidal war, both musket and powder horn being necessary to the soldier who wants to fire.[7] For once the natives had not really wanted to go to war. They regarded the dispute as the Europeans' own business, and they did not want to have anything to do with it. Being urged by the Europeans to take up arms, they did not want to offend them. So they agreed to appear with their muskets. They loaded them with gunpowder, but no bullets, and in this way they would produce a lot of noise and smoke without doing anybody any harm. At first everything went well. Then, for some unknown reason, some of the Osu loaded their guns with bullets, and when the Dutch natives saw some of their men being struck by them, they, too, began to fight in earnest.

When it proved impossible to settle the dispute locally the Christiansborg government, as the injured part, felt obliged to have it dealt with by the royal courts in Copenhagen and The Hague. At the same time the Christiansborg authorities demanded heavier artillery and the visit of a frigate from the royal navy to inspire respect for the Danish colors.

While the case was being slowly dragged through the labyrinths of diplomacy, the Danes in Guinea were left to their own devices. Their position was almost as dangerous as in 1729, when Wærøe had endured a most trying siege. Both Fort Christiansborg and Prøvesten had been damaged by Dutch cannon balls. It had been necessary to distribute quantities of gunpowder to the natives. As nobody could feel secure outside the fort, it was packed with human beings inside the walls. It was necessary to procure food for them all. The natives could not travel to their plantations, which were situated some distance inland. If the *Ada* had not brought supplies shortly before, it would have been utterly impossible for the Danes to take up the fight. As matters stood, they did not think they would be able to carry on very long. The Labadi advised the Danes to ask the Akwapim caboceer Atiambo for help. He promised them his support, but the Danes stressed their inability to pay him. All they could do was to flatter him with presents. Nevertheless, he allowed himself to be persuaded because of his blood ties with the Labadi. With a force of 1,000 men, he marched against the above-mentioned native plantations, burnt down the plantation buildings of the Dutch Africans, and carried off their millet and fruit. This remedy proved so effective that the Dutch natives stayed at home.

Next Atiambo marched down to Christiansborg with 600 men "and entered into the Danish service for a monthly pay of 8 rixdollars, slave price." We are further informed that he "ate fetish to swear everlasting loyalty and service to us Danes in whatever cases might befall, as also for the safety of the trade-routes for us Danes and for themselves likewise never to enter into the service of, or accept pay from, the English and Dutch here at Accra, to confirm which his successor and other grandees likewise ate fetish." In addition, he ate fetish to confirm his everlasting friendship with the headmen of the Danish native towns and promised mutual support in all emergencies. The treaty thus signed was called an alliance by the Christiansborg government. It had been costly, but was defended as absolutely indispensable. And it had the added advantage that Atiambo was closely allied with Ashanti.

For some time, there were only minor episodes, such as the kidnapping of individual natives. It was difficult to get a cargo for the *Ada*, but soon trade with Ashanti improved. To get fresh supplies of goods, the Danes traded with French captains, and for some time things went tolerably well. Then, on January 14, 1777, the Dutch commissioners informed the Danes that they had tried in vain to persuade their natives to refer the settlement of the dispute to the diplomats in Europe.[8] The Dutch Africans demanded recognition of their sovereign rights over the Danish African towns. If this proved unacceptable, the Dutch would have to leave the Danish Africans to their fate. Of course, Fort Christiansborg refused to submit to this claim. Soon it was rumored that the Dutch were arming themselves, hiring people from Fanti and Krobbo, and planning the bombardment of the Danish forts. So the Danes again sent for Atiambo, and risked reminding the Ada of their oath of allegiance of 1731. The Dutch tried to buy Atiambo by offering him goods worth 60 ounces of gold, but this was in vain. After a further exchange of letters, on January 30 the Dutch informed the Danes that they had given their natives freedom of action. Several times the Dutch Africans seemed on the point of attacking, but the storm did not break until February 21. On this occasion the guns of Fort Crèvecoeur fired at Fort Christiansborg even before the natives had launched their attack. The attackers did not succeed in subduing the Danes this time either. Like the year before, they were driven back. Afterward they renewed the attack three times, twice with no better results; but on the third time on May 25, 1777, they managed to set fire to Osu with their guns and afterward pillaged it.

A month later, when Governor Hemsen reached the coast on board the frigate *Christiansborg*, he found everything in this sorry state. It was not very fine property which was returned to the Danish king. The Danes and their Africans with wives and children were still sheltered in the fort, while the surrounding native towns had been burnt down. Some of the garrison, including Kiøge, were wounded, and the morale of the natives was very low. Aarestrup had appealed for help to Dadecon, king of Akwamu, by promising him 3,200 rixdollars slave price. If, thanks to this alliance, the Dutch agreed to pay compensation without hostilities breaking out, he was to have a further 1,600 rixdollars. However, Dadecon received an offer from the Dutch also and sided with them. Shortly afterward, when an Ashanti trade expedition turned up outside Christiansborg, it was attacked and robbed by exiled Obrincoran and the Krobbo, acting on an agreement with the Dutch. Next the Danes turned to Approffo, king of Akim. In the meantime, a couple of so-called grand-lieutenants arrived from Ashanti; the Dutch flatly refused to have anything to do with them. On October 19, a favorable reply was received from Approffo. He, however, first had to come to an agreement about the matter with his Ashanti overlord. Now a Dutch government solicitor, van Leefdael, arrived at Fort Crèvecoeur, so that proper negotiations could be initiated. To attend these, Atiambo arrived with all the loyal natives of the Volta district. All these swarms were reducing Christiansborg to starvation. Finally, on November 28, the preliminary drafts for the terms of the armistice were exchanged. After debates on numerous proposals and counter-proposals, the terms were agreed upon. Another month went by, because the Dutch Africans refused to confirm the treaty by eating fetish. They were willing only, under oath, to promise the commandant of their fort to observe the terms of the treaty. So the document could not be dated until February 10, 1778. By this treaty a two-year armistice was arranged while the case was transferred for settlement to Copenhagen and The Hague. In the meantime, the trade routes were to be kept open. Nevertheless, the Dutch Africans stuck to their demand that the Danish Africans recognize them as their lords and masters, and that they beg their permission to rebuild their towns. So the Christiansborg government did not feel secure with them, and the Dutch did not refrain from attempts to buy the native allies of the Danes.

On January 31, the frigate *Christiansborg* was allowed to sail, but only after another, a newly built royal frigate, the *Fredensborg* had arrived.[9] This ship remained in the road until August 1778, and was folowed by the frigate *Rio Volta* which remained until October, and the frigate *Accra* which remained until April 1779. Thus care was taken that there was always support at hand in case fresh attacks were launched. By special royal order the *Fredensborg* brought six cannons, including two heavy ones for twenty-four pound balls, which would be able to deal with Fort Crèvecoeur if need be. From the start the Dutch fort had possessed guns for only eighteen-pound balls. The Copenhagen government tried a diplomatic *démarche* at The Hague, but the Dutch Foreign Affairs Department answered provisionally that it had not been informed about the dispute so far. Annoyed by this official Dutch attitude and enervated by Governor Hemsen's constant clamors for help, in the summer of 1779 the Danish government finally decided to dispatch to the Gold Coast a man-of-war, the *Holsteen*, commanded by Commodore Ulrich Kaas.[10] Its purpose was to strike the Dutch with a holy terror, awe the natives, as well as to keep an eye on events in case the armistice expired before the conflict had been finally settled. The man-of-war was going to the Cape of Good Hope, anyhow, to convoy Danish vessels returning from China and India, so, it could easily make a secret call at Christiansborg. Commodore Kaas was allowed a free hand to do what was needed after consultation with Hemsen. In case the Dutch had broken the armistice before it expired, he was to use his full powers to revenge this crime. Otherwise, he was to work either for a peaceful settlement or for the prolongation of the armistice. During his stay off Christiansborg, Kaas was given no opportunity to use force. So, to stabilize the position, he landed some artillery and thirty soldiers, and thus temporarily enabled Hemsen to hit back, if he were attacked. By negotiations in January 1780, therefore, the armistice was prolonged for two years to allow negotiations in Europe to come to a conclusion.[11] The European governments, too, had agreed upon a two-year prolongation of the armistice.

The diplomatic negotiations ended inconclusively. The Danish minister to The Hague, a Swiss named A. F. de Saint-Saphorin who was one of the elder Bernstorff's protégés, was not very talented, for he made a number of contradictory proposals for the settlement of the dispute. He had been instructed to demand compensation and satisfaction for the Dutch insults against the Danish king's dignity and territorial rights. In addition, he was to put out feelers with a view toward obtaining the cession of Fort Crèvecoeur and perhaps other forts to the Danes as part of the compensation. The Dutch first tried to get out of it by reprimanding their representatives on the coast and recalling van der Penÿe; afterward they retorted by a number of counter claims. The Danish government left the reply to these claims to former Governor Aarestrup, a man deeply versed in the history of the coast. Much time was spent in proposals and counter proposals, the Dutch evidently trying to gain time, but meanwhile a train of events started in Guinea which completely changed the balance of power.

After the prolongation of the armistice the Dutch in Guinea had indulged in no further hostilities against the Danes other than the capture of a boat with its cargo. By the summer of 1780 they had become very tractable. The reason for this change of attitude was the war which had broken out between Holland and England, because Holland had joined the Armed Neutrality Alliance. The war ended in disaster for Holland's colonial power, and ramifications of these struggles reached even remote places like the Guinea coast. During the end of February 1781 an armed English trading vessel made prizes of several Dutch traders off the coast, while a privately owned Danish vessel in the road off Elmina was left unmolested. Under these circumstances the Dutch deigned to offer the Christiansborg Danes compensation for the boat they had captured and, as the armistice was again expiring, to make proposals for its prolongation for another year. Fort Christiansborg was now under the command of energetic Jens Adolph Kiøge, who became temporary governor[12] after Hemsen had died on December 2, 1780. He tried to make his own conditions. He demanded that the Dutch release all their prisoners, and that their Africans eat fetish with the Danish Africans. The Dutch, however, would not agree, so Kiøge had to be content with the prolongation of the armistice. In March he received a Dutch document to which he was asked to add his signature.

But now the hand of fate descended upon the Dutch. They managed to hold out at Elmina, though the smaller Dutch forts in Fanti fell into the hands of the English, and at last the time was ripe for Fort Crèvecoeur. Beforehand, the Dutch governor-general, Volckmar, sent word to the Danes, warning them that they should be careful as there were rumors that Denmark, too, was at war with Britain. At the last minute, when danger was imminent, this gentleman did not shrink even from calling upon the Danes for assistance. The English had captured six Dutch merchantmen but had allowed two of them to return with Dutch refugees to Europe. Now the Dutch feared that these vessels might be captured by other English men-of-war while homeward bound. So they asked that these ships be allowed to sail under Danish colors and with

Danish sea-passes. How could Kiøge escape the thought that this proposal was intended to create difficulties for him with the English?

On April 1, 1782, the English opened an attack on the Dutch fort. With the support of the Accra, the Dutch garrison put up a brave defense until April 18, when, under cover of night, they spiked the guns and stealthily left the fort. In the morning the Danes informed the English of this fact, and added that they had heavy counterclaims to make for all the crimes the Dutch had committed against them. Of course, the English would not hear of delivering the fort into the hands of the Danes. Instead, they offered them one of the small forts in Fanti, but Kiøge did not care to accept. The English carried the best part of the artillery off to Fort James, broke up the rest, and set the woodwork of the fort on fire. Thus, Fort Crèvecoeur was demolished, but not razed to the ground. Nevertheless, a thorn in the flesh of the Danes at Christiansborg was removed, and their situation looked somewhat brighter.

During the hostilities between the Dutch and British, the wives and children of both the Danish and Dutch Africans sought shelter in the Danish fort. After Crèvecoeur was silenced, the commandants of the lesser Dutch forts at Temma and Ponny on the Lower Coast thought that they had no possibility of defending themselves. They relinquished their posts and came running to Christiansborg, begging for protection. Finally, the commandant of Fort Crèvecoeur turned up with a few attendants. For a fortnight they had undergone every kind of hardship among the interior peoples. While there they had been sent some food supplies by the Danes. Nevertheless, they had been reduced to starvation, and now humbly begged for protection. This appeal to Governor Kiøge's generosity was successful. He received them all on the condition that they remain strictly neutral. This change in his relations with the Dutch cannot but have pleased him.

Meanwhile, he thought about the matter, and found the time ripe for action. He had received the Dutch terms for the prolongation of the armistice, but he did not sign them. So it was up to him to end the armistice. When he learnt that the governor of Elmina wanted the Dutch refugees to remain at Fort Christiansborg, because he hoped that the natives would again help them regain their former power and honors, Kiøge considered that the refugees had broken their promise of neutrality. Consequently, on May 25 he sent the document back unsigned, and demanded that the refugees be ordered to leave Fort Christiansborg. In reply to the Dutch protest he said that he did not feel authorized to sign an armistice with them, because they were unable to fulfill its terms. Nevertheless, he was willing to live up to the rules regulating the friendship of Holland and Denmark.

However, he did not allow these rules to limit him. Instead, he made prompt use of the possibilities offered by the new situation. He arranged a meeting at Fort Christiansborg for July 2, 1782. The caboceers, head-men, and lieutenants of Osu and Labadi, Tessing, and Little (now called Small) Ningo came together. The Tessings, who had joined the Danish service in the 1750's, now came forward demanding readmission to the service of their former masters. Governor Kiøge explained to them that the Danes were willing to accept their offer on condition that they would, on all occasions, remain loyal and obedient to the Danes and work for the good of their trade exclusively without ever entering into al-liance with other European nations. Within their own territories they were to protect and defend the Danish king's flag with such prerogatives as were customary there. They replied that they had often bitterly re-gretted their defection, and that they were now prepared to eat fetish to confirm their acceptance of the Danish conditions. In return for this, they asked for Danish protection and alliances with Osu and Labadi so that they would stand as one man and brother on all occasions. After this, fetish was eaten as was the custom of the country.

Kiøge's defense of these doings was as follows: the Tessings had de-fected to the Dutch, when the latter paid their debts for them. For this they had repaid the Dutch by risking their own lives in the defense of Fort Crèvecoeur. After the departure of the Dutch, their Africans were free to choose a European protector. This protection was indispensable for them, for without it they would be captured and sold into slavery by the interior peoples. The natives were masters in their own country and could deliver it to whomever they preferred, as long as it had no European fortifications. Kiøge's contract with the people of Tessing (and Small Ningo) implied, according to the political thought of the day, that he received them and their territories "into the king's rights, protection, and defence." In modern terms this meant that Tessing had become a Danish protectorate.

The other natives of Accra and surrounding area, of course, wished for a short respite, but after six months Kiøge thought that the time was ripe for binding them over to the Danish king, too. On December 28, 1782, caboceers, grandees, and some of the young warriors from the Danish native towns of Osu, Labadi, Tessing, Small Ningo, Great Ningo, and Ada were assembled with their peers from Accra (the town next to Fort Crèvecoeur), Temma, and Ponny.[13] They had all agreed in advance to eat fetish on the same conditions as had already been accepted by Tessing. The Accra were the first to take the oath; but afterward when the Ponny people were about to do so, the Danes noticed a kind of wavering among the Accra. So they stepped forward and said that they would protect only those who were truly loyal. They would not allow other nations to take that oath that day; on the contrary, they were willing even to ab-solve the Accra from the oath they had already sworn. This the Accra could not face, and the caboceer of Ponny declared that he and his people had formerly belonged to the Danes. Both he and his father had served the Danes of old. Now his country belonged to himself alone; he was dependent on no one, and he did not share his country with anyone. Consequently, he was entitled to enter into an alliance with the Danes. Nevertheless, the Danes refused to let him take the oath that day. Kiøge wanted everything to be correct, but did not change his policy. Otho (Otto), the caboceer of Accra, was granted a monthly gratuity of 8 rixdollars bos, another Accra grandee, half as much, with the reservation that this agreement must be approved by the Danish king. Left to themselves, Ponny and Temma realized that they had to retain their application for Danish protection. A week later, on January 4, 1783, the Ponny turned up and, in the presence of all the Accra, swore an oath of friendship and loyalty to the Danes. After another week, on January 11, it was the Temma's turn to swear the same oath. Both caboceers were granted gratuities of two rixdollars each, and each of them was presented with one of the Danish Trade Office's maces. Afterward, the ruins of the lesser Dutch forts, or fortified lodges, were destroyed. Thus, having extended the power of the Danes, Kiøge invited the Krobbo down from their hills, and made peace with them after they had given him their prisoners.

With cunning and daring Kiøge had seized the opportunity to expand the Danish sphere of influence and to obtain some compensation for the disasters caused by the Dutch. The truth was that they had garnered their harvest as a result of the British exploits. The Copenhagen government, as far as we know, was very pleased with Kiøge's work. In the meantime, the total losses caused by the Dutch attacks had been calculated.[14] According to Aarestrup's calculation, Bargum's Society had lost 91,824 rixdollars, the Royal Danish Trade Office had lost 50,000 rixdollars, and the total losses amounted to 200,000 rixdollars or 2 barrels of gold. There was no financial compensation to be hoped for, so it was thought just as well to cling to the newly acquired territories. The Danish government was quite pleased to possess an unbroken territory, stretching from Christiansborg to Keta. The only foreign fort on the whole of this stretch of land was a small English one at Prampram. If this strip could be preserved in Danish hands, government circles were inclined to take an optimistic view of Crèvecoeur, whose natives might prove unreliable and troublesome. In any case, the Danish government decided to let Kiøge maintain the new contracts with the natives. In Europe it could, as a matter of form, continue the pressure on the Dutch for financial compensations. The actual occupation by the Danes of the Dutch forts was not to be attempted, unless all European attempts to get compensation proved fruitless. The Foreign Office asked for and obtained royal assent for this policy.

A formal settlement with the Dutch was never reached. By the Peace of Paris in 1784, Britain agreed to return its Guinean forts to Holland.

So, in the autumn of 1785 the transfer of a great number of forts took place, including even Crèvecoeur, which still lay in its demolished state. The Dutch application to the British commissioner for the delivery of Tessing, Temma, and Ponny was refused, and the commissioner reminded them that these places had never been occupied by Britain. So the Dutch had to try to get hold of these three places without British assistance. Some months before, an assistant had been sent to Christiansborg to look after the Dutch affairs; but finding that he had been provided with goods for sale to the natives, Kiøge sent him back. Thus a native chief of Dutch Accra had to look after the Dutch slaves working on the millet plantations farther upcountry. When, in September, the Dutch tried to regain possession of Tessing, Temma, and Ponny, they met with a flat refusal from the Danes. (On the other hand, Kiøge did not try to prevent the Dutch from repossessing Accra, the native town situated below the ruins of their former fort. He demanded merely that, if the Accra were to be absolved from their oath of alliance to Denmark, their debts to the Christiansborg government must be paid first.) A complaint of this refusal was sent from Elmina to Holland. It was then sent on to Copenhagen through diplomatic channels, but there the matter ended. In 1790-1791, the Dutch authorities at Elmina were still demanding the return of the three native towns. However, when the governor of Fort Christiansborg asked for instructions from Copenhagen, he was reassured by being informed that the state of utter confusion which presently prevailed in the affairs of the Dutch West India Company made it highly improbable that the Dutch would have recourse to arms.

The war between Britain and Holland put an end to Dutch usurpation of colonies throughout the world. From then on, the Danes were no longer seriously bothered by their neighbors at Fort Crèvecoeur. Fate had been good enough to grant the Danes revenge for all the wrongs suffered from these troublesome neighbors throughout the previous half-century. At the same time, very important changes were made in the state's legal rights to the Danish territories. Formerly, it had been generally accepted that the Danish forts stood on rented land, that the sovereign rights belonged to the native princes, and that the contracts made by the Danes with certain African nations must be regarded as alliances. Now the Danish government began to use a more precise terminology and to aim at the claim for sovereign rights on the coast. The Christiansborg government now made their native allies swear by an oath to be loyal subjects of the Danish king.

Thus the foundations of a real colony were being laid. It seemed likely that, except for the English fort at Prampram, this colony would extend along an unbroken coastal strip for 150 kilometers and would have incalculable possibilities for inland expansion.

17 / THE BALTIC-GUINEA TRADING COMPANY AND FORTS KONGENSTEN AND PRINSENSTEN

AFTER THE LIQUIDATION of Bargum's Trading Society, the Guinea traffic remained open not only to ships sent by the Kongelige Handels-Direktion (Royal Trade Office), but also to privately owned ships according to a royal decree of May 12, 1777.[1] So the traffic was subject to no other restrictions than those inherent in the new law concerning the rights of citizenship. The ships had to be built and fitted within the king's territories, be manned with subjects of His Majesty, and only in emergencies was it permissible to hire foreign sailors. The maritime trade was still exempt from duty in Guinea proper. Nevertheless, private citizens seldom used their right to trade in Guinea. The traffic was left to the Royal Trading Office, which had a number of new ships built for it.

This system was short-lived, for the government was not satisfied with it. By royal order in council of January 4, 1779, plans were initiated for the improvement of the Guinea trade. The Government Tax Office proposed an investment of 50,000 rixdollars in the slave trade. Trade was booming at the time; so after the airing of various projects, a charter was granted to the Kongelige Danske Østersøiske og Guineiske Handels-Compagnie (Royal Danish Baltic-Guinea Trading Company).[2] The aim of this company was the same as that of the private company which had gone out of business in 1774: namely, to combine Copenhagen's Baltic trade with its westward trade. An added incentive to the establishment of the new company came from the new Baltic-North Sea canal. Digging of the canal had just begun in Holstein, and it aroused great expectations. The company not only took over ships built for the Guinea trade but also the fleet of the Greenland Trade Office. They amounted to a total of 37 ships—everything connected with the company was on an equally grand scale. The boom in Danish overseas shipping because of the American Revolution made prospects seem golden. To give the com-

143

pany a quick start, the government presented it with ships and also warehouses, yards, etc., as well as large sums of money. Property that the Guinea Trade Office surrendered was valued at 501,661 rixdollars, that of the Greenland Trade Office at 806,060 rixdollars, and real estate in Copenhagen at 250,000 rixdollars. To this the government at once added 628,896 rixdollars, so that the assets totalled 2,276,612 rixdollars. The total aimed at was 3,000,000 rixdollars. In return 30,000 shares each worth 100 rixdollars were issued, which the shareholders could buy from the Stats-Balance-Direktionen (Government-Balance-Office). In this way the Government recovered the huge sum it had invested in the Guinea traffic since 1776.

By royal mandate of April 10, 1782, the company was granted a monopoly of the trade to the Danish forts and lodges in Guinea. Although 9000 rixdollars annually for repairs on the forts had been granted since 1776, the sum was increased to 25,000 rixdollars per annum.[3] As usual the government was very liberal with promises of exemption from duties, and, in addition, it promised a premium of 16 rixdollars per commercial last for armed ships and 10 rixdollars for ordinary trading vessels.

The privileges granted also included full protection for foreign crews. The company was ordered to preserve the king's rights on the Coast, such as the property rights to the banks of the Rio Volta. Expenses incurred in the opening of new factories would be refunded by the government. The company was governed by a board of directors who were paid on a commission basis, the first members being appointed by the king. The board was always to include three representatives of the Government Balance Office and three members elected by the shareholders.

The time for the foundation of the company was well chosen, and the shares were quickly sold. At the outset 1,500,000 rixdollars' worth were sold in two days, and afterwards 9,000,000 rixdollars' worth were sold in four hours. Observing this keen interest, the government only sold 2,000,000 rixdollars' worth and kept the third million rixdollars' worth of shares in its own treasury until 1783, when the Baltic-Guinea Company was allowed to buy them in installments.

The company's warehouses in Copenhagen were situated near the Customs House, but its offices were installed in the Almshouse in Amaliegade. About Easter 1784 three statesmen, Counts J. G. Moltke, Ernst Schimmelmann, and Chr. D. Reventlow, with Rear-Admiral Count Adam Ferdinand Moltke, Councillor of Conferences J. Fr. Heinrichs, and Councillors of State Fr. C. Trant and J. D. Vett are mentioned as directors. J. G. Moltke gave up his membership on the board when he resigned as prime minister in April 1784. J. D. Vett was succeeded by Councillor of Justice E. G. Meer. After that, the only count still on the board was Count Schimmelmann, while among the members we again meet N.U. Aarestrup, the former governor. Throughout all these vicissitudes, however, the control of the company remained firmly in the hands of the government. The position of the West Indian Company, founded in 1778, was somewhat similar.

The Guinea traffic had prospered in the days of the Royal Trade Office and continued to do so after the Baltic-Guinea Company had taken over. If anything, trade became brisker. About one third of the company's ships were constantly plying the triangular route between Copenhagen, Guinea, and the West Indies. Besides, many ships left Copenhagen for Guinea and returned directly. Four ships, the *Accra*, *Count Bernstorff*, *Fredensborg*, and *Christiansborg*, left Copenhagen for Guinea in the autumn of 1780. They all returned safely from the West Indies in June or July 1782. In the course of 1781 no less than five ships were sent to Guinea: the *Kammerherre Schack*, *Upernavik*, *Gehejmeraad Gregers Juel*, *Ningo,* and *Grev E. Schimmelmann*. Similar numbers were sent in the following years. Some of these, strangely enough, bore Greenland names. In the course of three years the following ships had to be written off as lost: the *Accra* in 1783, the *Printz Friedrich Haab* and the *Geheime-Raad Stampe* in 1785. In addition to the company, a few individual shipowners sent ships to Guinea, but not, as far as we know, to the Danish forts.[4] Only a little more than half of the ships loaded up with slaves at the Danish settlements; the rest purchased their slaves on the Upper Coast. Nonetheless, the number of slaves shipped from the Danish places increased, and Danish Guinean holdings grew and prospered commercially as well as politically under Kiøge's rule.

Danish political activity in Guinea did not come to a standstill after the treaties were signed with the former Dutch natives of Tessing, Temma, and Ponny. Having brought these towns within his sphere of influence, Kiøge made up his mind to put conditions around the Volta River under control. Here the Danes had opened the lodge on the island of Ada in 1731, the Keta lodge in 1744, had been trying to run a lodge at Way since 1757, and built the Popo lodge much farther east in 1772. The first three of these lodges had gone through various times of trouble. Sometimes under stress they had had to be abandoned, then later reoccupied; at other times they were threatened by the natives and saved only by cunning and/or money. Often, when in the hands of sick or fraudulent factors, they had lost money. At other times they had given considerable compensation by providing abundant slaves for the cargoes. Conditions had been most peaceful at the fourth lodge, because the power of the king of Popo, who befriended the Danes, was relatively stable. Life at each of these outposts could have provided the raw materials for a novel.

The greatest damage to the Danish settlements was caused by Awuna's inroads.[5] This nation had frequently sacked towns and villages and blocked the roads, so that trade was brought to a standstill. Contrary to the customs of the country, they would keep all runaway slaves from the forts and trading stations. Worst of all were their attacks upon the native allies of the Danes, especially the Ada. With them they waged perpetual wars over the boundary of their fishing rights on the river. In 1769 they had completely destroyed the town of Ada. Now they were at war again. They preferred to attack when the waters of the Volta River were rising and the island in the river was flooded. On October 26, 1780, 1,900 Awuna took the Ada by surprise. With only a couple of hours in which to prepare a defense, only the aristocrats and the young warriors were carried to safety on the mainland. Two hundred Ada women and children were taken prisoners, some were beheaded, and the island town was burnt for the second time. The Awuna then threatened the Danes and promised death to Governor Kiøge. Two years later, they sent an armed band up the river to destroy a Danish building which they feared would be turned into a fort. Finally, in the summer of 1783, they planned to demolish the Ada factory and set upon a Danish force headed by Governor Kiøge, which was marching towards Keta.

So Kiøge had been given sufficient reason to interfere. Earlier, Hemsen had chosen a spot west of the river suitable for a fort. The Ada now declared that they were no longer able to defend the lodge on the island, though it was covered by a small redoubt with a couple of guns. Kiøge adopted the plan of erecting a fort on the mainland, and to cover himself against Awuna, he entered into alliances with a number of native nations. While a mixed army from various localities was encamped by the riverside, the cornerstone was laid on October 15, 1783, for a fort which was to be called Kongensten. It was situated at a distance of about seven kilometers from the sea and within musket-range of the river. As the delta offered no stones for miles around building materials had to be brought at great cost from far away. Most of them came by canoe from Fort Christiansborg and were dragged over land from the river mouth by the natives. The fort was designed to be fairly large, ninety meters long and almost equally wide, and a small bastion was to be at each corner. At first, however, only the two bastions nearest to the riverbend were completed. Close to the river a redoubt was built to hinder enemy attacks across the river.

On February 14, 1786, on the open ground between the fort and the redoubt the general of the united native forces was solemnly appointed. The choice fell upon Otho, the already mentioned caboceer of Dutch Accra. The Danes did not regard him as absolutely reliable, but he proved worthy of his high office and did not disappoint them in any way. Among those present was Atiambo, the caboceer of Akwapim, who on this occasion was given the title of "Duke." A few days later there was another ceremony, and the whole army swore the oath of allegiance. On March 21, the Danes occupied the new fort. Preparations completed, a campaign was launched against Awuna on March 25. Governor Kiøge and other Danes took part in this campaign, which was graphically described in some published letters by another participant, the physician Paul Isert. A peace offer by the Awuna had been rejected, because they had not been willing to send hostages demanded by the Danes.[6]

First the troops traveled by canoes and on foot to the mouth of the Volta River, trying, after a couple of days, to cross the river under cover of large canoes armed with cannon. However, the enemy had ensconced itself on the opposite bank, and the allies of the Danes dared not force the landing. Instead, they marched around the enemy. Under the cover of night, the Danes and their allies were rowed up the river to the land of the Krepis. This expedition was made by 2,000 men. For want of sufficient numbers of boats, it had to be made in two sailings. All the next day was spent marching through districts east of the river, towards the sea. In the course of the following night a terrible storm came up. At last, on the third day, the thirtieth of March, 1784, after wading through almost impassable reed-covered swamps, they found themselves face to face with the Awuna, who lay in ambush among thickets and reeds. The Danish victory in the battle of Atocco was won by the Ada and other Danish Volta natives. Wading through swamps with the water up to their necks and carrying the muskets on their heads, they crept round the enemy and attacked them from the rear, exposing them to double fire. This victory cost the Danish party three lives and about fifty wounded. After the rout of the Awuna, Atocco and several other native towns were burnt by the victors. Before nightfall, they reached the town of Awuna, which was also devoured by flames. The enemy dead were decapitated, and the spoils of cattle and poultry provided food for a grand feast, which ended with the natives "saluting the victory" in an orgy of African savagery. The plantations of the defeated enemy were destroyed.

Afterward the expedition continued eastward along the narrow isthmus separating the sea and the Keta lagoon, a swampy lake, 70-80 kilometers in length with an outlet into the Volta River. On the march the expedition passed Way, which was also sacked, and the animals which the retreating enemy had been forced to leave behind were ruthlessly slaughtered. On their arrival at Keta, the Danish expedition found both the Danish lodge and the native town empty. The inhabitants feigned neutrality, but earlier they had signed an alliance with Awuna and were hiding in the inland bush. The factor of the Danish trading station had fled into the forest and taken refuge in the friendly town of Aflahu. On April 4, with reinforcements from Aflahu, Popo, and other towns, the Danish army numbered 3,000 men. Some days later it marched on by

way of Augoja, another friendly town, to Pottebra. Since the inhabitants
had fled, the Danish party made this town their camp. They stayed for
a month there at the eastern end of the Keta lagoon, while allies came
crowding in and increased the army to 4,000 men. On May 11, they
broke camp and marched inland, very doubtful about the reliability of
this huge mixed crowd of warriors belonging to various nations. On
May 14, an enemy camp was sighted, and a regular battle was fought. The
camp was successfully conquered, and the enemy retreated. This did not
amount to a decisive victory. For want of munitions and provisions the
Danish party withdrew to Pottebra. The battle had cost them 12 lives
and 60 wounded; the enemy had 60 killed and 150 wounded. Thus, it
could be reckoned a victory for Governor Kiøge and his European
attendants.

In the course of the following days Ofoly Bossum, son of the late
Assiambo, king of Popo, arrived. He swore the same oath of allegiance
as other natives who had come pouring in, but immediately he set to
work as a peacemaker. Before opening negotiations Awuna demanded ten
hostages, but received only six. On the other hand the Danes had
promised four but only sent three. After a fortnight's negotiation, the
peace treaty was signed on June 18, 1784. In it, the Danes secured the
right to build a fort near Keta and a free passage through Awuna. They
were also given permission to set up a trading station in the capital of
Awuna, and Awuna ate fetish to swear that they would never trade with
any other European nation than the Danes.

A few days later, on June 22, 1784, the foundation stone of Fort
Prinsensten was laid.[7] Several earlier Danish governors had wanted a
fort in this locality. Now the king of Popo and his brother took part in
the ceremonies and provided the military forces necessary to cover building operations. The fort was built to the same design as Fort Kongensten.
It was situated at a distance of 200-300 meters from the beach which was
exactly the width of its strip of white driftsand. The adjacent native town
was relatively large and well provided with fresh water, game cattle and
fish from a nearby arm of the Volta. On the whole, the Keta did not
particularly care to become dependents of a fort. But, not having helped
the Awuna, their former allies, in the war, they thought it the safest
plan to have a refuge, if the Awuna should decide to seek vengeance.

The permission given to build a lodge in Awuna-land led to the
setting up of a lodge in Aflahu. Andreas Riegelsen Biørn became commander of Fort Prinsensten and Paul Isert, the physician, commander of
Fort Kongsten. Both had taken part in the war.

After these great exploits, Governor Kiøge hastily returned to Fort
Christiansborg to send reports about his war successes to his employers
in Copenhagen and to persuade them to sanction the building of the two
forts and the peace treaty. He had given proof again of his ability to

grasp the possibilities inherent in a political situation, widened the Danish sphere of influence on the Gold Coast, and prepared the ground for a real colonization of the country. With the support of the king of Popo, he had struck terror into the hearts of Awuna and prevented the natives east of the Volta from entering into permanent relations with the other European nations.

These tidings, of course, must have seemed highly gratifying to the board of the Baltic-Guinea Company in Copenhagen.[8] The board felt obliged to explain to the government all the advantages resulting from the building of the Forts Kongensten and Prinsensten. By so doing, they hoped to secure financial aid for the erection of the two forts as laid down in the charter. They asked for no less than 28,000 rixdollars for the completion of the forts and 6,000 rixdollars annually for repairs, plus compensation for the war against Awuna. Startled by these enormous requests, the government ordered Chamberlain Poul Rosenørn and State Councillor F. C. Trant of the West Indian and Guinea Finance and General Customs Office to examine whether the forts were necessary and the war was justified. Their findings were favorable to the company.

So early in 1785 a royal assent was passed, sanctioning the Awuna war and promising a contribution to the erection of the forts.[9] On the other hand the government refused an annual grant for repairs on the forts. The slave market still seemed so favorable that this aid seemed superfluous. On the other hand, the company was ordered to send suitable presents to the king of Popo out of gratitude for his loyalty to Denmark. Kiøge, who earlier had been awarded the *Pro Meritis* medal, was raised to the rank of colonel, the highest military rank ever to be attained by a Danish governor in Guinea.

While the trading company's prospects in Africa seemed quite promising, its position in the home country soon changed. In 1784 the dividend was still 10 per cent for the previous year, and in the winter of 1784-85 the government was prepared to entrust the company with new tasks and offer further subsidies. Then the recession set in. It was caused by the decline of Danish shipping after the conclusion of the American War of Independence, when the powers of Western Europe were again able to concentrate on trade and shipping. The value of the company's property was reduced; its shares slumped. All calculations proved wrong. The sums needed for installments payable to the Royal Exchequer for the last third of the shares could not be found. So in the autumn of 1785, the board of directors appealed to the government, wailing loudly and asserting that it was the government's duty to help them. At the same time the West Indian Company faced similar troubles. The Finance Collegium (ministry of finance) admitted that, since His Majesty had founded two such companies, invited all his subjects to become shareholders, kept the management almost entirely in his own hands, and encouraged the launching of great schemes, the public could not but expect to profit from them. Consequently, the government was liable to pay compensations for any losses incurred. As a matter of form, the company was ordered to set up a committee to look into the state of affairs. Next the government remitted most of the debts payable to the Royal Exchequer, as, obviously, the sale of the company's assets would entail still heavier losses. Further, by assent of July 14, 1786, the king took over the company's bank debts. His Majesty even opened new credit for the company at the bank greater than the old one. To this he added the promise to pay the interest on 400,000 rixdollars spent by the company on raw materials for Danish industry and on the products of this industry. Out of this arrangement grew the Industry and Manufacture Fund, which tendered considerable loans for the advancement of industry. The total subsidies paid to the company amounted to more than 2,000,000 rixdollars. Nevertheless, the king left it to the shareholders to decide whether the company was to continue. If it was to continue, the shareholders who preferred to withdraw could obtain bonds guaranteed by the king in exchange for their shares. When a majority of the shareholders decided to carry on, 5,333 shares were annulled, and their owners accepted a bond worth 75 rixdollars for each 100 rixdollars share. In the end, therefore, the Baltic-Guinea Company involved the government in very considerable losses. What had seemed a brilliant idea in 1781 turned into a major fiasco.[10]

Even the government's enormous subsidies were not considered sufficient to stabilize the company. When some independent businessmen came forward, declaring themselves willing to carry on the Guinea trade, the Finance Collegium jumped at the offer. Most of the remaining shareholders were paid off with bonds worth 70 rixdollars per share, and the company formally became royal property. On August 11, 1787, Finance Minister Ernst Schimmelmann and the Finance Collegium signed a 28-year contract for the continuation of the Guinea trade with Frederic de Coninck, a Dutch-born Copenhagen merchant and shipowner. Other signatories to the contract were de Coninck's partner, Niels Lunde Reiersen, and his son-in-law, W. Pingel. One or two other merchants also joined the firm, for instance, Jeppe Praetorius, a former bookkeeper of Bargum's Society who now was an independent shipowner. The new firm assumed the name of Pingel, Meyer, Praetorius, and Company, and afterwards changed to Duntzfeld, Meyer, and Company. It was known to its contemporaries as "The Guinea Entrepreneurs." [11] By its contract, this firm was to buy the company's assets with 2,333 Baltic-Guinea Company shares, which would then be annulled; it was to pay 400,000 rixdollars to the banking-office at Altona and 84,000 to Statens Synkende Fond (The Government's Decreasing Fund); and lastly it was under obligation to pay 37,000 rixdollars per annum interest and installments on the bonds not guaranteed by the king, a total of 9,000 shares minus the already mentioned 2,333. Thus, the Baltic-Guinea Company was ended, even before the accounts of Bargum's Society had been finally settled. Numerous accounts were kept running on; claims and counter claims continued circulating between the Royal Exchequer and the two companies throughout the 1780's, adding to the complications of the accounts of the Guinea trade.

In consequence of the contract of 1787, the old regulations and conditions under which the Baltic-Guinea Company had worked were to remain in force until, after careful consideration, new regulations would be introduced. The king promised annual subsidies for repairs on the forts amounting to 25,000 rixdollars. His Majesty even granted 4,550 rixdollars for the new forts, and afterwards the total annual subsidy amounted to 30,000 rixdollars. In return for these favors the government retained a certain control. The finance minister, or the first deputy of the West Indian and Guinea General Interest and Customs Office, was to sign all outgoing correspondence to the coast concerning war and peace and sovereignty. The same officials were also to sign instructions for the Christiansborg government. On the other hand, the king also promised to free the entrepreneurs from all risks due to enemy raids and the preservation of Danish sovereign rights. In fact, the terms granted to the entrepreneurs were very favorable. Finance Minister Schimmelmann himself secretly invested 24,000 rixdollars in the venture.

The number of sailings to Guinea was very sensibly reduced in consequence of the difficulties of the Baltic-Guinea Company. In 1781 five company ships had been sent to Guinea, five in 1782, seven in 1783, nine in 1784, and eight in 1785. Now the number of ships was reduced: in 1786 to three, in 1787 to three, in 1788 to two, and in 1789 to two. There was no such decline in the numbers of slaves bought and sold at the Danish settlements as long as Governor Kiøge remained on the Coast. In 1777, 485 slaves had been shipped, 745 in 1778, 699 in 1779, and 462 in 1780; the numbers rose in 1781 to 1,258, in 1782 to 819, in 1783 to 1,011, in 1784 to 1,155, in 1785 to 1,257, in 1786 to 1,363, and in 1787 to 1,226. Only in 1788 did the number sink to 995, and in 1789 to 594. The total number of slaves sold by the Danish settlements during the period from the opening of the royal trade on July 1, 1777, to the end of October, 1789, amounted to 12,060. Of these slaves 3,945 had been bought at Fort Christiansborg, 2,641 at Fort Fredensborg, 1,667 at Keta-Prinsensten, 1,566 at Ada-Kongensten, and 1,520 at Popo. Besides from May 1, 1783, a total of 227 slaves had been shipped at Ponny, and from June 1, 1784, a total of 484 slaves at Aflahu. Of the total number of slaves for this period 9,679 were carried in Danish ships belonging to the king or the company. These ships also bought 7,434 slaves on the Upper Coast. During the passage 2,706 or 15.7 per cent died. Of the rest 6,229 were sold in the Danish West Indian Islands, and 8,176 to other islands. From other sources it appears that in 1785, a total of 4,000 slaves were sent from the Danish settlements in eight ships, four of which were Danish. That the Africans were not the only sufferers during the voyages will be seen from the fact that, of 2,004 Danish sailors who sailed in the Guinea ships in the period 1777-1789, no less than 691, or more than a third, died during the voyage.[12]

While the trade changed hands in Copenhagen, Governor Kiøge continued his constructive work in Guinea. In 1787 he built a small fort near Tessing and named it Augustaborg for Crown Prince Frederick's beautiful sister. He also had time to lay the foundation stone for a fort near Ponny, which he named Isegram or Isegrace. In the meantime, Kiøge's health was broken. He resigned and left Fort Christiansborg on April 21, 1788. He reached Copenhagen safely, and by royal order of January 21, 1789, he was formally relieved of his governorship. The fact that Kiøge was granted 1,000 rixdollars as an annual retirement allowance until another post could be found for him is sufficient proof of His Majesty's appreciation of his services.[13]

Still the home-coming was made bitter for him. Before leaving Guinea, he had paid 39,000 rixdollars out of his own fortune into the treasury at Fort Christiansborg. Now, on his arrival at Copenhagen he was not allowed to draw this sum. The company looked into the state of his affairs and came to the conclusion that he had saved up more money during his governorship than he could have made by legal methods. His pay was 2,000 rixdollars per annum plus a percentage on the slave trade which yielded him almost as much again. Even if, over and above his income, certain small profits would be permissible, it was impossible to reach the mentioned amount of 39,000 rixdollars. Nor was he known to have possessed a large fortune at his appointment to the governorship. So Pingel, Meyer, Praetorius, and Company refused to let him draw the money. Kiøge took the case into court, but he died in 1789 from "chagrin" as his widow declared. For 28 years he had served energetically in Guinea, consolidated Denmark's power on the coast, and laid the foundations of a real colony. Also due to his splendid business acumen he raised Danish trade to its all-time height. His private thrift may have been a blot on his escutcheon but it must be remembered that the investigation of his conduct was left almost entirely to his successor, A. R. Biørn. As it will soon be made clear, Biørn was not a friend of Kiøge. It must be borne in mind how difficult it was to find an able man who was willing to expose himself to the rigors of the hot African climate, especially if he was not allowed to try to look to his own profit. Kiøge's case raises the question of whether the Danish authorities were not too strict in the treatment of their officials. Who would run the enormous risks if deprived of the dream of a golden home-coming? Kiøge never forgot the interests of the Danish Government and the company. He had deserved a happier conclusion of his active life.

There was no one as able to carry on after Kiøge. His successor had great difficulty in keeping his acquired sphere of influence from falling apart. On Kiøge's departure, Johan Friedrich Kipnasse took over as temporary governor.[14] He had been chief trader and commandant of Fort Fredensborg, but was narrow-minded and took the squabbles with the natives too seriously. Dangerous unrest arose in the neighborhood of Fort Prinsensten. An African aristocrat named Dekkenie had been killed by persons from the fort, and his brother, Bontzi, had moved to Pottebra. From thence he tried to hinder Danish trade, and gradually the trade routes beyond the Volta district were blocked. Later the roads to Ashanti were closed for months, because a couple of native lieutenants felt that they had been badly treated at Fort Christiansborg. They even maintained that they had been whipped. This business was to cost the Christiansborg government goods worth quite a few benda, before it was finally settled.

Kipnasse's rule was shortlived. When Kiøge was allowed to retire, Andreas Riegelsen Biørn was appointed governor, and given the rank of captain.[15] Like Kiøge, he had spent many years on the Coast and had taken part in the 1784-85 campaign against Awuna. At the time of his appointment to the governorship, Biørn was in Copenhagen. On the same occasion a new commandant of Fort Fredensborg was appointed. This was Baron Chr. Fr. von Hager, who was given the rank of first lieutenant. On their arrival in Guinea these two gentlemen took over the forts for the new entrepreneurs on November 1, 1789. If Kipnasse had been narrow-minded and close-fisted, Biørn seems to have been too open-handed and full of a feeling of Danish grandeur. This was revealed as early as 1788 by a report he wrote concerning the Danish forts and native towns. In it he calculated the numbers of armed forces that native towns which were the allies of the Danes would be able to provide, and what tributes were or should be paid to them. According to his calculations, the "Danish" native towns had about 2,300 warriors. If Awuna, Aflahu, and their allies were included the number would be increased by about 6,000 warriors. The annual tributes paid to the kings of Ashanti, Akim, and Popo besides various caboceers and native aristocrats amounted to far more than 2,000 rixdollars in gold. To this must be added the so-called New Year's "custom," the tribute paid on the occasion of the yam festival (a kind of harvest festival), and other annual tributes. In regard to the last item Biørn was especially liberal. If his proposal had been carried out, the annual presents would have amounted to at least 5,000 rixdollars in gold. This was a rather stiff price to pay for the luxury of possessing "property rights" in Africa.

All Biørn's doings were influenced by his illusions of grandeur. He was dissatisfied with his rank as a captain, and he would have liked to

be a major. He pressed for regulations ordering Danish officials in
Guinea to wear uniforms. His own domestic economy was equally extravagant. He claimed that Kiøge had been lavish and had spoiled his
entourage by his generosity; he had recourse to the old and tried method
of blackening the record of his predecessor, especially in the picture
he painted of the condition of the forts. At Kiøge's departure, Fort
Christiansborg was in need of repairs; Fort Prinsensten was almost completed and only needed some warehouses; but at Fort Kongensten the
fortifications of the two last bastions had not been completed. Augustaborg was half completed, and work on Fort Isegram had only just
begun. The summer of 1788 brought unusually heavy rains. At Fort
Christiansborg one flank of the seaward battery collapsed, and a couple
of cannon fell into the sea. Also part of the tower of Fort Prøvesten and
two ravelins at Augustaborg fell down.[16] Thus Biørn's complaints were
justified, but they were not grounds for accusations against Kiøge. Nonetheless, the forts were not suitable residences for a man of Biørn's rank.
They were hardly habitable, and the new governor boldly estimated the
cost of repairing all the forts at more than 100,000 rixdollars. Now it is
worth noting that Kiøge had spent about 5,000 rixdollars on the erection
of Fort Kongensten. Prinsensten had cost 30,000 rixdollars, but most of
this enormous sum was paid for the military protection of the Popo
army during building operations. Obviously Biørn's estimate was too
high. In Copenhagen a dispute broke out between the numerous Guinea
authorities about the right to draw up his instructions; the entrepreneurs
feared that the government offices would order him to spend too lavishly.
Actually, during Biørn's term, Fort Christiansborg was thoroughly repaired, new slave rooms and barracks were added, and foundations were
laid for a new church. Prinsensten needed only slight repairs, and the
other forts were allowed to remain in a state of decay.

Biørn's relations with the natives were no better.[17] His subordinates
plainly said that he acted like a fool. The trouble seems to have started
after the death of Assiambo, when rivalry broke out between two
claimants for the throne of Popo. Attempts were made on the life of
Okaitkie, the rightful heir to the throne; he fled the country. The exiled
prince tried to win the support both of Akoto, king of Akwamu, to whom
he sent all his treasures, and of the Danes, to whom he pawned all his
children for war materials. This angered the Popo, who began robbing
the Danish factory near their town and encouraging the inhabitants of
Augoja and Pottebra to make attacks on Fort Prinsensten. Pottebra was
already hostile to the Danes, and now its inhabitants attacked them
several times. The climax was reached when they killed the factor, Thessen, on June 22, 1790. This was done to revenge the murder of an aristocratic native named Dekkenie which had occurred several years earlier

near Fort Prinsensten. In Biørn's opinion, this crime cried out for strong punishment to serve as an example. First he turned to King Approffo of Akim with a present, asking him to settle the account. This the king was unwilling to do. Biørn then wrote home and asked for 200 soldiers and a number of "amusettes" (one-pounder brass cannons), and howitzers, so he could undertake the punitive expedition himself. Of course, such support was not obtainable. A new danger arose when thousands of Awuna poured in toward the Volta River. The reason is said to have been a quarrel between Niels Lather, the commander of Fort Kongensten, and the Agraffy, allies of the Ada who lived farther up the Volta River and were normally allies of the Danes. Lather is said to have been ignorant of previous events and bribed Awuna to punish them. Of course, Awuna was ready and willing to make the river people suffer. They even threatened to kill all Ada. Only then did Lather sense the danger and sent for Biørn. The governor arrived as soon as possible, accompanied by all the forces he had been able to lay hands on—a few hundred. He also ordered an armed schooner to the Volta River, and started negotiations with Awuna; he managed to stop hostilities and made peace with them. The Awunas agreed to avenge the murder of Thessen and, of course, receive generous rewards for their services. On the other hand, Awuna had no quarrel with the people of Keta, Augoja, and Pottebra, who were their relatives. They regarded their agreement with Biørn as a splendid business transaction, pocketed the bullets and gun powder they could squeeze out of him, and sent word to the three towns warning them of their approach. After the inhabitants had fled, the three towns were burned down. However, the Awuna quarreled among themselves, many of them maintaining that they ought to have marched against the Ada instead of burning the property of their own relatives. A Danish factor named Christian Schiønning took part in the expedition to see that the three towns got what was due to them.

It has been said that Biørn sent word to Commandant Richter at Fort Prinsensten, ordering him, before the arrival of the Awuna, to try to lure the people of Keta into the fort and then to take them prisoners. They were not deceived, however, so Richter is said to have attacked the town and taken eight prisoners who were sold out of the country. The tolerable relations with the inhabitants of Keta brought about in Kiøge's days were thoroughly spoiled by Biørn and his contemporaries. All roads to Fort Prinsensten were now blocked by the people of the three towns which the Danes had burned down.

It must have been poor consolation for Biørn that the Akwamu caboceer wanted the Danes to build a fort at Popo, and that the powerful king of Dahomey and his brother sent letters inviting the Danes to build factories in their territories. There were not sufficient resources for such efforts, so Biørn had to reply that, before anything could be done, he would have to ask permission from Denmark. On the contrary, the Popo lodge had to be closed down.

In fact, the Danes had lost control of the situation around Fort Prinsensten. Before long, they again had to ask the Awuna to take up arms against the natives of the destroyed towns, who were hiding in the countryside. By promises of fixed salaries to the important Akwamu caboceers and a hundred benda slave price, they were induced to launch the campaign; but this time fate was against them. One of Biørn's lackeys, Børgesen, the factor of Aflahu trading station, took part in the campaign, and a battle was fought on February 22, 1792. Its outcome is said to have been as follows: after several hours' bombardment the caboceer Dacon, one of the Awuna leaders, drove the enemy out of his trenches and set a town on fire. He thought that he had won the victory, but then the majority of the Awuna deserted. The enemy rushed into the breach, and soon Dacon saw himself surrounded. He took out a knife and "slit his stomach open to the heart." Another caboceer, on seeing himself betrayed by his own children, chose the same exit. The next day thirteen caboceers were captured and executed. "Fortunately for Børgesen he had good, long legs." The crushing defeat inflicted upon the Awuna may have been due partly to their own improvidence. On the eve of the battle they had marched 60 kilometers without any water.

The situation had become critical. A number of young Awuna turned up "with tears in their eyes," demanding vengeance for the death of their parents, and declaring that "they had no other friends in the world than us Danes." After some deliberation, the Christiansborg government sent Børgesen to Osei Kwamina, king of Ashanti, to ask for his support. Afterward, he was sent to Akoto of Akim. The latter was ordered by Osei to wait for Ashanti's army, but he died before it arrived. At about the same time that mainstay of the Danes, Atiambo of Akwapim, died. His successor was Ejkufrenne, who marched to Christiansborg with 1,000 men to renew the alliance with the Danes. Unfortunately, we have no account of Børgesen's journey to Ashanti. It was the first time a white man ventured into that country. Biørn reported that he had asked for 10,000-12,000 men. The English were scared by the prospect of the arrival of this huge Ashanti army on the coast and vainly tried to prevent it. The king of Ashanti was willing to send 10,000 men, and in December 1792 Børgesen returned to Fort Christiansborg accompanied by a number of lieutenants and an ambassador from the Great King. The price of his assistance was 500 prequain (20,000 rixdollars), half of it payable in advance. Biørn thought this amount a mere trifle. He passionately desired to close the deal and gave lurid descriptions of the insolence of the Popo and the English schemes to conquer all trade beyond the Volta River.

Biørn's days were over, however.[18] His boasting and swaggering had gradually been recognized for what they were. Before his departure from Copenhagen in 1789, he had acquired from the entrepreneurs the right for himself and three partners, commanders Hager, Richter, and Lather, to freely carry on their private trade from the Danish forts in return for an annual payment of 50,000 rixdollars. It soon became clear that the four gentlemen were unable to pay the annual rent. The chief reason was, they said, that they had signed a contract for slaves with a French firm, Premord & Fils of Honfleur, which, because of the French Revolution, the firm was unable to fulfill. Biørn asked, but in vain, for a reduction of the annual rent payable to the entrepreneurs. Instead of a reduction they sent him, via Captain Andreas Hammer of the *Gregers Juel,* the choice between fulfilling the contract or resigning from the governorship. Biørn was forced to resign, and Hammer took over as interim governor. This was in July 1792, but Biørn remained another six months on the coast. With his habitual "superiority complex," he thought that during this period he ought to help the captain with everything. However, all major decisions, such as those concerning relations with Ashanti, seem to have been made by Hammer himself. He did not care to spend enormous sums to obtain the support of the Great King against the towns beyond the Volta. He is reported to have sent Ashanti's ambassadors home with a present for Osei of 250 ounces of gold (4,000 rixdollars) to persuade him to break off the campaign. According to Biørn's statement, Hammer asked for a postponement while he sent to Copenhagen for instructions. Biørn did not sail for Europe by way of the West Indies until January 27, 1793. Before his departure, he high-handedly installed Hager as interim governor, although, by virtue of the entrepreneurs's orders, Hammer was still governor. While in France on the way home Biørn succeeded in getting some guarantees out of Premord & Fils.

After his departure confusion became complete. Hammer, who was a peevish old man, was unable to inspire others with the necessary respect. Of Kiøge's wise administration and thrifty trade there was but little left. Sales at the forts had declined disastrously. Fort Prinsensten had been cut off from all inland communications. Several forts had sunk into ruin. The Popo lodge was lost forever. The trading boom had been closely followed by a slump, and a total reorganization was needed. Nevertheless, it had been a vivid and eventful chapter in the history of the Danish settlements. An attempt had been made to control the policies of the native peoples, the slave trade had been carried on energetically for some time, and new ideas had been tried. Kiøge's gains had been durable, and Biørn, in spite of his extravagance, did not have time to lose them all. Later generations managed to preserve important parts of these gains. From then on, the Danish holdings in Africa were far more extensive than before.

18 / LIFE AT THE FORTS

THE DANISH TERRITORIES in Guinea reached their greatest expansion during the days of Governor Kiøge. Gradually life at the forts and lodges had developed a characteristic pattern. The number of Danes on the coast was sufficiently large to develop a definite social order; individually they were no longer exposed to the same hazards and vicissitudes as in the early decades of the history of settlements. Miniature civil and military services had evolved, and everyday life was ordered by rules and customs. Some of these were like those of the home country, and some were necessarily adaptations, arising from intercourse with the natives. A local community came into being. It would be too much to say that a local Danish culture developed, but, at least, the lives of all Danish residents in Guinea conformed to the same general pattern.

When newly appointed civil servants, traders, or soldiers arrived at Fort Christiansborg and set foot on the sun-bleached beach, they were happy just to be ashore again after the long voyage. For three to six months they had been confined to the ship. In the northern sea, they would experience gales and seasickness. When they had crossed the stormy Bay of Biscay, they would often enjoy the passage, for the tropic seas were often calmer. The rising temperatures made promenades on deck enjoyable, and unknown species of birds and fish attracted their attention. In the distance the travelers might sight the rocks of Madeira or Teneriffa rising above the horizon. When they neared the African continent, their eyes would strain to catch the first glimpse of the land which was to be their world for years. There was, in fact, plenty of food for the imagination. About the same time, however, provisions on board usually began to run short. The bread became mouldy, and only salt meat would be left. The water would often have to be rationed. Then, outbreaks of disease often followed. Few ships reached Guinea without one or more death on board. In addition there was the mental strain of being shut up for weeks and months within such narrow confines and of seeing only a very few, mostly morally lax, individuals. Many a quarrel which broke out on board ship was continued within the garrisons of the forts.

The pleasure of arrival was often mixed with feelings of anxiety and dismay. Before leaving the ship, the traveler might have seen swarms of noisy Africans climbing on board. Then, there was a dangerous trip through the breakers. A short distance from the shore the traveler would be eased from the ship's barge into the African canoe, which the remidors skillfully steered shoreward on the crest of a wave. For the last part of the trip he would be carried on black shoulders. No sooner would the traveler have been deposited on the beach, than he would be surrounded by impudent natives. These apparently undisciplined ruffians would drag away his precious luggage. Lastly, he would be carried in triumph into the yard of the fort. Upon the arrival of governors and captains the roar of saluting cannon added to the din. Not even the escort of his countrymen from the fort could protect the newcomer from the curiosity of the natives.

The fort had originally been built from a definite plan. In the course of time, however, buildings frequently collapsed, and repairs and additions gave it a most irregular appearance. Altogether, it contrasted curiously with the eighteenth-century ideal of architectural order and symmetry. Outside the main wall was the outwork with warehouses and living quarters. Many of the building materials, especially lime and timber, had to be brought from Europe. Some stones came from local quarries. Wærøe had tried to start a brickyard and made plans for a limekiln.[1] In Boris' days lime was burnt from sea shells which the natives were ordered to collect. However, the worst hindrance was the labor shortage. The natives had no knowledge of European building techniques, and were extremely indolent as well. At the start, the work on the buildings had to be done exclusively by the Europeans. It was only in the late eighteenth century that the Danes succeeded in training the slaves who belonged to the fort to be useful handymen as bricklayers and carpenters. Often the completion of projected and even partially erected buildings would come to a standstill when the skilled bricklayers died, for the training of new ones was a slow process. Great skill was required to build the vaults which covered many of the rooms of the central parts of the fort. The water supply was of paramount importance.[2] In the innermost part of the fort there was an old cistern. Later on, another cistern was usually built in the outwork. Kiøge built two more. Attempts were made to transform a river into a reservoir by a system of dams, but again and again local wars and floods disturbed this work.

The Danish forts, or fortresses as they were often called in the eight-

eenth cenutry, were quite large for their day. Nevertheless, they were
quite inadequate for defensive purposes. All rooms at Fort Christiansborg were too small. Often two or more had to share a small room, and
this increased mortality. Letters sent home from the fort are full of
complaints about the lack of privacy.[3] As late as 1768, the governor
himself had only a bedroom and a side room at his disposal; but he
could use also the council hall, which is believed to have been on the
first floor. In 1754 an office is said to have been located on the emplacement. Still, it must have been quite gay when everybody gathered in the
hall for a festive dinner or dance. The food was not bad, unless war or
bad harvests caused a shortage of supplies. At any rate there were long
periods when officers and civil servants ate at the governor's table. Some
provisions were sent out from Europe. Game, fish, and several kinds of
delicious fruits were obtainable in the country, and generally the fort
had an excellent wine cellar. Meals would be particularly luxurious
when ships' captains or important persons from other forts came for a
visit. If one was planning to stay a long time, it was wise to get used to
the native diet. In a way, the natives made quite good cooks. Above all,
millet was a wholesome item of the diet, though many Danes in Guinea
preferred heavy meals which were too heavy in the tropics and thus
shortened their lives.

Now and again, attempts were made to establish gardens near the
fort.[4] These attempts were unsuccessful, since the soil probably was not
very good. Commander Suhm, for instance, had seeds sent out from
Europe, and his garden survived for some years. On the whole, however,
the Danes had to depend on supplies from the Osu inland plantations,
where the soil was better. Similar attempts were made to keep European
animals. The common, local domestic animals were the goats, or *cabrits*,
which might be either the long-legged, or the short-legged, variety. The
Danes tried also to keep cows.[5] Commander Rost had a number of them,
some of which were still alive in Herrn's days. A couple of years later, a
leopard bit and killed 15 of them in one night. The greatest threat to
the goats were snakes. Besides, the natives liked to steal them. On the
night that Herrn died, for instance, they stole 30 goats. They did this
again on the night when Østrup died. Later on, Dorph kept cattle on
the island of Ada. In 1793 it was reported that there were 177 head of
cattle belonging to the forts. Poultry and pigs could be bought from the
natives. In ordinary circumstances, therefore, the means of sustenance
were quite sufficient.

The daily routine of the white inhabitants of the forts was bound up
with the trade, which was carried on largely by barter. The export
articles of the Guinea Coast, such as slaves, gold, or ivory, usually were
obtainable only in exchange for other commodities which were in demand among the natives. So European ships bound for Guinea carried

composite cargoes which became more and more varied in the course of time.[6] Above all, the natives wanted muskets and gunpowder. In the days of the flintlock, flints were much in demand, too. When the African states were at war, these articles were all they wanted. There was a good market for such metal goods as iron bars, knives, pewter dishes, brass basins, and padlocks. The black customers were greatly interested in dry goods. The Africans did not wear many clothes but they loved beautiful pantjes. The forts always had to have a fine assortment of fabrics for this purpose. The natives' taste was subject to constant changes of fashion, so the textile trade was more hazardous than any other. In the old storehouse inventories the strange names of various fabrics, such as *broullis, nikones, salempuris, platillias, gingang, chellos, sej, perpetuan, bassein,* and *callevapuris,* are listed. Some of the fabrics came from Britain, a few were of Danish make, and others had been obtained by Danish ships from India and China. The Guinea trader was a regular customer at the auction sales of the Asiatic Company. The natives were very fond of the good Danish liquor. They were prepared to do almost anything to get hold of a bottle of it, and it was the greatest treat at local banquets. There was also a market for tobacco and pipes. Tobacco was one of the articles which the Christiansborg traders preferred to purchase from the Portuguese or from Dutch "interlopers." Lastly, at various times there were markets for corals for ornaments; and cowries, a species of snailshell used for small change, were always in demand.

Even if most of the trade was carried on by direct barter of commodities, prices were often given in terms of money. The local currency system was quite complicated.[7] As mentioned the cowry was in everyday use among the natives. Forty bos (cowries) made 1 damba, and 25 damba made 1 rixdollar bos. Two rixdollars bos equaled 1 cabes, 4 rixdollars bos, 1 big cabes. One rixdollar bos was also called 1 rixdollar slave price. The value of this rixdollar compared with the Danish rixdollar varied constantly. The Danish rixdollar had a fixed gold value until 1813; that is, the equivalent gold value of 3 Danish kroner in today's currency. In Guinea, however, the price of gold varied with the quantity of gold on the market. About 1750 the average value of 1 rixdollar gold price was 40 damba bos, and about 1780 it was 50 damba bos, i.e., 2 rixdollars bos or slave price. A few of the governors quarreled with their subordinates because they wanted to pay their salaries in rixdollars slave price instead of gold price.

Large amounts were calculated in ounces or benda. Eight gold rixdollars equaled 1 lod (about half an ounce), 16 rixdollars equaled 1 ounce, and 32 rixdollars equaled 1 benda. One prequain (perguin) was 400 rixdollars. In early days the following European currencies were used: 1 gold mark was at first worth 160 rixdollars, but later, about 1740 for instance, it was worth somewhat less than 130 rixdollars. One gold tonder (barrel) equaled 100,000 rixdollars. In the nineteenth century it was often calculated in piasters, of which 16 equaled one ounce of gold, or in guinea rixdollars of which, at one time, 1⅕ equaled a piaster.

The good were carried ashore by the remidors, or black canoemen, whose everyday occupation was fishing or the transportation of goods along the coast. Some of the remidors were slaves belonging to the forts, others seem to have been paid regular wages. Besides the canoes of the natives, there was often a rather larger European-made boat used for transporting supplies of goods to the forts and factories on the Lower Coast and for obtaining slaves from there. In some periods there were small ships for this local traffic, which were often partly manned by black crews. Manual labor at the forts and the work of carrying goods from the beach to the storehouses was done by the fort slaves. Of these some lived at the fort, others in the native towns. They were commanded by a black bos (bas) or bomba. In early days, there were only 10-20 fort slaves, but in the course of time this number increased. Around 1800 at Fort Christiansborg alone there were more than 150. The total number for all the Danish forts and lodges was 300-400. Gradually the custom evolved that unless they committed a criminal act, those slaves were not to be sold out of the country. Besides the slaves which were the property of the forts, there were also the pawned slaves. When a native was short of merchandise to use as payment, he would pawn a slave or a relative for the amount, until such time as he would be able to pay. If these pawned slaves were members of distinguished families, it was not proper to make them work; this would be rather awkward if many years went by before they were redeemed.

When natives from the interior came down to the coast to trade, they would, at least in the early days, first turn to one of the black traders of Dutch Accra or Osu. These were the mercadors, whom the Danes also called *klaploppere*.[8] They were a sort of agent, a title often given to them, and they served also as interpreters. In the early days, they mastered the Portuguese trade jargon which was spoken all along the coast. Later on they taught themselves Dutch and English, and some mastered even Danish, too. Such men were indispensable in the neighborhood of a fort. A European trading station could prosper only in the immediate vicinity of a native town. When competition was keen, the *klaploppere* were made to lie in wait along the inland paths and catch customers in time to prevent them from buying from the foreign forts. When customers arrived at Fort Christiansborg, they would be allowed to inspect the goods in the storerooms. They would often take their time to be able to pick and choose. When doing business with the natives, the trader always had to be ready with a small present. And, of course, the deal had to be closed with a small drink.

Often several days would elapse without the appearance of any customers. On other days regular embassies would turn up, and their leaders would be formally received by the governor. On such occasions, the courtyard of the fort would become the scene of great activity, and tumults might easily ensue, if the parties failed to agree. Even on ordinary days there was constant traffic going out and coming in. The sentry at the gate was hardly sufficient protection. In fact, it is a wonder that native bands did not sneak in to take the whites by surprise more often, and thereby make themselves masters of the fort. This, in itself, is sufficient proof that the inhabitants of the adjacent native town understood how useful the fort was to them, and that they supported it in every way.

When the governor wanted to travel from one fort to another, everybody would be astir before dawn. The journey would have to begin before sunrise, to make full use of the cool hours of the morning. The natives carrying lanterns marched in front and were closely followed by an armed escort. The governor and, as a rule, other white travelers would be carried in hammocks made of fiber. A regular procession of slaves carrying food and luggage on their heads would make up the rear. They would travel along at considerable speed. Twigs would lash the white faces on the way through forest and bush for the Negroes did not walk, they ran. Often they sang, too. They would wade across small lakes and rivers, but their clothes and bodies would dry almost instantly. The distance from Christiansborg to Fredensborg was covered in one day, with only a short rest in the hot noon hours. The run from Fredensborg to Kongensten was made at the same fantastic speed, and they even had time to call on the caboceers of the native towns en route. Nevertheless, the whites found traveling most fatiguing. The blazing heat of the day followed the cool morning hours. They would feel the heat less if enormous umbrellas were carried above their perspiring faces. In the interior, the dry, stagnant air would produce unbearable thirst, and the atmosphere of the swamps seemed infected with fever. The health of many white men was ruined by such excursions.

In the hot climate the Danes were often fatigued from drinking and attacks of fever. They had to have strong constitutions, or in the long run they would not be able to take any interest in the trade and government of the settlements. To maintain order, account books had to be filled in daily, and detailed reports to the home country had to be ready for the departure of every ship. This required many late hours of work. In the hope of pleasing the authorities at home, the local government would often write of events in the most favorable light. It was extremely difficult to produce general accounts. In the early days, there would be large gaps in accounts sent home during periods when the garrison was dying off. Usually, the Christiansborg government was several years behind in the rendering of its accounts. This was the reason why many of the governors who were lucky enough to get home to Denmark alive had great difficulty in accounting for their management of affairs.

The government of the Danish establishments was in the hands of the governor and a council, which was generally known as the *Sekretraad* (Secret Council). The governors usually assumed command immediately after their arrival. (The interim governor was elected following a service in the chapel.)[9] Afterward the newly appointed governor received the oaths of his subordinates. During the following days, he was acquainted with the forts and storehouses where he took part in the stock accounting and gave his receipt. In the course of time, the membership of the secret council underwent certain changes. Originally the councilors included the chief trader of Fort Christiansborg, one or two head clerks, and sometimes the chaplain. Later on, the council was chiefly made up of the commandants of the other forts and the more important trading stations, sometimes assisted by an officer from Fort Christiansborg. The council shared in all important political decisions, and all councilors present at its sessions signed letters from the council to the home authorities, as well as other important documents. It would, however, not be safe to conclude that the governor was entirely dependent on the council. His power varied quite considerably, according to his personality and those of the councilors. There seems to have been a degree of snobbery in the attitude of the council to the governors, though more often it was the governor who controlled the council than the opposite. The system of government reflected European constitutional ideas, and in practice the governor was a kind of petty, absolute monarch.

Especially in early days, it was often difficult to find suitable persons for the highest posts. The history of the Danish Guinea settlements too often bears witness to the fact that unsuitable characters were sent out. In a letter to the directors of the company, Commander Lygaard complained that he "had daily injury and tribulations from some naughty people . . . babble and wretches, who in the Mother Country have found it impossible to enter the service of decent people because of their own licentiousness, debts, or other faults." He found that many were mere boys, who ought to have been subjected to the discipline of a good schoolmaster, rather than to have served as advisers of a commandant; they demanded preferment to offices they did not deserve. So, naturally, he came to the conclusion that greater power should be vested in the governor.[10]

The governors preferred to have their subordinates sent out as assistants, so the governors themselves could promote them according to their merits and talents. If they were to assume a high office immediately upon arrival, they might do incalculable damage through their ignorance of Guinean conditions. A good assistant had, in fact, to possess many talents. Besides some knowledge of the law and commerce of the mother country, he had to speak several European languages, so he could associate with the other nations on the coast. He needed sufficient strength of character not to eat, drink, and fornicate himself to death. He had to have also a sufficient sense of justice to make both blacks and whites feel that neither were being wronged in his dealings with them. With their different background, the natives were extremely sensitive in their relations with the whites. They had to be ruled with a firm hand, but they loved whomever was good to them and gratefully remembered those who had helped them in emergency.

The whites were often completely ignorant of political developments and the historical background of events on the coast. If their stay at the forts had been short or if they died soon after their arrival, they did not have time to form any idea of the customs of the country. For a European to gain such knowledge, it was necessary to stay on the coast for many years. From about the middle of the eighteenth century when housing and water supply improved, Europeans would often last 15 to 20 years on the Guinea coast. In 1758 mention is made of a sergeant who had seen more than twenty-one years' service there.[11] The few whites who had been born and had spent most of their lives on the coast were the toughest.

The life of the white soldiers was extremely dull. At first, they were a chance-chosen lot who had been hired by the companies, but from 1779 onward both officers and privates of the Royal Danish Army were detailed for service on the coast. Often soldiers who had been trained as craftsmen were preferred, since they could be employed on buildings and repairs. Sometimes they were sent on expeditions along the coast or into the interior, but most of their time was spent on sentry duty, gambling, and drinking. Strict discipline had to be maintained if the *soldatesque,* as the garrison was often called, was to preserve its morale. A deserter, who had run off to Fort Crèvecoeur but been sent back by the Dutch, was sentenced to run the gauntlet of the garrison fifty times every day for three days. After this he was put in irons and placed with the slaves until he could be returned to the home country. He then had to spend the rest of his life in the slave prison of Bremerholm.[12] The great majority of the military personnel was stationed at Fort Christiansborg. The other forts usually had one or two soldiers, and their garrisons were made up of the fort slaves.

The numbers of civil servants, traders, and soldiers at the forts were repeatedly fixed by regulations, but the documents concerning this are of little interest. There might be a super-abundance of staff at a fort immediately after the arrival of a ship, but mortality was high, so it was rare that all posts were filled. When all forts had commandants, and all lodges had factors; when Christiansborg had its chaplain, schoolmaster, surgeon, bookkeeper, and 3 or 4 assistants; when Fredensborg had a surgeon and an assistant; and when the rest of the forts each had an assistant, the total number might be more than twenty. In addition to this there were a couple of artisans, twenty to thirty soldiers, and a few white private individuals, wives and children. So the grand total would amount to sixty persons, a small number, considering that there would be seven or eight times as many fort slaves and pawn slaves in the periods of good trade.

Usually, salaries were lower than at the Dutch and British forts.[13] Only commandants and governors were fairly well paid, though until the latter half of the eighteenth century, they were never paid more than 1,000 rixdollars per annum, and often not even that much. In 1753 the salaries were as follows: the commandant was paid 800 rixdollars, the trader of Fort Fredensborg 300 rixdollars, the bookkeeper 240 rixdollars, a head clerk 168 rixdollars, a subclerk 120 rixdollars, the chaplain 240 rixdollars, the schoolmaster 144 rixdollars, the surgeon 192 rixdollars plus extras for health examinations in connection with the slave trade, a sergeant and a corporal 192 rixdollars each, a constable 144 rixdollars, a drummer and a private 84 rixdollars each including free uniforms.[14] Thus, the total spent annually on salaries was 4,784 rixdollars, calculating an average of four subassistants. During difficult times, the staff could not live on their salaries. If they had not, regardless of whether their employers in Denmark liked it, been able to carry on some private trade, they would have succumbed to poverty and starvation. Bargum's Society was the first to raise salaries. They paid governors 2,000 rixdollars, and in a few cases 3,000 rixdollars and a percentage on the slave trade. The rest of Bargum's staff were paid proportionate salaries. Consequently, in 1794, the total spent on salaries amounted to 22,812 rixdollars; and disregarding Biørn's extravagant proposal, the salaries of the native princes were fixed at 1,344 rixdollars.[15]

When subordinates received their board at the governor's table, their household expenses were few. They would need only one black "boy." Nevertheless, many would live on a more expensive scale. With the exception of some of the chaplains, few Danes brought their wives out from Europe. Nevertheless, it was the rule for Danish officials to have families. For the period of time that he spent on the coast, the European would take a native woman into his house. This was called to *cassare*. In such cases the white man paid her keep, and she cooked his meals and bore his children. She always kept her property separate, and, presumably, at his death or departure she would get her share of what he left behind. This was a practical arrangement, which served to prevent sexual promiscuity; however, the chaplains did not always approve.[16] Occasionally one of them insisted that these concubines were lawful wives, who should accompany their husbands when they left for Europe. Fortunately, they never had their way. The black wives would never have been happy in the cold Scandinavian climate. It was said by some that they did not really love their white husbands. Nevertheless, competition was keen for the honor and profit.

The result of these "marriages" was the mulatto children, of whom there were a considerable number after awhile. At first, the Danes hardly knew what to do with these creatures. Gradually, however, a system evolved whereby those who kept black women paid money into a mulatto fund. Especially at their departures, such fathers would leave sums of money to this fund to provide for their children. Even if the black mother educated the children herself, the problem of the grown mulattoes remained. The Danes did not like to see them live exactly like the natives, so, in 1722 the chaplain, Elias Svane, in cooperation with Commandant David Herrn, opened the first mulatto school.[17] One aim was to bring up these children in the Christian religion. A soldier was hired to teach them, and skirts and caps were bought for them. A few years later, four mulatto boys were baptized. One of them was sent to St. Thomas, and the three others enlisted as soldiers. The black mothers hated to send their children to the West Indies, fearing that they would fall into slavery. These first attempts to educate the mulattoes were not entirely successful. In Wærøe's opinion, it did not pay to try to teach them. He thought that, in their hearts, they remained heathens and were prone to running away. By nature they were inferior to the natives: "So I trust a black rogue better than a seemingly honest mulatto." Later he complained that they give themselves up to "fetishism and idleness." Gradually it became the custom to make the mulatto boys, from the age of ten, serve as soldiers. There were long periods when the forts were manned almost exclusively by mulattoes. In fact, the mulatto girls presented a far more difficult problem. One of the first to be baptized was Anna Sophie, the daughter of a mulatto named Christian Pedersen Widt. She married one of the white assistants, and after his death was about to marry another white assistant. After they had quarreled, she bore him a fine looking white girl "almost like one from the Old Country." Keeping the mulatto girls on the straight and narrow path proved a Sisyphean task for the heavy Lutheran clergymen and their still slower deacons. On the other hand, there was never any intention of leaving them to become the whores of the Danes.

A couple of the mulattoes attained the rank of deacon. One, Frederik Svane, was the son of a clergyman named Elias Svane.[18] His father brought him to Denmark where he went to a good school. He went to the University of Copenhagen and became a resident of the Regensen College (Domus Regiae). Altogether, his career was most unusual; the decisive factor was his pathetic, melancholy turn of mind. When he joined the "Pietists," he quarreled with his first protector but was supported by Carl Adolph von Plessen. He became Guinea's first missionary.

In 1735 he set out for his native Guinea on board the *Jomfruen* to try to convert his black relatives. His attempt was a complete failure. Instead he became a deacon and schoolmaster, and afterward he did clerical work. His wife, whom he had brought out from Denmark, was a constant source of sorrow to him. She was coveted by Commander Boris, and in the end she had to be sent home. After that Frederik Svane is said to have kept four black wives.[19] When he became involved in the troubles of Billsen's days and was put in prison, he became a champion prisonbreaker, whom neither chains nor prison walls could hold, but who, nevertheless, allowed himself to be recaptured after each escape. Commander Platfuss dismissed him, after which he gave a detailed description of his life and adventures in a curious book dedicated to Plessen. In the end he became schoolmaster at Tersløsegaard, the estate of Ludvig Holberg the great Danish dramatist.[20] Christian Protten, another remarkable mulatto, had also gone to Copenhagen, because of the efforts of Elias Svane.[21] He studied at the university, hoping to become a missionary, and in the 1750's he became a good schoolmaster for the young mulattoes of Christiansborg. He must, however, have been prone to fits of uncontrollable fury, for in 1761 he was unfortunate enough to shoot and kill a mulatto child. This, however, did not stop His Majesty from granting the sum necessary for his return to Guinea as a schoolmaster in 1764. He was given free passage for himself and his wife and 250 rixdollars per annum to feed and clothe the little mulattoes. That same year he published in Copenhagen *En nyttig Grammaticalsk Fndle delse til Tvende hinindtil gandske nbekeindte Sprog Fanteisk og Acraosk* ("A Useful Grammatical Introduction to Two Hitherto Completely Unknown Languages: Fanti and Accra").

The type of education given to the young mulattoes is best revealed by the list of books sent out for their use.[22] At first, besides the spelling book, it included only the Lutheran Catechism, Pontoppidan's Explanations of the Catechism, the Hymn-Book, and the New Testament. In the 1760's the number of pupils had risen to forty, and in a small way an attempt was being made to teach the mulatto children of Fort Fredensborg.[23] In 1775 two mulatto boys were sent to Denmark to learn a trade. They were the sons of commanders Engman and Hackenburg. When Kiøge left, the school had 63 pupils, and the mulatto fund was endowed with ample sums for their keep.

The Christian congregation at the fort was not so flourishing. Not all pupils of the mulatto school were baptized, and some who were afterward reverted to their mothers' heathenish religion. By and large, the Church was not much respected. The efforts of the chaplains were too short-lived, subject to interruptions, and devoid of plan. The chapel built by the Portuguese in 1680 had fallen into decay by Elias Svane's time. He calls it a ruin, more useful as an antechamber than as a chapel, since all visitors to the governor had to pass through it.[24] It was also used for the washing and ironing of clothes, and the tailor cut out suits there. At night it was the sleeping quarters of the black servant boys. "The table which served as an altar, is so rickety that it is with great anxiety and watching my every movement that I stand before it," writes Svane. "These is no altar-piece, there are no candlesticks, much less any light in the chapel. The altar-cloth is very old and worn, as also the surplice, which is, besides, very dirty . . . There being here usually a shortage of soap. Nor is there any chasuble!" Though, by and by, some of these deficiencies were remedied, and a new house was built for the chaplain, the divine service did not gain much in dignity until Governor Biørn had a new chapel built inside the fort.

Nor were the clergymen models of Christian morality. One would seek to enrich himself by dabbling in trade, another would quarrel with the "government," and a third would drink with the soldiers. Some collapsed into sickness and death, or their minds were darkened by loneliness for want of anyone with whom to share their interests. Probably, the Reverend Mr. Kop was the worst case. In 1755 he went stark raving mad and began to sing and dance and challenge the sentry to a fight. After vain attempts to cure him by means of native medicine, he was put in a room near the guard room, where he could be carefully watched. "Sometimes he climbs up to the window, puts his legs out between the wooden bars, and bleats like a goat or crows like a cock." [25] The hot climate, the reprobates around him, and the constant fear of the dangerous fever, were more than enough to drive a poor European out of his mind.

Death struck down many when they least expected it. Most were attacked by fever shortly after their arrival; it killed some in a few days. If one was planning a long stay, it was almost a necessity to catch the fever at once and to survive it. He who had to wait too long for his attacks of fever, was looked upon as the certain prey of death. He whose constitution was hardened against the fever risked falling a victim to diseases of the digestive tract or to intestinal hemorrhages. Others suffered excruciatingly from Guinean worms. Some were felled by epidemics. Hardly any European lived to old age on the coast. Those who escaped alive, remained human wrecks for the rest of their days, for the most part, skinny, pock-marked, sallow, prematurely aged.

The funeral would take place immediately after the death of the sufferer; if possible it would be on the very same day, but never later than the day after. Otherwise, the body would be decomposed by the heat. If there was a chaplain at the fort, the ritual would be followed; if not, the only ceremony would be a prayer said at the graveside by one of the officials. Near the beach at Fort Christiansborg there is still a Danish graveyard, fraught with memories, and with several tombstones which still reveal Danish names and inscriptions. The property of the deceased was taken charge of by the official whose duty it was to see to the settlement of the estate. His goods and personal belongings were sold by auction. On such an occasion, new arrivals among the assistants would often be able to pick up fine furniture and elegant clothes very cheap. If there was anything left when all debts had been paid, and if the company directors at Copenhagen did not find a pretext and prevent it, the deceased's relatives in the old country might hope to get their legacies. It was rare that large sums reached the mother country from such sources.

It can be safely said that the Europeans who found happiness on the Guinea Coast were few and far between. Still, a few were pleased with the constant servility of the natives, African cooking, the wine on the governor's table, and by their black concubines. Or a man might love the children born to him in this foreign land. Such men settled down, made life as comfortable for themselves as possible, and paid for this pasha's life with an early death. Most lived there only a few months, however, before they started groaning and complaining of "this rotten country." They called it the white man's grave, and wished they were safely back under the low, grey, and cold skies of the Sound. Most had signed for a number of years, usually four or six, but many sent home abject letters, begging to be relieved before the end of their term. The sad, plaintive tone of these letters is often deeply moving in its simplicity. Frequently these men died before they could be relieved, but a few were able to settle their accounts, bid farewell to their black servants and concubines, and embark on the long voyage home by way of the West Indies. We are led to believe, however, that the homeward voyage lasted long enough to produce a kind of retrospective optimism, which made some of them forget their worst sufferings. It was not at all rare for people who had spent years on the African coast to be seized by a longing for the hot climate after their home-coming. Those who went out a second time usually settled down and very rarely returned to Denmark again.

It is no secret that the presence of the Danes on the tropical coast of Africa produced a fairly large number of individual tragedies. It seems surprising that it was still possible to get men to apply for posts in the Guinean service and to run the enormous risks which were involved in travels in the tropics before the birth of modern medical science. Presumably, the majority of those who volunteered were either men to whom all doors in Denmark were closed, or young victims of unhappy love. Even so, we have irrefutable proof that persons who would have been able to make satisfactory careers at home went to Africa in search of adventure, to satisfy their curiosity, or to win power. A few went there to preach the Gospel to the heathen. The urge to travel was very strong in these descendants of the Vikings. It cost them strife, danger, suffering, and death, and their work on those foreign shores brought no blessing. Denmark's African adventure was strange rather than creditable. It was a colorful episode in the history of the Danish people, but not a happy one.

19 / PLANTATIONS AND THE ABOLITION OF THE SLAVE TRADE

A FEW YEARS after Danish influence on the Guinea coast had been consolidated by treaties with the former Dutch Africans, an event occurred which completely changed the prospects of the settlements, ruined their economy, and made their continued existence seem almost absurd: the king of Denmark forbade his subjects to take part in the slave trade. This trade had been the chief source of revenue of the Danish forts; therefore, its abolition was to entail drastic changes.

Ernst Schimmelmann is usually given credit for the Royal Ordinance of March 16, 1792, concerning the slave trade.[1] There can be no doubt about this nobleman's humane philosophy. His surprise upon finding himself one of the directors of the Baltic-Guinea Company was unquestionably sincere. He would have much preferred to bring happiness to the Africans instead of plunging them into despair. It cannot have been a matter of indifference to him, either, that the Guinea trade was unprofitable. According to our present knowledge of Schimmelmann's character, the question must remain open whether it was the first or the second consideration which spurred him to action. Wishing to bring about a change in the African situation, he allowed his lively imagination to toy with a number of solutions to the problem. In July 1786, he sent a professor of divinity named D. G. Moldenhawer to Madrid to negotiate an exchange.[2] Spain was to have the forts on the Volta, and in return cede Crab Island (or Bique) in the West Indies to Denmark. The mission was abortive; but on November 29, 1786, even before this was obvious, Schimmelmann set up a committee to look into the Guinea trade.[3] This committee had six members, three of whom represented the company. It not only was to work for the success of the company, but also to examine the prices of goods sent out, the costs of fitting ships, the long sojourns of expeditions in Guinea and the West Indies, and circumstances connected with the purchase of slaves at the forts. The committee's report of June 4, 1787, proved that, no matter how accounts were made, the Danish slave trade was not even supporting itself.

Existing documents do not reveal the considerations occasioned by this report, but in the first instance the decisive factor was neither humanity nor the prospect of quick profits. Instead, plans were made for starting plantations in Africa to encourage the Africans to cultivate their native soil, instead of dragging them off to America. An important part was played by Paul Isert, the physician who had marched with Kiøge in his campaign beyond the Volta.[4] He returned home by way of the West Indies toward the close of 1787. He brought collections and observations concerning the geography and nature of Guinea, and was in addition very interested in attempts at cultivation. "Why," asked Isert, "did our ancestors not have the common sense to start plantations for the production of these commodities in Africa, where one can obtain plenty of labor at lower wages?" If they had done so, there would have been no need to send the Africans off on the risky voyage across the Atlantic. "Willingly would the Blacks allow us to take possession of the largest and best districts, which have been lying in waste for thousands of years. And for moderate wages they would even help to cultivate them, if we come to them bearing in our hands the olive branch instead of the murderous steel."

Isert was not the first Dane to suggest the possibility of plantations in Africa. It seems that the idea was first conceived within Bargum's Trading Society. The first project was for a garden similar to the ones that occasionally had been laid out near some of the forts, and that were always found outside the English and Dutch strongholds on the Gold Coast. In 1769 G. F. Wrisberg mentions seeds which had been sent out, but which would not grow. The Moravian brethren were called in expressly for the purpose of starting plantations. It was found, at the time, however, that the distrust and indolence of the natives were insurmountable hindrances. So, it was suggested that the company slaves should be allowed to marry three or four wives each, so multitudes of children would be produced. In this way, there would be a supply of fresh labor for the plantations after fifteen years.[5]

Where Bargum's Trading Society had failed, Isert was successful. He actually started a plantation.[6] Provided with a royal license and the rank of an army captain, he sailed out in the summer of 1788 on board the *Fredensborg*. He had further obtained a letter of instructions from His Majesty's ministers, Schimmelmann and Brandt, and a grant of 1,795 rixdollars from the Ad Usus Publicos Fund. Immediately after his arrival at Christiansborg on November 14, he set out for the island of Malfi, about 50 kilometers up the Volta River. Finding the climate there hot and unhealthy, he pushed on to Akwapim, a mountainous forest district with a fertile soil and suitable climate. Atiambo, Isert's old comrade-at-arms from the Awuna campaign, was still caboceer of Akwapim, and with his assistance Isert succeeded in persuading the tribal council to grant him a piece of unused land. He also got the blacks to build a house for him and cut a road through 11 kilometers of forest in the direction of Fredensborg. On December 21, 1788, he moved into his new house built on the land that was to become his plantation. Atiambo himself and two important natives planted the Danish flag before the front door of the house, swearing everlasting loyalty and friendship as in the treaty of alliance between Akwapim and the Danes. A formal treaty was signed with the republic of Krobbo, by which the Danish king bought from its inhabitants all unused land. The land thus purchased could be used for plantations, but the natives might settle there, too, provided they obeyed the laws of the settlement. Whites of other nations, on the other hand, were not allowed to settle there without special permission from the government of the colony. Krobbo undertook the defense of the establishment against foreign attacks, and the Danes promised to supply them with war materials. Atiambo was to be paid a price of 512 rixdollars, a monthly salary of five rixdollars, and New Year's gifts worth 60 rixdollars. The new settlement had been founded by government authority and was independent of the entrepreneurs of the Baltic-Guinea Trading Company. On the other hand, the company's employees on the coast were ordered to supply Isert with men and materials. By the wording of the treaty, the land must be considered bought as private property in allied territory. Afterward it was said that Isert had made a mistake in not dealing directly with the king of Ashanti as overlord of the country.[7]

When the formalities were finished, Isert began clearing the forest and planting. Some craftsmen who had come out with him started laying the foundations of a stone house. The intention was to build a fort and a town encircled by walls. Isert called this town Frederiksnopel, but afterward it was known mostly as Frederikssted. When everything was well under way, Isert went to Fort Christiansborg. Unfortunately he died at the fort on January 21, 1789, and his wife followed him into the grave a month later. Isert had unique talents for dealing with the native people, a thorough knowledge of the nature of Guinea, and unshakeable faith in his own mission. He would, no doubt, have been able to make a success of the settlement. His death brought the work to a standstill, and afterward it never developed along the lines laid down by him. The most important Danish project for the cultivation of plantations on the Guinea Coast had failed.

Not that there was any dearth of men who wished to carry on. The post of governor of the colony was given to Jens Nielsen Flindt. He worked hard clearing the forest and trying to make bricks; and with the assistance of a blacksmith named Ole Fynberg, he built a lumber mill.

However, when Biørn assumed office as governor of Christiansborg at the close of the year he made such demands on Flindt that the latter gave up and sailed for home. Thus Biørn succeeded in disturbing the results of Isert's work, much as he had disturbed Kiøge's. In this case, Biørn may have been justified. He thought that a couple of new plantations which had now been started by private individuals near the coast would prove more successful, since they did not require the long transportation by land necessary from Isert's plantation.[8] One of these plantations was founded by Peder Meyer. He had been a trader in the service of the Baltic-Guinea Trading Company, but had resigned when the entrepreneurs took over. His plantations were situated between a freshwater and a saltwater arm of the river near Tubreku. He had houses built in the native style and soon cleared 13-15 acres and planted 12,000 cotton plants. The second plantation, called Jaegerslyst, was started by Niels Lather, commandant of Fort Kongensten. Even before Isert's day, he had examined the quality of the land, and, in 1786, had reported to Copenhagen about it. Both men applied for government grants for bringing further areas under cultivation and for the purchase of agricultural implements. They are not known to have received any subsidies.

At first the harvests were probably not worth much. Nothing could thrive under Biørn's inefficient rule. Another handicap was the small number of ships sent out from the home country. Lather's plantation was wrecked after his unfortunate interference in the quarrels of the natives, for Biørn made him pay for Awuna's campaign against the river natives by confiscating his slaves and implements. He left Guinea in 1791 on a North American ship bound for the West Indies and died at sea. Meyer, also thwarted by Biørn, had to give up. All the efforts lavished on these plantations bore no fruit.

In the meantime, reports reached Copenhagen that it was possible to cultivate the African soil. This information profoundly influenced the renewed discussion of the slave traffic between Africa and America. The incentive to abolish the slave trade finally came from Britain, where, in the 1780's, a number of orators and writers, headed by William Wilberforce, had aroused great indignation against the treatment of the Negroes. While the position of Negroes in the Danish West Indies was being considered in Copenhagen, Schimmelmann closely followed the discussion in Britain and introduced reforms at his own West Indian plantations. When a bill for the immediate abolition of the slave trade was rejected by the British Parliament on April 18, 1791, Schimmelmann wrote a report on the question, demanding that a Danish committee be set up to deal with the problem.[9] He thought that before the slave trade could be prohibited, there should be a period of transition, during which the West Indies could get abundant supplies of slave labor. If, afterward, the Negro slaves of the West Indian plantations were well treated, they would breed large families, their numbers would increase steadily, and there would be no need to import slaves from Africa. Consequently, in the summer of 1791, a committee for the better management of the slave trade in the West Indies and on the Guinea Coast was established. The secretary of the committee was E. P. Kirstein, Schimmelmann's private secretary. Its report was ready on December 28, 1791.[10] Of course, this document dealt mostly with West Indian conditions and tried to make the proposition appear advantageous to the planters of the islands. As far as Guinea was concerned, the report simply referred to the attempts to start plantations, without making new proposals. This report led to a Royal Order of February 24, 1792, which put the realization of reform into the hands of the West Indian and Guinea Interest and General Customs Office.[11] On the recommendation of this office the Royal Ordinance of March 16, 1792, received the royal signature, after which the slave trade was prohibited from New Year's Day, 1803.[12] Until that date, all nations were to be allowed to import Negroes into the Danish West Indies. To encourage importers, ships were allowed to export a certain quantity of sugar for each slave they imported. As Negresses were most in demand, they could be imported duty-free, while the exportation of Negroes from the islands was strictly prohibited.

Thus Denmark was the first country to prohibit the slave trade within its colonies, the first to introduce one of the most important humanitarian reforms known to mankind. That Austria had already introduced this reform in 1782 could be of only theoretical interest. For the Danish settlements in Guinea, however, the consequences would be disastrous, unless the local authorities succeeded in stimulating interest in plantations. This interest, of which Isert's Frederikssted had been the first manifestation, was the one on which governmental people in Copenhagen seemed to have set their hearts. Neither the Baltic-Guinea Trading Company nor its entrepreneurs were willing to keep the settlements after the abolition of the slave trade. The king had to take back the forts and trading stations.[13] On November 11, 1792, A. R. Biørn, who had been appointed governor by the entrepreneurs, was discharged. In his place Bendt Olrik was appointed and given the rank of an infantry major. On the same day, the Guinea trade monopoly was abolished. From then on, Danes and foreigners were to be allowed to trade with the Danish forts and factories. To pay for the forts, an export duty of 10 rixdollars per slave was imposed as long as the slave trade was still permitted. Of this sum, 5 rixdollars would be refunded for each adult Negress landed alive in the Danish West Indies. It was estimated that the settlements would cost 36,000 rixdollars annually; and it was hoped that the slave-duty would earn about 16,000 so that the government would have to pay out only 20,000 rixdollars annually.

A couple of weeks later the new governor with an escort of 20 soldiers sailed from Copenhagen on board the *Hertug Ferdinand*. At first, however, he got no farther than the Dogger Bank. There the ship was damaged by huge breakers and had to go back to Norway for repairs. So Olrik did not reach Fort Christiansborg until June 26, 1793. On his arrival, he found everything in the same state of confusion in which Biørn had left it at his departure in January. There was a feud between Captain Hammer, the governor appointed by the entrepreneurs, and Baron Hager, whom Biørn arbitrarily had installed as temporary governor. Fort Prinsensten was still being besieged on the landward side and had to receive all supplies by sea. Fort Christiansborg was partly in ruins. The governor's rooms were packed with assistants, and there were swarms of slaves for whom no employment could be found. Monthly salaries swallowed more than 2,000 rixdollars, but, for his own safety, he dared not discharge anyone. Wherever he turned, he was faced with disaster, and by August 3 he was dead.[14]

Now Hager was formally appointed temporary governor, and he restored law and order. He installed Christian Fleischer as commandant of Fredensborg. Johan David Ahnholm became commandant of Kongensten, and Johan P. D. Wrisberg, a former temporary governor, received Prinsensten. At Fort Christiansborg, Hager created a new position for a master of the equipage and storehouse, later called the *monstrskriver* (tally clerk). He was to keep control of the stores and to prevent the slaves from revolting or deserting. This new position was given to Christian Schiønning. In addition, Hager had at his side a legal commissioner named Hans Moe, who was to look into the state of affairs and report on the settlements.[15] Also, the government had ordered Lieutenant-Colonel J. Ph. B. von Rohr, an expert on cotton growing, to go from the West Indies to Guinea to study the possibility of plantations in Guinea.[16] Rohr never reached Guinea; the ship on which he sailed disappeared without a trace. On the other hand, Flindt had been sent out again because the Ad Usus Publicos Fund granted him 1,370 rixdollars to pay for presents for the native princes and other necessities.[17] Since Rohr's departure had been delayed by illness, Flindt had been authorized to take over Isert's plantation. Between May 1793 and March 1795, he planted no less than 4,730 cotton plants, started 3 grain plantations, and built a house 35 alen[18] long.

In spite of the fact that a number of able men had been installed in positions of leadership, developments at the forts and trading stations after 1792 were far from encouraging. The French Revolution brought trade with the French West Indies to a standstill. In the preceding decades, the French islands had been great purchasers of slaves from the Danish forts. And the boom in the slave trade to the Danish West Indies, which had been expected in the last years before the abolition, failed to materialize. Worst of all, the Copenhagen government did not know what to do with its Guinea settlements when the slave trade had ceased. There was as yet little action taken to promote the plantations. The future of the Guinea forts remained uncertain.[19] Hager was never promoted to the full governorship, salaries were not to be raised, and no new posts created. The government did not send ships with supplies, but left the Guinea traffic to private enterprise. The government merely sent out the necessary minimum by private ships. In 1794, no cargo arrived from the home country, and afterwards there would often be intervals of more than a year between the arrivals of supplies. Under these circumstances, the Christiansborg government would often have to purchase goods from foreign ships and traders, paying them with checks on Copenhagen. The private Danish Guinea traffic amounted to one or two ships a year, most of them sent by a shipowner named Captain Jens Lind. A couple of times a ship came out from Altona.[20] Supplies were bought for the government by Praetorius in return for 2 per cent commission. Usually each cargo cost about 20,000 rixdollars, the freight costing about a quarter of this amount. Until New Year's 1803, the ships sailed on to the West Indies with cargoes of slaves. Finally, because of the Christiansborg export duty on slaves, it was more profitable for the ships to obtain their slave cargoes elsewhere on the coast.

So the Danish settlements continued with reduced vitality. The only novelty was the arrival of individual Europeans, who began to settle round the forts as private traders.[21] Hager kept wondering how they could be made to pay duty on all the slaves passing through their hands. The garrison of the fort had no influence on those out of reach of their guns. Moe came to the conclusion that the civil servants ought to be allowed to trade. Even if private traders would try to evade the customs, he thought it would always bring in some money—mutual jealousies would see to that. In fact, the slave trade proved far less lucrative than had been estimated; but as several posts were left vacant, the amounts overspent were not too enormous.

Both Hager and Moe came to the conclusion that, in the long run, the best thing would be the sale of the settlements. Neither of them believed in the plantation experiments. Hager thought that it would be difficult to maintain discipline among the slaves;[22] and Moe was convinced that, even in the best circumstances, only the plantations on the islands of the Volta River which could be defended could be made to pay.[23] It was this pessimistic view which made the Copenhagen government decide to give up Isert's plantation. Flindt was recalled from there in 1795, just as the plantation was beginning to flourish. On the same occasion, a couple of African slaves, who had come out by ship from Denmark, spread the rumor that the Danish settlements were to be evacuated, and their slaves sold out of the country.[24] Consequently, all the fort slaves and pawn slaves deserted from Christiansborg to Ada, so that

Peder Meyer, who was now a private trader, lost all the slaves he owned.

After Moe's return to the mother country the Danish government decided at length to pass an ill-advised order of May 18, 1796, whereby forts Christiansborg and Prinsensten, the two best-equipped strongholds, were to be evacuated, and only Fredensborg and Kongensten maintained.[25] If private individuals wanted to establish themselves around the latter two forts, they were to be helped to do so. A number of soldiers and civil servants were to be discharged. Annual grants for the establishments must not exceed 22,460 rixdollars. Fredensborg was to be the seat of the government. For the time being, nevertheless, a token garrison was to stay at the evacuated forts.

It was first of all due to Johan P. D. Wrisberg that nothing came of these decisions, and that the Danish settlements did not fare so badly after all.[26] After Hager's death on August 17, 1795, there was a period of confusion, before Wrisberg could take over as company governor. He had no intention of reducing the Danish sphere of influence. Step by step, he tried to get things going again. Before long he obtained the Copenhagen government's permission for the civil servants on the coast to engage in trade. Most of the runaway slaves were returned to him, though a few took refuge with the fetish priests. A slave who had sought the protection of the fetishists could not return to his master, but he could usually expect to be well treated by the black priests. Although Wrisberg was aware that Isert's plantation was situated too far from the coast, he temporarily manned it with a caretaker and some slaves belonging to the fort. Only in 1802 was it finally abandoned. He bought himself a small ship, which he sent off to Benin with salt and which returned with a cargo of slaves.[27] He hurriedly sent home samples of cotton that he had grown near Fort Prøvesten. Finally, in July 1797 he beban work on a plantation within artillery range from Fort Christiansborg. Wrisberg's plantation afterwards became known as Frederiksberg.[28] There he immediately had 17 acres cleared for cotton and gardening, a house built for a caretaker, and cabins for the natives. At the same time he announced that he would buy all the cotton that the natives could grow. By and by the Frederiksberg plantation grew, until it covered about 100 acres.

Understandably, Wrisberg and his entourage did not dream of obeying the royal order for the evacuation of Fort Christiansborg.[29] On the contrary, it was answered very boldly by enumerations of the unfortunate consequences which would ensue: the natives would be furious, the whites would be killed, the king's property go to waste. Therefore, Wrisberg asked for fresh instructions. If some of the mulatto soldiers were discharged, all of them would desert; and this would necessitate the sending of a large force from Denmark. The Christiansborg government did not venture to reduce their pay, but rather it thought that it would be possible to keep all four forts going with their present garrisons and the grants received. In Copenhagen these protests were referred to the Slave Trade Committee. This body did not venture to contradict Guinean expert opinion. So, on May 12, 1799, a royal order was issued to the effect that the forts were not to be abandoned, but that expenses must be reduced to a minimum.[30]

As proof of the usefulness of the African settlements, in 1798 the Christiansborg government sent home the first bale of cotton harvested at Frederikssted and Frederiksberg. Several more followed. Copenhagen thought the quality excellent. The bales fetched a good price at the stock exchange, and samples of fabrics made from them were sent back to the coast. For some time there were plans to have cotton gins sent out to separate the cotton from the seeds; but when one finally arrived, it was found to be impossible to use.[31]

Fortunately for Wrisberg and his helpers, they were not disturbed by any major native wars. Still, the enmity of Awuna and Keta had not been forgotten.[32] In 1797 an armistice was made, which was to be confirmed by a grant from the king of Denmark of 800 rixdollars compensation to Awuna. By the following year, however, the armistice was broken, and peace was not made until 1802. A few other minor squabbles did not last long, and various revolts and a couple of demises of the crown in Ashanti did not disturb the peace of the Danes.[33]

A dangerous situation did arise in 1799, when a quarrel broke out between two quarters of Osu.[34] There was some shooting and several casualties, after which one party left the town under cover of night and took refuge at Dutch Accra. A few days later, 200-300 Accra came marching up under a Dutch flag, crossed the border of the Danish territory, and marched on Osu. The next morning the attackers were permitted to enter the market place, but later they refused to withdraw and shooting broke out. Consequently, Ahnholm, who was the acting governor from 1800-1802 while Wrisberg was on a visit to Denmark, had to fire the guns as a warning to drive them out. The next day, when they again attacked, they had to be driven off by gunfire from Fort Prøvesten. Ahnholm at this point appealed to the governor-general at Elmina. The war was stopped, and an arrangement was made for the exchange of prisoners. The Danes would have liked to have appealed to Akwapim for help, so as to get vengeance, but they feared the cost and contented themselves with the peace they could obtain. Peace was not made until the return of Wrisberg on October 3, 1802.[35] At last the Copenhagen government had seen fit to appoint him as full governor.

In an attempt to economize, Ahnholm tried not to pay the dues to the natives in 1801, but he soon had to give up this brilliant idea.[36]

After Copenhagen had been persuaded not to abandon the forts, interest in the future of the settlements again revived. Thus, shortly afterwards, the General Customs Office sent to Guinea a medical student, named Peter Thonning, who was to study Guinean botany and investigate the possibility of growing plants for the production of dyes and other useful purposes.[37] He arrived at Fort Christiansborg on board the *Generalinde Schimmelmann* on January 12, 1800. From there he made excursions in the environs, collecting plants, and making experiments in cultivation. He found several species of indigo and various kinds of dyewoods. In addition, he declared himself satisfied with the Frederiksberg plantation. He was, nevertheless, rather critical of what he had seen. In his opinion, the interior was too damp for cotton. The Volta River district seemed beautiful to him, but not as fertile as rumor would have it. The soil was too salty, but he believed that rice and sugar would thrive on the islands in the river. In the spring of 1801, he sent home by way of the West Indies nine boxes full of natural curiosities. At the same time, he began writing a description of the country, and its inhabitants, and he sent home the best map of the country, drawn while the Danes were in residence there. He did not get back to Copenhagen until 1803, bringing still more plant materials and descriptions. Unfortunately, his collections were burnt during the bombardment of Copenhagen by the British in 1807. Fortunately, the duplicates he had given to various friends were saved and became the foundation of Professor F. C. Schumacher's description of Guinean plants in the publications of the Danish Academy of Science (Videnskabernes Selskabs Skrifter, 1827).

Fresh enterprise for plantations was also offered. During his second stay at Isert's plantation, F. N. Flindt,[38] his sister, and Hans Christophersen, the son of a Hvidovre smallholder, had engaged in brewing and distilling, using maize grown in Guinea. Therefore, in 1798, Flindt applied for a loan for the continuation of these activities; the next year he applied for the post of commandant of Fort Kongensten. It was his plan to start plantations in the Volta district with the assistance of slaves from the fort. So he managed to be sent to Guinea a third time. The Finance Collegium granted him a loan of 6,000 rixdollars. In 1801 he began the work on a plantation near Fort Kongensten which he called Ejebo. He was fairly successful with the cotton plants. In 1805 he had 5,000 cotton plants which yielded a fine harvest. The coffee shrub was more sensitive. Some years were too dry for them, and to save them he had to plant them in shady places. Sugar grew well in places which could be flooded. If the seeds were planted in June, the cane would be over two yards high in September. Tobacco would grow as willingly as in America, and bananas were useful as food for the natives on the plantations. A yellow root grown for dyeing and ginger yielded very meagre crops. The maize harvest would sometimes fail too; but then Flindt hit upon the idea of making liquor of palm wine, which sold at higher prices than any other kind of spirits. Palm wine could also be boiled to yield a kind of syrup which Flindt found particularly efficacious against tuberculosis. Hans Christophersen was the expert distiller. Another industry was started, because Flindt's sister dyed and spun yarn which the natives liked, and which was widely sold for native pantjes. On the plantation Flindt built large houses, but he did not acquire any property rights to the land. It had, in the course of time, passed through so many hands that it was impossible for him to find out with whom he should sign the contract.

For some time Wrisberg himself thought of finding more peaceful places for his plantation experiments. His eyes fell on the native republic of Bimbia near Cameroun.[39] In 1800 he bought an island from the republic. He intended to open a trade in dye-woods, wax, oil, and ivory there. During his stay in Denmark, on January 4, 1801, he was granted royal approbation of the purchase deed. A royal order of May 19, 1802, authorized his purchase of land on other islands in the district. Again he worked out plans for a colonization and sent the schooner *Experiment* to the islands. Since this ship was to be manned by slaves, the fort slaves deserted for the second time, and only a few craftsmen took sail. They successfully built various houses, but several men died during the trip. The most important result was the slave cargo which the schooner brought back, and which was sent on to the West Indies. The factory set up on the island was sacked in 1803, when some Liverpool merchants inflamed the natives to drive the Danes out. Afterwards, Wrisberg dreamed of exchanging the forts on the Lower Coast for the Portuguese island of Principe.[40]

Meanwhile, the interest in plantations was still widespread among the Danes on the coast. The trader, P. Meyer, starting afresh planted cotton and nursed his coffee shrubs, which yielded him ripe beans.[41] His orange trees and tamarinds bore fruit too. This time he laid out his plantations about 25 kilometers inland, just below the Akwapim hills where he found the soil most fertile, and where there was a forest and good water close by. It was located close to the small native town of Ojadufa. Soon he had more coffee shrubs planted; and in 1803-1804, at the expense of the Exchequer and with the aid of publicly and privately owned slaves, he built a road to his plantations. Then he entered into negotiations with the natives for the purchase of the land. The inhabitants of the town of Blegusso (Blaccusse, afterwards known among the Danes as Blaekhuse or Blaekhuso) asked the same price as Isert had paid.[42] The place where the plantation was laid out was also called Bimbiasch or Bibiase. In the end, however, he did not buy the land, but only the usufruct. The price was a 128-rixdollar gratuity, a "salary-custom" of 2 rixdollars, and monthly quantities of liquor and tobacco. The right to build fortifications was included in the purchase but never used. The work was delayed in 1804, when war broke out between Akwapim and Dutch Accra.[43] There was a great battle in which Akwapim was victorious and lopped off the heads of 23 distinguished Accra. The Christiansborg government refused to mediate for fear of the costs. The pause, which the war caused in the work on the plantations near the Akwapim hills, was utilized to plant 2,000 coffee shrubs at the Frederiksberg plantation. Flindt also planted coffee shrubs at Ejebo.[44] Afterwards, the Danes tried to remain friends with Akwapim. In 1807 the caboceer was called to Fort Christiansborg to receive an advance payment of 456 rixdollars, for which he left his sister's son as a pawn at the fort.

Mention must also be made of extensive plantations called Dacubie, laid out at the foot of the Akwapim hills by Christian Schiønning, who became temporary governor in the spring of 1807 when Wrisberg made his second visit to Denmark. Dacubie was nearly two kilometers in length, and in 1809 it had no less than 40,000 coffee shrubs, and a nursery garden with 100,000 plants.[45] The cultivation of coffee on a really large scale was well under way. Proof had at length been given that it would be possible to bring African soil under cultivation and make it yield important products for densely populated Europe. There was every reason in 1808 for Britain to send a deputation to Africa for the purpose of finding out about the possibilities of colonization on the Guinea Coast.[46]

After the cessation of the slave trade, the Danish settlements would never pay a dividend, unless the plantations prospered. After January 1, 1803, life at the forts and trading stations changed considerably. Until that date, duty was still paid for numerous slaves exported in Danish vessels, for instance, in 1798 there were 737.[47] After January 1, 1803, there were no more large-scale shipments of slaves in Danish ships. Only a couple of small vessels were given permission to exceed the time limit.[48] This is not to say that the slave trade at the Danish forts ceased on the date fixed by the king. One captain was fined for having sailed slaves to the island of St. Croix, and the Christiansborg government simply tried to ignore the prohibition.[49] The Christiansborg authorities reasoned that it was only for the sake of trade that the natives were willing to tolerate the presence of Europeans in their country. Until the new plantations had been consolidated, it would be necessary, in order to remain on good terms with the natives, to permit the continuation of the slave trade at least for some time. The opposite course would not only lead to political unrest and enormous expenses, but it also would endanger the very lives of the Danes on the coast. So the Christiansborg government did not immediately fully comply with the royal ordinance of 1792. It could not risk the existence of the settlements and would not forfeit the respect of the natives for the Danes.[50]

Of course, Copenhagen could not tolerate such independent action. When an explanation was demanded, Christiansborg had humbly to declare that the slave trade was no longer allowed at the forts. That was on August 5, 1805. Possibly, this assurance should not have been taken too seriously. Shortly afterwards, the Christiansborg government reported on the harmful effects on trade with Ashanti caused by cessation of the slave trade. After the slave trade had stopped, it was impossible to send as valuable gifts to the natives as before. So some great families in Ashanti had given orders that no one of their nationality, on pain of death, should trade with the Danes or so much as supply them with food. To get out of this impasse, the Danes had to "lend" Ashanti one thousand pounds of gunpowder, half of which was paid for by the private traders of Osu. One reason why Ashanti was so difficult to satisfy may have been that, shortly before, Christiansborg had turned down their request for a large loan. There is a great deal of evidence to support the fact that the slave trade at the Danish forts continued, even if on a smaller scale than before. Even in 1821, when P. S. Steffens came out to be installed in the governorship, the free mulattoes maintained that the abolition of the slave trade had never been announced to them; so they knew nothing about it. Consequently, in Copenhagen the question was raised whether the Danish king had any right to forbid the natives to deal in slaves. It was only in the 1820's, apparently, that a real effort was made to put an end to the slave trade in the Christiansborg district.

It seems natural to ask what the clergymen were doing. They do not seem to have been very active. In the first few years of the new century, two brothers of Nikolaj Frederik Severin Grundtvig, the well-known Danish poet and divine, died after having served for short periods as chaplains in Guinea.[51] The first of them, Jacob Grundtvig, arrived at Christiansborg in January 1800, and died in the autumn. After his death he was given the highest praise ever bestowed upon any Danish clergyman in Africa, especially for his tireless work for the school. He must have been a brother worthy of Denmark's great hymnist. Neils Grundtvig, the poet's second brother, left for Guinea in the summer of 1802 and died in May 1803. He quarreled with Governor Wrisberg and was put in prison for having had sexual intercourse with a Negress. Posthumous praise for him was somewhat less; Wrisberg called him a "disreputable character." On the other hand, his successor, H. C. Monrad, who served as a chaplain on the coast from 1805-09, vindicated his character.[52] Monrad, too, fell out of favor with Wrisberg, merely because he opposed the slave trade. He declared that as long as the government of the settlements remained in the hands of hardened old slave traders nothing much would come of the plantations. His letters are full of complaints; how useless is a clergyman in a country where reason, virtue, and religion are of no account, and where men's consciences and all that should be held sacred must bow to mere egoism. In his opinion, the natives of the coast simply regarded the Christian clergymen as fetish-priests and magicians. So he gave thanks to Almighty God when he escaped unhurt and was again able to set foot on his native soil. After his departure, many years passed before a Danish clergyman came to Osu again.

Later on, when Monrad had had time to calm down in a Danish parsonage, he collected his memories and impressions in a humane and sympathetic book. He called it *Guinea Kysten og dens Indbyggere* ("The Guinea Coast and Its Inhabitants"). It was published in 1822 with a preface by C. Molbach. Of all the books about the subject, Monrad's is the one most likely to give the modern reader some idea of what it was like to be a Dane in Guinea. Above all, he describes the plantations which were beginning to spread about the time when he left the coast. Thus, he gives his reader some idea of what the Danes might have achieved in Africa, if it had not been for the rampant bellicosity of the natives.

20 / THE ASHANTI WAR

THE CONTROL WHICH ASHANTI had held over the Christiansborg and Fredensborg districts since 1742 might seem somewhat sporadic. Sometimes there would be long intervals between payments of "custom" from the European forts. Sometimes the tribes of the neighborhood were allowed an illusion of independence. But every time Ashanti chose to demonstrate its military supremacy, they and the Europeans had to submit and do homage to His Majesty, the king of Ashanti.

The empire built by Ashanti was, by African standards, quite powerful, supposedly the mightiest African state.[1] Its nucleus was a union of closely related tribes, in which the king of Ashanti had been *primus inter pares* at first. In the cousre of time he won absolute control of home affairs, while for foreign affairs he had to take the advice of a council of caboceers, or captains. The satellite nations had to pay tribute in gold and slaves. Their chiefs had to go to Kumasi, the capital of the kingdom, for the annual yam festival, a kind of harvest festival, in September when the new crop was ready to be harvested. The population was always well trained for war. When launching an attack, the swift and fearless Ashanti would spring straight at the throats of their opponents. For large-scale campaigns the satellite nations would be mobilized, too. Sometimes, when a neighboring tribe was to be punished, the king of Ashanti would entrust one of his vassal princes with special tasks. An Ashanti officer was decked with enormous feather ornaments, gold, elephants' tails, and a lot of tawdry fetishes. The soldiers were armed with muskets and swords. The royal bodyguards carried long-barreled Danish muskets, which they themselves had adorned with bands of gold. On festive occasions there would be endless salutes from the muskets. A good deal of the gunpowder sold from the European forts went to Kumasi, so that His Majesty's might could be displayed by the roar of his muskets on all occasions.

The Ashanti were far better warriors than traders. They had no real understanding of transit trade. They imported sufficient arms, munitions, rum, and liquor to serve their own needs, by paying with gold or slaves. Because their own craftsmen were highly skilled, purchases of other commodities were negligible. They were expert gold- and silver-smiths, for the golden treasures of the king of Ashanti were remolded every year in new and original patterns. Many of the textiles they imported were unraveled, and the threads used for new and very beautiful fabrics. Their fine houses were solidly built and were models of cleanliness and order. The king and his noblemen surrounded themselves with riches, color, and splendor. Their material culture was inferior to none.

Nevertheless, Europeans were shocked by the barbarism which the Ashanti demonstrated. The laws and customs of darkest Africa were such as to make the whites thankful that they had been born among civilized nations. Europeans were hardly surprised when told that the king of Ashanti had 3,333 wives occupying an entire secret quarter of is capital, or when they witnessed their wild dances at the great festivals. But the amount of torture and human sacrifices for ritualistic purposes exceeded even the wildest imaginations of the most hardened Europeans. When a great caboceer had arrived at Kumasi, his first duty was the sacrifice of a slave. When feasts were nearing their climax, groups of human beings were led to the slaughter. They had already been prepared for their lot by having had knives thrust through their cheeks and sometimes behind their shoulder blades too. Then, one hand was lopped off before they were mercifully put to death. Not only slaves and prisoners of war were sacrificed; in the course of funerals among the "better families," a free man among the mourners would be struck from behind by a slave. His body would fall in such a way as to cover the deceased, after which they would both be hastily buried. Royal funerals were the worst. When the mother of Osei Bonsu died, 3,000 were sacrificed, of whom 2,000 were Fanti prisoners. At the death of a king all his *ocras,* that is, free men who had devoted their lives to his service and had been supported by him at court, would be sacrificed. Homer's hecatombs were child's play compared with this. And, as if this were not enough, human sacrifices would continually be made at the royal tombs at Bentama near Kumasi to keep the earth soaked with blood. So it is hardly surprising that, while a battle was being fought, the heads of fallen enemies would be taken to the general and arranged in careful piles. At the same time, to show his indifference to the outcome of the battle the commander-in-chief, reclining carelessly in his seat, would play a board game while issuing his orders.

So it was a formidable, savage, and indomitable enemy that the Europeans were faced with when, in the opening years of the nineteenth century, a war broke out between them and the Ashanti.[2] The cause of the war was a sacrilege perpetrated in 1805 by robbers plundering a tomb in the country of Assin, situated between Ashanti and Fanti. This gave rise to a quarrel between the local chiefs. When Osei Bonsu, king of Ashanti, was asked to pass sentence in the dispute, he demanded that the chief of the robbers' party be delivered into his hands. The chief took off, however, and sought the protection first of the Fanti, and afterwards of the English. Now the Ashanti sent an army to the coast. The most dramatic event at this early state of the war was the Ashanti's storming of Anamabo in 1807. The town was captured, and the fort narrowly escaped the same fate. For many years afterwards there were numerous battles between the Ashanti and the English. In the following pages mention will be made only of events which directly concern the Danes.

The disastrous turn of events was due partly to the unfortunate behavior of Torrane, the English governor. In the opinion of Wrisberg, his Danish colleague, he was a man so discourteous that Fort Christiansborg simply broke off all correspondence with him. So the Danes did not feel called upon to side with the English when the war broke out. Besides, in the previous year the Danes had paid a great tribute in an attempt to remain on good terms with the Ashanti. Thus when, after the battle of Anamabo, Ashanti's army was expected at Accra, the Danes were not particularly nervous. Still, forts Christiansborg and Prøvesten were made ready for the defense, but the Ashanti failed to appear. Osei Bonsu marched home and gave thanks to his gods by innumerable human sacrifices. Nevertheless, the Danes were made to suffer daily from the arrogance of the victors. The Ashanti robbed and blackmailed the inhabitants of the coast in every possible way, and the interim Governor Schiønning had to lend considerable sums to their victims. At the same time, Ashanti leaders with their attendants, under cover of friendship, would descend like locusts on the forts. They would remain there with threats of violence for weeks and months while the Fanti were threatening from the outside, because they had not received the support promised them by the Danes.

When the second round started, it was no longer possible for the Danes to avoid the ravages of war. By 1809 preparations were being made for another conflict between Fanti and Ashanti, and in 1811 Ashanti sent two armies toward the coast.[3] The eastern force under Opoku Ferefere invited the Akim chief, Abuakwa, to take part in the campaign. Abuakwa, however, had the Ashanti messengers put to death. Afterwards he entered into an alliance with Kwao Saforo Twie, chief of Akwapim, and in February 1811 he made a stand against the enemy on the River Pra. At this point, the Dutch Accra and the towns of Osu and Labadi sent an army to Osei Opoku. The Akim and Akwapim then retreated, the former westward and the latter towards the east. The combined forces of Akim and Fanti beat back the western army of

Ashanti; but Akwapim's army disintegrated, and Kwao fled. Opoku's Ashanti army took up the pursuit and reached Ada. The town was burnt down, and Flindt, the Danish commander of Fort Kongensten, was taken prisoner. The Ejebo plantation as well as Schiønning's, Meyer's, and Truelsen's plantations in Akwapim were completely destroyed. Threats of attack were uttered against the Danes, unless they handed over Kwao. The Danish forts were far too short of munitions to take up the fight. To the great vexation of the Osu, the Danes declared their neutrality and tried to get out of their difficult position by giving the Ashanti presents worth nearly 2,000 rixdollars. It was hoped that this amount would also suffice for the ransom of Flindt, but some time was to pass before he was set free.

The situation soon changed. Kwao had escaped safely to the Akim. Now he turned up again, backed by Akim and Fanti, and called up his own men. On August 27, 1811, these combined forces together with the Danish natives along the coast fought a decisive battle against Opoku's Ashanti army. The latter were not defeated; but they had already been weakened by the battles of the Pra, and now they again suffered great losses. Afterwards Akwapim retreated to the top of Mount Krobbo which, in spite of two Ashanti attacks, they managed to hold. In September the king of Ashanti called his army home. This made the coast people so insolent that no European could feel safe from them. The Osu issued strong proclamations. Every hope of saving some of the crops of the Akwapim plantations had to be abandoned. It was estimated that 36,000 coffee bushes could have yielded 100,000 pounds of coffee.[4] Now the natives stole and sold the coffee. Nobody was allowed to tend and weed the plantations so that there might be a chance for a crop the next year. Nature was allowed free play. The cultivated plants were soon smothered and everything laid waste. Frederiksberg plantation was lost, too. A beautiful avenue of trees leading from Fort Christiansborg to the plantation was destroyed, and in November the natives forced the gate of the compound and robbed all that was of value to them. Thus the native wars reduced to total ruin all that the Danes had tried to build up for two decades. The belief that plantations would enable Denmark's Guinea settlements to bring in revenue in the future had been fundamentally shaken.

The local governments completely lost control of the natives.[5] Those mulattoes who were not soldiers in the service of the forts threw off their allegiance with the Europeans. Some of Fort Christiansborg's slaves, who were of great importance because the mulatto garrison was small, were lured away. The Dutch Accra, without the support of the Dutch, gained supremacy over Osu and Labadi. They were reinforced when Akwapim made peace with them, and became their vassals.

Trouble was also brewing to the east of the Volta.[6] Awuna tried to collect 6,000 rixdollars from the Danes. They claimed Governor Biørn had borrowed this amount from them years ago; but, as far as we know, he had not. The old enmity of Awuna and Keta constantly flared up. On September 17, 1819, a pitched battle was fought which cost Fort Prinsensten 1,500 rixdollars, besides money out of the governor's own pocket. Afterwards Schiønning proposed to the Danish authorities that the fort be abandoned. Following the abolition of the slave trade the fort was useless, for the soil of the district was not suitable for plantations. Copenhagen was of the opinion, however, that the fort should not be given up as long as the Danes wanted to keep control of the Volta River.

The helplessness of the Danish Guinea government against the inroads of the natives was due to the war that was being fought in Europe between Denmark and Britain. Neither in 1801 nor in 1807 were the Danish forts in Guinea occupied by the British, as was the case in the Danish East and West Indian territories. But the war of 1807-1814 prevented the sending of a ship from Copenhagen for nine years. Fortunately, the mortality rate among the Danes on the coast was low in those years. Throughout this period Christian Schiønning held the post of governor *ad interim*. New regulations for the forts had just come into force when he took up the reins after the departure of Johan P. G. Wrisberg in 1807.[7] At the same time, the Christiansborg government took over great quantities of goods from Wrisberg's private stores, so business was quite good at first. The authorities even found strength enough to pull down the old government hall dating from 1725 and replace it with more comfortable rooms.[8] After a couple of years, however, the shortage of goods and other resources became considerable. Also, the commandants of the forts on the Lower Coast complained that they did not get their share of Wrisberg's merchandise.[9] In spite of the war a few letters got through to Copenhagen. In one of them Schiønning proposed that a cargo of goods be sent from the United States to the Danish Guinea forts.[10] The attempt was made, but in vain. For some time Schiønning carried on by paying out of his own pocket. Then, after 1810 he succeeded in persuading English merchants to supply him against drafts on Copenhagen.[11] To start with he drew £1,500, next year, £1,086, and a year later, £3,500. In 1813, the amount which passed through the hands of a merchant of Elmina rose to £4,000. In spite of the war these drafts were duly paid. In this way the Danes in Guinea staved off starvation and poverty, but there were many other difficulties. The officials did not receive their full salaries; and the native chiefs did not get their tributes, which in itself sufficed to make them lose all respect for the Danes.[12] The war cost the Danes great sums. About New Year's 1812, Flindt was finally ransomed;[13] the Danish authorities had to buy 27 Ashanti prisoners of war from the coast natives in exchange for him. Schiønning's health broke down under this constant strain. Gradually he seems to have lost control, neglected his account books, and let things slide.

After the catastrophic war years, Denmark had great difficulty in resuming contacts with her overseas possessions.[14] As late as the autumn of 1815, it was impossible for the government to find the money to equip a ship for Guinea although several shipowners offered their assistance. For a long time the only manifestation of any interest in Guinea on the part of the government was the appointment of Philip Wilhelm Wrisberg, the brother of Governor Johan P. D. Wrisberg, on August 28, 1814, as chief of His Majesty's military forces in Guinea. The king appointed him captain, afterwards permitted him to call himself commandant of Fort Christiansborg, and gave him a seat in the secret council. When the Prøven, which belonged to Tutein Bros., left for Guinea in November 1815, only a few of the barest necessities were sent at the king's expense; but Ph. W. Wrisberg himself sent some goods. Proper supplies for the forts were finally sent by the brig Turbulent, which took on board 96,264 rixdollars' worth of goods and sailed from Copenhagen in December 1816. There were no plans for immediate changes in the position of the Guinea settlements. On November 8, 1815, the king merely resolved that accounts were to be kept as usual. He also fixed the rate of exchange for Guinean rixdollars at 1⅗ Danish Rigsbank silver dollars, that is, a far better rate than paid for Danish rixdollars after the National Bankruptcy of 1813. It was only after the royal order of December 13, 1816, that reductions of Guinea expenses were decreed, because the loss of Norway and of Denmark's and Norway's combined navy made this urgent. Nearly all Guinea officials were discharged with full pay for the period they had remained on the coast. In addition, they were to receive a free passage home and retirement allowances at home in silver "with the difference in the currencies." Next, it was laid down that normal annual expenses for the forts must not exceed 24,000 silver rixdollars. Christiansborg was to remain the seat of the Guinea government, and all other forts were to be dismantled. Superfluous mulattoes were to be discharged with a gratuity of one year's pay. The governor was authorized to stop expenses for useless slaves, now called "serfs." To encourage planters the Guinea government was authorized to buy coffee and cotton at fixed prices.

The Guinea government was still forced to buy against drafts. In 1815 it drew £2,500 and in 1816, £24,000. In October 1815 Schiønning had an apoplectic stroke, lost the use of his voice, and became completely helpless. The reins passed into the hands of the commandant of the fort, Johan Emanuel Richter, who was appointed governor and given the rank of a major of His Majesty's Army on December 12, 1816.[15] He formally took over after Schiønning's death on March 3, 1817.

However, the Ashanti were now threatening war again. A huge army under the command of Amankwa Abinowa had appeared on the coast in August 1815. When the Akim and the Akwapim tried to stop them, they were vanquished. Now the Ashanti pitched their camp on Mount Abodé in Akwapim. From there they sent an embassy of their greatest nobles to Fort Christiansborg, who accused Schiønning of having spoken ill of the king of Ashanti and demanded payment of 2,000 rixdollars, "using proud words against us." After some negotiations, the fort was let off with a fine of 160 rixdollars, but the stay of the distinguished guests was not gratis. After five months' stay in the camp, the army invaded Fanti, advanced on Cape Coast Castle and Elmina, and did not return until the black inhabitants of these places had paid £2,000. Next, they returned to Accra in June 1816 and camped 15 kilometers inland on the plantations of the coast peoples, so that the Accra could harvest neither grain nor fruit. On that occasion the Christiansborg government completely lost patience with the Ashanti as friends. "May Merciful God at length deliver us from this villainous pack of robbers." However, the paramount duty of the Ashanti forces was to arrest the runaway chiefs of Akim and Akwapim and re-establish Ashanti supremacy over the rebellious tribes. So when they succeeded in laying their hands on the two chiefs, sent their carefully smoked heads to Kumasi, and pacified the natives, the army at last marched home. On the way, they made another vain attempt to conquer Mount Krobbo. Kwao's successor as caboceer of Akwapim, Ado Dankwa, came to the Danes and asked for money to pay the Ashanti for their peace. Fort Christiansborg's treasury was empty, so he only received 250 rixdollars, while Akwapim had to pay Ashanti 200 slaves and about 2,000 rixdollars.

Thus, as long as possible, the Danes used the oft-repeated method of buying their peace when the natives threatened attack. After the arrival of the *Turbulent* in March 1817, the blacks again pressed for goods and salaries; and the Danes succeeded in restoring respect for the government on the coast. However, the bustle and business of the heyday of the slave trade could not be restored. Often there would be intervals of more than a year between the arrivals of supplies from Copenhagen. These cargoes were bought for the king by Praetorius, who hired space for them in the holds of small vessels leaving for the coast. Often these vessels carried privately owned goods, besides those sent by the government. But it seems that only very rarely did private shipowners send their ships to the Danish Guinea settlements. When the *Prøven* was sent out again at Christmas time 1817, it was wrecked in the Tannis Bay.[16] As the arrivals of ships became fewer, life at the forts slowed down to a quieter pace than in the eighteenth century.

An additional reason for this slackening was the reduction of staff ordered by the king.[17] The governor was to have only two assistants.

Richter chose Jens Nicolaj Reiersen as chief assistant and Christian Svanekiaer as second assistant. Ph. W. Wrisberg sailed on the *Turbulent* to see whether the settlements could be advantageously exchanged for the Portuguese island of Principe in the Gulf of Guinea.[18] While there, however, he fell ill and returned directly to Europe, where he was discharged by the king with the rank of major. Richter was not to hold office very long. He died on October 5, 1817, and was succeeded by Reiersen as governor *ad interim*.[19] It was not easy to carry on the government's business with the reduced staff. The planned revision of Schiønning's accounts, which were chaotic, or had not been kept for years, simply had to be given up in the end.[20] To make matters worse, there were some years when the staff changed constantly. Mathias Thonning, who had tried to run a couple of plantations, had to be sent home when his eyesight began to fail. Reiersen had died on May 6, 1819, and was succeeded by Svanekiaer as interim governor. At this point, Ph. W. Wrisberg was appointed governor. He seems, however, to have been suspected of having a part in the upsetting of a canoe, whereby the white passengers had been in danger of their lives. So he was discharged with a waiting allowance a month later on November 25, 1819, before he had even set out for Guinea. His Majesty's government had to look for somebody else. The government dared not appoint Svanekiaer; he was not thought fit for the post. The Ashanti were threatening to launch another campaign against the Fanti and the British, and Svanekiaer lost control of the Accra in the general unrest. An expedition made up of thirty hired, free natives and headed by Sergeant Palm was sent to Kumasi with gifts for the Ashanti king. They brought back his demand for bullets and gunpowder in lieu of an advance on the king's normal "custom." [21] Svanekiaer was unwilling to grant this advance, so the Ashanti prohibited all trade with Fort Christiansborg. By royal order of May 6, 1820, in Copenhagen, Peter Svane Steffens, an infantry officer, was appointed governor and major.[22] Having been provided with new regulations for himself and the Danish officials in Guinea, he arrived at Fort Christiansborg on board the *Emerald*. About New Year's 1821 he stepped ashore, accompanied by Mathias Thonning, now restored to health, and various new men. Among them was L. G. Poulsen, who had been sent out "by His Majesty's express order," although he was a half-crazy eccentric, who, it was rumored, was the son of King Frederik VI.[23]

Having thus augmented his staff, Steffens set to work with great energy. He found that the Osu were agreeable neighbors provided they received the "custom" due to them. (Reiersen and Svanekiaer, in obedience to the strict economy demanded by the home government, had vainly tried to avoid these payments.) Steffens praised the natives, too. Since they themselves were now beginning to cultivate the land, their harvests provided him with export goods. He had no difficulty in getting as-

sistance for the arrest of some Portuguese and English slave traders at
Temma. He did all he could to keep the Danish mulattoes from entering
the service of the English, who were recruiting energetically for the war
against Ashanti. He still had seventy-six able-bodied men left. First he
presented them with a banner on behalf of the king and made them
swear an oath of loyalty. Next he organized them as a militia, which
seemed to him necessary for the defense of Fort Christiansborg. The
permanent garrison of the fort counted only twenty men. Trade was at
a low ebb, most of it had fallen to the traders of English Accra. In Osu
only a mulatto merchant named H. Richter carried on important trade.
Frederiksberg plantation had again been fenced in, and in the neighborhood of the fort there was "The King's Garden," which had also been
fenced in and fertilized.[24] Steffens himself bought the ruins of Bibiase
plantation, including fifty-two natives of both sexes. He further planned
excursions into the district to find out where the soil was most suitable
for cultivation. He also applied for loans for the native planters. On
October 22, 1822, the king granted 2,000-3,000 rixdollars annually for a
three-year period for these loans. However, this grant was never used, for
the information given to the natives about it "had no effect on this
thriftless people."

It was evident that Steffens was planning for a revival of Danish
influence on the coast, and he was hoping to get the necessary revenue
from new large-scale plantations. Unfortunately, nothing came of his
plans. Steffens died on September 5, 1821, and Mathias Thonning took
over as governor *ad interim*.[25] After that a long time elapsed before he
was replaced by a full-fledged governor. It was not until September 17,
1822, that the Copenhagen government had finished its deliberations and
made the appointment. The choice had fallen upon Johan Christopher
Richelieu, who was appointed governor and major.[26] His departure was
delayed in every conceivable way. The first ship in which he was to sail,
the *Kammerherre Rosenkrans,* got only to Penzance in Cornwall. Here
the passengers had to be put ashore and the cargo stored, because the
ship was rotten. After that, six months were spent on intrigues and
arguments before another ship, the *Marie,* could be sent off. Richelieu,
who had drawn large advances on his salary and used too much money
in England, had to ask to be received in audience by King Frederik VI
and beg his pardon. He did not reach Fort Christiansborg until about
New Year's 1824.

In the meantime Thonning had had difficulties, also. In 1821 the
British government had taken over the Guinea Coast possessions of the
British African Company. They had been annexed to the territories
governed by the joint governor of all British West African territories.
This was Sir Charles McCarthy, whose official residence was in Sierra
Leone.[27] During his first visit to the Gold Coast in March 1822, he

came to the conclusion that the British government would have to break the back of Ashanti. When he arrived at Cape Coast Castle a year later, he meant to take stern measures. Immediately after his arrival Captain Blenkarne, commander of Fort James near Accra, without telling the Danes, invited the natives of Osu, Labadi, and Tessing to come to him. The natives are said to have gone to Thonning to ask his advice, but he flew into a rage and had them thrown out of the fort. Others of them asked him just to remain neutral. They went to the English, and, in their indignation against Thonning, accepted the British invitation to join the alliance against Ashanti. Inflamed by the English, they went home and killed all the Ashanti who were visiting in their towns on business. Several hundred are said to have been massacred. It seems that the skulls of the murdered Ashanti were brought to Fort Christiansborg to be sent on to Fort James. In any case, the breach with Ashanti was now irremediable. So the Danish coast natives joined the English for a successful campaign against Akwapim.

In November 1823, however, a huge Ashanti army marched into Fanti. On January 21, 1824, in the battle of Nsamankow, the Ashanti defeated part of the Fanti and the English. McCarthy pressed on too eagerly, got into difficulties, and took his own life. The Ashanti cut off his head and carried it to Kumasi. On the day of the battle, intelligent and energetic King Osei Bonsu of Ashanti died. Since his successor was seventeen-year-old Osei Yaw Akoto, at first the country was ruled by a regency. The fighting continued. The Ashanti harried the country far and wide. Fort Christiansborg was making preparations for its defense. Then, on July 11, 1824, the combined English and Danish forces, each supported by their native allies, inflicted a crushing defeat on the Ashanti army.[28] The Christiansborg government had appointed L. G. Poulsen, the assistant, captain of the Danish force, but it was the bravery of the Danish natives which carried the day. The greatest gallantry was shown by Queen Dokua of Akim, who led her army into battle herself, and by Nothay Davunna, caboceer of Osu, who with his own hand felled one of the most important Ashanti leaders. When informed of these feats, King Frederik VI commanded that both should be presented with silver swords. The costs of the war were paid by the English with a check for £2,000 sterling.

After that, there was peace for awhile. Richelieu made a journey to the forts on the Lower Coast and found them more or less in ruins. At Fort Prinsensten he found a soapworks run as an enterprise of Major Wrisberg. He had to fire Svanekiaer[29] and Poulsen[30] and send them home as embezzlers, but his own accounts were not in very good order. Fresh difficulties arose in 1824 when the crops failed. Richelieu himself suffered attacks of one disease after another. So after little more than a year's stay on the coast, he sailed for home on May 7, 1825.[31] At his departure an assistant named Niels Brock took over as interim governor. On their return to Copenhagen, both Svanekiaer's and Richelieu's accounts were carefully audited. L. G. Poulsen died in 1825. An investigation committee, whose members were Assessors Rottbøll and Witt, had great difficulty proving Svanekiaer guilty of some minor offences, and afterward he established himself in Guinea as a businessman.[32] Richelieu, on the other hand, was taken to task for spending some of the £2,000 which the English had paid for the defeat of the Ashanti and was never able to recover.[33] The revision of their accounts was made very complicated by the fact that goods were sold to the whites at invoice prices, to mulattoes at higher prices, and to the natives at still higher prices.[34] Also for a considerable length of time, the defendants and Major Wrisberg were busy incriminating each other.

Niels Brock had landed in Guinea at the age of 16 and was a mere 21 when he succeeded to the governorship.[35] For more than a year, he carried on singlehanded. Only then were a couple of assistants sent to him from Europe. Under these circumstances, he could hardly be expected to have put affairs into better shape. Nevertheless, he showed common sense and evidently was supported by the good advice of the trader, Richter.

Before long, the Ashanti again made a nuisance of themselves. As might have been expected, they were out to wreak vengeance for their defeat. During 1825 the Akim had frequent clashes with them. The British tried to win the friendship of the warlike queen of Akim by presenting her with a palanquin. She was not satisfied with it, however, and is said to have declared that she recognized no other overlords than the Danes. In 1826 the Akim were put to flight when another Ashanti army marched out. This time they marched directly toward the Danish territories. Christiansborg dared not ask the English for assistance, for fear of the compensation which would have to be paid afterwards. The Danes had to be content with such support as they could request from the tribes which were regarded as under Danish protection. However, the English themselves offered their assistance and an Anglo-Danish pact was signed. The two nations were bound to mutual assistance without compensations to either party. The English governor, Lieutenant-Colonel Purdon, came over from Cape Coast Castle with several officers, considerable quantities of munitions, four field-guns with Congreve rockets, and part of the garrison. Over and above this, the English called up 6,000-7,000 of their natives. Purdon's plan was to await the arrival of the enemy under the guns of Fort Christiansborg, but the Danes could not get provisions for their great force. Besides, the Osu preferred to meet the enemy north of their plantations, so they would not be starved out. Therefore, the Danish natives formed the vanguard, and the combined forces marched into the hills of Akwapim. There, on the morning of

Monday, August 7, 1826, the Ashanti attacked them.[36] Thus began the battle of Dodowa (or Dudua) about 60 kilometers northeast of Accra.

The English and Danish reports of the battle do not agree. Nevertheless, they both say that "pressed by the furious onslaught of the enemy," the Fanti had to give way. So the Ashanti stormed against a reserve of Europeans which, supposedly, included the trader, Richter, and his slaves. This reserve was in charge of the Congreve rockets, which the Ashanti had never come up against before. Great numbers of them were slaughtered, and yet the outcome remained in the balance. Now the English reported that the victory was secured by Akwamu and Denkyera, which, having been victorious on either wing, were called to the assistance. The Danes, on the other hand, would have it that the Akwamu force, numbering two thousand men, neatly turned the enemy's flank and attacked the Ashanti from behind, capturing their supplies. This spread confusion in their ranks, so of the total Ashanti army of 10,000-12,000 men, 5,000-6,000 were killed or captured, including 37 generals and nobles. Among the spoils taken by the Danish natives was Governor McCarthy's head, sewn up in a leopard's skin. When the English demanded that it be handed over to them, this was done. The Danes were represented in this campaign by Brock and the mulatto, Lindendorff, with 20 soldiers of the garrison, who were distributed among the native chiefs to dole out the reserve of munitions. Besides this, there were the traders, Aarestrup, Lutterodt, Balch, and Richter, each with his own slaves. Richter received a wound in the thigh, and a slave who had served as a bricklayer was killed. The munitions for the battle cost a total of 6,800 rixdollars.

Shortly after the battle a new British governor, Sir Neil Campbell, arrived on the coast. Hoping that the trade routes to the interior could soon be reopened, he at once made peace overtures to Ashanti.[37] This met with the opposition of the coast natives. For, according to their code, the victor could not ask for peace, and besides, they feared that the British would again deliver them into the hands of the Ashanti. So it was a long time before a peace could be settled.

Meanwhile, in Copenhagen on September 28, 1826, the king appointed an investigation committee to be sent to Guinea.[38] Its members were Lieutenant Commander Jens Peter Flindt and judge-advocate Ludvig Vincent Hein. Flindt was to be interim governor pending the investigations. The committee did not leave Copenhagen until the following year, and it finally arrived at Christiansborg on board the *Lille Cathrine,* which belonged to a merchant L. N. Hvidt, on September 29, 1827. The ship brought also all the necessary materials for a "Dutch" mill, plus a millwright and a couple of journeyman millers. The mill was ready for use in March 1828. The purpose was to make a serious attempt to create an export of maize flour from Guinea to the West Indies, so that the

triangular route would again be profitable. The new article would take
the place of the former export of slaves. These attempts to export flour
to the West Indies brought only a deficit. On its arrival at the islands,
the flour was fit only for the pigs.[39]

At the same time, the sloop *Laurine Mathilde* set out on an expedition
to the Volta River. The chief aim of this expedition was to ascertain the
value of the forests along the river. The commander of this expedition
was first lieutenant of the Navy, Henrik Gerhard Lind. He left Christiansborg on Christmas Eve 1827 and returned on February 1, 1828.[40] On
its way up the river, the ship passed the native towns of Agraggi,
Tjerrekoi, Tefferie, Hume, Blappa, and Malfi before reaching Mafe.
Since Kiøge's days at least, the inhabitants of all these towns, being
close relatives of the Ada, had been more or less attached to the Danes.
The ship could not sail any farther than Mafe, but Lind continued by
canoe to the town of Asjotale. He mentions Bataa as the last Danish
native town, and toward the end of his journey he reached places which
no white man had seen before. He drew a map of the river, indicating the
most important shallows. Investigations made by him and two carpenters
of the forests along the river were not very promising. The Copenhagen
Admiralty had hoped to find timber usable for shipbuilding there; but
tall trees were too few, transportation costs too high, and, above all, the
climate too dangerous. Lind and most members of his expedition were
seriously ill when they returned. So the attempt to make use of the
forests was given up.

This investigation committee worked faster and better than any of the
other committees which had been sent to Guinea. A number of reports
were sent home on the political situation of the settlements, "customs,"
Brock's administration, schools and languages, probate courts, and a
cultivation plan submitted by Major Ph. W. Wrisberg, which among other
innovations proposed setting up a penal colony on the Volta River.[41]
It said that the school was run by two mulattoes who had been confirmed
by Monrad. Neither of them spoke decent Danish, and the native language was too primitive and inarticulate to be suitable for teaching or
for writing. An attempt by Major Wrisberg to translate the Sermon on
the Mount into the language of the Accra had not been very successful.
The language of Wrisberg's book was very different from either Protten's
or Schiønning's translations of the Ten Commandments. (Of all the
Europeans, Schiønning was thought to have the greatest proficiency in
the native language.) So the committee came to the conclusion that the
school language ought to be Danish, which would help to raise the
natives out of the "slough of barbarism and anarchy in which they are
now living." [42] In its report on the political situation in regard to the
natives, the committee said that in 1826 the Akwamu had sworn an
oath of loyalty to the Danish king. It proposed that the king of Akwamu

be paid half the salary which until recently had been paid to the king of Ashanti. It would not do to deprive any caboceer of his salary, seeing how interested the natives were in this income. In regard to colonization, the committee proposed that plantations be started at Bibiase. The committee advised against the plan for a penal colony on the Volta River, since the climate of the district was too unhealthful. In order to consolidate the position of the settlements, the committee advocated the establishment of an artillery corps of mulattoes. Having handed in their reports, both Flindt and Hein left the coast in 1828.[43] Flindt went home by way of the United States. Hein sailed directly for Europe. After the departure of Flindt, H. G. Lind served as governor *ad interim*. The proposals of the committee did not result in any important changes on the part of the Danish government. The most significant one may have been the king's assent of September 17, 1828, to the creation of the artillery corps.[44] In addition, Lind, like Steffens, organized a militia of four to five hundred men.[45] The committee's work resulted also in new and detailed instructions for the Guinea probate courts.[46]

Another result of the revival of Danish interest in the settlements was the sending of missionaries to Guinea.[47] On June 3, 1826, the king had ordered the Danish Mission Society (founded in 1821) to take the matter in hand. Shortly afterwards, the order was reversed; the mission was to be sent by the Basle Mission Society. So four missionaries, headed by Johan Phillip Hencke, came to Denmark to be ordained by the Bishop of Sealand. They reached Christiansborg by way of London in December 1828 and were accompanied by an African named Noi, the son of an Osu caboceer who was baptized as Frederik Dawunna. Rasums Rask, the great Danish linguist, after studying Frederik Dawunna's mother tongue, wrote a guide to the Accra language for the use of the missionaries.[48] The results of the four men's activities were meagre. They were critical of the Danish administration on the coast, so the Christiansborg government tried to persuade them to move to the native villages on the plantations in Akwapim. However, three of them died in August 1829. Afterward Hencke was made catechist and schoolmaster at Christiansborg,[49] where he died in 1831. His appointment had been an attempt to improve the school. The Christiansborg government wanted better schools, so an effort was made to start a girls' school with a female teacher qualified to teach needlework. This project received the royal assent on April 24, 1830. After Monrad's time there had been no chaplains at the Danish settlements, and now after the death of Hencke, catechists instead were sent out to teach in the schools on the coast.

A great individual contribution was made by a physician, J. J. Trentepohl, of Tönning.[50] On board the Asiatic Company's ship *Christianshavn* he had visited China and had brought home many scientific observations and collections. Now he applied for the position of surgeon in Guinea;

and, with an annual grant of 400 rixdollars for two years, he arrived in Guinea in 1829 and bought a plantation. However, he died on January 15, 1830. Nevertheless, he found time to make a collection of insects, which was sent home. He also started very detailed meteorological observations which were carried on by an assistant named R. Chenon and a surgeon named F. Sannom; the results were published by Videnskabernes Selskab (the Academy of Science) in 1845 in Copenhagen.

While these attempts were being made to develop the Danish settlements, a long time passed before peace was made with the Ashanti. Only after many months did an embassy from the king of Ashanti arrive at Cape Coast Castle with offers of peace. The English commandant thought that the Danes and their native allies had better take part in the negotiations. The allies of the Danes did not want peace, for they regarded it as an insult that the embassy had gone to the English and not to the Danish fort. The Christiansborg government, however, was willing to make peace, so Flindt sent Lind to Cape Coast Castle. Here he found the peace terms drawn up by the English unsatisfactory, and he protested. Since the Ashanti would not accept the peace terms, either, no treaty could be signed at the time. Afterwards squabbles broke out between Fanti and the Elmina natives, who had sided with the Ashanti. In the meantime in 1828 the British government handed its forts over to a company of merchants trading on the coast. The new rulers at Cape Coast Castle took a purely mercantile view, and for the sake of trade they were even more desirous of peace than the old ones. Still, negotiations dragged on. The Danes hoped to make a separate peace; so to prepare the way, they sent presents to the queen of Akim, but all was in vain.

Instead, the Danes and English signed a treaty on March 2, 1830, forbidding either of the parties to seek a separate peace, and binding both to make peace with the Ashanti on equal terms. At length, Ashanti offered a pawn of 600 gold ounces and two youths of their best families as hostages to be educated at the schools of the forts. These terms were accepted, so an Ashanti embassy came to Accra and afterwards to Cape Coast Castle, where they made peace with the English and their allies on April 27, 1831. The Danes and their allies did not sign this treaty. Problems of etiquette prevented their presence, so from Cape Coast Castle the Ashanti embassy returned to Accra, where on August 7 of that year a separate peace treaty was signed by Denmark and Ashanti. Strictly speaking, the treaty of March 2, 1830, had been disregarded.[51]

Nevertheless, the terms of the Danish treaty were practically the same as those of its English counterpart, only more detailed. Besides rules for trade and slavery, it was expressly laid down therein that "those African Chiefs who were allies of His Majesty the King of Denmark: and who were signatories of the peace treaty, should be completely independent of the Ashanti." The cosigners were a number of caboceers from towns on the coast and from the Volta River district. There were none from the mountains or from Akim or Akwapim. As for the 600 ounces of gold paid by Ashanti as a pawn, it was to be refunded if peace was not broken for five years. The Danes were willing to allow the pawn to remain at Cape Coast Castle, provided the English gave a written security for half the amount to the Christiansborg government. Afterwards the English refused to hand over the guarantees, unless the Danes paid half the costs of the campaign, which they had no intention of doing. The promissory note which the Danes finally obtained seemed to them a poor security, but the Ashanti did not break the peace and were repaid the pawn by the English.

Before the peace treaty had been formally signed, Lind was permitted to leave Guinea for reasons of health and on September 19, 1830, L. V. Hein was appointed governor.[52] His second arrival at Christiansborg on board the *Aurora* took place on January 27, 1831. A few days later he assumed his post. Before long, however, he fell out with the trader, Richter; he tried to reduce the wages of the native slaves of the fort, and for some time was troubled with unrest among the Osu.[53] This friction disturbed the peace conference, and the influence of the Danes declined. The Danes split into two parties, after which Hein sent home an assistant, Balthasar Mathias Christensen,[54] who sided with Richter. The quarrel was of short duration, however, for Hein died on October 21, and was succeeded by his A.D.C., Helmuth von Ahrensdorff, a gentleman-in-waiting, who became interim governor.

After the conclusion of the peace treaty, the Ashanti never regained control of the coast natives. From then on, neither the English nor the Danes paid tribute for the forts, whereas the Dutch continued to do so. The salaries still paid to the caboceers of the coast natives and the Akwapim hill towns could no longer be taken as signs of submission. The thought that by these payments the Danes became the subjects of a black monarch from now on was absurd. The native tribes of the coastal towns were too weak to make themselves masters of the country. The balance of power had shifted in favor of the Europeans and their mulatto descendants, however few they might seem to be compared with vast numbers of pure-blooded natives. At long last, there was reason to think that Denmark possessed an extensive colony in Africa. Steffens had already openly referred to the natives of the hill regions of Akwapim as "subjects of the Danish King," and what he called "the Danish Territories." [55] The peace treaty of 1831 spoke of "allied" African chiefs, but the governor's instructions remained in force, demanding "defence of the Danish Territory." So, in the following years, a number of native tribes were considered to be living in Danish territory. With sovereign rights followed some responsibility for the life of the inhabitants of the country. The first dawnings of this feeling were beginning to be perceptible in Copenhagen. Also, the hope of making the colony bring a revenue through cultivation remained alive. Even if, for the time being, the territories did not pay, there was still the possibility of improvements; thus, the future did not look too bad, and the maintenance of the settlements might still seem reasonable.

21 / QUARRELS WITH THE BRITISH

AFTER PEACE HAD BEEN MADE with the Ashanti, there were several relatively quiet years during which the Christiansborg government was not very active, being hampered by constant changes of personnel. H. von Ahrensdorff, the interim governor, died of a fever at the close of 1831,[1] after which Niels Brock again took command.[2] On July 8, 1832, the home government appointed H. G. Lind, the former leader of the Volta expedition, temporary governor.[3] With his wife and sister he reached Christiansborg in February 1833 on board L. N. Hvidt's ship Der junge Heinrich. This time his work on the coast was to be of short duration. He died on July 21 that year.[4] His wife passed away during the homeward voyage; only his sister returned safely to Europe. Lind was succeeded by the head assistant, a second lieutenant named Edvard von Gandil, but on August 12, 1834, the home government appointed First Lieutenant Frederik Siegfred Mörch of the Royal Danish Navy interim governor.[5] He arrived at Accra on the Den danske Eeg on December 26, 1834. He was promoted to the full governorship on August 19, 1837, and his term of office was to be of somewhat longer duration than those of his immediate predecessors on the Guinea Coast.

The constantly changing chiefs of the Christiansborg government were still interested in plantations.[6] In 1829 Lind spent some weeks in Akwapim and had a great quantity of coffee beans sown. Afterwards he had the inhabitants of Osu, Labadi, and Tessing promise that each one alternately for a year would clear the road to the Akwapim plantation. For this service they were to be paid in liquor, pipes, and tobacco. In addition, he tried to find the former native servants of the fort who, during the 1817 reduction of staff, had been discharged as superfluous. These he settled in the plantation district. Hein, too, became interested in these plans. He bought the plantation from Lind for 2,400 rixdollars, so that it became government property. The king gave his most gracious permission to name it Frederiksgave. On November 9, 1832, he gave orders for the appointment of a committee to consider the advisability of launching a new cultivation scheme. At the same time, the king followed Lind's advice and granted 4,000 rixdollars for the expansion of the areas under private cultivation. Lastly, he assented to the setting up of a militia to protect the plantations. The king also approved the purchase of a horse and carriage for transportation from the plantation to the coast. In 1829 Lind had sent the snow *Laurine Mathilde* to purchase donkeys and goats from the Cape Verde Islands, and the former hospital in the outwork of Fort Christiansborg was converted into stables for these donkeys. Most of the imported animals died in less than a year.[7] Lind was no more successful with four horses which, on his outward voyage, he had bought at the Cape Verde Islands. They produced a few foals, but died after a couple of years. Early in 1835, when the road to Akwapim had been completed, the journey was made by bullock cart. One example of Lind's efforts to civilize the population was his attempt to introduce Danish law for dealing with cases of murder and manslaughter.[8] He tried also to introduce townplanning, so that the homes would not be built too close together as had been the old unsanitary custom.

The Basel Mission Society, also, continued its attempts to help the natives.[9] Three more missionaries were sent out in 1831. Two died very soon after their arrival, while the third man, an inhabitant of Southern Jutland named Andreas Riis, worked in Guinea until 1845. At first he was allowed to prepare the Christiansborg mulattoes for confirmation. Afterwards he went to live at Akropong in Akwapim, and relations between him and the Guinea government became anything but friendly. In the 1840's he set up a small colony of Christian Negroes from Jamaica at Akropong and built a small church. In all the long years he spent in Guinea, he did not baptize a single native. Afterwards it was generally said of him that he had been too busy meddling in politics.

The most important reform in Guinea, however, was forced upon the settlements from outside. In spite of the order for abolition of the slave trade, it was still carried on more or less openly in the Danish territories during the 1830's. At this time the British decided upon more serious measures, and in 1833 slavery was abolished within the British Empire. In that year Denmark was invited to subscribe to the Anglo-French Conventions of November 30, 1831, and March 22, 1833, whereby the signatories allowed each other's warships to examine any ship sailing under their flags to see if they carried slaves. Frederik VI readily signed the conventions on condition that, should the occasion arise, Danish ships were to be sentenced by Danish courts of law on St. Croix in the West Indies, at Christiansborg in Guinea, and at Tranquebar in India. This necessitated the appointment of judges to serve the Christiansborg government, and consequently higher salaries for the assistants. The accession document was dated July 26, 1834,[10] and was followed by a complicated decree of July 3, 1835, concerning the suppression of the slave trade.[11] The Danish government, however, sent out no warships for the purpose of examining vessels at sea, for it was feared that by capturing English or French ships, the Danish government would become liable to damages in cases where judicial decisions went against the capturer.

Hitherto, slaves had frequently been taken on board east of the Volta River, especially at Popo and Wydah.[12] The slavers would often call beforehand at Fort Prinsensten for water and animals, and the slave transports went through the towns of Awuna. The drastic measures taken by the British Navy reduced the exportations of slaves somewhat.[13] The risk was too great, and around the Danish forts the slave trade dwindled considerably. For the time being there was no thought of abolishing slavery itself within the Danish territory, as the English had already done within theirs. Nor was there any manifestation of increased military might. On the contrary, by royal order of August 3, 1834, the small garrisons left at forts Fredensborg, Kongensten, and Prinsensten were still further reduced.[14] From now on each fort was to have only one soldier, whose duty would be to hoist the flag on national holidays, Sundays, and when ships passed by. Thus only the absolute minimum was done to demonstrate territorial sovereignty.

While, as we have seen, a few uncertain steps had been taken towards civilization, Danish supremacy had not been secured. On the contrary, the political situation was anything but clear. The Dutch reoccupation of Fort Crèvecoeur brought no improvement in the situation; but after both the Dutch and the Ashanti had been defeated, relations with the English came to the fore. These relations presented a most complicated problem. Since the Napoleonic Wars, British trade on the Gold Coast had increased enormously, and in time the competition of British traders was felt everywhere.[15] As early as Steffen's days, the traders of English Accra were reported to have sent presents to Akwapim to obtain of the trade. After the battle of Dodowa, the Christiansborg government proposed to the home government that they send a silver sword and a salary as presents to the king of Akwamu in the hope of keeping him from entering the British service. In 1830 it was found that the English were actually trying to bribe the Akwapim and the Akim into showing coolness to the Danes. A new British governor had just arrived at Cape Coast Castle. His name was George Maclean, and he had been especially picked for the post to serve the needs of the merchants. Several years were still to pass before the rivalry between the English and Danes came into the open, but in the long run there was no escaping it. Maclean was a very able man. Nobody equaled his ability for making himself trusted by the natives and smoothing out their quarrels. The situation would become dangerous if he were to try to win over the Danish natives.

It was all too easy to find a cause for conflict. The quarrel started over Akwapim and Akim. The Ashanti peace treaty had not brought real peace there. It was a long time before the direct trade routes were again opened, although the road to Ashanti by way of Fanti soon became passable.[16] Queen Dokua of Akim was having a quarrel with Adjemang, caboceer of part of Akim who remained loyal to the Ashanti. Now Adjemang took refuge at Fort Christiansborg. On the other hand, Boatrim, who was opposed to the government of Ashanti, fled to Queen Dokua.[17] After the death of Osei Yaw, a king of Ashanti, in 1834, his successor, Kwasi (Kwaku) Dua, sought a reconciliation with Boatrim. The question of the refugee's return to Kumasi was often discussed; but in 1839 he was still in Akim, and shortly afterwards he died. No important Danish measures were taken, until Governor F. S. Mörch arrived at Christiansborg. He was as zealous and patriotic as Maclean. Unavoidably the two of them had to collide in the execution of their plans.

It all began when, shortly after his arrival, Mörch sent soldiers to escort Ashanti traders through Akim, while at the same time he sent small presents to the native villages along the route. Afterwards, he attempted with some degree of success to reconcile Boatrim and his enemies and to obtain recognition of the treaty Isert had signed with Krobbo. Meanwhile, Maclean was still trying to make light of Mörch's successes. Peace was necessary for trade, and for the sake of peace he even punished English soldiers who had offended the Danes in Akwapim.[18] But Mörch was reckless. His observations had convinced him that Akwapim was pro-British, rather than pro-Danish. To find out if this were really so, he made a journey to Akwapim in November 1835. Afterwards he wrote that he had done this "partly for the sake of his health, and partly to find out if it would be possible to plant a colony there." When he got there, however, he "learnt" that there was a serious quarrel between Akwapim and Krobbo. They now appeared to be separate nations, though in Isert's days—perhaps because of a misunderstanding on his part—they had seemed united. Mörch said that he tried to mediate, but that the Krobbo refused to obey him. So he decided upon a punitive expedition. Forty soldiers from the garrison, a few pieces of field artillery, and natives from Osu and Labadi combined with the force of Akwapim. After that, most of the coast people joined the expedition, so that Mörch's army numbered no less than 8,000-10,000 men. Thus being overwhelmingly outnumbered by an array far larger than Mörch really cared to have, the Krobbo soon had to sue for peace. On January 12, 1836, there was a battle in which Krobbo lost 42 dead and 60-70 wounded while the Akwapim and its allies had only 14-15 dead and 30 wounded. Krobbo sued for peace, gave up hostages, and paid the costs. Among those who took part in the expedition were Riis, the missionary, and the merchants Richter, Holm, Lutterodt, and Svanekiaer. As a reward for their exploits Mörch and Richter were afterwards made Knights of the Order of Dannebrog, two sergeants were awarded the Cross of Dannebrog for gallantry in action, and others were presented with tokens of His Majesty's satisfaction.

Not having any other means of paying the compensation, Krobbo was compelled in the ensuing period to hand over to the Danes their harvest of palm oil. To the English this looked like an attempt to monopolize trade. To this was added the question of the conduct of the English soldiers in Akwapim and Akim. Under the impression created by these events, Maclean began looking into the matter of territorial rights and came to the conclusion that the Danes had no right to the two territories. So a meeting was held on March 8, 1836, at Fort James, attended by the two governors and the most prominent Europeans. There they agreed to refer the case to the home governments for decision, and Maclean had to promise that he would not in the meantime present Akwapim with a British flag and a salary book.[19]

Mörch, on the other hand, continued his activities in the hope of further binding the debatable nations to Denmark.[20] The Krobbo came down to Fort Christiansborg to redeem their hostages, and by eating fetish confirmed their dependence on the Danes. Akwapim proper proved more difficult to handle. Mörch vainly tried to summon the chiefs of the country to appear before him. Ado Adankwa, the chief caboceer, sided with the English, but Mörch learned that two of the most powerful caboceers were loyal to the Danes. So, when Maclean sailed away on home leave, Ado got frightened and tried, through the Dutch Accra, to contact the Danes. This attempt was prevented by the English traders. Now Mörch wanted to demonstrate to the natives that the Danes were independent of the English. Consequently, on July 18, 1836, he deposed Ado and made Kwasum (Quasung) chief of Abodé, caboceer of part of the country. Next, on January 9, 1837, in the presence of all the chiefs who had recognized the Danes as their overlords, Addum was installed as the successor to Ado.[21] They all ate fetish and took the oath of loyalty and mutual friendship. Addum left his sister's son as a hostage at Fort Christiansborg. He himself had to be escorted to his home, for Ado, who had sought refuge at Fort James, set a price upon Addum's head. After that, the Danes began to interfere whenever murder or manslaughter threatened the peace in Akwapim. Nevertheless, Addum was never allowed to rule in peace. Even after Ado's death, there was unrest, because he did not possess the lawful royal stool and the lawful insignia of a caboceer, which the English refused to relinquish. A new stool had to be consecrated, a most solemn event, seeing that the natives believed that the stools had supernatural powers.

Mörch's perseverance gave the English constant grounds for complaint to London.[22] Meanwhile, the negotiations in Europe tried their patience. The London merchants, who were, presumably, under the influence of Maclean, painted the Danish governor in even darker colors than did the authorities of Cape Coast Castle. "He has reduced the district round our settlement at Accra to a state of war by constantly stirring up trouble." Certainly when the British minister to Copenhagen, H. H. Wynn, handed over the complaints demanding independence for Akim and Akwapim, H. Krabbe-Carisius, the Danish foreign minister, seemed very meek. Krabbe-Carisius believed that no great wisdom could be expected from Mörch, a mere lieutenant of the navy; it was most regrettable that, owing to the climate, it was impossible to get better candidates for the governorship. Nevertheless, the Copenhagen authorities took their time.[23] When Mörch's opinion was asked, he wrote a long historic dissertation, but it did not finally arrive until March 31, 1838. It said that there was no intention of preventing the natives from trading with the English, but stated that Akim, Akwapim, and Krobbo received *appointements réguliers* (regular salaries) from the Danish Guinea government, and that Mörch had interfered only to put down a rebellion. The Danish government maintained that the native tribes in question could not be dependents of the English, but hinted that it might be open to doubt whether they were independent of or dependents on the Danes. Afterwards, Mörch was given promises of support; but with the condition that he be cautious in his dealing with the British, since independence on the part of a small power in its affairs with a far-flung Empire was intolerable. Maclean was still in London and was asked his opinion of the Danish government's reply.[24] He asserted that Mörch had stirred up Akwapim against Krobbo, when he saw that the latter nation had received a British flag. He also wrote in his reply that during the 1836 campaign, Akwapim had cut down entire forests of palms, which had brought the oil trade to a standstill, and prevented the natives from paying their debts to the English merchants. Maclean thought the place which the Danes had taken over from the Dutch ought rightfully belong to the British. About Akim and Akwapim he told a downright lie, saying that their independence had been established by the Ashanti peace treaty of 1831.

It was on such unreliable assertions that the British government based its renewed complaint which was submitted to Copenhagen in the spring of 1838. This time the Danish government acknowledged defeat. It was up to Krabbe-Carisius to decide, and he bowed in complete submission to the British demands. Mörch was ordered to refrain from taking any step which might, "even if only apparently," hurt British trade, to re-establish normal relations with the British Guinea government, and "more than had so far been the case, to give up his own personal ideas in favor of superior political considerations."

Simultaneously with Mörch's reception of this reprimand, Maclean returned to the Gold Coast. There stood Mörch deprived of the support of his government and without any military means of maintaining his position. In the meantime, he became an alcoholic and on March 19, 1839, he died at Frederiksgave plantation.[25] He must also have been embittered by the energetic opposition of Riis, the missionary.[26] The latter had called him "one of the most unprincipled and licentious individuals who ever lived" and accused him of having taken part in the slave trade. We must, therefore, state as clearly as possible, that, against the complaints sent home by Riis, Mörch had his government's full support, and that Riis had been threatened with recall.

After the death of Mörch, Hans Angel Gjede, the second assistant, was made temporary governor, since Lucas Dall, the chief assistant, had not asked to be appointed. There seems to have been peace with the English for some time but Gjede was active in other directions. In July 1839 he launched an expedition against Atocco, a native town close to the east bank of the Volta estuary. In previous years, this town had again and again been suspected of trading in slaves. In the neighborhood of another town up the Volta, Gjede succeeded in laying hands on one of the worst slave traders, a Spaniard named José Mora. Unfortunately, he was merely banished to the opposite bank of the river. Afterwards, he made a nuisance of himself, and the government had to chase him from the Atocco and Way areas, after which he escaped eastward to Popo or Wydah.[27] Immediately after the Atocco expedition, Gjede died on August 18.[28] Now Dall was compelled to take up the governorship. First, he had to endure insistent complaints from the English about the slave trade on the other side of the Volta, and second, the enmity of Akwamu and Krepi caused him much trouble.[29] In previous years, these two nations had repeatedly been at war with each other. In the spring of 1841, the king of Akwamu agreed with Awuna to attack Krepi town of Asjotjale. This town consequently appealed to the coast natives and Krobbo for help. When, with the permission of the Christiansborg government, these two armies turned up, the Awuna forces at once went home, and Akwamu dared not attack.

In Copenhagen on December 31, 1841, Bernhard Hohan Christian Wilkens, an officer of the Royal Danish Navy, was appointed temporary governor.[30] On that occasion, the British government carefully inquired if, this time, a companionable man had been chosen. When answered in the affirmative, the British chargé d'affaires in Copenhagen took the liberty of proposing that London should provide him with a letter of recommendation to Maclean. Wilkens arrived at Christiansborg on May 14, 1842, and was installed as governor on May 24. Due to an enterprising clerk, a Jew named Wulff Josef Wulff who had been sent out in 1836, Wilkens found everything in perfect order.[31] Wulff had diligently carried out his official duties; and since he was also a merchant, he had built himself a fine house and storehouse, which he named Frederiksminde. The forts and plantations were shipshape, the accounts in order. So Wilkens could devote his energies to more difficult tasks. With a force of 20-25 men, he left in a hired English schooner to sail to Way and Atocco to catch Mora. The culprit escaped, and local people assured the Danes that he was now too poor to have any trade. However, there were plenty of other problems. Preparations were again being made for a war with Krepi. So Wilkens busied himself with attempts to maintain order and peace. While engaged in these pursuits, he learned that in many places the natives believed that the Danish Guinea government was subject to the British. He was not allowed time to uproot this error, for shortly after his return to the Danish stronghold, he died of dysentery on August 26, 1842. Under these circumstances, the second assistant, a lawyer named Edward James Arnold Carstensen, took command. On July 30, 1844, he was made full-fledged governor, thus becoming the last chief of the Danish territories in Guinea. During his term of office he paid two visits to the home country. His first absence from the coast was from March 15 to October 9, 1844, an exceptionally fast voyage; the second from April 10, 1847, to February 20, 1850. During his first departure, he left affairs in the hands of Edward Julius Ericksen, an assistant. After Ericksen's death, on July 5, Georg Lutterodt took over. His management was so bad, that afterwards the king gave orders that he should never again be entrusted with important government posts. During Carstensen's next absence, an assistant named Rasmus Emil Schmidt became acting governor.

Edward Carstensen had come to Guinea at the same time as Wilkens.[32] He gave proof of extraordinary powers as a government official who was well able to preserve the loyalty of the allies of the Danes in Guinea. In spite of the shortage of staff, he sent home a number of informative reports on the situation on the coast. He also tried to evolve a system of organization which would make possible the maintenance of Danish supremacy without great economic sacrifices. But it was by no means an easy task. Like Mörch, he was very loath to give up Akim and Akwapim to the British. He scored one point at the start, for a new Akim caboceer, Attia, son of Dokua, was installed in office under Danish auspices on August 25, 1842; and afterwards was admonished not to strip his people by means of fines, nor to exact duty on the transit trade through Akim.[33] Carstensen even had time to confirm Adjemang in his new dignity, so that Akim became even more extensively linked up with the Danes. Before long, however, the English were again causing trouble. They complained that the village of Blaekhuse possessed a Danish flag, although it belonged to an Englishman,[34] and the commandant of Fort James sent seven soldiers to demand that the Danish flag be delivered into their hands. The inhabitants of the village, however, inquired at Fort Christiansborg. Carstensen admonished them to hand over English private property but not the flag, advising them, if need be, to seek the protection of the caretaker at Frederiksgave plantation. Afterwards Carstensen and Maclean agreed to refer the case to the respective royal courts in Europe.

In his reports to Copenhagen on this quarrel, Carstensen explained at some length the great changes that had been taking place on the Gold Coast in recent years.[35] While, formerly, Europeans had avoided interfering with the fetishism of the natives, the English were now openly making war on it, explaining the tricks of the fetish priests and even destroying the fetish temples. Everywhere the natives humbly submitted to the English; the inhabitants on the coast did so, because without them they would fall into the hands of the more powerful inland nations, and these, because without the British they would be at the mercy of the Ashanti. Besides, a demand had grown up among the natives for European manufactured goods, while in return they wanted to sell gold, ivory, and palm oil. Of the Danish traders, Richter was the only one to have any trade, and he had to pay for it with relatively expensive presents to the caboceers. Under these circumstances, it would be both useful and economical if the quarrel with Britain about Akim and Akwapim could be settled by treaty.

Later Carstensen also made clear the insufficiency of Danish enterprise on the coast. In the 1830's the plantations were devastated several times by drought and grasshoppers, and by 1843 there were only four coffee plantations with a total of a little more than 10,000 shrubs left in Danish territory. Of these, only Frederiksgave earned a small profit, because the servants provided it with cheap labor. Lutterodt's, Svanekiaer's, and Richter's plantations yielded little or nothing.[36] The state of education was equally depressing. The school at Christiansborg was ineffective. It was utterly impossible to teach the Danish language there. The Accra language was mostly used for religious instruction and arithmetic. If any results were produced at all, they were mainly due to the monitorial system of teaching which Frederik VI had so eagerly advocated. Church was attended only by school children and soldiers, for whom attendance was compulsory. Around the British forts things were quite different. The English language was really spreading over the Gold Coast. So it was wise, even if not patriotic, of the missionary Riis to seek English contacts and speak English at the school he started at Akropong. As an example of the understaffed conditions under which the Danes in Guinea lived, it might be mentioned that during his first stay in the country, Carstensen had himself to perform the confirmation of twelve mulatto boys and four girls. The next catechist to come out, C. Th. Jørgensen, died after only a few months' work at Christiansborg, and there were still intervals without a chaplain at the settlement.[37]

All this was discouraging. Still the Danish government did not give up. When the British brought up the Blaekhuse affair in Copenhagen, they now possessed, in the person of H. Reventlow-Criminil, a very capable foreign minister. When Wynn brought his note, Reventlow-Criminil received him coolly. This was followed by a note in reply, which simply referred to the Danish note of March 31, 1838.[38] There both parties let the matter rest. In fact, in the following years the Christiansborg government settled quite a few disputes in Akwapim. So the country could still, with some truth, be regarded as a Danish dependency.

But there were complications. One affair, particularly, gave rise to many difficulties. In 1844, during Carstensen's absence, the missionary Riis and Lutterodt started an expedition to Akropong and to Addum's residence at Mampong. Evidently, the missionary disliked Addum. He asserted that the caboceer had become addicted to alcohol. Addum was also said to have captured nine Akropongs, shot one of them, and sold the rest. The Danes then summoned a meeting at Akropong, but Addum and his men failed to turn up; so they were fined, and the Danes promised a salary to Ursu Akim, caboceer of Akropong. Consequently, on Carstensen's return, he found the country in a state of utter confusion, and he summoned all parties to appear before him at Christiansborg. While negotiations were going on at Osu, there was an exchange of fire between the Osu and the Akropong party. The latter party fled, but Ursu Akim was killed in flight. The next night at Osu, Addum and the grand-interpreter Sebah Akim, as general of the Osu, sacrificed two children from Akropong, which had once offended Addum. Sebah himself wielded the knife, and the blood was poured over the great drum of the town. Now the cry for civilization became so loud, and the British so scandalized, that the Danes could not let such a crime pass unpunished. Addum and Sebah Akim were put in prison, and the town of Osu was fined. Some Osu, who went to Akropong afterwards, were to have been slaughtered by way of vendetta, but were ransomed by Riis. Five Akropong children, whom the Osu were taking to the slave market at Way where Mora happened to be staying, were stopped at Ada and carried safely home. Still later, peace was made between Akropong and Osu with Carstensen's assistance.[39]

But there was more to come. On the day following Sebah Akim's arrest, when, after a formal visit to a French brig, Carstensen was on his way back to Fort Christiansborg, Sebah's men were waiting at the landing place to kill him. Carstensen escaped from them, but as a punishment fired his guns at Osu. A large part of it was burnt down, but not the business quarter, the home of the traders. After that, Addum and Sebah Akim were chained together in their cell. The news of all these events stirred Copenhagen to action. There had, in accordance with Carstensen's wish, been talk of sending a Danish man-of-war to the coast to make the natives respect the Danes. Now the king resolved that, when the ship arrived at Accra, an examination committee should be set up. The captain of the man-of-war was to be chairman, and the committee was to pass sentence on the two natives. The committee sentenced the culprits to death; but Carstensen was permitted to commute the sentence to deportation, and he made use of his privilege. They were sent to the West Indies and thence to Copenhagen. There they were imprisoned in the Citadel, where they remained as long as Denmark kept her Guinea territories. For his conduct of the whole business, Carstensen was made a Knight of the Order of Dannebrog, and the blood-smeared drum is now on view in Denmark's National Museum.

The next caboceer of Akwapim was not installed in office until December 1845. His name was Okinne-Kuma.[40] He was obedient to the Danes; so after the departure of Riis, the country quieted down. Koffi Krah, a supporter of Ursu Akim, still turned to Ashanti for support. He offered the king of Ashanti the return of the treasures he had lost in the battle of Dodowa in 1826. When his treachery was discovered, he was sentenced to death, but his execution was prevented by the presence of a Danish soldier. He was taken to Fort Christiansborg, where he hanged himself in the cell. After that, Akwapim caused trouble only once more. That was in the spring of 1847, when there were complaints that Ashanti traders, traveling through Akim with gold dust and ivory, were being waylaid. So ambassadors were sent by Ashanti with orders, in case the traders were not handed over to them, to travel on to Akropong. There they were to shoot themselves before the eyes of the people, after which the king of Ashanti would come and take what Akwapim had not been willing to hand over to him. R. E. Schmidt, the temporary governor, had to go to Akropong, where, by seizing the person of the caboceer, he compelled the leaders to give up the traders.

The Danes were not alone in their attempts to keep order in Akwapim. Now and again the English would interfere, too. Even as late as 1849 this gave rise to a dispute. The English tracked down a native criminal in the disputed territory, after which the Danes demanded that he be handed over to them for punishment. In the course of the ensuing correspondence, the English maintained that they, too, often settled disputes in Akim. Nevertheless, an Akim chief who was summoned by the English, refused to appear, arguing that he was a Danish subject.[41] The correspondence about these matters was interrupted when the Anglo-Danish negotiations for the sale of the settlements were opened in 1849.

Awuna, beyond the Volta River, remained as troublesome as Akwa-pim. The slave trade had not been entirely stamped out in those parts. In 1845, when the caretaker of Fort Prinsensten caught a transport of 62 slaves, he was forced to obey the command of the king of Awuna and give them up. So, a couple of months later when a man-of-war, the *Ørnen,* arrived, it was sent to Keta to scare the native king, who promptly swore the oath of allegiance to the Danes. He also promised to assist in repairs on the Danish fort, which were then carried out under the leadership of Lieutenant Johan Vilhelm Svedstrup. In 1847, how-ever, Svedstrup sent word that the natives were rebellious and aimed to destroy the fort; consequently, his soldiers had killed a native, and now the fort was surrounded by 500-600 men. R. E. Schmidt had to set out with sixty soldiers to relieve the fort. When he arrived, the natives had scattered, but next day he gathered their chiefs and fined them 100 piastres. If the fine was not paid, their town would be burnt down. On the second day he caught two of the important men of the town, but one of them died of shock while being taken to the fort. So the fine was paid at once; but the town was evacuated, and Schmidt was told that he would be intercepted on the homeward journey. To ascertain the truth of this, he made a sortie and got safely back to the fort, which was then besieged by 6,000-7,000 natives. Fortunately after a week, when they were on the verge of starvation, a French armed brig, the *Abeille,* ar-rived. So when the natives set the town on fire to launch the attack under cover of smoke, they were battered by the guns of both the fort and the brig, and "a good number" of them were killed. After the fort had been provisioned from the ship, Schmidt embarked with his forces and re-turned to Fort Christiansborg. From there he sent word to all caboceers on Danish territory, asking them if they were willing to join him in a campaign against Awuna. When it was found that they were willing to do so, Awuna was graciously pleased to ask forgiveness, after which they were ordered to pay the costs of the war with 2,000 piastres. Neverthe-less, now and again they would return and besiege the fort. Svedstrup was only able to keep them at a distance by means of hand grenades and rockets. In the autumn of 1847, after the return of the *Ørnen,* captained by C. Irminger, Schmidt again arranged a raid on Keta. On the way, some people of the town of Way were captured, and the town of Tebwy was bombed. After their arrival at Keta, the Danes threatened to set all the coast towns on fire, unless the natives obeyed orders. Since this was of no avail, they bombed Kiddy, a town six to seven kilometers east of Fort Prinsensten, where many had fled when Keta was devoured by the flames. The tall coconut palms crashed down on the native huts; and when the natives had had time to think this over, they sued for peace. At last, on October 23, 1847, all the chiefs gathered, and Awuna swore the oath of loyalty to the Danish king and begged for pardon. The roads were to be kept open, and the liberty of some prisoners was to be paid for with ransoms. The peace was saluted by two gunshots from the forts. Small wonder that, shortly afterwards, when the French brig *Abeille* was wrecked about a mile from Prinsensten, both ship and crew were robbed by the natives. Nor is it very surprising that when the Danes sent a lieutenant and some soldiers to Awuna to collect some fines in 1849, they returned empty-handed. They had, in fact, no control of the country beyond the Volta River.[42]

The Danish sovereignty or protectorate was undisputed only in the coastal towns from Accra to the Volta River. In the interior and on the flanks in Akwapim and Awuna, Danish power was in the nature of a postulate rather than a reality. There can be no doubt, however, that had the Danish government been prepared to make the necessary sacrifices and use all its resources, the territories, and probably Akim, too, might have been won for Denmark—and that in the future Denmark would have been the richer by an extensive tropical colony. Formally, the English were still claiming sovereign rights only within their forts. When, after Maclean had resigned the governorship in 1843, the British Crown again took the administration out of the hands of the merchants, no change was made in this respect. In practice, the English merchants were sure to claim that British rights covered far more extensive territories; but if the Danes had actually occupied the disputed countries and brought law and order to the natives, it would have been quite possible to defend the legality of the Danish claim.

This was, in fact, what Governor Carstensen was working for. In numerous reports and reflections on the government, judicial system, schools, church, and civilization of the coast, he sketched lines of developments which might have been followed. During his stay in Copenhagen in 1844, he managed to obtain from the government the promise that, from now on, the man-of-war sent on annual visits to the West Indies should sail via Guinea.[43] Thus the Danish settlements on the African coast were visited in 1845 and 1847 by the armed brig *Ørnen*, and in 1846 by the armed brig *Mercurius*. After that, the war in the home country made it impossible to send out men-of-war. Only one transport ship was sent to the coast in these years, the bark *Heinrich Sørensen*, in 1846.[44] Carstensen also put an end to the custom of paying salaries to the native chiefs.[45] He did not think it necessary to pay them money for good conduct. Firstly, he had recourse to extensive reductions, and secondly, he seized suitable opportunities to fine them. The chiefs knew of only one way of paying the fines: they had to give up their salaries for a number of years. As early as 1843 he sentenced Osu to five years' loss of salaries. And lastly, it was Carstensen who realized that it was a mistake to abandon Fort Prinsensten.[46] On May 13, 1846, with the support of the Ministry of Foreign Affairs he persuaded the king to give the necessary orders for its restoration, so that the fort could again be garrisoned and become a serious hindrance to the slave trade in Awuna.

Carstensen's proposals for an "African System of Emigration and Immigration" to make the slave trade unnecessary were abortive.[47] On the other hand, his request to be permitted to free the remaining royal slaves in Guinea was granted by the remarkable royal order of February 16, 1848. This was remarkable, since the British had sent a note to the Danish Court, calling upon it to forbid Danish subjects in Guinea to buy or own slaves.[48] At the same time, certain changes, which had also been proposed by Carstensen, were introduced in the government of the settlements.[49] The Guinea government was authorized to permit both Danes and foreigners to establish business firms under the sovereignty and protection of the Danish Crown. All exports of goods from Denmark to the coast at the government's expense were prohibited, the stores in the royal warehouses were sold out, and the officers and civil servants were no longer allowed to dabble in trade or traffic.[50] The governor was to have two councilors and one or two assistants. In accordance with the principles of liberalism, all necessary repairs on the forts were to be carried out in the best and cheapest way after bids had been received and contracts made. Shortly before, by royal order of December 20, 1847, annual expenditure on the Guinea budget was fixed at 30,080 rixdollars.

It is an act of justice to call attention to the good intentions expressed in these hitherto unnoticed decrees of moribund absolutism. The liberation of the royal slaves was the more remarkable because it took place before P. von Scholten proclaimed the abolition of slavery in the Danish West Indies. It must be regarded as an expression of the government's humane intentions that old and feeble slaves were allowed to remain in the service and to be pensioned off. In practice, however, the administration of this charitable system proved rather difficult. At first, the Guinea government found it necessary to apply for permission to keep the slaves until certain important work had been completed. Afterwards, there were complaints that it was impossible in Guinea to contract with the person who made the cheapest bid. Nevertheless, on March 16, 1848, the slaves of the fort were gathered and informed of their liberation. Four days later, the same scene was enacted on Frederiksgave plantation. Only five old native women and two elderly men remained in the service. The blacksmith's and carpenter's workshop were sold to the most skillful craftsmen. A year later, the Guinea government begged to inform the home authorities that it was impossible to find new laborers to replace those who had been allowed to go. Or, more to the point, wages would have to be raised, if the work was to be done.

Further, Carstensen was preparing plans for the consolidation of the positions of the officers and civil servants.[51] He wanted them to be paid traveling allowances, as well as half of the palaver-fees paid by the natives for the settlement of their disputes. A policy of reform was developing in many directions, when, as far as Denmark was concerned, all the Guinea problems were solved, solved by the sale of the settlements to Britain.

AFTER THE PUBLICATION of the decree of 1792 prohibiting the slave trade, Hager and Moe were the first to suggest that, since they were no longer useful as suppliers of slaves to the Danish islands in the West Indies, it might be better to sell the Danish settlements. However, it was only after 1803, when the decree had been put into force, that the plan became the subject of serious consideration. Next there was a period when the Danish government partly put its trust in the cultivation experiments, and partly laid plans for an exchange of the settlements for the Portuguese island of Principe. Then came the 1807-1814 war, and many years elapsed before there was again any thought of offering the Danish forts to a foreign power.

An offer was made during the Congress of Vienna, when Niels Rosenkrantz, the Danish foreign minister, mentioned the possibility of a sale to Lord Castlereagh, the British representative.[1] Since Castlereagh did not seem interested, Rosenkrantz dropped the matter. Afterwards, in 1818 the Danish government tried to sell the territories to the United States, which was looking for a suitable home for freed slaves and mulattoes, but these American efforts led to the founding in 1822 of Liberia, instead.[2] A Swedish plan for the exchange of the West Indian island of Saint Bartholomew for the Danish forts, which were then to have been used as a penal colony, was not favorably received in Denmark.[3] Thus various plans for the sale of the settlements proved abortive, and later the wish to get rid of the forts cooled somewhat. In his old age, King Frederik VI was loath to give up any part of his paternal heritage.

On the other hand as their trade on the coast increased, the British gradually became interested in the Danish settlement.[4] As early as Steffens' days, John Hope Smith, the British governor, asked if the Danish territories were for sale, a question which Steffens, of course, could not answer. The English commissioner, Dr. Madden, who was to report on the coast, visited Christiansborg in 1842 and asked the same question. By this time, however, there was a new Danish king, who took a different view of the matter. On his accession to the throne, King Christian VIII was very desirous to reduce the government's budget. So, on November 2, 1840, he resolved that, if opportunity offered, both the Guinea and East Indian territories were to be sold.[5] Until the sale could take place, he granted 27,000 rixdollars annually for repairs on the forts.

From two different points of view the British were interested in the Danish offer. The first was that of the merchants. They maintained that the Danish territory included some of the best soil on the Gold Coast, that much of the palm oil was produced there, and that some of the export of this product was in the hands of the Danish merchants. Dr. Madden, the commissioner, stated that in one year Christiansborg had shipped no less than five or six shiploads of palm oil. Bannermann, an English merchant at Accra, described how the ground nuts and maize, sheep and poultry, which he and his colleagues sold, came from the Danish territory. In the words of the British governor, "there is no doubt that from a commercial point of view, the Danes possess the finest part of the Coast; and were they commercially an enterprising people, their possessions here would be of great importance to them." [6] Another argument in favor of the purchase, said the governor, was that if Britain held more of the forts, she would be able to impose customs duties, which would cover government and military expenses. Lastly, he emphasized that it would be an achievement worthy of British humanity to stamp out slavery, human sacrifices, and other kinds of barbarism, which the Danes could hardly cope with. The latter argument, especially, was well received by the British public. But they were not sufficient to convince the London government, which had no desire to burden itself with further obligations to preserve law and order and civilize primitive countries. The Gold Coast merchants' first attempts to persuade the government to accept the Danish offer met with a flat refusal.

There was another point of view, which, no doubt, seemed more important to the British government. There was the risk that a third power should acquire the territories. There was France, which just then was very actively at work acquiring colonies and apparently was also interested in the purchase of the Danish forts in Guinea. The merchants of Marseille wanted palm oil for their soap factories, while the merchants of Bordeaux sent expeditions to West Africa. About 1840 the leader of these expeditions, a naval officer named Bouet-Willaumez, signed treaties with native chiefs at Grand Bassam and Assene on the Ivory Coast and at Gabon near the Equator. In addition the Prince of Joinville visited Fort Christiansborg in February 1843. A couple of months later, when two

French brigs arrived at Osu, Captain Baudin declared that the French would like to see the fort flying the tricolor.[7] Such events were bound to alarm the English at Accra.[8]

The British government, too, had to pay attention; and in 1843, when the Blaekhuse affair came up for discussion in London, it had to admit that there were more arguments in favor of the purchase than it had originally thought. Once the French had purchased the forts, they would not find it very difficult to extend their sovereignty to the disputed tribes. Probably, a discussion with them about this would only whet their appetite for the purchase. In spite of these considerations, the opposition to the purchase was so strong in London, that, for the time being, the British government refused to buy. To prevent misunderstandings, however, a declaration was sent to the Danish government, informing it that Britain would never allow a third power any sovereignty over the disputed tribes based on a cession by Denmark.[9]

At first, the Danish government does not seem to have realized that there might be a rivalry between the prospective purchasers of her Guinea assets. However, when informed of the visit of units of the French Navy in Guinea it resolved, by the royal assent of April 8, 1843, that the Danish minister in London should offer the forts to England; at the same time he should hint that France was interested, and that Belgium and the United States might also be prospective purchasers. In August of that year, when Wynn handed over his government's declaration concerning the Blaekhuse affair, Reventlow-Criminil informed him that there was reason to believe that France or Belgium would come forward as purchasers.[10] He added that, personally, he was against the sale, because the cost of keeping the settlements was low, and circumstances might arise which would make them vital to Danish trade. In the opinion of the Danish government, the Guinea territories represented a considerable value. There was talk, in connection with the offer to Britain, of demanding £285,000 for them. If this sum were ever mentioned to the British, it is obvious why they did not accept. At any rate the negotiations ended without result. The Danish minister to the Court of St. James informed his government that negotiations with other powers would be inadvisable. During his first visit to the home country, Carstensen had made a detailed statement about all problems involved in the maintenance of the settlements, and on July 30, 1844, the king resolved that, for the time being, his government was not to carry on negotiations for their sale, make plans for the cession of the territories to a foreign power, or abandon them.[11] Also, that the question of whether a foreign power should be allowed to occupy the territory east of the Volta was to be left open.

There the matter rested for some years. France was still interested, and in 1846 a French merchant, Regis of Marseille, received permission to set up a factory close to Fort Christiansborg.[12] It was, in fact, the Paris government's plan to open a station there similar to the trading stations near Grand Bassam and Assene. When negotiations were re-opened, Governor Carstensen became the driving force, evidently spurred on by the hope of not having to lay down his own life during a renewed stay at the settlements.[13] In 1847, with the king's permission, he entered into correspondence with Winniett, the British governor, about the transfer for the price of £40,000, a sum mentioned by him to the English on the coast as early as 1842,[14] before there was any possibility of a sale to the French. Carstensen succeeded in whetting the British governor's appetite for the deal; but London still thought the price too high, and Carstensen's attempt was doomed to failure. This news reached Denmark almost simultaneously with the abolition of absolute monarchy and the rise to power of new men, to whom the preservation of the Guinea territories seemed an untimely luxury. By April 3, 1848, a royal order was obtained to the effect that an attempt should be made to sell the settlements to Britain on as favorable terms as possible.[15] This time the price was £30,000, but not even this offer was acceptable to Britain. So the Danish government decided to make tentative offers to France, Holland, Belgium, and the United States, and as late as December 30, 1848, the Foreign Ministry declared that it must await the results of these feelers.[16] In the meantime, London was not given a chance to forget the matter. Governor Carstensen wrote privately to the interested London merchants, offering to rent them the Danish buildings on the Guinea Coast, so that Denmark could reduce her troops at each fort to just enough men to hoist the flag.[17] Seizing this opportunity, the merchants informed their government, adding that annual expenses would amount to only £500-600. This moved Lord Palmerston, the British foreign secretary, to propose negotiations for the purchase of the forts. However, Lord Grey, the colonial secretary, still thought them too expensive, and Carstensen's second attempt met with no better success than his first.

So, in the end, on the suggestion of the minister of France, the Danish government decided to make one more offer to Britain, asking payment only for the forts as buildings, but not as sovereign rights. With one stroke of the pen the government gave up the territorial rights upon which it had, for so many years, insisted. Application was made partly through Denmark's London minister, Count Fr. Reventlow, and partly through the Danish government's London banker, C. J. Hambro, to Foster, the leading merchant trading to Africa, who was also a Member of Parliament. This time the price was only £10,000, so Foster was quite enthusiastic. In a letter to the Colonial Office he explained that this was a fine bargain. The Treasury ought not to offer any opposition to this minimal expense. In case the government was not willing to enter into the agreement, Foster reserved his right to make a proposal which could both relieve Denmark of the cost of keeping up the forts and prevent their falling into the hands of a third power. This was "an aim so important with a view to the future of this part of Africa, that I shall neither spare trouble nor private risk to obtain it." These reflections had the desired effect on Lord Grey, but the Treasury refused to pay the total amount at once. Now the Danish minister spoke to Lord Palmerston, and, in a note of July 7, 1849, made the third official offer for the settlements.[18] Both Palmerston and Grey were in favor of the purchase; and after having asked Governor Winniett's opinion, they overwhelmed the Treasury with such a flood of arguments that it gave in, subject, of course, to the approval of Parliament.

Seeing that much time might elapse before Parliament could finish the matter, it was decided that Denmark might as well hand over the forts at once. The final negotiations between Palmerston and Reventlow took place on December 31, 1849.[19] On the same day a treaty was signed whereby, for a price of £10,000, Denmark ceded forts Christiansborg, Augustaborg, Fredensborg, Kongensten, and Prinsensten, with cannons and munitions, "together with all other possessions, property, and territorial rights whatever, belonging to His Majesty, the King of Denmark, on the said Coast." The House of Commons did not pass the bill concerning the treaty until July 19, 1850, after a debate on the timeliness of acquiring tropical colonies and the expenses necessitated by them in which Richard Cobden, Foster, and Palmerston took part.[20] The ratification documents were exchanged in London on September 11, 1850, when the price was also paid.[21]

Even before the treaty had been signed, Governor Carstensen arrived in London on his way to the Gold Coast, where he was to undertake the transfer to Governor Winniett. He arrived at Fort Christiansborg in the English brig Contest on February 20, 1850. The formalities were carried out with all speed.[22] By March 1, furniture and private belongings were sold at auction; and after Carstensen had recuperated somewhat, having been ill with a fever for several days, Fort Christiansborg was ceded to Britain on March 6, 1850. Next a journey was made to the forts along the coast. Since Carstensen was ill, G. C. Schiønning had to replace him. At each fort he introduced the native chiefs to their new masters and sold the Danish property at auction. East of the Volta River the reception given the new masters was extremely cold. The Awuna accepted British flags, but refused to give up their Danish and Portuguese flags. Only the utmost liberality on the part of Winniett and abundant rum rations prevented open hostilities. Finally, on March 17 the expedition struck inland from Prampram, Carstensen having joined it to arrange the transfer of the hill tribes. The journey took them to Shai, Krobbo, and Akwapim, but not to Akim. The expedition returned by way of Akropong, Abodé, and Frederiksgave to Accra, where it arrived on March 21. The Danes still held Fort Prøvesten, but on March 30, the Danish flag was lowered there also, marking the end of Danish rule in Guinea. Carstensen left on April 18, after a farewell party given by the new commandant of Fort Christiansborg. But Schiønning, who was exhausted by the hardships of the journey, had to remain behind. He died on May 10, the last victim of Denmark's Guinea adventure. Winniett, too, fell ill and died before the end of the year.[23]

For want of teachers, in 1848 R. E. Schmidt had turned over the school to the Basel Mission.[24] Now the British government agreed to grant money to the school and to pay certain pensions. A few pensions due natives still had to be paid by the Danish Exchequer, some of which were paid until as late as 1863.[25] Of the Danish merchants on the coast, Georg Lutterodt died within a year of the sale. The officials who returned to Denmark, that is, Carstensen, R. E. Schmidt, and lieutenants Svedstrup and Larsen, were discharged and granted allowances until new positions were obtained.[26] Carstensen retained his title of governor and the right to wear his uniform. He lived until 1898. Schmidt was given the honorary title of *kammerraad*, but resigned it in 1871.

There are still considerable remains of the buildings erected by the Danes in Guinea. After the transfer, the British governor moved from Cape Coast Castle to Fort Christiansborg, which was considered healthier than any of the forts which the British had, until then, possessed on the coast. Thus the former Danish stronghold became the seat of the British Guinea government. All the forts were badly damaged by an earthquake on June 10, 1862; but Christiansborg was repaired and on the gun emplacement a bungalow was built, which became the residence of the British governor of the Gold Coast. Above the gateway the monogram of King Christian VII and the year 1770 are still legible; and on the highest platform there are small brass cannon bearing the initials of Frederik V and Christian VII, while a few old iron cannon lie scattered on the beach below the fort. Near the sea, a short distance to the west of the fort, is the Danish graveyard surrounded by the wall built by Danish merchants. A few tombstones have been preserved, such as those of governors Hein and Wilkens. Among the inhabitants of Accra there are people bearing Danish names, such as the numerous members of the Svanekiaer family. One street is named Hansen Road, another is named after Lutterodt. The main street is Christiansborg Road, and some of the dark-skinned inhabitants still have stories to tell of the days when the coast belonged to Denmark and Dannebrog could be seen flying over rockborne Christiansborg.[27]

The natives seem to have regretted the disappearance of the Danes. True, no voice was raised in protest, but afterwards it was not easy for them to get used to British ways. They had been accustomed to great freedom, and now rebelled against attempts to make them dependent.

The English wanted to introduce a poll tax, which led to repeated rebellions in 1854. So a man-of-war shelled Labadi and Tessing, and with the assistance of Fort Christiansborg's guns destroyed Osu. Similarly, a rebellion of Krobbo was put down by a large English force. More than a generation was to elapse before warlike Ashanti was forced to give in to Britain's military might. In the meantime, Britain purchased the Dutch forts in 1871. After the whole country had been pacified, shortly after 1900, a rich economic expansion began. Since the turn of the century, roads and railroads have been built, cocoa and cotton grown, manganese and nickel mined, and timber cut from the great inland forests. Accra has grown into a town of 350,000 inhabitants. The former Danish territories on the Gold Coast are now among the richest areas of West Africa; and they have recently entered upon a rapid political evolution, which in 1957 led to the independence of the Gold Coast as a new state renamed Ghana.[28]

CONCLUSION

A BACKWARD GLANCE at Danish destinies on the African coast through two centuries must leave an impression of tragedy. However fertile and rich in gold the Guinea coast was, it seemed an inhospitable country to Scandinavians. Life in the heat of the tropics was burdensome and exhausting for the whites, and soon killed their spirit of enterprise. The impassable forests, the swamps of the Volta, the dry December wind, the rain squalls, and the fear of wild beasts, all wore down the health of the white men. When mosquitoes infected them with fever, they were faced with either almost instant death or long illness. Of the 90 persons sent from Denmark to the Guinea coast as officials in the period after 1820, 53 died there, and 33 of these within the first year of their arrival. Besides, of those that escaped 9 died soon after their departure. Not a third got home alive, and several of the survivors were broken by fever and alcohol. Before the days of quinine, a European state which wanted to possess colonies in tropical Africa had to be prepared to sacrifice a high percentage of human lives to the climate every year.

Nor can much good be said about the native population. Its early acquaintance with the Portuguese can hardly have had a salutary effect on its morals. The natives also suffered from the climate, even if it were not so unhealthy for them as for the whites. Seen through European eyes, many of them were lazy, thievish, and unreliable. On the other hand, the blacks had reason to think even less favorably of white morals. The Europeans entered their country by force. The natives had no reason to love these uninvited guests or to work for them willingly. But even so, their conduct often seems to have been disastrous. We are not referring here to the tricks and sharp practices of individual black traders, or to the fact that particularly unaccommodating whites were quietly disposed of. Far worse was the turbulent bellicosity of the natives, which drove them to greater extremes than could be justified by the love of liberty.

Their blocking, often for years, of the roads to the interior caused the Europeans greater losses than dishonesty and begging. The consequent disappointment to governments, shipowners, and companies in Europe was one reason why the traffic became irregular, and this irregularity made life difficult for the whites at the settlements. The natives did not always understand that the whites had come to trade. They could think only of their own political quarrels, in which the Europeans consequently got involved. So the whites were dragged into many predicaments, which, in their weakness, they had to scramble out of as best they could.

In the face of the great difficulties due both to the climate and to the inhabitants, the Danish efforts were mostly unavailing. The Danish king's first possessions on the Gold Coast were acquired by chance when, in his struggle with Sweden, Carlof, the adventurer, obtained Carlsborg, afterwards known as Cape Coast Castle, for him. The Danish government was unable to make use of this acquisition. A Glückstadt company tried to do so, but failed. Through the chaos of wars and political upheavals the well-situated Fort Frederiksborg was preserved in Danish hands. Then, however, the traffic failed for such a long time that the fort had to be pawned, and thus was lost by Denmark. To make up for this loss Fort Christiansborg was built near Accra. It was only after 1697, when the West India and Guinea Company made use of this fort in order to purchase slaves for its West Indian plantations, that a Danish settlement in Guinea gained a permanent place in the economy of the home country and was able to preserve it until the abolition of the slave trade on New Year's 1803. Gradually, Danish trade and influence expanded eastward, resulting in more forts and trading stations. Nevertheless, even in this, the most flourishing period in the history of the Danish Guinea settlements, ships were sent so sporadically that the forts were often short of both the staff and goods necessary for a steady flow of trade. The few expeditions sent out by the home country were, as a rule, quite well prepared. Unavoidably, however, there were disreputable characters, drunkards, and spendthrifts among the personnel. Real criminals were never sent to Guinea, and the personal relations of the Danes and their native neighbors were mostly friendly. The cargoes usually consisted of high-quality goods. Danish muskets and gunpowder especially were in great demand, and the goods were sold at competitive prices. But all this did not suffice. The work was carried on in fits and starts; what was gained one year was lost the next.

Thus Danish influence on the natives was insignificant and not distinguishable from that of other European nations on the Guinea coast. The imports of arms and gunpowder served only to increase the native wars. The importation of liquor was certainly received with genuine satisfaction, but served only to break down what little capacity for work the natives might have. The textiles appealed to the Africans' love of color, but the various articles made of metal, such as knives, kettles, and dishes, were probably the most useful. It cannot be said that the Danes raised the general level of African civilization. Their influence on the African soul was still less. They tried to teach the elements of the Christian religion only to the mulattoes. Missions under Danish flags produced no lasting results, and the doors of the school which gradually grew up at Christiansborg usually remained closed to individuals of pure African extraction. The best that the Danes were able to do for the natives was, undoubtedly, now and then to settle their disputes for them, thereby helping them to avoid savage feuds. But the good results produced by their efforts as peacemakers could hardly make up for the disastrous effects of the slave trade. As a constant incentive to war and kidnapping in large parts of Africa, it was so disastrous to the black race that the Africans would have been far better off if they had been left alone without any contact with the far too enterprising nations of Western Europe.

The Danes had little or nothing to give the natives, but the benefits that they reaped from their African adventure were just as dubious and negative. If the value of the Africans exported to the West Indies at the prices they fetched in the slave markets of the islands is totaled, the entire African trade must be regarded as a losing business for both the companies and the government. It is not clear whether "interlopers" and private shipowners made profits equaling the losses from the public coffers. We know that some such ships were sent out from Denmark, but usually we know neither what they brought home, nor if they called at the Danish settlements. The Danish lives lost in Guinea and in the Guinea traffic seemed a doubly tragic sacrifice of the manhood of the nation, because it was so utterly useless. Only if we consider it of paramount importance that sufficient labor was secured for the Danish West Indies can the importation of sugar and the money thus made by Copenhagen merchants be regarded as a kind of indirect compensation.

Because the African settlements were bad business propositions, the fact should not be overlooked that, everything taken into consideration, they brought the home country other advantages. The African expeditions brought direct and reliable information about the Africans and their civilization, which widened the Danish horizon considerably. The immediate result was a number of excellent travel books, which were Denmark's contribution to the international literature of exploration, and which ought to be reprinted today. Other results were some scientific investigations, and even a few linguistic studies, altogether the merest beginnings of attempts to make the territories useful to science. Most important was, presumably, the food for the imagination and the spirit of adventure which arrivals from afar brought their receptive fellow countrymen. This widened the horizon of the middle classes, and a valuable advance was made toward the evolution of a merchant class, capable of taking its share of world trade. A door was kept open, in case a commercial genius should appear in time to see his chance. In this view, no attempt to widen the nation's horizon was ever made in vain.

Throughout all the years that the Danes held them, the Guinea settlements were, in fact, nothing but a great shop with some branches. True, since they were doing business in a difficult neighborhood, they were armed with cannon and soldiers, but it must be remembered that the merchantmen of the day were armed too. However, in the course of time, this business firm laid claim to sovereign rights over the neighboring Africans, and territorial rights over the surrounding districts. This was repeated almost everywhere, when Europeans had settled among colored nations, and was a consequence of the superiority of European culture and especially of European technical civilization. If anything were able to give Denmark compensation for the financial losses incurred by the Guinea traffic, it must be the knowledge that it thereby had occupied a territory which some day could become valuable to Danish commerce, or could permit a really important cultural development. This was the only defense offered for keeping the settlements in Danish hands for nearly half a century after the abolition of slavery, in spite of the fact that, in all these years, they did not earn one penny. With the political situation which had prevailed for some years in the territories before they were sold, they might, in fact, have been made the foundation of a profitable economic expansion. The territory which could be regarded as Danish, and which included the coast district, the country round the Volta estuary, and Akwapim can be estimated at 10,000 square kilometers. To this must be added the possible expansion of Danish sovereignty to include Akim and countries farther inland.

In 1837 the Christiansborg government estimated that the population was 40,000, and that the number of men the country could call to arms would be one-fourth of the total population. In 1840 and 1845 the population was estimated at 53,000, but this time the armed men were estimated as one-fifth of the population. In 1847 Winniett estimated the population of the coastal district at 20,000-30,000. So there was room for a considerable increase of the population. Today a half million live in these districts. If Denmark had been willing to make sufficient investments of money and manpower, a rich economic expansion would have been possible under her flag.

If we look at the matter from this angle, it seems regrettable that the territories were sold so cheaply, and that the Danish government almost begged Britain to take them over. In fairness to the Danish government of the time, however, it should not be forgotten that for generations her African possessions had brought Denmark nothing but losses, and that it was impossible to foresee the advances of medical science, which would have made it possible a few decades later to keep them without the costly sacrifices of able-bodied men and without the endless procession of mourners at home. Nor was it possible to foresee that a time would come when it would be regarded as desirable for a state to be self-supporting for as many commodities as possible. Those were the days of liberalism, when there was no thought of converting national boundaries into trade barriers. But this much is certain: by the sale of her Guinea possessions, more than by any other government measure, Denmark made it impossible for herself to become self-supporting.

Future developments made the Guinea territories far more valuable than Denmark's East and West Indian possessions. The East Indian establishments had far more civilized, peace-loving populations, but their territories were so small and so densely populated, that they could never have become self-supporting. They had to import most necessities, so they were quite dependent on the neighboring countries. In a difficult international situation it would be equally impossible to defend them and to make them pay their way. The three West Indian islands were better off and would have been able to feed their own populations, but their area was too small for a large-scale production of fruit and other tropical goods. Only the Guinea possessions were extensive enough to make room for a more varied tropical vegetation from which the home country could benefit. By the close of the nineteenth century the Danish people produced so high a percentage of emigrants that it would have been possible to find the manpower necessary to carry on in Guinea. Since Danish businessmen and engineers extended their activities to nearly all the countries of the globe, they might just as well have helped civilize Danish Guinea. It would have been a rewarding, even if difficult, task for Danish missions and schools to have transformed the Africans so they could benefit from European social order and science.

In the eyes of the twentieth-century Dane, his country's African adventure looks tragic for two reasons: because of the tragic course it followed, and because the settlements were given away very shortly before they could have become a source of increased wealth and the scene of happy human activity from which, not only Denmark, but also the African inhabitants of the territory would have benefited.

Notes

Chapter 1 / The Gold Coast

1. Herodotus, II, 158, IV, 42.
2. *Hannonis Carthageniensium Ducis Navigatio* (Zurich, 1559). Several later editions in divers languages often bear the Greek title: Periplus.
3. Giouan Lioni Africano [Leo Africanus], "Della descritione dell'Africa," in Giovanni B. Ramusio, *Primo volume & terza editione delle navigatione et viaggi racolto* (Venice, 1563), 77-80. English translations: Joannes Leo Africanus, *A geographical historie of Africa,* trans. and collector Iohn Pory (London, 1600), 284-296; Joannes Leo Africanus, *The History and description of Africa . . .* ed. Robert Brown (London, 1896), III, 819-854; Heinrich Schurz, "III. Afrika," in Hans F. Helmolt, *Weltgeschichte* (Leipzig & Wein, 1901), III, 507-520.
4. The classical description of the discovery of Guinea is Gomez Eannes de Azurara, *Chronica do descobrimento e conquista de Guiné,* ed. Visconde da Carreira (Paris, 1841); English trans. Charles R. Beazly & Edgar Prestage, *The Chronical of the Discovery and Conquest of Guinea,* 2 vols. (London, 1896-1899).
5. French priority as discoverers of Guinea is claimed mainly by [Nicolas] Villault, Escuyer sieur de Bellefond, *Relation des costes d'Afrique appellées Guinée* (Paris, 1669). Among more recent works about the question, Charles de la Roncière, *La découverte de l'Afrique au Moyen Age* (Caire, 1925), II.
6. Richard Hakluyt, *The Principal Navigations' Voiages, Traffiques and Discoveries of the English Nation* (London, 1599), II, pt. 2; *Purchas his Pilgrimage or Relation of the World* (London, 1613), I, Book 6, Chap. 14; *Ibid.* (London, 1625), II, Book 7; *The Golden Coast or a Description of Guinney* (London, 1665); [T. Astley], *A New General Collection of Voyages and Travels* (London, 1745), I. More important among later works on the English on the Gold Coast are: William W. Claridge, *A History of the Gold Coast and Ashanti,* 2 vols. (London, 1915); a textbook, William E. F. Ward, *A Short History of the Gold Coast* (London, 1935); numerous later editions such as, William E. F. Ward, *A History of the Gold Coast* (London, 1948). Useful information on all aspects of the history of the Gold Coast is given by Allan W. Cardinall, *A Bibliography of the Gold Coast, issued as a companion volume to the Census Report of 1931* (Accra, 1932).
7. [Peter de Marees], *Beschreyvinge van de Goudt-Kust Guinea* (Amsterdam, 1602); new edition by S. P. l'Honoré Naber in *Werken uitgeven door de Linschoten-Vereenigung* (s'Gravenhagen, 1912); French translation, *Description et recit historical de riche royaume d'or de Guinea* (Amsterdam, 1605); German translation, *Wahrhaftige Historische Beschreibung des gewaltigen Goltreichen Königreichs Guinea,* trans. Gotthardt Arthus von Dantzig (Frankfurt am Main, 1603); *Trou-Hertighe Onderrichtinge aen alle hooft Participanten en Lief-hebbers van de Ge-octroyeerde West-Indische Com-*

231

pagnie nopende het open stellen van den handel op de Cust van Africa, namentlyckle St. Thomé, Guinea, Angola, St. Paulo de Loando (1643); later summaries, J. K. J. de Jonge, *De oorsprong van Neerland's Bezittingen op de Kust van Guinea* (s'Gravenhagen, 1871); C. M. Kan, *Nederland en de Kust van Guinea* (Utrecht, 1871); I. F. Doorman, "Die Niederländisch-West Indische Kompagnie an der Goldküste," *Tijdschrift voor Indische Taal-, Land-en Volkenkunde,* XL (1898), 389-496; Herman Wätjen, "Zur Geschichte des Tauschhandels an der Gold-Küste um die Mitte des 17. Jahrhunderts, nach holländische Quellen," *Forschungen und Versuche, zur Geschichte des mittelalters und der neuzeit; Festschrift Dietrich Schäfer* (Jena, 1915), 527-563.

8. Kay Larsen, *De danske i Guinea* (København, 1918).

9. *To ortse der Zeevardt verlichtende West-Indien, Brasilien, Guinea en Angola* (Amsterdam, 1648), 182; Villault, *Relation,* 180.

10. Villault, *Relation,* 9.

Chapter 2 / The Danish-Swedish Rivalry

1. G. N. Ligtenberg, "Willem Usselinx," *Utrechtsche bijdragen voor letterkunde en geschiedenis,* IX (1914).

2. Nils Jacobson, *Svenska öden vid Delaware 1638-1831* (Stockholm, 1938), with full bibliography; Christopher Ward, *New Sweden on the Delaware* (Philadelphia, 1938).

3. DKanc., B54, *Sjæll. reg.,* XVIII (1624-1626), 3b, KB. 313.

4. DKanc., B54, *Sjæll. reg.,* XIX (1632-1637), 397b, KD. III, 16off.

5. The Swedish Riksarkiv, Stockholm, possesses under "Handel ock Sjöfart" four volumes of documents concerning their African company; P. I. Coyet, "En kort Relation om Swenska Africanske Compagniets inrättande ock förlop indtil år 1663," *Historiska Märkwärdigheter,* I (1768), 22-26; Victor Granlund, "En svensk koloni i Afrika eller Svenska-Afrikanske Kompagniets Historia," *Historiskt Bibliotek,* VI (1879), 285-420; about the earliest years, E. W. Dahlgren, *Louis de Geer* (Uppsala, 1923), II, 333-350.

6. Nicolaas de Roever, "Twee Concurrenten van de eerste West-Indische Compagnie," *Oudh-Holland,* III (1889), 195-222.

7. Wilhelm Johan Müller, *Die Africanische auf der Guineischen Gold-Cust gelegene Landschafft Fetu* (Hamborg, 1676), 9; N. A. Dyce Sharp, "Cape Coast," *Transactions of the Cape Coast Historical Society,* I (1936).

8. A. C. Lucht, *Glückstadt oder Beiträge zur Geschichte dieser Stadt und des dreissigjährigen Krieges in unserm Lande* (Kiel, 1854); D. Detlefsen, "Die städische Entwicklung Glückstadts unter König Christian IV," *Zeitschrift der Gesellschaft für Schleswig-Holsteinische Geschichte,* XXXVI (1906), 191-256; J. Wilcke, *Daler, Mark og Kroner 1481-1914* (København, 1931), 126-130; Heinrich Sieveking, "Die Glückstädter Guineafahrt im 17. Jahrhundert, ein Stück deutscher Kolonialgeschichte," *Vierteljahrschrift für Sozial- und Wirtschaftsgeschichte,* XXX (1937), 19-71; F. C. Rode, *Kriegsgeschichte der Festung Glückstadt und der Niederelbe* (Glückstadt und Hamburg, 1940), I.

9. "1630. 22. Okt. (Wismar). Traktat mellem Kong Christian IV af Danmark-Norge og Kong Filip af Spanjien angaaende Glückstadts Oprettelse til Stapelplads for Handelen paa Spanien fra Elben, Wasen og andre Steder ved Vestersøen," in Laurs R. Laursen, *Danmark-Norges Traktater* (København, 1917), IV, No. 6, 87-94; "1644. 10./20. Marts (Madrid). Handelstraktat

mellem Danmark-Norge og Spanien; med dertil hørende Biakter," *ibid.*,
No. 17, 258-323.

10. TKUA, Kopibog Latina 1632-1651, 409B.

11. TKIA, Inländisch registratur 1648-1649, 364 & 493b, July 14 & Oct. 18,
1649; TKIA, B 153, Jan. 4, 1650. On São Thomé as a sugar island: Hans
Jacob zur-Eich, *Africanische Reiszbeschreibung in die Landschaft Fetu*
(Zürich, 1677), 171-173; Wätjen, "Geschichte des Tauschhandels," 556.

12. TKIA, A 171, Diverse akter vedr. det Ostindiske Komp. og G. 1618-1659.
It also may be worth mentioning that Regeringskancelliet i Glückstadt 146,
Akter vedr. Glückstadt by of fæstning 1630-1703, contains an undated letter
to the king in which Behne and partners describe Louis de Geer's charter
and themselves apply for permission to sail to the coast of Coromandel.

13. Extract, section 7, quoted in a letter from burgomaster and town council
of Glückstadt to the king, Aug. 27, 1689, TKIA, Regeringskancelliet i
Glückstadt 146, Akter vedr. Glückstadt by og fæstning 1630-1703.

14. Ludvig Holberg, *Dannemarks Riges Historie* (København, 1735), III, 608,
states that in the early years of the reign of King Frederik III and two
years before the Swedes settled in Guinea, i.e., in 1648, the Danes had a
small factory near Accra; Claridge, *History of the Gold Coast*, II, 593, says
that the Danes built a factory near Orsu in 1642.

15. Roever, "Twee Concurrenten," 205.

16. TKIA, A 10, Patenten 1655-1656, 340.

17. Privilege, of Mar. 5, 1653, for "de vestindiske participanter" (the first
Danish West Indian Company); of Oct. 5, 1653, for Heinrich Müller; of
Oct. 19, 1653, for Jens Lassen and partners; of Aug. 29, 1655, for the shipowners of Elsinore: DKanc. B54, Sjæll. reg. XXIII (1653-1655), 335, 441,
445 & 656; KD III, 411-412; V, 365.

18. E. Gigas, *Grev Bernardino de Rebolledo, spansk gesant i Kjøbenhavn 1648-
1659* (København, 1883), 181, 377. The application was signed by Jens Lassen, Niels Friis, Morten Mikkelsen, and Christopher Gabel.

19. DKanc., B57, Sjæll. tegn. XXXII (1651-1653). 639b; XXXIII (1654-1656),
26, 61, & 72 (14 sailors from the Holmen signed up); DKanc., B54, Sjæll.
reg. XXIII (1653-1655), 702b & 704, and enc. Nov. 2, 1655; O. Nielsen,
Kjøbenhavns Historie og Beskrivelse (København, 1885), IV, 229-231, 320-
322.

20. Vilhelm Bergsøe, *Trankebar-Mønter 1644-1843 samt Mønter og Medailler
vedr. den danske Handel paa Ostindien, China og Guinea 1657-1777*
(København, 1895), 56-57.

21. Egeskabene, E, Letter, June 19, 1656, Vestindien og afr. handel angående,
1653. etc., No. 1.

22. DKanc., B54, Sjæll. reg. XXIII (1653-1655), 825b, with enclosures of June 28,
1656.

23. TKIA, A 10, Patenten 1657, 115; drafts in, Egeskabene, E., Vestindien og
afr. handel angående 1653, etc., No. 1.

24. Capitulation bearing Carlof's signature in TKIA, A 171.

25. Granlund, "En svensk koloni i Afrika," 308-313, which makes use of among
other documents, Krusenstierna's report to King Carolus Gustavus, June 25,
1658. In V-gK., 1, Designation "Guinea wie auch St. Thomas in Westindien,"
is a list of documents which proves that there must have existed several reports on the matter from Eberstein, June 15, 1658, and subsequent days. The
list, in addition, mentions several reports on the events of the following
years.

26. Michael Hemmersam, *Guineische und West-Indianische Reisebeschreibung von anno 1639-1645* (Nürnberg, 1663), 26-27.

27. *Grundeligh Underrättelse om the rättmätige Skääl* (Göteborg, 1656); S. Pufendorf, *Thaten Carl Gustavs* (Nürnberg, 1697), 449-452; L. F. v. Eberstein, *Beschreibung der Kriegsthaten des General-Feld-marshalls Ernest Albrecht von Eberstein 1605-1676* (Berlin, 1891), 188-192, with several printed documents but with mistakes. Carlof's letter to Eberstein from Antwerp, July 23, 1658, and Eberstein's letter to the king, Dec. 6, 1658, are to be found in TKIA, A, I, 93.

28. Granlund, "En svensk koloni i Afrika," 329-344; Laursen, *Danmark-Norges Traktater,* V (1920), 351, 354-356, 370.

29. Extract, "Schreibens von d. Commandanten Smitt aus Guinea, May 1, 1658," TKIA, A 171, Diverse akter vedr. det Ostindiske Komp. og G. 1618-1659, sent by means of an English captain to England by way of Barbados.

30. John Barbot, "Description of the Coast of North and South Guinea," in [A. & J. Churchill], *A Collection of Voyages and Travels* (London, 1732), V, 177.

31. *Memorial door syn E. den deenschen Resident Heer Petrus Charisius inghegeven aen de Heeren Staten generael der vereenichde nederlantsche Provincien, midtgaders de afghedronghen verantwoordinge ende rechtmatighe klaghten de daen aen Kon. Majesteyt van Denemarken* (Amsterdam, 1664), 13; *Afgedrongen en Welgefondeerde Tegen-Bericht der Conincklycke Deensche Geoctryeerde Affricaansche Guineesche, en in de Hooft-vestinghe Gluckstadt opgerichte Compagnie* (Glückstadt, 1665), 42-43; Holberg, *Dannemarks Riges Historie,* III, 279-280, says the Dutch fooled Smidt by telling him that Carolus Gustavus had conquered the whole of Denmark, captured King Frederik III, and carried him off to Sweden.

32. [B. Pilat], *La vie . . . du Sieur Michel de Ruyter* (Rouen, 1678), 154.

33. Coyet, "En kort Relation," 22-26; zur-Eich, *Africanische Reiszbeschreibung in die Landschaft Fetu* (Zürich, 1677), 101-105; Granlund, "En svensk koloni i Afrika," 344-352, 365.

Chapter 3 / The Glückstadt Company

1. TKIA, A 24, Inländisch 1659, 69 & 174; TKIA, A 171, Div. akter vedr. det Ostindiske komp. og G. 1618-1659, May 20, 1659. The most important sections of the agreement are printed in *Afgedrongen en Welgefondeerde Tegen-Bericht,* 44.

2. TKIA, A 10, Patenten 1600-1664, 64b, 65b, 175. The text of the charter of 1659 is not to be found in the Danish Rigsarkiv but is summarized in Sieveking, "Glückstädter Guineafahrt," 31.

3. TKIA, A 24, Inländisch 1659, 261.

4. TKIA, A 24, Inländisch July 24, 1661, & Regeringskancelliet i Glückstadt 146, akter vedr. Glückstadt by og fæstning 1630-1703, No. 21; cf. TKIA, B 5, Patenten 1671-1672, 155.

5. "Generalcapitulation über die Guineische Handlung, Jan. 14, 1672," Regeringskancelliet i Glückstadt 146, Akter vedr. Glückstadt by og fæstning 1630-1703, printed in Sieveking, "Glückstädter Guineafahrt," 42-43. At that time 1 mark gold was worth 368 marks.

6. TKIA, A 10, Patenten 1660-1664, 73.

7. For this traffic and events to which it gave rise, Müller, *Fetu,* and zur-Eich, *Africanische Reiszbeschreibung.*

8. Copy of the contract in TKIA, A 171, Div. akter vedr. det Ostindiske Komp. og G. 1618-1659.

9. Müller, *Fetu,* 105 & 109; V-gK., br. & dok. 1680, indk., apr. No. 24.

10. The existence of this contract is proved by V-gK., 6, Participanternes resolutionsprotokol 1671-1690, year 1680. Cong is mentioned in Eric Tilleman, *En liden enfoldig Beretning om det Landskab Guinea* (København, 1697), 78.

11. Besides pamphlets dealing with this episode, see, Lieuwe van Aitzema, *Saken van Staet en Oorlogh* (s'Gravenhagen, 1665), X, 277-278.

12. DKanc., C 8, Sjæll. tegn. XXXVI (1660-1663), 319; draft for note to the English and French kings, Sept. 15, 1663, in Egeskabene, E, Vestindien og afr. handel angående 1653, etc., No. 1; TKIA, A 27, Inländisch registratur 1664, 353, & A 28, Inländisch 1669, 84; *Klagh-Vervolgh von den Deenschen Koningk en dessels Ministers aen de Heeren Staten over de pretense volentie door de Nederlantsche West-Indische op de Deensche Africaensche Compagnie gepleectet* (Naer de Coppe, 1662); *Memorial door syn E. den deenschen Resident Heer Petrus Charisius Remonstrantie aen de Ho: Mo: Heeren de Staten Generael der Vereenighe Nederlanden, overgegeven den . . . Juny 1664 by de Heeren de Bewint-heeberen van de geoctroyeerde Westindische Compagnie der Vereenighde Nederlanden* (Amsterdam, 1664); *Afgedrongen en Welgefondeerde Tegen-Bericht;* the last mentioned also in German. Concerning a lawsuit which touched upon the Guinea dispute, see Brieven, *Confessie mitgaders Advisen van verscheyden Rechtsgeleerden in de saeck van Isaac Coymans gegeven: als mede de sententie daer op gevolgt* (Rotterdam, 1662); Aitzema, *Saken van Staet en Oorlogh,* XI (1668), 406-421, 429-460; *Brieven geschreven en gewisselt tusschen de Heer Johan de Witt . . . ende de Gevolmaghtigden van den Staedt der Vereenigde Nederlanden* (s'Gravenhage, 1724), IV, *passim;* Doorman, "Niederländische-West Indische Kompagnie," 449-451; Laursen, *Danmarks-Norges Traktater,* VI (1923), 2-5, 7, 10, 15-18, 62-63; Granlund, "En svensk koloni i Afrika," 366-370; C. O. Bøggild-Andersen, *Hannibal Sehested, en dansk statsmand* (København, 1946), I, 379, 423.

13. Claridge, *History of the Gold Coast,* I, 108.

14. *Afgedrongen en Welgefondeerde Tegen-Bericht,* 87; Müller, *Fetu,* 17-18, zur-Eich, *Africanische Reiszbeschreibung,* 105: Tilleman, *En liden enfoldig Beretning,* 72-73; *Brieven geschreven,* IV, 376; Granlund, "En svensk koloni i Afrika," 374; Claridge, *History of the Gold Coast,* I, 110.

15. Copy of Holmes' report, Apr. 19, 1664, and of H. Albrecht to R. Holmes & Fr. Sellwyn, Apr. 19, 1664, in V-gK., br. & dok., 1680, Udgåede, Oct. No. 48, 3 A-B; the latter also in V-gK., uordnede sager, 1670-1686.

16. [Pilat], *Michel de Ruyter,* 146-156; Doorman, "Niederländisch-West Indische Kompagnie," 453-460.

17. Villault, *Relation,* 200.

18. Aitzema, *Saken van Staet en Oorlogh,* XII (1668), 480-493; Laursen *Danmark-Norges Traktater,* VI (1923), 85, 115-119, 504, 570, 579, 583.

19. Granlund, "En svensk koloni i Afrika," 315.

20. Generalcalculation, Jan. 14, 1672, TKIA, Regeringskancelliet i Glückstadt 146, Akter vedr. Glückstadt by og fæstning 1630-1703, 146.

Chapter 4 / Fort Frederiksberg

1. Zur-Eich, *Africanische Reiszbeschreibung,* 98.

2. Barbot, "Description of the Coast," 172.

3. Müller, *Fetu*, 6.
4. Villault, *Relation*, 197. Mention must be made of Villault's statement (p. 142) that the Portuguese had conquered from the Danes the island of Cantozi "which they held in the River Niger," a position of which nothing else is known.
5. TKIA, A 10, Patenten 1664-1665, 192.
6. TKIA, A 10, Patenten 1666-1667, 364, & A 28, Inländisch 1667, 260, 261, 298; DKanc., C 61, henlagte sager 1671-1673, litr. V, Dec. 10, 1672; V-gK., br. & dok. 1680, udgåede Oct., No. 47; rescript to H. Albrecht in TKIA, Regeringskancelliet i Glückstadt 146, Akter vedr. Glückstadt by og fæstning 1630-1703.
7. Sea-pass for Cornelius Janssen in TKIA, A 10, Patenten 1664-1665, 185; TKUA, Koncepter til Latinske ekspeditioner, som ikke ses at være registrerede 1662-1669, last entry, Sept. 13, 1667.
8. TKIA, A 10, Patenten 1668-1669, 201b.
9. Sea-pass in TKIA, B 5, Patenten 1671-1672, 187.
10. Claridge, *History of the Gold Coast*, I, 119.
11. Letter of Dec. 4, 1675, from Frederiksberg, mentioned in V-gK., 12, Direktionsprotokol 1671-1680, 248 & cf. 255. According to V-gK., br. & dok. 1680, udgåede, Oct., No. 47, Peter Witt was appointed provisional commandant of Fort Frederiksberg on June 20, 1678.
12. Jonh Barbot, "Voyage de Guiné . . . 1678-1679," British Museum, MSS., additamenta 28.788, 44-47; Barbot, "Description of the Coast," 172-174.
13. Carl Behrens, ed. *Da Guinea var dansk, W. J. Wulffs Breve og Optegnelser fra Guldkysten 1836-1842* (København, 1917), 41-42.
14. V-gK., br & dok. 1680, udgåede, Oct., No. 46 A; copy of Lykke's agreement with the English of July 11, 1684, in V-gK., uordnede sager 1670-1686; contracts for the surrender of Fort Frederiksberg are mentioned in the list of documents V-gK., 1, Designation "Guinea wie auch . . ."; according to DKanc., C 24, Vestindiske sager 1671-1699, 151, the fort had been pawned for £ 3,221 6 s (plus interest); DKanc., C 24, Vestindiske sager 1671-99, 154, ratification of May 15, 1688; V-gK., 6, Participanters resolutionsprotokol 1671-1690, Dec. 2, 1685; V-gK., direktionsprotokol 1682-1688, Dec. 2, 1685; Mariager, "Historisk Efterretninger June 30, 1773," ny kgl. saml. 426, fol. 55, 80-81.
15. Guillaume Bosman, *Voyage de Guinée* (Utrecht, 1705), 61, 67, 69-70 (German translation, Hamburg, 1708); Sharp, "Cape Coast."
16. V-gK., direktionsprotokol 1682-1688, Dec. 2 & Dec. 4, 1685; a facs. of diplomatic negotiations in V-gK., uordnede sager 1670-1686; DKanc., C 24, Vestindiske sager 1671-1699, 111; Otto F. von der Gröben, *Guineische Reise-Beschreibung* (Marienwerder, 1694); Richard Schück, *Brandenburg-Preussens Kolonial-Politik 1647-1721* (Leipzig, 1889), I, 134-312.
17. TKIA, B 12, Inländisch registratur 1679, 215; cf. Barbot, "Description of the Coast," 173.
18. V-gK., 6, Participanternes resolutionsprotokol 1671-1690, Aug. 5, 1688; V-gK. direktionsprotokol 1682-1688, Feb. 18, 1686-Dec. 13, 1688; V-gK., 43, Brevkopibog 1682-1688, Nov. 11, 1686-Mar. 24, 1688, & kopibog 1688-1690, Apr. 3 & May 16, 1688; DKanc. C 24, Vestindiske sager 1671-1699, 142-145, 147-150; the list of documents in V-gK., uordnede sager 1670-1686, Apr. 28, 1686, mentions the company's report on the king's right to Fort Frederiksberg, and, Aug. 31, 1686, its report on the king's claims.

Chapter 5 / The Fetu

1. The text of this chapter is based upon Müller, *Fetu*, zur-Eich, *Africanische Reiszbeschreibung,* and Villault, *Relation.*
2. Zur-Eich, *Africanische Reiszbeschreibung,* 111.

Chapter 6 / Accra and Fort Christiansborg

1. Claridge, *History of the Gold Coast,* I, 49, 55, 59, 102; Doorman, "Niederländisch-West Indische Kompagnie" 441, n. 1, 444-445, 447, 481-483.
2. *Memorial door syn E. den deenschen Resident Heer Petrus Charisius,* 9, 18; *Afgedrongen en Welgefondeerde Tegen-Bricht,* 18.
3. German version in, V-gK., br. & dok. 1680, udgåede, Oct., No. 48, 2.
4. Tilleman, *En liden enfoldig Beretning* 91-94; thence incorporated in Ove Malling, *Store og gode Handlinger af Danske, Norske og Holstenere* (København, 1777), 42-44 (translated into English, French, and German).
5. Tilleman, *En liden enfoldig Beretning,* 97.
6. Claridge, *History of the Gold Coast,* I, 119-120; Olifert Dapper, *Umbständliche und eigentliche Beschreibung von Africa* (Amsterdam, 1670) dedicated to King Christian V of Denmark by the publisher Jacob van Meurs), 448-449; Barbot, "Description of the Coast," 182-183.
7. Ward, *Short History,* 16-28; Ward, *History of the Gold Coast.*
8. V-gK., br. & dok. 1681 indk., July, No. 7; Tilleman, *En liden enfoldig Beretning,* 95; Barbot, "Description of the Coast" 173, 183-184.
9. DKanc., C 24, 56-58; V-gK., br. & dok. 1681, udgåede, Aug., No. 2 & 1681, indk., Aug., Nos. 2 & 30, V-gK., 42, Brevkopibog 1676-1682, 241-245, 279-283; Mariager, "Historisk Efterretninger," fol. 79.

Chapter 7 / The West India and Guinea Company

1. TKIA, A 28, Inländisch, 1670, 316; TKIA, B 12, Inländische registratur 1671, 38, 42; TKIA, B 64, June 2, 1671.
2. Generalcalculation, Jan. 14, 1672, TKIA, Regeringskancelliet i Glückstadt 146, Akter vedr. Glückstadt by og fæstning 1630-1703.
3. TKIA, Regeringskancelliet i Glückstadt 146, Akter vedr. Glückstadt by og fæstning 1630-1703.
4. Rescript of May 25, 1672, and, relation of June 20, 1672, TKIA, Regeringskancelliet i Glückstadt 146, Akter vedr. Glückstadt by og fæstning 1630-1703; J. Lindbæk, *Aktstykker og Oplysninger til Statskollegiets Historie 1660-1676* (København, 1910), II, 293-296.
5. DKanc., C 24, Vestindiske sager 1671-1699, 16-17; *Patent om it Guineiske Compagnies Oprettelse i Københaffn, Dec. 10, 1672* (n.p., n.d.).
6. TKIA, B 48, Apr. 30, 1673.
7. V-gK., br. & dok. 1680, udgåede, Oct., No. 47; V-gK., 12, direktionsprotokol 1671-1680, 141ff.; DKanc., C 24, Vestindiske sager 1671-1699, 25-27, 36-37.
8. V-gK., uordnede sager 1670-1686; Mariager, "Historisk Efterretninger," fol. 21ff.
9. DKanc., C 24, Vestindiske sager 1671-1699, 37-38; order sent to the governor: V-gK., 41, Brevkopibog 1671-1676, Dec. 18, 1674, Feb. 8 & 20, Mar. 27, Apr. 22 & 24, 1675; V-gK., 12, direktionsprotokol 1671-1680, May 23, 1675, Sept. 8, 1679, May 12, 1680.

10. DKanc., C 24, Vestindiske sager 1699-1771, 18-19, 28-31, 39-40, 45-46; DKanc., C 6, Sjæll. reg. XXIX (1673-1675), 171, 498b; TKIA, B 5, Patenten 1675-1677, 372 & 1678-1680, 13; TKIA, B 12, Inländisch registratur 1676-1677, 333, 337 & 1680, 142; V-gK., 12, direktionsprotokol 1671-1680, June 26, 1676; the list of documents in V-gK., 1, Designation "Guinea wie auch St. Thomas in Westindien"; Mariager "Historisk Efterretninger," fol. 22.

11. V-gK., 12, direktionsprotokol 1671-1680, Sept. 8, 1679; V-gK., 6, Participanternes resolutionsprotokol 1671-1690, Sept. 10, 1679.

12. DKanc., C 24, Vestindiske sager 1671-1699, 48-53; *Verordnung wegen des West-Indischen und Guineischen Handels Mar. 3, 1680* [København] (n.d.); Mariager, "Historisk Efterretninger," fol. 31-34.

13. V-gK., 6, Participanternes resolutionsprotokol 1671-1690, Feb. 24, 1682; list of coach-owners in Copenhagen in V-gK., br. & dok. 1680, indk., Dec.; postponement of coach-tax: DKanc., C 8, Sjæll. tegn. XLIII (1681-1682), 210.

14. Numerous documents concerning the loading of the ship: V-gK., br. & dok. 1680, udgående; list of documents Prang was ordered to take to Guinea: V-gK., uordnede sager 1670-1686; Prang's patent of office, Sept. 30, 1680: V-gK., 6, Participanternes resolutionsprotokol 1671-1690; cf.: V-gK., 29, Instruktioner for komp's. embedsmænd i Guinea 1680-1746; Marinens arkivs; Skibsjournal 1680, No. 4, V-gK., br. & dok. 1681, indk., Aug., No. 3 & Sept., No. 3.

15. V-gK., br. & dok. 1681, indk., Sept., Nos. 4, 18, 23 & Oct., Nos. 11, 12.

16. V-gK. direktionsprotokol 1682-1688 Apr. 22, 1682.

17. V-gK., direktionsprotokol 1682-1688, Apr. 1, 7, 8, 22 & 27, 1682; V-gK., litr. B fra 1682 (table of contents for lost direktionsprotokol 1680-1682), Jan. 7, 1682, along with an invoice of what was sent with Thors to Guinea in V-gK., uordnede sager 1670-1686; cf. V-gK., 42, Brevkopibog 1676-1682, 388; sea-pass: DKanc., C 24, Vestindiske sager 1671-1699, 58-60.

18. V-gK., 6, Participanternes resolutionsprotokol 1671-1690, Feb. 24, 1682; Mariager, "Historisk Efterretninger," fol. 41-46; contracts with some of the participants in the *Havmandens'* expedition are in V-gK., 21, Kontrakt og instruksbog 1682-1684; vessel's journal, V-gK., 181, Skibsjournal for "Havmanden" 1682-83.

19. V-gK., 12, direktionsprotokol 1671-1680, Apr. 24, 1675; V-gK., 42, Brevkopibog 1676-1682, 291-292, 306-307; DKanc., C 24, Vestindiske sager 1671-1699, 58 and numerous later entries; TKIA, B 5, Patenten 1683-1684, 350; TKIA, B. 12, Inländisch registratur 1686, 380; V-gK., 6, Participanternes resolutionsprotokol 1671-1690, Mar. 25, 1684, draft, Jan. 24, 1689; V-gK., direktionsprotokol 1682-1688, Apr. 29, 1684, Feb. 5 & 6, Mar. 14, May 18, 1685, Nov. 6, 1686 Sept. 15 Oct. 14, 1687, May 15, Aug. 24, 1688; extract of instructions for Henriques, Apr. 17, 1686, in V-gK., uordnede sager 1670-1686; Mariager, "Historisk Efterretninger," fol. 54-58.

Chapter 8 / Nikolaj Jansen Arf

1. A part of Copenhagen where the Colonial Company's officers were located.

2. DKanc., C 24, Vestindiske sager 1671-1699, 166, 187-209; Mariager, "Historisk Efterretninger," fol. 58-60; Nielson, *Kjøbenhavns Historie,* V (1899), 96, 137.

3. TKIA, B 5, Patenten 1690, 475, sea-passes which state that ships sailed from Glückstadt.

4. V-gK., direktionsprotokol 1682-1688, May, 15, 1688; Fensman's account books 1687-1688 and 1698, and his daily register June 22, 1688-Apr. 7, 1689

(in Dutch), are in V-gK., br. & dok. fra G. 1687-1705; Mariager, "Historisk Efterretninger," fol. 81-82.

5. Documents in TKIA, Regeringskancelliet i Glückstadt 146, Akter vedr. Glückstadt by og fæstning 1630-1703.
6. Tilleman, *En liden enfoldig Beretning*, 12-13; Lucht, *Glückstadt*, 90, 98.
7. V-gK., guvernørernes kopibog 1690-1713, Aug. 5 & Sept. 23, 1695; V-gK., 15, direktionsprotokol 1697-1734, May 11, 1703.
8. H. Meyer's description, Mariager, "Historisk Efterretninger," fol. 82ff.
9. Tilleman, *En liden enfoldig Beretning*, 102-105; Bosman, *Voyage*, 73-75.
10. The text is based upon Tilleman, *En liden enfoldig Beretning*, 96; Bosman, *Voyage*, 76-77; Mariager, "Historisk Efterretninger," fol. 84-86. Claridge, *History of the Gold Coast*, I, 127-129, is based upon the more detailed description in *New General Collection*, II, 102-103, 618, which maintains that Assemoni's attack was arranged by the Cabuceer of Accra; he considered himself insulted by the Danes. The latter work is the source of *Almindelig Historie over Reiser til Lands og til Vands, eller Samling af alle Reisebeskrivelser* (København, 1749), IV, 319-320, which tells the story of Assemoni.
11. TKIA, B 12, Inländisch registratur 1693, 212.
12. Account of the reorganization in V-gK., 15, direktionsprotokol 1697-1734, Mar. 7, 1702; DKanc., C 24, Vestindiske sager 1671-1699, 238-240, with enc. May 1, 1697; Mariager, "Historisk Efterretninger," fol. 86-91.
13. V-gK., 29, Instruktioner for komp's embedsmænd i Guinea 1680-1746, July 10, Aug. 3, 10, 27, Oct. 21, 1697.
14. DKanc., C 24, Vestindiske sager 1671-1699, 241-246.
15. Concerning regulations and decree of May 29, 1699: DKanc., C 24, Vestindiske sager 1671-1699, 277-284; Mariager, "Historisk Efterretninger," fol. 108-109.
16. DKanc., C 24, Vestindiske sager 1671-1699, 249-279; orders and instructions for the employees on board the ships of kgl. octr. da. w. i. guin. komp. signed copies in V-gK., printed charters in the Danish Rigsarkiv.
17. V-gK., br. & dok. fra G. 1687-1705, Feb. 28, 1698; Mariager, "'Historisk Efterretninger," fol. 86-87.

Chapter 9 / Ado and Aquando

1. In this and subsequent chapters the commandants of Fort Christiansborg are indicated as correspondents even in cases where the letters also bear the signatures of the other members of the secret council of the fort, and could thus be classed as "letters from the council" (*general-breve*).
2. Trane's letters, Jan. 26, 1699-Apr. 12, 1703, V-gK., 121, br. & dok. fra G. 1687-1705; V-gK., 884, Dag-journal ført på Christiansborg, Dec. 23, 1698-July 23, 1700; A. M. Brun's letter, Aug. 8, 1705, V-gK., br. & dok. fra G. 1705-1716.
3. Trane's letters, Sept. 12, 1703-Mar. 28, 1704, and Meyer's letters, Jan. 2, 1703-Feb. 10, 1704, V-gK. br. & dok. fra G. 1687-1705; V-gK., dag-journal fra G. Sept 12, 1704-May 28, 1705; V-gK., 886, Kopibog fra G. Dec. 23, 1703-Mar. 19, 1705.
4. Sverdrup's letters, Feb. 3, 1703-Mar. 19, 1705, V-gK., br. & dok. fra G. 1687-1705.
5. Lygaard's letters, May 4, 1705-Oct. 5, 1710 and Boye's letter, Aug. 18, 1711, V-gK., 121, br. & dok. fra G. 1705-1716.

6. Mariager "Historisk Efterretninger," fol. 110.
7. G. L. Grove, "Nogle Oplysninger om Tordenskjolds første Langfart," *Personalhistorisk Tidsskrift,* 3. rk., IV (1895), 151-164.
8. Beside Lygaard's letters, letters also from Pheiff and Wærøe, V-gK., 121, br. & dok. fra G. 1705-1716; Mariager, "Historisk Efterretninger," fol. 110-111, 116; Georg Nørregård, "Forliset ved Nicaragua 1710," *Årbog for Handels- og Søfartsmuseet på Kronborg* (1948), 67-98.
9. Lygaard's letter, Sept. 19, 1709, Boye's letters, Aug. 18, 1711-June 19, 1716, V-gK., 121, br. & dok. fra G. 1705-1716 and July 19, 1716-Sept. 1, 1717, V-gK., 122, br. & dok. fra G. 1717-1732; Herrn's letter, Feb. 10, 1722, and Syndermann's letter, Mar. 21, 1724, *ibid.*
10. Letter, Feb. 28, 1714, V-gK., 121, br. & dok. fra G. 1705-1716.
11. V-gK., 15, direktionsprotokol 1697-1734, Feb. 20, Mar. 14, Apr. 15, 1713; Boye's letters, Jan. 7, Feb. 15 Apr. 3, 1714 and Wærøe's letter, Feb. 19, 1733, V-gK., 122, 123 br. & dok. fra G. 1717-1732 & 1732-1745. Wærøe says that the ship made a bad voyage, using its pumps all the time.
12. Rost's letters, Nov. 29, 1717-July 13, 1720, V-gK., 122, br. & dok. fra G. 1717-1732.
13. Herrn's letters, Feb. 10-Sept. 19, 1722, Elias Svane's letter, Feb. 6, 1722, H. C. Brock's, Jan. 27, 1723, N. J. Østrup's, Jan. 28, 1723, and Syndermann's, Mar. 31, 1724, V-gK., 122, br. & dok. fra G. 1717-1732.
14. Syndermann's letters, Dec. 29, 1723, Mar. 21, 1724, V-gK., 122, br. & dok. fra G. 1717-1732; V-gK., 886 Kopibog fra G. 1723-1724.
15. Suhm's letters Apr. 29, 1724-Sept. 20, 1725, V-gK., 122, br. & dok. fra G. 1717-1732; V-gK., 886, Kopibog fra G. 1725-1726.

Chapter 10 / Dutch Intrigues and the Rise of Akim

1. Suhm's letters, Mar. 14, 1726-Mar. 5, 1727, Pahl's, Apr. 14 & Sept. 10, 1727, Willemsen's, Nov. 18, 1727-Mar. 16, 1728, and Wærøe's, Dec. 18, 1729-Dec. 28, 1730, V-gK. 122 br. & dok. fra G. 1717-1732; V-gK., 886, Kopibog fra G. 1727-1729.
2. Herrn's letter, July 1, 1722, Willemsen's, Feb. 10, 1728, Wærøe's letters, May 16, Aug. 30 & Dec. 28, 1730, Niels Lange's, May 16, 1730, and Hammer's, May 17, 1730, V-gK., 122, br. & dok. fra G. 1717-1732; V-gK., 886, Kopibog fra G. 1729-Oct. 1, 1731.
3. Wærøe's letters, Dec. 24, 1730-Oct. 10, 1731, Sparre's, Dec. 24, 1730, Aug. 2, Sept. 27, 1731, V-gK., 122, br. & dok. fra G. 1717-1732; Wærøe's letters, Mar. 22, 1732-Mar. 30, 1734, V-gK., 123, br. & dok. fra G. 1732-1745; V-gK., Kopibog fra G. 1732-1734.
4. Wærøe's letter, Mar. 30, 1784, Erik Trane's, Mar. 23, 1734, and P. N. Jørgensen's, Mar. 30, 1734, V-gK., 123, br. & dor. fra G. 1732-1745.
5. Schiellerup's letter, Apr. 15, 1736, V-gK., 123, br. & dok. fra. G. 1732-1745.

Chapter 11 / The Slave Trade

1. William Snelgrave, *A New Account of Guinea and the Slave-Trade* (London, 1754), esp. Chap. II; Anthony Benezet, *Some Historical Accounts of Guinea . . . With an Inquiry into the Rise and Progress of the Slave-Trade* (Philadelphia, 1771); C. Alberti, "Den danske Slavehandels Historie," *Nyt Historisk Tidsskrift,* 2 rk., III (1850), 201-244.
2. V-gK., guvernørernes kopibog 1690-1713, Nov. 30, 1696.

3. Mentioned f. inst. in Hachsen's letter, Dec. 31, 1751, V-gK., 124, br. & dok. fra G. 1746-1754.
4. Wærøe's letter, Dec. 24, 1730, V-gK., 122, br. & dok. fra G. 1717-1732.
5. V-gK., 880, Sekretrådsprotokol fra Guinea, 1732-1730 (Sept. 9, 1726-Mar. 3, 1727 [ends really Sept. 9, 1727]) fort på.
6. Schiellerup's letter, Apr. 15, 1736, and Boris' letter, Nov. 14, 1739, V-gK., 123, br. & dok, fra. G. 1732-1745.
7. Jean B. Labat, *Voyage du Chevalier des Marchais en Guinée, isles voisines et à Cayenne fait en 1725, 1726, & 1727* (Paris, 1730), I, 312.
8. Instances quoted from letters of: Trane, July 27, 1700 & Apr. 30, 1701, Lygaard, May 4 & July 19, 1705, Boye, Feb. 15 & Sept. 13, 1714, Feb. 6, 1717, Østrup, Feb. 28, 1714, Rost, July 13, 1720, Pahl, Apr. 14, 1727, Wærøe, Mar. 30, 1732, P. N. Jørgensen, Apr. 2, 1742, Billsen, Mar. 30, 1744, Hackenburg, Mar. 17 & Aug. 20, 1746, Platfuss, July 9 & Aug. 10, 1750, and Hachsen, Jan. 5, 1752, all extracted from V-gK., br. & dok. fra G.
9. Postscript of Hachsen's letter, Jan. 6, 1752, V-gK., 124, br. & dok. fra G. 1746-1754.
10. Lygaard's letters, Sept. 1, 1705, V-gK., 120, br. & dok. fra G. 1705-1716.
11. V-gK., guvernørernes kopibog 1690-1713, Oct. 12, 1698 & Oct. 24, 1700; Platfuss' letters, Feb. 6 & May 15, 1747, Ole Erichsen's from St. Thomas, Feb. 3, 1749, V-gK., 124, br. & dok. fra G. 1746-1754; Waldemar C. Westergaard, *The Danish West Indies under company rule (1671-1754)* (New York, 1917), 320-326.
12. Johannes Rask, *En kort og sandfærdig Rejse-Beskrivelse til og fra Guinea* (Trondhjem, 1754), 75-76.
13. Engman's letter, Sept. 15 & 20, 1753, and further reports, f. inst. of the juridical examinations, Rtk., indk. div. g. br. 1755-1759; Georg Nørregård, "Slaveprøret på Patientia 1753," *Årbog for Handels og Søfartmuseet på Kronborg* (1950), 23-44.
14. V-gK., 9, Dok. til direktions-og generalforsamlings protokol 1725-1733, No. 135.
15. V-gK., 15, 16, direktionsprotokol 1697-1734 & 1734-1740; Mariager, "Historisk Efterretninger," fol. 134-167.
16. *Det kongelige Danske Westindiske og Guineiske Compagnies Participanters vedtagene Convention, Reglement og Foreening, indgaaet og sluttet den 26 Sept. 1733* (København, n.d.).
17. V-gK., 5, Trykte oktrojer, konventioner, plakater m.m.
18. *Octroy for det Kongelige Danske West-Indiske og Guineiske Compagnie den 5 Feb., 1734* (København, n.d.).

Chapter 12 / The Eastern Districts and Fort Fredensborg

1. Trane's letters, July 27, 1700, Feb. 26 & Aug. 13, 1701, Lygaard's, Mar. 9, 1706, Rost's, June 30, 1718, Wærøe's, Dec. 28, 1730 & Aug. 15, 1733, V-gK., br. & dok. fra G., Jan Conny's offer was made in 1717 to Capt. Wærøe and in 1721 to Hearn.
2. Lygaard's letter, Apr. 14, 1710, Boye's, May 30, 1713, Apr. 3, 1714, May 20 & July 20, 1716, Aug. 3 & Sept. 1, 1717, Rost's, Feb. 11, 1718, Mar. 19, June 15, & Dec. 10, 1719, Apr. 19 & July 13, 1720, V-gK., 121, 122, br. & dok. fra G. 1705-1716, 1717-1732; Rost was stationed as a trader at Keta in 1714.
3. Boris' letter, Nov. 14, 1739, V-gK., 123, br. & dok. fra G. 1732-1745; ex-

planation of the building of a saw mill on the Volta with a description of the river, V-gK., 124, br. & dok. fra G. 1746-1754.

4. Herrn's letters, Apr. 20 & July 1, 1722, postscript to Suhm's letter, May 27, 1724, Syndermann's letter, Mar. 31, 1724, seem to indicate that in Niels Østrup's time the Keta factory had been the scene of unhappy events, V-gK., 122, br. & dok. fra G. 1717-1732.

5. Suhm's letter, Sept. 28, 1726, Pahl's, Sept. 10, 1727, Willemsen's, Jan. 23, 1728, and Wærøe's, Aug. 30, 1727, V-gK., 122, br. & dok. fra G. 1717-1732.

6. V-gK., kopi af protokol holden på fortresset Christiansborg udi 1731-1733, 40-42; Sparre's letter, Sept. 27, 1731, Wærøe's, Mar. 22 & May 26, 1732, V-gK., 122, br. & dok. fra G. 1717-1732.

7. Wærøe's letters, Mar. 22 & Mar. 30, 1732, Nov. 10, 1734, Schiellerup's, Apr. 15, 1736, Boris', July 26, 1736, Feb. 1 & Sept. 30, 1737, May 3, 1738, V-gK., 123, br. & dok. fra G. 1732-1745.

8. V-gK., 189, Frederik P. Svane, "En kort, sandfærdig og tydelig og omstænde-lig general declaration og underretning om ti aars begivenheder paa fortet Christiansborg i Acra paa cysten af Guinee i Africa, June 1, 1748," 22; Ludvig F. Rømer, *Tilforladelig Efterretning om Negotien paa Kysten Guinea* (København, 1750), 39; Malling, *Store og gode Handlinger*, 45-46; Gerhard L. Grove, " Om Søren Schielderup, guvernør paa Guineakysten," *Personalhistorisk Tidsskrift,* 3 rk. IV (1895), 292-311.

9. Boris' letters, July 26, 1736-June 7, 1740, V-gK., 123, br. & dok. fra G. 1732-1745; V-gK., 190, br. & dok. vedk. det guld, som fra G. skal sendes til Amsterdam, 1738-39; V-gK., 136, Dok. vedk. afståelsen af de vestindiske øer og forterne i G. 1753-1754.

10. P. N. Jørgensen's letter, Apr. 2, 1742, Billsen's, Mar. 30, 1744, Platfuss', Sept. 9, 1746, V-gK., 123, 124, br. & dok. fra G., 1732-1745, 1746-1754.

11. V-gK., 189, Svane, "General declaration."

Chapter 13 / The Rise of Ashanti

1. Boris' letters, Sept. 30 & Oct. 28, 1737, Mar. 10, 1739, Feb. 15, Mar. 18 and May 23, 1740, P. N. Jørgensen's letter, Aug. 31, 1740, V-gK., 123, br. & dok. fra G. 1732-1745; Claridge, *History of the Gold Coast,* I, 199; Ward, *Short History,* 46-49.

2. Jørgensen's letters, Aug. 31, 1740-Apr. 2, 1742, Dorph's, July 11, 1743, V-gK., 123, br. & dok. fra G. 1732-1745; V-gK., 189, Svane, "General declara-tion," 28; about the "Kongen af Danmark": V-gK., 17, direktionsprotokol 1741-1752, Aug. 29, 1741.

3. Jørgensen's letter to Dorph, May 25, 1743, with other documents and en-closed copy of letter, July 11, 1743, Dorph's letter, Oct. 15, 1743, Billsen's, Mar. 30, 1744, V-gK., 123, br. & dok. fra G. 1732-1745; Dorph's letters of Nov. 22, 1746 & Jan. 28, 1747, V-gK., 124, br. & dok. fra G. 1746-1754; V-gK., 17, direktionsprotokol 1741-1752, Dec. 28, 1744.

4. V-gK., 17, direktionsprotokol 1741-1752, Nov. 17, 1742, Jan. 12, Mar. 15 & Aug. 15, 1743; Billsen's letters, Feb. 7 & Apr. 6, 1744, V-gK., 123, br. & dok. fra G. 1732-1745.

5. Billsen's letters, Mar. 30 & July 21, 1744, V-gK., 123, br. & dok. fra G. 1732-1745.

6. Hackenburg's letter, June 15, 1745, S. H. Klein's protest against his sus-pension, with numerous enc's., V-gK., 123, br. & dok. fra G. 1732-1745; Rømer's letter, Feb. 28, 1745, and other documents, V-gK., 124, br. & dok.

fra. G. 1746-1754; V-gK., 885, Diarie-bøger fra Christiansborg Feb. 3, 1744-Dec. 31, 1745; V-gK., 189, Svane, "General declaration," 103-125.

7. V-gK., 17, direktionsprotokol 1741-1752, Dec. 13, 1745; Hackenburg's letter, Aug. 20, 1746, V-gK., 124, br. & dok. fra G. 1746-1754.

8. Rømer's two books were translated into German: *Die Handlung verschied-ner Völker auf der Küste Guinea und in Westindien* (København, 1758) and *Nachrichten von der Küste Guinea* (København & Leipzig, 1767).

9. V-gK., 17, direktionsprotokol 1741-1752, May 20, Aug. 19, Nov. 26, 1745, Jan. 17 & Apr. 4, 1746, June 26 & Aug. 8, 1747; Hackenburg's letter, Mar. 17, 1746, Platfuss', Aug. 20, & Sept. 29, 1746, Jan. 18 & May 15, 1747, Sept. 21, 1748, V-gK., 124, br. & dok. fra G. 1746-1754; V-gK., diarie-bøger på Christiansborg June 21, 1746-Sept. 22, 1748; Mariager, "Historisk Efterret-ninger," fol. 174-185.

10. Platfuss' letters, Aug. 20, 1746-Jan. 16, 1751, V-gK., 124, br. & dok. fra G. 1746-1754. Concerning cessation of payment to Abonna: Engman's let-ter, Apr. 5, 1755, brevbog holden på fortet Christiansborg 1755, RGGA.

11. *Plan og Convention hvorefter det Kongelige Octroyerede Danske Westin-diske og Guineiske Compagnies Participanter til Compagniets have sub-skriberet, Feb. 6, 1747.* (København, 1748).

12. Schou, *Kongelige Forordninger og Aabne Breve* (København, 1777), IV.

13. *Placet om Føringen ved det Kongelige Octroyerede Danske Westindiske og Guineiske Compagnie, Oct. 10, 1747* (n.p., n.d.).

14. V-gK., 17, direktionsprotokol 1741-1752, Mar. 20, 1750; Hacksen's letter, May 28, 1751, V-gK., 124, br. & dok. fra G. 1746-1754.

15. Hacksen's letters, May 28, 1751-Apr. 9, 1752, V-gK., 124, br. & dok. fra G. 1746-1754.

Chapter 14 / The Crown Takes Over

1. V-gK., 136, Dok. vedk. afståelsen af de vestindiske øer og forterne i G. 1753-1754; Edvard Holm, *Danmarks-Norges Historie 1720-1814* (København, 1897), III, 2, 238-239. Presumably the negotiations leading up to the trans-fer occasioned the manuscript about the company by P. Mariager, the com-pany's bookkeeper, entitled "Historisk Efterretninger, June 30, 1753," ny kgl. saml. 426.

2. V-gK., 5, Trykte oktroyer, konventioner, plakater, m.m.; Schou, *Kongelige Forordninger.*

3. Schou, *Kongelige Forordninger.*

4. In Danish, "Vestindisk og Guineisk Rente-og General-Toldkammer."

5. V-gRtk., Kgl. resol. [vedk. V. og G.] 1759-1760, Jan. 11, 1760.

6. V-gRtk., Kgl. resol. [vedk. V. og G.] 1754-1758, Nov. 13, 1754, Mar. 18, 1755, Sept. 13, 1756.

7. V-gRtk., Guineiske sager og aktstykker (ujournaliserede) 1765-1802.

8. Holm, *Danmarks-Norges Historie*, III (1897), 2, 246; Poul P. Sveistrup, "Det almindelige Handelskompagni 1747-1774," *Meddelelser om Grønland*, CXXXI, No. 9 (1944), 9.

9. The northern part of Norway, Sweden, and Finland—Lapland.

10. Engman's letter, Aug. 26, 1755, V-gRtk., Brevjournal for europæiske og V. samt g. br. 1754-1760.

11. Engman's letters, Aug. 26 & Nov. 7, 1755, RGGA, brevbog holden på fortet Christiansborg 1755; Schmidt's letter, Mar. 31, 1757, Rtk., indk. div. g. br. 1755-1759.

12. Jessen's letters, Apr. 23, & Aug. 15, 1757, RGGA, brevbog 1757, his letters, Apr. 23 & Oct. 22, 1757, Rtk., indk. div. g. br. 1755-1759.
13. Engman's letter, Nov. 7, 1755, Sept. 24 & Oct. 27, 1756, RGGA, brevbøger holdt på fortet Christiansborg 1755-1756.
14. Quist's letter, Apr. 23, 1757, Jessen's, Aug. 16, 1757, with other complaints of Engman's conduct, Rtk., indk. div. g. br. 1755-1759.
15. Jessen's letters, Feb. 2 & June 4, 1758, V-gRtk., Det. Kgl. guvern. archiv, Brevbog 1758; his letters, July 14 & Sept. 4, 1759, May 28, July 2 & Dec. 17, 1760, V-gRtk., Indk. eurp. og V. [samt g.] br. 1760-1764; complaints that Danish ships did not call at the Danish forts; Engman's letters, Sept. 24 & Oct. 27, 1756, V-gRtk, Det. Kgl. guvern. archiv. brevbog 1756.
16. Jessen's letter, Oct. 22, 1757, Rtk., indk. div. g. br. 1755-1759.
17. Jessen's letters, Apr. 23, 1757, June 4, 1758, Rtk., indk. div. g. br. 1755-1759; his letter, July 12, 1760, V-gRtk. Indk. eurp. og v. [samt g.] br. 1760-1764.
18. Jessen's letter, Apr. 23, 1757, V-gRtk., Det. Kgl. guvern. Archiv, brevbog 1757; his letters, Oct. 22, 1757, June 4, 1758, Rtk., indk. div. g. br. 1755-1759.
19. Jessen's letter, July 10, 1760, V-gRtk., Indk. eurp. og v. [samt g.] br. 1760-1764; Resch's letter, June 17, 1765 (No. 220), V-gRtk. Indk. eurp. og v. [samt g.] br. 1764-1768.
20. Jessen's letters, July 12 & Dec. 27, 1760, Feb. 27, June 12 & Sept. 26, 1761, V-gRtk., Indk. eurp. og v. [samt g.] br. 1760-1764.
21. V-gRtk., Kgl. resol. [vedk. V. og G.] 1760-1763, Aug. 24, 1761 & Mar. 22, 1762; concerning Schmidt's letter, July 21, 1760, V-gRtk., Indk. eurp. og v. [samt g.] br. 1760-1764.
22. V-gRtk., journal over de fra g. indk. br. 1759-1768, Nos. 60, 76, 101, 134, 139, 140, 144, 162, 206, 232, 280; letters are in V-gRtk., Indk. eurp. og V. [samt g.] br. 1760-1764 & 1764-1768.
23. Enclosures in Kgl. resol. May 15, 1775, V-gRtk., Kgl. resol. vedk. v. [og g.] 1773-1775, No. 36.

Chapter 15 / Bargum's Trading Society

1. V-gRtk., Kgl. resol. [vedk. V. og G.] 1764-1768.
2. H. Trier, "Om Gaarden Nr. 14 ved Stranden," *Historiske Meddelelse om København,* rk. 1, I (1907-1908), 175ff.; *Fonden ad usus publicos,* udgivet af Rigsarkivet, I (1897), 3-4.
3. Charter in KODGKA, I, Oktnoj 1763.
4. V-gRtk., Kgl. resol. [vedk. V. og. G.] 1764-1768, No. 25a; the concession is in KODGKA, I, Koncession 1765; calculations occasioned by application for recovery of expenses for repairs, fasc. 1756-1764, V-gRtk., g. sager og aktstykker (ujournaliserede) 1765-1802.
5. Schou, *Kongelige Forordninger.*
6. The convention of Feb. 19, 1766, and royal confirmation of Aug. 4, 1766, in KODGKA, I, konfirmation 1766; German translation in Finanskollegiets Arkiv, Diverse sager, Schimmelmanns papirer vedk. det ø.-g. handelskompagni og de danske besiddelser på Guineakysten 1765-1802.
7. Extract enclosed in kgl. resol. May 15, 1775, V-gRtk., Kgl. resol. vedk. V. [og G.] 1773-1775, No. 36.
8. Tychsen's letter, Nov. 12, 1766, KODGKA, Brevbog 1766, 155-158, and his letter, Feb. 20, 1767, KODGKA, Kystdokumenter 1767; the king's con-

firmations of appointments for Guinea from then on are mostly to be found in V-gRtk., V. (later, indiske) forestillinger og resolutioner.

9. It worked on the coast from July 7-Oct. 15, 1768; its protocol in Kystdokumenter; its instructions of Mar. 29, 1768, in Direktionens skrivelser til guvernøren 1765-1771, all KODGKA.

10. Kuhberg's letters, Apr. 21, 1768-Apr. 6, 1769, entered in, KODGKA, Brevbog 1768 & 1769; the letters themselves in KODGKA, Kystdokumenter.

11. Wrisberg's letters, July 18, 1769-Apr. 28, 1770, entered in KODGKA, Brevbog 1769 II, and in KODGKA Indk. br. 1770-1773; original letters in KODGKA Kystdokumenter; Aarestrup, KODGKA, Indk. br. 1770-1773, Nos. 174-176, 200. For the years 1770-1775, there are also special letter copybooks.

12. Kuhberg's letters, Apr. 21 & Sept. 9, 1768, Apr. 6, 1769; Wrisberg's, Mar. 9, July 18 & Aug. 30, 1769, entered in KODGKA, Brevbog 1768 & 1769; original letters in KODGKA, Kystdokumenter; Frölich's letter, July 26, 1770, Aarestrup's, July 17, 1772 & Apr. 14, 1773, Kiøge's, Nov. 24, 1773, KODGKA Indk. br. 1770-1773, and 1773-1777.

13. Tychsen's letter, Feb. 20, 1767, Kuhberg's, Apr. 21, July 21 & Nov. 1, 1768, Wrisberg's, July 18, 1769 & Feb. 18, 1770, entered in KODGKA Brevbog 1767, 1768, 1769 and 1770; KODGKA, Indk. br. 1770-1773, Nos. 287, 311, 405, 419, 432, 634, 677, 687, 727, 730, 755, 760, 806, 870; original letters in KODGKA, Kystdokumenter.

14. Letters from directors to governor, Sept. 30, 1768, Direktionens skrivelser til guvernøren 1765-1771; Frölich's letter, July 26, 1770, Kystdokumenter 1770; his letter, Feb. 15, 1771, Brevbog 1770 II; Aarestrup's letters, Feb. 19, Mar. 21, Aug. 15, 1772, Brevbog 1772; his letters, Jan. 3, Apr. 14, June 4 & Aug. 26, 1773, Brevbog 1773; his letter, Aug. 17, 1774, Brevbog 1774; Indk. br. 1770-1773, Nos. 112, 297, 298, 408, 477, 496, 595, 601, 646, 669, 670, 739, 838; Indk. br. 1773-1777, Nos. 1, 57, 67, 148, 217; original letters in Kystdokumenter; all KODGKA.

15. Wrisberg's letters, Feb. 6 & 28, 1770, Frölich's, Feb. 15, 1771, Aarestrup's, Aug. 15 & Oct. 31, 1772, Jan. 3 & June 28, 1773, Apr. 26, 1774, Feb. 24 & May 28, 1775, entered in Brevbog 1770, 1771, 1772, 1773, 1774, 1775; original letters in Kystdokumenter; all KODGKA.

16. Kiøge's letter, Mar. 26, 1772, KODGKA, Indk. br. 1770-1773, No. 838; Aarestrup's letter, Apr. 14, 1773, and Kipnasse's, Dec. 24, 1774, entered in KODGKA, Brevbog 1773 & 1774.

17. Aarestrup's letters, July 26 & Aug. 15, 1772, Apr. 21 & June 8, 1774, Indk. br. 1770-1773 and 1773-1777; his letter, June 15, 1775, Brevbog 1775-1778; original in Kystdokumenter; all KODGKA.

18. KODGKA; Direktionens resolutionsprotokol 1770-1777, May 15 & July 22, 1774, Eiler Nystrøm, ed., Luxdorph's Dagbøger (København, 1915-1930), I, 264, 266, 279, 290, 291, 362; Henrik Koppel, "En 'advokat de la cour du Roy de Dannemarck' i Danton processen," Personalhistorisk Tidsskrift, 9 rk., IV (1932), 242-252.

19. KODGKA, Direktionens resolutionsprotokol 1770-1777, Jan. 4, 1775; afterward the society moved to rented offices because vermin ate the papers; several documents, such as the shareholders' resolution of Apr. 6, 1775, are in J. G. Moltke's privatarkiv, C5b, Papirer vedk. det kgl. oktr. da. guin. komp. 1765-1777; V-gRtk., Kgl. resol. vedk. V. [og. G.] 1773-1775, No. 36, kgl. resol. May 15, 1775, with enc. of the directors' letter to the king, Apr. 12, 1775; the company's view of the matter is revealed by Bredahl's and Thalbit-

zer's memoranda of Dec. 16, 1775 in Finanskoll. arkiv, Div. sager, Schimmelmannske papirer vedk. det. ø.-g. handelskomp. 1765-1802, encs. in the
latter parcel give an estimate of the Guinea traffic of Bargum's society.

20. Direktionens resolutionsprotokol 1770-1777, Dec. 28, 1774; Aarestrup's letters, Oct. 13, 1773 & July 17, 1774, Feb. 26 & Mar. 30, 1775, entered in
Brevbog 1773, 1774 & 1775-1778; original letters in Kystdokumenter; all
KODGKA.
21. KODGKA, Direktionens resolutionsprotokol 1770-1777, July 24, Oct. 13
& Dec. 1775; V-gRtk., Kgl. resol. vedk. V. [og. G.] 1773-1775, No. 37;
minutes of July 24, 1775, in J. G. Moltke's privatarkiv, C5b.
22. KODGKA, Indk. br. 1773-1777.
23. V-gRtk., Kgl. resol. vedk. V. [og. G.] 1776, No. 46; KODGKA, Indk. br.
1773-1777, Nos. 999, 1029, 1034, 1049, 1051, 1058, 1060, 1064, 1070, 1073,
1076; a directors' letter, Mar. 26, 1777, Overskattedirektionens Arkiv. Korr.,
A XXXVII (1777); order for Hemsen in KODGKA, Direktionens skr. til
guvernøren 1771-1778; V-gRtk., v.j., 1778, No. 49.
24. KODGKA, Direktionens resolutionsprotokol 1770-1777, June 12, 1776;
KODGKA, Indk. br. 1773-1777; calculations for the transfer of stores in
V-gRtk.; Gamle guineiske dok., forterne vedr. 1765-1787; sjæll. tegn. 1777,
No. 525 (the committee archives 1788); DKanc. F 71, Kommissonen til at
likvidere det forrige oktrojerede guineiske kompagni [1777]-1788.
25. KODGKA, Direktionens skr. til guvernøren 1765-1771, Dec. 12, 1767.
26. Copy of the society's agreement with the Moravian Church, Sept. 2, 1767,
in J. G. Moltke's privatarkiv C5b; Kuhberg's letter, Nov. 1, 1768, KODGKA,
Brevbog 1768; Wrisberg's letter, Feb. 28, 1770, Frölich's, Nov. 23, 1770,
Aarestrup's, Dec. 31, 1773, KODGKA, Indk. br. 1770-1773 and 1774-1777;
original letters in KODGKA, Kystdokumenter.

Chapter 16 / At War with the Dutch

1. Most documents dealing with the war against the Dutch are to be found, at
least in copies, in DfuA., Alm. korr.s. Litr.G., Korrespondansager vedr. de
på kysten af Guinea i året 1775 opkomne stridigheder mellem de danske
og hollandske kolonier 1775-1809; most important are the memorial of July
19, 1782, and the extract 1784; Doorman, "Niederländisch-West Indische
Kompagnie," 436, 467-477.
2. Aarestrup's letter, Mar. 3, 1776, June 25, 1776, in copy enc. with his letter,
Aug. 19, 1776, KODGKA, Kystdokumenter 1775-1778; KODGKA, Indk. br.
1773-1777, No. 1108.
3. The word is used f. inst. in Bernstorff's letter to Admiral Kaas, July 19,
1779, in parcel from DfuA. Litr.G, 1775-1809.
4. V-gK., 884, Dag-journaler ført på Christiansborg, Dec. 23, 1698-July 23,
1700; Billsen's letter, Mar. 30, 1744, V-gK., 123, Br. & dok. fra G. 1732-
1745.
5. About flags: Herrn's letter, Feb. 10, 1722, Wærøe's, Aug. 30, 1730, V-gK.,
122, Br. & dok. fra G. 1717-1732. V-gKtk., journal over de fra G. indk. br.
1759-1768, No. 220.
6. Johan F. W. Schlegel, Statistisk Beskrivelse af de fornemste europæiske
Stater (København, 1793), I, 501.
7. Ward, Short History, 89.
8. Aarestrup's letters, Dec. 27, 1776, Jan. 31 & Feb. 1, 1777, KODGKA, Indk.

br. 1773-1777, Nos. 1123, 1124, 1130; v.j. 1777, Nos. 245, 477, v.j. 1778, Nos. 62, 546, 698; originals in parcel DfuA, Litr.G, 1775-1809.

9. List of ships sent out by the Royal Trade Office in V-gRtk., g. sager og aktstykker (ujournaliserede) 1765-1802; V-gRtk., Kgl. resol. vedk. V. [og. G.] 1777, No. 106.

10. Copy of letter from Bernstroff to Admiral Kass, July 19, 1779, parcel from DfuA., Litr. G, 1775-1809; Marinens arkiv, Skibsjournal No. 531a, 1779-80 ("Holsten"); copy of document concerning arms and goods landed in V-gRtk., guin. sager og aktstykker (ujournaliserede) 1765-1802.

11. G.j. 1776-1798, No. 78; further documents concerning the diplomatic negotiations in parcel from DfuA., Litr. G, 1775-1809.

12. Kiøge's letters, Mar. 23 & Dec. 26, 1781, in parcel from DfuA., Litr. G, 1775-1809.

13. According to Jessen's letter, Aug. 15, 1757, V-gRtk., Det kgl. guvern. arkiv, Brevbog 1757, Ponny had been ignominiously surrendered by Dorph to the Dutch in 1743 or 1744.

14. Beside a facs. of calculations in parcel from DfuA., Litr. G, 1775-1809; v. j. 1781, No. 810; 1783, Nos. 87, 401, 817; 1784, No. 623; 1786, No. 694.

Chapter 17 / The Baltic-Guinea Trading Company and Forts Kongensten and Prinsensten

1. Accounts of Den Kongelige Handels-Direktion are J. G. Moltke's privatarkiv, C5c; Overskattedirektionens arkiv, G, Ektrakter over udskibede varer til St. Eustace, Guinea og Østindien 1778-1781, & Generalbalancer over den islandske, finmarkske, færrøske, grønlandske og guineiske handel 1775-1781.

2. Holm, *Danmark-Norges Historie,* V (1906), 518-522; the company's archives are not preserved; a few relics are enclosed in guineiske journal numbers; besides these there are: V-gRtk., G. sager og aktstykker (ujournaliserede) 1765-1802, which includes printed instructions for trade-clerks, sea captains, etc. and, Finanskoll. Arkiv, Div. sager; Schimmelmannske papirer vedk. det ø.-g. handelskomp. 1765-1802; Overskattedirektionens arkiv, G; Subskription på aktier i det ø.-g. handelsselskab; General-balance December 1781 and 1782, J. G. Moltke's privatarkiv, C5c, Papirer vedk. det ø.-g. handelsselskab 1781-1785; in the latter archives are also the printed charter of July 5, 1781, and a list of the 37 ships.

3. Fasc. in V-gRtk., "Gamle g. dok., forterne vedr. 1765-1787."

4. V. j. 1781, No. 756 mentions a Norwegian ship, the *Johanne;* according to a sheet addressed "Til hendes Naade frue Grevinde Reventlow" March 16, 1784, in Finanskoll. Arkiv, Div. sager, Schimmelmannske papirer vedr. det. ø.-g. handelskomp. 1765-1802, the company temporarily had shares in a limited liabilities company which in 1781 sent to Guinea the ships *Geheime-Raad Stampe, Grev Scheel, Prins af Bevern,* and *Geheime-Raad Gregers Juul;* only one of these ships produced a deficit.

5. G.j. 1776-1798, Nos. 56, 113; account enclosed in V-gRtk.'s letter to Bernstorff, Jan. 14, 1785, and other documents in the parcel, DfuA, Litr. G, 1775-1809; Biørn's not quite accurate account in letter of Jan. 25, 1793, Finanskoll. Arkiv, Div. sager, Schimmelmannske papirer vedk. det. ø.-g. handelskomp. 1765-1802.

6. The main source, is, Paul E. Isert, *Reise nach Guinea und den Caribäischen*

Inseln in Columbien in Briefen an seine Freunde Beschrieben (København, 1788); 2nd ed., *Neue Reise* . . . (Berlin und Leipzig, 1790); Danish translation in *Samlig af de bedste og nyeste Reisebeskrivelser* (København, 1790), III, 247-512; condensed Danish translation by Ingeborg Raunkiær (København, 1917), French trans., 1793; condensed Swedish trans., 1795; Dutch trans., 1797; Isert's record differs somewhat from the account of Jan. 14, 1785, and it is impossible at present to ascertain which source is the more reliable.

7. Earlier governors of a fort near Keta: Hachsen's letter, Dec. 31, 1751, V-gK., 124, Br. & dok. fra G. 1746-1754; Jessen's letters, Apr. 23, 1757 and June 4, 1758, V-gRtk., Indk. div. g. br. 1755-1759; Frölich's letter, Apr. 19, 1771, Indk. br. 1770-1773; and KODGKA, Direktionens resolutionsprotokol 1770-1777, Nov. 1772; A number of documents concerning the erection of the fort are included in an enclosure to g.j. 1847, No. 218.

8. V. j. 1784, Nos. 570, 623, 856; 1785, Nos. 4, 37, 213, 241; 1787, Nos. 263, 370; a general account, Dec. 31, 1784, Finanskoll. Arkiv, Div. sager; Schimmelmannske papirer vedk. det. ø-g. handelskomp. 1765-1809; Julius V. Schovelin, *Fra den danske handels empire* (København, 1899), I, 249; (1900), II, 4, 10, 126-139; Holm, *Danmarks-Norges Historie* (1907), VI, 1, 151-157.

9. The royal assent is printed in, E. Gigas, "En theologisk Professors diplomatiske Mission," *Historisk Tidskrift* (København), 8 rk. I (1907), 187.

10. Schimmelmannske papirer vedk. det. ø-g. handelskomp. 1765-1802, throw some light on various plans for the future of the company; Designation med bilag over det. ø-g. handelsselskabs ejendele i anledning af dets overdragelse til finanskollegiet 1787; Trækningsprotokol over obligationer, udstedte af det. ø-g. handelsselskab June 11, 1786, 1787-1811; Trækningsprotokol ved finanskollegiet til indløsning af det. ø-g. handelskompagnis aktier og obligationer af July 1, 1787, 1788-1812; Trækningsprotokol for det. ø-g. handelskompagnis obligationer 1811 (with enclosed examples of cancelled bonds); Regnskab over udbetalt kapital og rente i det. ø.-g. handelsselskabs obligationer à 75 rd., 1797-1807; all these parcels are in Finanskoll. Arkiv, Div. sager.

11. The archives of this firm no longer exist; for its contract with the Finance Collegium 1787, *vide* v. j. 1787, No. 735; copy 1788, No. 776; Camillus Nyrop, *Niels Lunde Reiersen* (København, 1896), 268.

12. Details in, V-gRtk., Dokumenter vedk. kommissionen for negerhandelens bedre indretning og ophævelse samt efterretninger om negerhandelen og slaveriet i Vestindien 1783-1806; for the total number of slaves exported from Africa on all Danish vessels, *vide,* Schlegel, *Statistisk Beskrivelse,* I, 520; P. Bonnassieux, *Les Grandes Compagnies de commerce* (Paris, 1892), 443.

13. His letter, Aug. 6, 1787, and Kipnasse's, May 22, 1788, in V-gRtk., g. sager og aktstykker (ujournaliserede) 1765-1802; v. j. 1788, Nos. 500, 511, 541, 597; 1789, Nos. 5, 15, 310, 604.

14. His letters, May 22, July 3, and Sept. 16, 1788, extract from his letters, Mar. 11 & Feb. 4, 1789, in V-gRtk., g. sager og aktstykker (ujournaliserede) 1765-1802; v. j. 1788, No. 511.

15. V. j. 1789, Nos. 15, 29; transfer on Nov. 1, 1789, in V-gRtk., g. sager og aktstykker (ujournaliserede) 1765-1802; Biørn's report in, "Biørns Beretning 1788 om de Danske Forter og Negerier," *Archiv for Statistik, Politik og Huusholdings,* Udgived af Professor Frederik Thaarup (København), III (1797-1798), 193-230.

16. V. j. 1788, No. 511; 1789, Nos. 66, 155; 1797, Nos. 32, 154, 773; 1792, Nos. 25, 627; Kipnasse's letters, May 22, 1788, with survey of July 30, 1788, & July 5, 1788; Cortnum's and Wrisberg's, June 21, 1791, Biørn's, Apr. 24, 1792, V-gRtk., g. sager og aktstykker (ujournaliserede) 1765-1802; letters Aug. 11, 1787, & May 18, 1789, with instructions of Apr. 30, 1789, in Finanskoll. Arkiv, Div. sager, Schimmelmannske papirer vedk. det. ø.-g. handelskomp. 1765-1802.

17. V. j. 1701, Nos. 25, 134; Biørn's letters, Apr. 24, 1792 & Jan. 24, 1793, in V-gRtk., g. sager og aktstykker (ujournaliserede) 1765-1802; Ward, *Short History*, 107; Claridge, *History of the Gold Coast*, I, 223, 224.

18. V. j. 1793, No. 915; Biørn's letter, Dec. 3, 1793, V-gRtk., g. sager og aktstykker (ujournaliserede) 1765-1802; Biørn's letters, May 15 & 30, 1794, Finanskoll. Arkiv, Div. sager, Schimmelmannske papirer vedk. det. ø.-g. handelskomp. 1765-1802, g. j. 1793, No. 3.

Chapter 18 / Life at the Forts

1. Herrn's letter, Apr. 20, 1722, Wærøe's, Dec. 24, 1730, Boris', May 3, 1738, V-gK., 122, 123, br. & dok. fra G. 1717-1732, 1732-1745.

2. Wrisberg's letter, Oct. 25, 1769, Aarestrup's, Dec. 31, 1773, KODGKA, Indkomne br. 1770-1773 & 1773-1777; v. j. 1788, No. 511.

3. Engman's letter, Oct. 6, 1754, V-gRtk., Brevjournal for europæiske og v. samt g. br. 1754-1760; Kuhberg's letter, Apr. 21, 1768, KODGKA, Kystdokumenter.

4. Suhm's letter, Aug. 15, 1724, Wærøe's, Aug. 30, 1730, V-gK., br. & dok. fra G. 1717-1732.

5. Herrn's letter, Feb. 10, 1722, Syndermann's, Mar. 31, 1724, Suhm's, Mar. 5, 1727, Hackenburg's, Sept. 9, 1746, V-gK., br. & dok. fra G.; g. j. 1793, No. 98.

6. Lists of goods sent by ship to Guinea are found in scattered documents, particularly informative are the 1722-1725 lists in V-gK., 122, br. & dok. fra G. 1717-1732. The "general letters" sent by the Christiansborg government; Georg Nørregård, "Varer til Guinea," *Årbog for Handel- og Søfartsmuseet på Kronborg* (1951), 56-66.

7. Most informative is Engman's letter, July 29, 1752, V-gK., 124, br. & dok. fra G. 1746-1754; a quarrel caused by the currency, Engman's letter, Apr. 2, 1760, V-gRtk., Kgl. resol. [vedk. V. og G.] 1760-1763.

8. Rask, *Rejse-Beskrivelse*, 138-139.

9. Syndermann's letter, Dec. 29, 1723, & Engman's, July 29, 1752, V-gK., 124, br. & dok. fra G. 1746-1754.

10. Lygaard's letter, Mar. 6, 1711, V-gK., 120, br. & dok. fra G. 1705-1716.

11. Jessen's letter, July 14, 1758, V-gRtk., Indk. eurp. og v. [samt g.] br. 1760-1764.

12. P. N. Jørgensen's letter, Aug. 31, 1740, V-gK., 123, br. & dok. fra G., 1732-1745.

13. Among the English, Jessen's letter, Sept. 4, 1759, V-gRtk., Indk. eurp. og v. [samt g.] br. 1760-1764.

14. Memorandum of Oct. 13, 1753, V-gK., 136, Dok. vedk. afståelsen af de vestindiske øer og forterne paa G. 1753-1754.

15. G. j. 1794, No. 16.

16. Suhm's letter, Sept. 28, 1726, Pahl's, Sept. 10, 1727, N. Lange's, Dec. 24, 1730, V-gK., 122, br. & dok. fra G., 1717-1732.

17. Svane's letter, Feb. 6, 1722, Herrn's, Feb. 10, 1722, Syndermann's, Mar. 21, 1724, Suhm's, Mar. 5, 1727, Pahl's, Sept. 10, 1727, Wærøe's, May 28, 1729, & Mar. 30, 1734, N. Lange's, Dec. 24, 1730, V-gK., 122, 123, br. & dok. fra G. 1717-1732, 1732-1745.

18. V-gK., 189, Svane, "General declaration," *passim.*

19. Svane's letters, Nov. 13, 1739, Mar. 14, 1740, Boris' letter Mar. 3, 1738, Hackenburg's, Sept. 9, 1746, V-gK., 123, 124, br. & dok. fra G. 1732-1745, 1746-1754.

20. *Holberg Blandinger* (København, 1939), 28ff.

21. Jessen's letter, June 12, 1761, V-gRtk., Indk. eurp. og v. [samt g.] br. 1760-1764, No. 19; V-gRtk., Kgl. resol. [vedk. V. og G.] 1764-1768, No. 32.

22. Resch's letter, May 29, 1762, V-gRtk., Indk. eurp. og v. [samt g.] br. 1760-1764, No. 41; Aarestrup's letter, Dec. 31, 1773, brevbog 1773, 163, KODGKA.

23. Hyltoft's letter, Apr. 27, 1763, V-gRtk., Indk. eurp. og v. [samt g.] br. 1760-1764, No. 134; Resch's letter, June 17, 1765, V-gRtk., Journal over de fra G. indk. br. 1759-1768, No. 224; Aarestrup's letter, Feb. 24, 1775, brevbog 1775, KODGKA; v. j. 1788, No. 511.

24. Svane's letter, Feb. 6, 1722, copy of Suhm's letter, Aug. 15, 1724, V-gK., 122, br. & dok. fra G. 1717-1732.

25. Kop's letter, Oct. 22, 1755, brevbog holden på fortet Christiansborg 1755, RGGA.

Chapter 19 / Plantations and the Abolition of the Slave Trade

1. Louis Bobé, *Efterladte Papirer fra den Reventlowske Familiedreds* (København, 1900), IV, 14.

2. Gigas, "Diplomatiske Mission," 185-253.

3. Schimmelmannske papirer vedk. ommende kommissionen betraeffende Guinea og negerhandelen samt forskellige vestindiske papirer 1778-1809, V-gRtk.; this committee must not be mistaken for a committee working on the Negro law, from which are preserved drafts and memoranda 1783-1789, and 2 vols. of proposals of June 29, 1785, and which deliberated on the condition of the Negroes in the West Indies. That the Finance Collegium and the V-gRtk. were carrying on a correspondence about the changes in the slave trade is shown by v. j. 1788, No. 776; original text in V-gRtk., g. sager og aktstykker (ujournaliserede) 1765-1802.

4. Isert, *Reise nach Guinea*, 338-340; for a bibliography of Isert's works *vide* Bobé, *Efterladte Papirer,* IV, 301.

5. Wrisberg's letter, Oct. 25, 1769, Frölich's, July 25, 1770, & Mar. 23, 1772; indk. br. 1770-1773, Nos. 36, 329, 835; Aarestrup's letter, Dec. 31, 1773; indk. br. 1773-1777, No. 297; direktionens resolutionsprotokol 1770-1777, Nov. 1772; all from KODGKA.

6. *Fonden ad usus publicos,* udgivet af Rigsarkivet (København, 1897), I, 112; Schimmelmannske papirer vedk. kommissionen betr. G. 1778-1809; V-gRtk., g. sager og aktstykker (ujournaliserede) 1765-1802; original text of treaty with Krobbo in German in enc. to g.j. 1891, No. 311; a few documents printed in "Nogle Bidrag til Kundskab om den danske Strækning paa Guinea Kysten," *Archiv for Statistik, Politik og Huusholdings,* Udgived af Professor Frederik Thaarup (Kjøbenhavn), III (1797-1798), 231-268.

7. Kipnasse's letter, Dec. 7, 1791, Schimmelmannske papirer vedk. kommissionen betr. G. 1778-1809, V-gRtk.

8. Lather's letter, Sept. 16, 1790, & P. Meyer's letter, Sept. 18, 1790, V-gRtk., Schimmelmannske papirer vedk. kommissionen betr. G. 1778-1809; Biørn's letter, May 15, 1794, Finanskoll. Arkiv, Div. sager, Schimmelmannske papirer vedk. det. ø-g. handelskomp. 1765-1802, g.j. 1793, No. 12; 1802, No. 174; 1804, No. 491.

9. V-gRtk., Dok. vedk. kommissionen for negerhandelens bedre indretning og ophævelse 1783-1806, og om negerhandelens afskaffelse betr. [correspondence with the committee, etc.] 1788-1847.

10. Extracts printed in Rahbek's periodical *Minerva*, XXVIII (1792), 43-46, 257-265, 311-318.

11. Printed in Frederik Thaarup, *Udførling Vejledning til det danske Monarkis Statistik* (København, 1819), VI, 665-672.

12. V-gRtk., V. forestillinger og resol. 1791-1792, No. 5; Schou, *Kongelige Forordninger* (1793), X, 584-586.

13. V-gRtk., V. forestillinger og resol. 1791-1792, Nos. 15a & 16; v.j. 1792, No. 749; Schou, *Kongelige Forordninger* (1793), X, 645-646; quarrel between the entrepreneurs and the Finance Collegium, g.j. 1795, Nos. 202, 204.

14. V.j. 1793, Nos. 1, 27, 39, 877, 915, 933; g.j. 1793, Nos. 1, 3, 4, 5, 7, 8, 10; protest of Jan. 26, 1793, V-gRtk., Schimmelmannske papirer vedk. kommissionen betr. G. 1778-1809; Biørn's letter, May 15, 1794, Finanskoll. Arkiv, Div. sager, Schimmelmannske papirer vedk. det. ø.-g. handelsselskab 1765-1802.

15. Rescript of Nov. 2, 1792, Schimmelmannske papirer vedk. kommissionen betr. G. 1778-1809, V-gRtk.; extract of Moe's letter, Dec. 31, 1793, in V-gRtk., g. sager og aktstykker (ujournaliserede) 1765-1802.

16. V-gRtk., V. forestillinger og resol. 1791-1792, No. 15; Camillus Nyrop, "v. Rohr, Julius Philip Benjamin," Carl F. Bricka, ed., *Danske Biografisk Leksikon* (København, 1900), 158-159.

17. *Fonden as usus publicos* (1897), I, 140-141; letter from the West Indies, May 26, 1795, in V-gRtk., g. sager og aktstykker (ujournaliserede) 1765-1802; Flindt's letter, Oct. 28, 1799; Schimmelmannske papirer vedk. kommissionen betr. G. 1778-1809, V-gRtk.

18. One alen = 68.8 cm.

19. G.j. 1794, No. 35; 1797, No. 299.

20. G.j. 1798, No. 413; 1799, No. 1; 1805, No. 631; 1806, No. 746; the first ship was lost.

21. G.j. 1794, No. 91.

22. G.j. 1793, No. 18.

23. G.j. 1795, Nos. 126 & 209.

24. G.j. 1795, No. 138.

25. G.j. 1796, No. 218.

26. G.j. 1796, Nos. 206, 216, 225; 1797, Nos. 273, 276; 1798, No. 406; 1801, No. 129; 1803, No. 407.

27. G.j. 1797, Nos. 297, 298.

28. G.j. 1798, Nos. 365, 415; 1802, No. 179.

29. G.j. 1798, No. 385.

30. G.j. 1799, Nos. 19, 41.

31. G.j. 1798, No. 415; 1799, Nos. 15, 75; 1800, No. 18; 1801, Nos. 130, 162, 167, 168; 1803, No. 420; enc. g.j. 1849, No. 659.

32. G.j. 1797, Nos. 302, 306, 337; 1798, No. 404; 1799, Nos. 15, 29; 1802, No. 329.

33. G.j. 1798, Nos. 365, 389, 405; 1799, No. 33; 1801, No. 252; 1802, No. 329;

1803, No. 409; about Ashanti, g.j. 1797, No. 305; 1798, No. 365; 1799, No. 15.

34. G.j. 1800, Nos. 38, 112; 1801, No. 243; 1803, No. 409.

35. G.j. 1802, No. 195; 1803, No. 409.

36. G.j. 1802, No. 285.

37. G.j. 1799, Nos. 51, 88; 1800, Nos. 27, 31, 98; 1802, Nos. 182, 266, 269, 270, 271; 1803, Nos. 392, 434; 1805, No. 656; Carl F. Christensen, *Den danske Botaniks Historie* (København, 1924), I, 142.

38. G.j. 1798, No. 370; 1799, Nos. 90, 101; 1800, Nos. 5, 9, 13, 17, 24, 43, 50; 1801, Nos. 132, 133; 1802, Nos. 181, 449; 1804, Nos. 490, 524; 1805, No. 650; 1819, No. 1765; applications of Oct. 28, 1799, Schimmelmannske papirer vedk. kommissionen betr. G. 1778-1809; V-gRtk.; report on Ejebo of April 29, 1805, V-gRtk., Dok. vedk. kommissionen for negerhandelens bedre indretning og ophævelse 1783-1806.

39. G.j. 1800, Nos. 67, 73, 85; 1801, No. 95; 1802, Nos. 186, 197, 211, 224, 284; 1803, Nos. 366, 408, 426; 1804, Nos. 465, 468; 1808, No. 969; a description of Bimbia (Njoffra), C. H. Bonne, *Søreiser paa Europas Kyster og Kysten af Guinea* (Thisted, 1833), 49ff.

40. G.j. 1804, No. 455; 1806, No. 728.

41. G.j. 1804, Nos. 466, 491, 498; 1807, No. 864.

42. G.j. 1804, No. 502.

43. G.j. 1805, Nos. 595, 596, 669; 1806, Nos. 792, 796, 844; 1807, No. 871.

44. G.j. 1805, No. 650; 1806, No. 728.

45. G.j. 1809, Nos. 1030, 1080; 1810, No. 1124.

46. G.j. 1809, No. 1083.

47. G.j. 1799, Nos. 34, 75.

48. G.j. 1804, No. 465.

49. About Captain Lind's fine, g.j. 1805, No. 692; g.j. 1804, No. 502; 1805, No. 706; 1806, Nos. 796, 844; copy in Andreas R. Biørn, *Tanker om Slavehandelen* (København, 1806).

50. G.j. 1806, Nos. 844, 856; 1821, Nos. 34, 52.

51. G.j. 1800, Nos. 27, 39; 1801, Nos. 106, 126, 243; 1802, No. 188; 1803, No. 426; Frederik Rønning, *Den grundtvigske slaegt* (København, 1904), 112-142.

52. G.j. 1804, Nos. 536, 550; 1807, Nos. 656, 894; 1809, No. 1086; Hans C. Monrad, *Bidrag til en Skilding af Guinea-Kysten og dens Indbyggere* (København, 1882), 315, 367, 371.

Chapter 20 / The Ashanti War

1. Thomas E. Bowdich, *Mission from Cape Coast Castle to Ashantee* (London, 1819); material from this book summarized by L. Zinck, "Guldkysten og Ashanti," *Fra alle Lande* (København), I (1874), 101-126, 219-247, 279-304, 400-418, 464-486; II (1874), 142-176.

2. G.j. 1806, Nos. 741, 749, 750; 1808, No. 923; 1809, Nos. 1034, 1073. Detailed accounts both of these and subsequent events in several English books: Henry Meredith, *An Account of the Gold Coast of Africa* (London, 1812), 129ff.; Brodie Cruikshank, *Eighteen Years on the Gold Coast of Africa* (London, 1853), 2 vols.; John D. Hay, *Ashanti and the Gold Coast and what we know of it, a sketch* (London, 1874); Carl Reindorf, *The History of the Gold Coast and Ashante* (London, 1889); Alfred B. Ellis, *A History*

of the Gold Coast of West Africa (London, 1893), 107ff.; Claridge, *History of the Gold Coast*; Ward, *History of the Gold Coast.*

3. G.j. 1810, No. 1122; 1811, Nos. 1208, 1217, 1221; 1813, No. 1309.
4. G.j. 1814, No. 1348.
5. G.j. 1814, No. 1348.
6. G.j. 1809, Nos. 1035, 1045; 1810, Nos. 1118, 1122; 1813, Nos. 1309, 1310; 1814, No. 1353.
7. G.j. 1807, No. 885.
8. G.j. 1809, No. 1028.
9. G.j. 1809, Nos. 1078, 1090.
10. G.j. 1810, Nos. 1123, 1126; 1811, Nos. 1184, 1189, 1203; 1812, No. 1220.
11. G.j. 1811, Nos. 1194, 1218; 1812, Nos. 1237, 1238; 1813, Nos. 1309, 1310; 1814, Nos. 1329, 1348, 1349, 1366; 1816, No. 1454; 1817, No. 1498.
12. G.j. 1811, No. 1221.
13. G.j. 1812, No. 1254; 1813, No. 1309; 1814, Nos. 1341, 1350.
14. G.j. 1814, No. 1362; 1815, Nos. 1410, 1416, 1422, 1433, 1437; 1816, Nos. 1458, 1482, 1487, 1488; 1817, No. 1498.
15. G.j. 1816, Nos. 1460, 1489; 1817, Nos. 1497, 1508.
16. G.j. 1817, No. 1615; 1818, No. 1620.
17. G.j. 1817, Nos. 1561, 1562, 1599.
18. G.j. 1817, Nos. 1560, 1587, 1613; 1819, Nos. 1779, 1787, 1791, 1797.
19. G.j. 1818, Nos. 1625, 1629; 1819, Nos. 1732, 1750, 1773; 1820, No. 1828.
20. G.j. 1828, Nos. 205, 207.
21. G.j. 1819, Nos. 1759, 1768, 1772; 1820, Nos. 1833, 1848, 1852.
22. G.j. 1820, Nos. 1853, 1898; 1821, Nos. 13, 14, 22, 23, 24, 25, 30, 42.
23. *Collegialtidende* (København), Oct. 14, 1820; J. Davidsen, *Fra det gamle Kongens Kjøbenhavn* (København, 1881), II, 110-130.
24. G.j. 1820, No. 1834; 1821, Nos. 26, 42, 83, 84; 1822, Nos. 159, 160, 174; 1825, No. 512; enc. g.j. 1849, No. 702.
25. G.j. 1822, Nos. 146, 153; 1824, No. 338.
26. G.j. 1822, Nos. 157, 185; 1823, Nos. 264, 308; 1825, No. 613; his despatches, g.j. 1822, Nos. 177, 215, 223, 224, 231, 277; 1823, Nos. 234, 245, 246, 255, 256, 258, 260, 262, 265, 280, 285, 296, 305, 308, 313, 322, 324; his debt, enc. g.j. 1848, No. 545.
27. Claridge, *History of the Gold Coast*, I, 334-355; g.j. 1824, Nos. 336, 337, 361; 1825, No. 580.
28. G.j. 1825, Nos. 462, 512; 1826, Nos. 676, 702; 1827, No. 884.
29. G.j. 1825, Nos. 463, 467, 512, 557; 1826, Nos. 669, 816; 1827, Nos. 844, 969.
30. G.j. 1825, Nos. 507, 558, 566, 602, 604; 1826, Nos. 663, 669, 719.
31. G.j. 1826, Nos. 719, 749, 793, 807, 819; 1827, Nos. 837, 850, 886, 891, 895, 949, 1027; enc. g.j. 1844, No. 663; 1848, No. 545.
32. Edvard E. T. Svanekiær, "Personalhistoriske Meddelelser om Slaegten Svanekiær," ms.; Th. Winther's manuscript notes, "Fra Guinea" (København, 1920), the property of Mr. Poul H. Winther.
33. A. C. Forsberg, *Røst fra Kysten Guinea eller Beretning om den i Aaret 1822 dertil sendte ekspedition under Major von Richelieu, som daværende Gouverneur* (København, 1827).
34. G.j. 1826, No. 727.
35. G.j. 1825, No. 613; 1828, No. 98.
36. G.j. 1825, No. 613; 1826, Nos. 732, 869, 910, 1052; *Statstidende* (København), Apr. 30, 1827.

37. G.j. 1827, Nos. 882, 1063.

38. G.j. 1826, No. 795; 1827, Nos. 899, 946; 1828, No. 5.

39. G.j. 1824, Nos. 384, 393; 1826, No. 825; 1827, Nos. 856, 925, 956; 1828, Nos. 6, 93, 100, 101, 150, 151; 1829, Nos. 301, 308, 361; 1831, No. 158; 1837, No. 484; 1839, No. 747; in the end the mill was demolished.

40. G.j. 1827, Nos. 911, 929, 958; 1828, Nos. 32, 34, 44, 93, 127, 141; Henrik G. Lind, "Undersøgelser foretaget op ad Floden Volta i 1827 og 1828," *Archiv for Søvæsenet* (København), VI (1834), 1-16.

41. G.j. 1828, Nos. 93, 98, 147, 175; 1829, Nos. 243, 248, 264, 391.

42. *Jesu Biergprädiken oversat i det Accraiske Sprog, med nogle tillæg af Luthers lille Cathecismus,* Forord af Fr. Münter (n.p., n.d.); g.j. 1826, No. 745; in 1805, Schiønning had a small book printed containing the Ten Commandments, the Apostolic Creed, and the Lord's Prayer translated into the Accra language, but this opusculum consisted of only a half sheet and there were only 100 copies, none of which were for sale to the public.

43. G.j. 1828, Nos. 73, 93, 210.

44. G.j. 1828, No. 130.

45. G.j. 1830, No. 469.

46. G.j. 1830, No. 486; 1832, No. 470; Schou, *Kongelige Forordninger* (1832), 460-464.

47. G.j. 1826, Nos. 661, 710, 758, 787; 1827, No. 999; 1828, Nos. 43, 55, 92, 170; 1829, Nos. 314, 330, 376, 467; 1830, Nos. 614, 620; 1831, No. 2; enc. g.j. 1850, No. 29; Christian Kalker, *Den evangeliske Missions Historie* (København, 1857), 133; Niels Bundgaard, *Det danske Missionsselskabs Historie* (København, 1935), I, 14, 42, 49-51, 62-63.

48. Rasmus Rask, *Vejledning til Akra-sproget paa Kysten Guinea med et tillæg om Akvambuisk* (København, 1828).

49. G.j. 1826, No. 791; 1830, Nos. 457, 511, 523.

50. J. J. Trentepohl, R. Chenon, F. Sannom, "Observationes meteorologiecae per annos 1829-1834 & 1838-1842 in Guinea factae," Introduction: H. C. Ørsted, J. F. Schouw, P. Pedersen, *Collectanea meteorologica sub auspiciis Societatis Scientiarium Daniae, edita.* Hauniae, fasc. III (1845).

51. G.j. 1828, Nos. 6, 35, 197, 259; 1829, Nos. 317, 318, 332, 391; 1830, Nos. 536, 617, 623, 638; 1831, Nos. 78, 133, 134, 143, 252, 301, 303, 311, 312; 1832, Nos. 341, 445; 1834, No. 795; 1835, Nos. 24, 84, 91; 1838, No. 580; enc. g.j. 1850, Nos. 87, 126; copy treaty of March 2, 1830, in C.O. 96/3 & 267/131; the English peace treaty of April 27, 1831, C.O. 267/112, Public Record Office (PRO), London; the latter treaty printed in Claridge, *History of the Gold Coast,* I, 409-411; copies of the Danish treaties, enc. g.j. 1891, No. 311.

52. G.j. 1830, Nos. 642, 643, 644; 1831, Nos. 77, 78, 130, 131; 1832, Nos. 288, 289, 296.

53. G.j. 1832, Nos. 283, 285, 300, 301, 303.

54. During his stay in Guinea he published in the periodical *Valkyrien,* "Correspondents-Efterretninger fra Christiansborg, fra Kysten af Guinea," I (1831), 272-274; "Breve fra og om Guinea," II (1831), 262-278, III (1831), 56-63; "Om slavehandel," I (1832), 251-258; "Nogle Bemaerkninger om fremmede Kolonier paa Vestkysten af Afrika," I (1832), 258-278; "Om Colonien Princes-Island," II (1832), 46-50.

55. G.j. 1821, Nos. 24, 84.

Chapter 21 / Quarrels with the British

1. G.j. 1830, No. 656; 1832, No. 304.
2. G.j. 1833, No. 367.
3. G.j. 1832, Nos. 351, 364; 1833, Nos. 622, 674, 693.
4. B. M. Christensen's obituary sketch of Lind, "Nekrolog over H. C. Lind," *Dagen*, Nr. 278-279 (1833).
5. G.j. 1834, No. 847; 1835, Nos. 37, 450.
6. G.j. 1830, Nos. 613, 637, 644, 662; 1837, Nos. 7, 14, 111, 117, 118, 119, 251; 1832, No. 474; 1834, No. 825; enc. g.j. 1849, No. 709; the committee of Nov. 9, 1832, handed in its report in 1848, g.j. 1848, No. 536 (with encs.).
7. G.j. 1830, Nos. 466, 509; 1831, No. 13; 1832, No. 474; 1833, No. 622; 1834, No. 797; 1835, Nos. 5, 7, 36, 83.
8. G.j. 1830, Nos. 637, 647.
9. G.j. 1831, Nos. 83, 164; 1832, Nos. 413, 414, 472, 515, 706; 1843, No. 433; enc. g.j. 1848, No. 576; C.N. Lorenzen, "Sønderjyden Andreas Riis," *Nordisk Missions-Tidsskrift*, III (1892), 289-340; C. H. Friis, *Andreas Riis* (København, 1932); Bundgaard, *Danske Missionsselskabs*, I, 51.
10. G.j. 1833, No. 704; 1834, Nos. 739, 741, 753, 754, 765, 766, 770, 910, 923; F.O. 84/142, 84/158, PRO; Korrespondancesager vedr. slavehandelens under-trykkelse, I, DfuA, alm. korr. litr. S; the treaty is printed in "Treaty be-tween Great Britain and France and Denmark, containing the Accession of Denmark to the Conventions of 1831 and 1833, between Great Britain and France, for the more effectual suppression of the Slave Trade.—Signed at Copenhagen, 26th July, 1834," *British & Foreign State Papers*, XXII (1833-1934), 218-222; in Schou, *Kongelige Forordninger* (1834), 118-131; in *Danske Tractater efter 1800*, I, Politiske Tractater, I, 1800-1863, 143-159; Georg Nørregård, "Englands Køb af de danske Besiddelser i Ostindien og Afrika 1845 og 1850," *Historisk Tidsskrift* (København), 10 rk., III (1936), 375.
11. G.j. 1835, No. 73; Schou, *Kongelige Forordninger* (1835), 197-214.
12. G.j. 1835, Nos. 10, 83.
13. G.j. 1834, No. 821; 1835, No. 10; 1836, No. 318.
14. G.j. 1834, No. 835.
15. G.j. 1821, No. 87; 1827, No. 883; 1830, No. 617.
16. G.j. 1832, No. 415; 1833, No. 693.
17. G.j. 1833, No. 647; 1834, Nos. 799, 821, 875; 1835, Nos. 5, 83, 84, 89, 142; 1836, Nos. 168, 209; 1837, No. 480; 1838, Nos. 579, 680, 729; 1839, Nos. 748, 887; 1840, Nos. 932, 997.
18. G.j. 1835, No. 142; 1836, Nos. 108, 224, 329; Gtk.'s historic explanation in DfuA, alm. korr.s., Litr. G., Korrespondancesager vedranende de danske establissementer på kysten af Guinea 1804-1848, Nørregård, "Englands Køb," 359-373.
19. G.j. 1836, No. 324; Residents of British Accra to the President & Council of Cape Coast Castle, July 4, 1836, F.O. 211/32, PRO; copy in DfuA., alm. korr.s., litr. G. vedr. de etablissementer på Guinea 1804-1848.
20. G.j. 1836, Nos. 324, 338; 1837, Nos. 411, 418, 480, 482, 498; 1838, No. 611; 1839, No. 748.
21. G.j. 1837, Nos. 442, 480; 1839, Nos. 814, 861, 887; 1840, No. 997; 1841, No. 144; African Merchants to C.O., Feb. 11 & Oct. 12, 1837, C.O. 267/144, PRO.
22. President & Council of Cape Coast Castle to African Merchants, May 17 & July 14, 1837, C.O. 267/144; the same to the same, Mar. 1, 1838, C.O.

267/150; African Merchants to C.O., Dec. 5, 1836, C.O. 267/136; F.O. to Wynn, Feb. 19, 1837, F.O. 211/32; Wynn's note with enclosures in DfuA., alm. korr.s., litr. G.; Korres. vedr. de etablissementer på Guinea 1804-1848, g.j. 1836, Nos. 399, 464.

23. Gtk.'s historic record, Dec. 5, 1837; draft for note to Wynn, Mar. 31, 1838; instructions for the Danish minister at the Court of St. James, Mar, 29, 1838; DfuA. to Gtk., Mar. 29, 1838; all in DfuA., alm. korr.s., litra G. Korres. vedr. de etablissementer på Guinea 1804-1848, instructions for Mörch, Apr. 7, 1837, enc. in g.j. 1891, No. 311; g.j. 1837, Nos. 399, 464; 1838, No. 592; Wynn to F.O., Apr. 12, 1838, C.O. 267/150, PRO.

24. Maclean to African Merchants, June 4 & 9, 1838, C.O. 267/150; F.O. to Wynn, July 24, 1838, F.O. 211/33, PRO; copy of report, Wynn's note, July 28, 1838, Krabbe-Carisius' resolution, Aug. 8, 1838, and Gtk.'s instructions for Mörch, June 29, 1838, in DfuA., alm. korr.s., litra G, Korres. vedr. de etablissementer på Guinea 1804-1848, g.j. 1838, No. 644.

25. G.j. 1839, No. 793.

26. Quotation from dispatch from Copenhagen to F.O., Feb. 5, 1842, C.O. 267/177, PRO; g.j. 1837, Nos. 440, 441, 475, 476; 1838, No. 565; 1839, No. 888; 1842, No. 104.

27. *Dagen*, No. 49 (Jan. 26, 1834); g.j. 1834, No. 763; 1835, Nos. 24, 83, 142; 1836, No. 224; 1839, Nos. 861, 887; 1840, No. 902; 1841, No. 48; 1842, Nos. 144, 184, 626; 1845, No. 82; Claridge, *History of the Gold Coast*, I, 457.

28. G.j. 1839, No. 887.

29. G.j. 1830, No. 616, 637; 1836, No. 323; 1837, No. 480; 1838, No. 611; 1841, Nos. 5, 48.

30. G.j. 1842, Nos. 105, 181, 216; F.O. to Browne, Mar. 29, 1842, F.O. 211/37, & Browne to F.O., Feb. 5, 1842, C.O. 267/177, PRO.

31. G.j. 1842, No. 226; his letters, Behrens, *Da Guinea var dansk;* Wulff died on Dec. 16, 1842.

32. G.j. 1842, No. 270; his travels and deputies, g.j. 1843, No. 413; 1844, Nos. 626, 652, 726, 758; 1846, No. 440; 1847, No. 8. His reports are published in Georg Nørregård, ed., *Guvernør Edward Carstensens Indberetninger fra Guinea 1842-1850* (København, 1964).

33. G.j. 1842, No. 270; 1843, Nos. 287, 363.

34. G.j. 1843, No. 288; enc. in g.j. 1891, No. 311.

35. G.j. 1845, Nos. 289, 433.

36. G.j. 1835, Nos. 83, 142; 1836, No. 226; 1839, No. 885; 1843, No. 364; drought: g.j. 1835, No. 83; 1836, Nos. 219, 314; 1845, No. 187; 1846, No. 225; locusts: g.j. 1834, No. 799; 1839, Nos. 814, 861.

37. G.j. 1843, Nos. 433, 490; enc. in g.j. 1844, No. 708; copies of letters from C. Th. Jørgensen and his wife's letters to Denmark have been preserved and are the property of Lauritz Jørgensen, Frederiksyndest Manor, Fredensborg, Denmark.

38. F.O. to Wynn, July 31, 1843, with encs., F.O. 211/38; Wynn to F.O., Aug. 21, 1843, F.O. 84/474, PRO; Wynn's note, Aug. 21, 1843, and draft for a reply, in DfuA., alm. korr.s., litra G. Korres. vedr. de etablissementer på Guinea 1804-1848.

39. G.j. 1844, Nos. 726, 728; 1845, Nos. 81, 82, 83, 93, 187; 1846, Nos. 201, 203, 205, 242, 243, 245, 246, 348, 376, 403; 1850, No. 28; encs. in g.j. 1850, No. 125; Jens Yde, "Ethnografisk Samlings Taletrommer," *Fra Nationalmuseets Arbejdsmark* (København, 1945), 18-24.

40. G.j. 1846, Nos. 323, 431, 442; 1847, Nos. 131, 293.

41. Fitzpatrick to C.O., Sept. 19, 1849, with encs., C.O. 96/15, PRO; printed in *British & Foreign State Papers*, XXXVIII (1849-1850), 67ff. (Fitzpatrick's letter only in suitable extracts); g.j. 1849, Nos. 824, 825, 948; Finansministeriet to Udenrigsministeriet, Jan. 15, 1850, in encs. to g.j. 1891, No. 311.
42. G.j. 1845, Nos. 154, 165; 1846, Nos. 202, 204; 1847, Nos. 98, 293; 1848, Nos. 374, 389, 407, 435, 488; 1849, Nos. 773, 826, 829, 950; 1850, No. 112; 1851, No. 235; encs. in g.j. 1850, No. 142; R. Hammer, "Fra Orlogsbriggen 'Ørnen's' Togt til Marokko, de danske Kolonier paa Guineakysten og til Vestindien i 1845-1846," *Tidsskrift for Søvæsen*, XXXI (1922), 281-331; C. Irminger, "Erindringer fra Kysten Guinea fra Togtet 1847," *Fra alle Lande*, VII (1868), 353-370; C. Irminger, "Slavehandelen paa Guinea," *Dansk Maanedskrift*, I (1859), 261-272; a very biased account in Claridge, *History of the Gold Coast*, I, 457-458; and in Ward, *Short History*, 152-153; Johan W. Svedstrup's copious diaries from his stay in Guinea (from 1844) were used by his son, Alexander Svedstrup, for his novel, *Erik Gudmand* (København, 1923-1925); his drawings of the forts are in the Handels- og Søfartsmuseum, Kronborg, Elsinore, Denmark.
43. G.j. 1844, Nos. 646, 651, 680; 1845, Nos. 46, 48, 164, 258; 1846, Nos. 288, 301, 353, 451; 1847, Nos. 4, 144, 148; 1848, No. 389; encs. in g.j. 1849, No. 921.
44. G.j. 1846, No. 364; 1847, Nos. 27, 98.
45. G.j. 1843, Nos. 504, 540; 1844, No. 628.
46. G.j. 1845, Nos. 135, 178; 1846, Nos. 299, 312, 343.
47. G.j. 1847, No. 290; encs. in g.j. 1849, No. 658; g.j. 1846, Nos. 224, 362, 430.
48. G.j. 1846, No. 384; 1848, Nos. 396, 401; encs. in g.j. 1850, No. 39; g.j. 1848, Nos. 478, 616, 617; 1849, Nos. 711, 828.
49. G.j. 1846, No. 384; 1847, No. 240.
50. G.j. 1847, No. 291; 1848, No. 385.
51. G.j. 1846, No. 218; 1847, No. 129; 1848, No. 624; 1849, No. 696.

Chapter 22 / The Sale

1. Niels Rosenkrantz, *Journal du Congrès de Vienne 1814-1815*, publié par G. Nørregård (Copenhague, 1953), 137; orders for the Danish Minister to the Court of St. James, Feb. 11, 1815, & Instructions for Moltke, May 23, 1821, in DfuA., alm. korr.s., Litr. Ø, Korrespondance vedr. Ostindien, II, Trankebar 1800-1846.
2. DfuA., alm. korr.s., litra G., Korres. Vedr. de establissementer på Guinea 1804-1848.
3. P. Videl, "Krabbe-Carisius, Hans," C. F. Bricka, ed., *Dansk biografisk Lexikon* (København, 1895), IX, 410.
4. G.j. 1821, No. 24; 1843, No. 288; "[Madden] Report of H.M.'s Commissioners of Inquiry on the State of the British Settlements on the Gold Coast, at Sierra Leone and the Gambia, with some Observations on the Foreign Slave Trading Factories along the Western Coast of Africa in the Year 1842," *Parliamentary Papers*, XII (1842); Georg Nørregård, "Englands Køb," 383ff.; a preparatory study in Georg Nørregård, "The English purchase of the Danish possessions in the East Indies and Africa 1845 and 1850," *Revue française d'histoire d'outre-mer*, XXI (1933), between pp. 186-187 (74 pp).
5. Guineisk resolutionsprotokol 1816-1850; g.j. 1840, No. 1040.
6. African Merchants to C.O., Dec. 8, 1840, C.O. 267/162; Bannermann to

Hutton, Dec. 19, 1842, C.O. 96/2; Winniett to C.O., Dec. 31, 1847, C.O. 96/11; all in PRO; "[Madden] Report," 11, 76.

7. Winniett to C.O., July 28, 1849, C.O. 96/15, and July 24, 1850, C.O. 96/19; both in PRO.

8. G.j. 1843, Nos. 365, 444; encs. in g.j. 1891, No. 310; Christian Schefer, "La Monarchie de Juillet et L'expansion coloniale," *La Revue des deux mondes*, II (Sept. 1912), 177ff; Christian Schefer, *Instructions generales données de 1763 à 1870 aux gouverneurs . . . français en Afrique Occidentale* (Paris, 1927), II, 133, 142, 146, 564, 565.

9. African Merchants to C.O., Mar. 7, 1843, C.O. 96/2; Stephen's opinion on Danish Claims to the Sovereignty adjoining the Danish Settlements on the Gold Coast, Mar. 13, 1843, C.O. 96/3, PRO.

10. C.O. to F.O., Apr. 17, 1843, C.O. 401/1; F.O. to Wynn, July 31, 1843, with encs., F.O. 211/38, both in PRO; Wynn's note, Aug. 21, 1843, DfuA., alm. korr.s., litra G. Korres. vedr. de etablissementer på Guinea 1804-1848, g.j. 1844, No. 528.

11. G.j. 1843, No. 339; draft for orders for the Danish Minister to the Court of St. James, Apr. 10 & June 21, 1843, DfuA., alm. korr.s., litra G, Korres. vedr. de etablissementer på Guinea 1804-1848; Wynn to F.O., Aug. 21, 1843, F.O. 84/474, PRO.

12. Gtk., Guineisk resolutionsprotokol 1816-1850; g.j. 1844, Nos. 104, 646, 650.

13. G.j. 1846, Nos. 375, 410; 1848, No. 596; note from French Minister to Copenhagen, Aug. 7, 1846, & Gtk. to DfuA., Oct. 4, 1846, in DfuA., alm. korr.s., litra G. Korres. vedr. de etablissementer på Guinea 1804-1848.

14. G.j. 1847, No. 290; 1848, No. 457

15. Bannermann to Hutton, Dec. 19, 1842, C.O. 96/2, PRO.

16. Gtk., Guineisk resolutionsprotokol 1816-1850; encs. in g.j. 1891, No. 310; g.j. 1848, Nos. 458, 475.

17. G.j. 1848, Nos. 577, 581; 1849, No. 655.

18. Hutton to C.O., Nov. 7, 1848, enc. Carstensen to Hutton, Oct. 27, 1848, C.O. 96/14; Eddisbury to Merrivale, Dec. 11, 1848, C.O. 96/13, PRO; encs. in g.j. 1891, No. 319; g.j. 1848, Nos. 579, 584.

19. G.j. 1849, Nos. 690, 753, 793, 881; Foster to C.O., Apr. 30, 1849, Reventlow to F.O., July 7, 1849; Winniett to C.O., & Trevelyan to Merrivale, Dec. 12, 1849, C.O. 96/17, PRO, "Correspondence relative to the Purchase by Great Britain of the Danish Possessions on the Coast of Africa—1849, 1850," *British & Foreign State Papers*, XXXVIII (1849-1850), 61-98.

20. Documents in C.O. 96/17 & 402/3; treaty in F.O. 94/112, PRO; Danish documents enclosed in g.j. 1891, No. 310; g.j. 1849, Nos. 939, 960; 1850, No. 4; the printed treaty: "Convention between Her Majesty and the King of Denmark, for the Cession of the Danish Possessions on the Coast of Africa to Great Britain," *Parliamentary Papers*, LVII (1851), 1-6; John J. Crooks, *Records Relating to the Gold Coast Settlements 1750-1874* (Dublin, 1923), 322; *Danske Tractater efter 1800*, I. Politiske Tractater, I, 1800-1863, 218-219; Larsen, *De danske i Guinea*, 129-131.

21. Hansard, 3rd Series, CXIII (1850), 37ff.; *Daily News* (Apr. 2, 1850), which rails against the purchase; g.j. 1850, No. 17.

22. F.O. to C.O., Sept. 14, 1850, C.O. 96/2, PRO; g.j. 1850, Nos. 97, 108, 109.

23. G.j. 1849, Nos. 962, 965, 968, 971; 1850, Nos. 1, 19, 56, 57, 151; encs. in g.j. 1891, No. 311; Winniette's diary in C.O. 96/18, printed as: "A Journal of a Tour through an extensive part of the Danish Settlements now transferred to the British Crown," *Parliamentary Papers*, XXXVIII (1850),

3-12, and under the same title in *British & Foreign State Papers*, XXXVIII (1849-1850), 80-98; Claridge, *History of the Gold Coast*, I, 475-476.

24. G.j. 1850, No. 81.
25. G.j. 1848, No. 615.
26. Treasury to F.O., July 30, 1850, C.O. 96/20, PRO; g.j. 1851, No. 178; 1854, No. 288; 1862, No. 303.
27. G.j. 1850, Nos. 115, 116, 117; 1851, No. 308.
28. Claridge, *History of the Gold Coast*, I, 477ff.; E. Nissen, "Guldkysten," *Under Dannebrog* (1916), 79-80; Sophie Petersen, *Danmarks gamle trope-kolonier* (København, 1946), 272-286

Bibliography

Printed Works

Afgedrongen en Welgefondeerde Tegen-Bericht der Conincklycke Deensche Geoctryeerde Affricaansche Guineesche, en in de Hooft-vestinghe Glückstadt opgerichte Compagnie, Glückstadt, 1665.

Aitzema, Lieuwe van. *Saken van Staet en Oorlogh, in ende omtrent de Vereenigde Neerlanden,* s'Gravenhagen, X (1665), XI (1668), XII (1668).

Alberti, C. "Den danske Slavehandels Historie," *Nyt Historisk Tidsskrift,* Kiøbenhavn, 2 rk., II (1850), 201-244.

Almindelig Historie over Reiser til Lands og til Vands eller Samling af alle Reisebeskrivelser, København, 1749, Vol. IV.

Barbot, John. "Description of the Coast of North and South Guinea," in A. Churchill, comp., *Collection of Voyages and Travels,* London, 1732, Vol. V.

Behrens, Carl, ed. *Da Guinea var dansk, W. J. Wulffs Breve og Optegnelser fra Guldkysten 1836-1842,* København, 1917.

Benezet, Anthony. *Some Historical Account of Guinea . . . With an Inquiry into the Rise and Progress of the Slave-Trade,* Philadelphia, 1771.

Bergsøe, Vilhelm. *Trankebar-Mønter 1644-1843 samt Mønter og Medailer vedr. den danske Handel paa Ostindien, China og Guinea,* København, 1895.

Bjørn, Andreas R. "Beretninger om de Danskes Forter og Negerien paa Guineakysten, 1788," *Archiv for Statistik, Politik og Huusholdings-Videnskaber, Heftskrift,* Udgivet af Professor Frederik Thaarup, Kjøbenhavn, III (1797-1798), 193-230.

———— *Tanker om Slavehandelen,* København, 1806.

Bobé, Louis. *Efterladte Papirer fra den Reventlowske Familiekreds,* Kjøbenhavn, 1900, Vol. IV.

Bøggild-Andersen, C. O. *Hannibal Sehested, ed dansk statsmand,* København, 1946, Vol. I.

Bonassieux, P. *Les grandes compagnies de commerce,* Paris, 1892.

Bonne, C. H. *Søreiser paa Europas Kyster og Kysten af Guinea,* Thisted, 1833.

Bosman, Guillaume. *Voyage de Guinée,* Utrecht, 1705.

Bowditch, Thomas E. *Mission from Cape Coast Castle to Ashantee,* London, 1819.

Brieven, Confessie mitgaders Advisen van verscheyden Rechtsgeleerden in de saeck van Isaac Coymans gegeven: als mede de sententie daer op gevolgt, Rotterdam, 1662.

Brieven geschreven en gewisselt tusschen de Heer Johan de Witt . . . ende de Gevolmaghtigden van den Staedt der Vereenigde Nederlanden, s'Gravenhage, 1724, Vol. IV.

Bundgaard, Niels. *Det danske Missionsselskabs Historie,* København, 1935, Vol. I.

Cardinall, Allan W. *A Bibliography of the Gold Coast. Issued as a companion volume to the Census Report of 1931,* Accra [1932].

Christensen, Balthasar M. "Correspondents-Efterretninger fra Christiansborg, fra Kysten af Guinea," *Valkyrien,* I (1831), 272-274.

––––––– "Breve fra og om Guinea," *Valkyrien,* II (1831), 262-278; III (1831), 56-63.

––––––– "Nekrolog over H. C. Lind," *Dagen,* No. 278-279 (1833).

––––––– "Nogle Bemærkinger om fremmede Kolonier paa Vestkysten af Afrika," *Valkyrien,* I (1832), 258-278.

––––––– "Om Colonien Princes-Island," *Valkyrien,* II (1832), 46-50.

––––––– "Om slavehandel," *Valkyrien,* I (1832), 251-258.

Christensen, Carl F. A. *Den danske Botaniks Historie,* København, 1924, Vol. I.

Claridge, William W. *A History of the Gold Coast and Ashanti,* London, 1915, 2 vols.

Collegial-Tidende for Danmark, København, 1820.

"Convention between Her Majesty and the King of Denmark, for the Cession of the Danish Possessions on the Coast of Africa to Great Britain," *Parliamentary Papers, Accounts and Papers,* LVII (1851), 1-6.

"Correspondence relative to the Purchase by Great Britain of the Danish Possessions on the Coast of Africa—1849-1850," *British & Foreign State Papers,* XXXVIII (1849-1850), 61-98.

Coyet, P. I. "En kort Relation om Swenska Africanske Compagniets inrättande ock förlop indtil år 1663," *Historiska Märkwärdigheter,* Stockholm, I (1768), 22-26.

Crooks, J. J. *Records Relating to the Gold Coast Settlements 1750-1874,* Dublin, 1923.

Cruickshank, Brodie. *Eighteen Years on the Gold Coast of Africa,* London, 1853, 2 vols.

Dagen, Newspaper, København, 1833 and 1834.

Dahlgren, Erik W. *Louis de Geer, 1587-1652.* Uppsala, 1923, Vol. II.

Daily News, London, 1850.

Danske Tractater efter 1800. I. Politiske Tractater, I, 1800-1863, København, 1877.

Dapper, Olifert. *Umbständliche und eigentliche Beschreibung von Africa,* Amsterdam, 1670.

Davidsen, J. *Fra det gamle Kongens Kjøbenhavn,* København, 1881, Vol. II.

Detlefsen, D. "Die städtische Entwicklung Glückstadts unter König Christian IV," *Zeitschrift der Gesellschaft für Schleswig-Holsteinische Geschichte,* Kiel, XXXVI (1906), 191-256.

Doorman, I. F. "Die Niederländisch-West Indische Kompagnie an der Gold-Küste," *Tijdschrift voor Indische Taal-, Landen Volkenkunde,* Batavia, XL (1898), 389-496.

Eannes de Azurara, Gomez. *Chronica do descobrimento e conquista de Guiné,* Visconde da Carreira, ed., Paris, 1841. English translation by Charles R. Beazley and Edgar Prestage, *The Chronical of the Discovery and Conquest of Guinea,* London, printed for the Hakluyt Society, 1896-1899.

Eberstein, Louis F. *Beschreibung der Kriegsthaten des General-Feldmarschalls Ernst Albrecht von Eberstein 1605-1676*, Berlin, 1891.

Ellis, Alfred B. *A History of the Gold Coast of West Africa*, London, 1893.

"Fonden ad usus publicos," *Udgivet af Rigsarkivet*, København, I (1897).

"Fonden ad usus publicos," *Udgivet af Rigsarkivet*, ved Henny Glarbo, København, III (1947).

Forsberg, A. C. *Røst fra Kysten Guinea eller Beretning om den i Aaret 1822 dertil sendte ekspedition under Major von Richelieu, som daværende Gouverneur*, København, 1827.

Friis, C. H. *Andreas Riis*, København, 1932.

Gigas, Emil L. *Grev Bernardino de Rebolledo, spansk Gesandt i Kjøbenhavn 1648-1659*, København, 1883.

———— "En theologisk Professors diplomatiske Mission," *Historisk Tidsskrift*, Kjøbenhavn, 8 rk., I (1907), 185-253.

The Golden Coast, or a Description of Guinney . . . Together with a relation of such persons, as got wonderful estates by their trade thither, London, 1665.

Granlund, Victor. "En svensk koloni i Afrika eller Svenska-Afrikanske Kompagniets Historia," *Historisk Bibliotek*, utgifvet af Carl Silferstolpe, Stockholm, VI (1879), 285-420.

Gröben, Otto F. von der. *Güineische Reise-Beschreibung*, Murjerwerder, 1694.

Grove, Gerhard L. "Nogle Oplysninger om Tordenskjölds første Langfart," *Personalhistorisk Tidsskrift*, Kjøbenhavn-Christiania, 3 rk., IV (1895), 151-164.

———— "Om Søren Schielderup, guvernør paa Guineakysten," *Personalhistorisk Tidsskrift*, København-Christiania, 3 rk., IV (1895), 292-311.

Grundelig Underrättelse om the rättmätige Skääl, Göteborg, 1656.

Hakluyt, Richard. *The Principal navigations, voiages, traffiques and discoveries of the English nation*, London, 1599, Vol. II, part 2.

Hannonis Carthageniensium Ducis Navigatio, Conrad Gesner, trans., Zürich, 1559.

Hammer, R. "Fra Orlogsbriggen 'Ørnen's' Togt til Marokko, de danske Kolonier paa Guineakysten og til Vestindien i 1845-1846," *Tidsskrift for Søvæsen*, København, XXXI (1922), 281-331.

———— *Kaptajn lejtnant O. C. Hammer*, København, 1928.

Hansard, London, 3rd. Series, CXIII (July 19, 1850), 37-69.

Hay, John D. *Ashanti and the Gold Coast and what we know of it, a sketch*, London, 1874.

Hemmersam, Michael. *West-Indianische Reisebeschreibung, 1639-1645*, Nürnberg, 1663.

Herodotus. Bks. II, IV.

Holberg, Ludvig. *Dannemarks Riges Historie*, København, 1735, Vol. III.

Holberg Blandinger, København, 1939.

Holm, Edvard. *Danmarks-Norges Historie 1720-1814*, København, III (1897), V (1906), VI (1907).

Irminger, C. "Erindringer fra Kysten Guinea fra Togtet 1847," *Fra alle Lande*, København, VII (1868), 353-370.

———— "Slavehandelen paa Guinea," *Dansk Maanedsskrift*, København, I (1859), 261-272.

Isert, Paul E. *Reise nach Guinea und den Caribäischen Inseln in Columbien in Briefen an seine Freunde beschrieben,* København, 1788. Several other editions. One recent edited version, Ingeborg Raunkiær, ed., *Laegen Paul Iserts Breve fra Dansk Guinea 1783-87,* København, 1917.

Jacobson, Nils. *Svenska öden vid Delaware 1638-1831,* Stockholm, 1938.

Jesu Biergprädiken oversat i det Accraiske Sprog, med nogle tillæg af Luthers lille Cathecismus, Forord af Fr. Münter (n.p., n.d.).

Jonge, J. K. J. de. *De oorsprong van Neerland's Bezittingen op de Kust van Guinea,* s'Gravenhagen, 1871.

Kalkar, C. H. *Den evangeliske Missions Historie,* København, 1857.

Kan, C. M. *Nederland en de Kust van Guinea,* Utrecht, 1871.

Klagh-Vervolgh von den Deenschen Koningk en dessels Ministers aen de Heeren Staten over de pretense volentie door de Nederlantsche West-Indische op de Deensche Africaensche Compagnie gepleectet, Naer de Coppe, 1662.

Det kongelige Danske Westindiske og Guineiske Compagnies Participanters vedtagene Convention, Reglement og Foreening indgaaet og sluttet den 26 Sept. 1733, København (n.d.).

Koppel, Henrik. "En 'advokat de la cour du Roy de Dannemarck' i Danton-processen," *Personalhistorisk Tidsskrift,* København, 9 rk., IV (1932), 242-252.

Labat, Jean B. *Voyage du Chevalier des Marchais en Guinée, Isles voisines et à Cayenne fait en 1725, 1726 & 1727,* Paris, 1730, Vol. I.

La Roncière, Charles G. M. B. de. *La découverte de l'Afrique au Moyen Âge, cartographes et explorateurs,* Le Caire, 1925, Vol. II.

Larsen, Kay. *De danske i Guinea,* København, 1918.

Laursen, Laurs. *Danmark-Norges Traktater, 1523-1750,* København, IV (1917), V (1920), VI (1923).

Ligtenberg, G. N. "Willem Usselinx," *Utrechtsche bijdragen voor letterkunde en geschiedenis,* Utrecht, IX (1914).

Lind, Henrik G. "Undersøgelser foretaget op ad Floden Volta i 1827 og 1828," *Archiv for Søvaesenet,* København, VI (1834), 1-16.

Lindbaek, J. *Aktstykker og Oplysninger til Statskollegiets Historie 1660-1676,* København, 1910, Vol. II.

Lioni Africano, Giouan. "Della descritione dell'Africa," in Giovanni B. Ramusio, *Primo volume & terza editione delle navigatione et viaggi racolto,* Venice, 1563. Later English editions, tr. and collected by John Pory, *A Geographical historie of Africa,* London, 1600; Hakluyt Society edition, London, 1896.

Lorenzen, C. N. "Sønderjyden Andreas Riis," *Nordisk Missions-Tidsskrift,* København, III (1892), 289-340.

Lucht, A. C. *Glückstadt oder Beiträge zur Geschichte dieser Stadt und des dreissigjährigen Krieges in unserm Lande,* Kiel, 1854.

[Madden, R. R.] "Report of H.M.'s Commissioners of Inquiry on the State of the British Settlements on the Gold Coast . . . ," *Parliamentary Papers, Reports from Committees,* XII (1842).

Malling, Ove. *Store og gode Handlinger af Danske, Norske og Holstenere,* København, 1777. English translation, *Great and Good Deeds of Danes, Norwegians and Holsteiners,* London, 1807.

[Marees, Pieter de] *Beschreyvinge van de Goudt-Kust Guinea,* Amsterdam, 1602.

New edition by S. P. l'Honoré Naber, *Werken uitgeven door de Linschoten-Vereenigung*, s'Gravenhagen, 1912.

Memorial door syn E. den deenschen Resident Heer Petrus Charisius inghegeven aen de Heern Staten generael der vereenichde nederlantsche Provincien, midtgaders de afghedronghen verantwoordinge ende rechtmatighe klaghten de daen aen Kon. Majesteyt von Danemarken, Amsterdam, 1664.

Meredith, Henry. *An Account of the Gold Coast of Africa*, London, 1812.

Minerva, København, XXVIII (1792), 43-46, 257-265, 311-318.

Monrad, Hans C. *Bidrag til en Skilding af Guinea-Kysten og dens Indbyggere*, København, 1822.

———— "Voyage de Monrad, de 1805 à 1809," C. A. Walckenaer, *Collection des relations de voyages en Afrique*, Paris, 1842, Vol. XII, 366-432.

Müller, Wilhelm J. *Die Africanische auf der Guineischen Gold-Cust gelegene Landschafft Fetu*, Hamburg, 1676.

A New General Collection of Voyages and Travels, London, printed for T. Astley, 1745, Vols. I & II.

Nielsen, Olaf A. *Kjøbenhavns Histoire og Beskrivelse*, Kjøbenhavn, IV (1885), V (1889).

Nissen, E. "Guldkysten," *Under Dannebrog* (1916).

"Nogle Bidrag til Kundskab om den danske Straekning paa Guinea Kysten," *Archiv for Statistik, Politik og Hussholdings-Videnskaber, Heftskrift*, Udgived af Professor Frederik Thaarup, København, III (1797-1798), 231-268.

Nørregård, Georg. "Englands Køb af de danske Besiddelser i Ostindien og Afrika 1845 og 1850," *Historisk Tidsskrift*, København, 10 rk., III (1936), 335-412.

———— "The English purchase of the Danish possessions in the East Indies and Africa 1845 and 1850," *Revue d'histoire des colonies*, Paris, XXI (1933).

———— "Forliset ved Nicaragua 1710," *Aarbog for Handels- og Søfartsmuseet paa Kronborg* (1948), 67-98.

————, ed. *Guvernør Edward Carstensens Indberetninger fra Guinea 1842-1850*, København, 1964.

———— "Slaveoprøret på 'Patientia' 1753," *Aarbog for Handels og Søfartsmuseet paa Kronborg* (1950), 23-44.

———— "Varer til Guinea," *Aarbog for Handels- og Søfartsmuseet paa Kronborg* (1951), 56-66.

Nyrop, Camillus. *Niels Lunde Reiersen, et mindeskrift*, København, 1896. "v. Rohr, Julius Philip Benjamin," Carl F. Bricka, ed., *Dansk biografisk Leksikon*, Kjøbenhavn, 1900, XIV, 158-159.

Nystrøm, Eiler, ed. *Luxdorphs Dagbøger*, Kjøbenhavn, 1915, Vol. I.

Octroy for det Kongelige Danske West-Indiske og Guineiske Compagnie den 5 Feb. 1734, København (n.d.).

"Papers respecting the Danish Possessions of the Coast of Africa," *Parliamentary Papers, Accounts and Papers*, XXXVIII (1850), 1-15.

Patent om it Guieneiske Compagnies Oprettelse i Københaffn, Dec. 10, 1672 (n.p., n.d.).

Petersen, Sophie. *Danmarks gamle Tropekolonier*, København, 1946.

[Pilat, B.] *La vie . . . du Sieur Michel de Ruyter*, Rouen, 1678.

Placat om Føringen ved det Kongelige Octroyerede Danske Westindiske og Guineiske Compagnie, Oct. *14, 1747* (n.p., n.d.).

Plan og Convention, hvorefter det Kongelige Octroyerede Danske Westindiske og Guineiske Compagnies Participanter til Compagniets Augmentation have subskriberet, Feb. 6, 1747, København, 1777.

Pufendorf, Samuel. *Thaten Carl Gustavs,* Nürnberg, 1697.

Purchas, Samuel. *Purchas his Pilgrimmage,* London, 1613, Vol. I, book 6.

[Purchas, Samuel] *Hakluytus posthumus,* London, 1625, Vol. II, book 7.

Rask, Johannes. *En kort og sandfærdig Rejse-Beskrivelse til og fra Guinea,* Trondhjem, 1754.

Rask, Rasmus. *Vejledning til Akra-sproget paa Kysten Guinea med et tillægøm Akvambuisk,* København, 1828.

Remonstrantie aen de Ho: Mo: Heeren de Staten Generael der Vereenighe Nederlanden, overgegeven den . . . Juny 1664 by de Heeren de Bewinthebberen van de geoctroyeerde Westindische Compagnie der Vereenighe Nederlanden, Amsterdam, 1664.

Reindorf, Carl C. *The History of the Gold Coast and Asante,* London, 1889.

Rode, F. C. *Kriegsgeschichte der Festung Glückstadt und der Niederelbe,* Glückstadt and Hamburg, 1940, Vol. I.

Roever, Nicolaas de. "Twee Concurrenten van de eerste West-Indische Compagnie," *Oudh-Holland,* Amsterdam, III (1889), 195-222.

Rømer, Ludvig F. *Die Handlung verschiedener Völker auf der Küste Guinea und in Westindien,* København, 1758.

―――― *Nachrichten von der Küste Guinea,* København and Leipzig, 1767.

―――― *Tilforladelig Efterretning om Nogotien paa Kysten Guinea,* København, 1750.

Rønning, Frederik. *Den grundtvigske slægt,* København, 1904.

Rosenkrantz, Niels. *Journal du Congrès de Vienne 1814-1815,* publié par G. Nørregård, København, 1953.

Schefer, Christian. *Instructions générales données de 1763 à 1870 aux gouverneurs . . . français en Afrique Occidentale,* Paris, 1927, Vol. II.

――――"La Monarchie de Juillet et L'expansion coloniale," *La Revue des deux mondes,* Paris, II (Sept. 1912), 152-184.

Schlegel, Johan F. W. *Statistisk Beskrivelse af de fornemste europæiske Stater,* København, 1793, Vol. I.

Schou, Jacob Henric: *Chronologisk Register over de Kongelige Forordninger og Aabne Breve* (reprint of laws 1670), 1 vol., Copenhagen, 1777, still continued by other editors under the title: *Love, Anordninger, etc.*

Chronologisk Register over de Kongelige Forordninger og Aabne Breve, som fra Aar 1670 til 1775 Aars Udgang ere udkomne, tilligmed et nøiagtigt Udtog af de endnu gieldende, for saavidt samme i Almindelighed angaae Undersaaterne i Danmark og Norge. Forsynet med et alphabetisk register ved Jacob Henric Schou . . . København. (The first volume of this reprint of Danish laws was published 1777 and contained laws from 1670, onward. This series is continued until now, since 1850, under the title: *Love og Anordninger.*)

Schovelin, Julius V. *Fra den danske Handels Empire,* København, Vol. I (1899), Vol. II (1900).

Schück, Richard. *Brandenburg-Preussens Kolonial-Politik unter dem Grossen Kurfürsten und seine Nachfolgern (1647-1721),* Leipzig, 1889, Vol. I.

Schurz, Heinrich. "III. Afrika," Hans Helmolt, *Weltgeschichte*, Leipzig and Wien, 1901, Vol. III, 389-574.

Sharp, N. A. Dyce. "Cape Coast," *Transactions of the Cape Coast Historical Society*, I (1936).

Sieveking, Heinrich. "Die Glückstadter Guineafahrt im 17. Jahrhundert. Ein Stück deutscher Kolonialgeschichte," *Vierteljahrschrift für Social- und Wirtschaftgeschichte*, Stuttgart, XXX (1937), 19-71.

Snelgrave, William. *A New Account of Guinea and the Slave-Trade*, London, 1754.

Statstidende, København (April 30, 1827).

Svedstrup, Alexander. *Erik Gudmand*, København, 1923-1925.

Sveistrup, Poul P. "Det almindelige Handelskompagni 1747-1774," *Meddelelser om Grönland*, København, CXXXI, No. 9 (1944), 1-110.

Thaarup, Frederik. *Udførlig Vejledning til det danske Monarkis Statistik*, København, 1819, Vol. VI.

Tilleman, Eric. *En liden enfoldig Beretning om det Landskab Guinea*, København, 1697.

To ortse der Zeevadrt verlichtende West-Indien, Brasilien, Guinea en Angola, Amsterdam, 1648.

Trentepohl, J. H., R. Chenon and F. Sannom. "Observationes meterologicae per annos 1829-1834 & 1838-1842 in Guinea factae," introductio, H. C. Ørsted, J. F. Schouw, P. Pedersen, *Collectanea meteorologica sub auspiciis Societatis Scientiarium Daniae, edita*, Hauniae, facs. III (1845).

Trier, H. "Om Gaarden Nr. 14 ved Stranden," *Historiske Meddelelse om København*, København, rk. 1, I (1907-1908), 167-185.

Trou-Hertighe Onderrichtinge aen alle hooft Participanten en Liefhebbers van de Ge-octroyeerde West-Indische Compagnie nopende her open stellen van den handel op de Cost van Africa, nementlycke St. Thome, Guinea, Angola, St. Paulo de Loando, 1643.

Verordnung wegen des West-Indischen und Guineischen Handels Mar. 3, 1680 [København, n.d.].

Videl, P. "Krabbe-Carisius, Hans," in Carl F. Bricka, ed. *Dansk biografisk Leksikon*, Kjøbenhavn, 1895, Vol. IX, 409-412.

Villault, Nicolas. *Relation des costes d'Afrique applées Guinee*, Paris, 1669.

Ward, Christopher. *New Sweden on the Delaware*, Philadelphia, 1938.

Ward, William E. F. *A History of the Gold Coast*, London, 1948.

—— *A Short History of the Gold Coast*, London, 1935.

Wätjen, Herman. "Zur Geschichte des Tauschhandels an der Goldküste um die Mitte des 17. Jahrhunderts, nach Holländische Quellen," *Forschungen und Versuche zur Geschichte des Mittelalters und der Neuzeit*, Festschrift Dietrich Schäfer, Jena, 1915, 527-563.

Westergaard, Waldemar C. *The Danish West Indies under Company Rule (1671-1754)*, New York, 1917.

Wilcke, Julius. *Daler, Mark og Kroner, 1481-1914*, København, 1931.

Yde, Jens. "Etnografisk Samlings Taletrommer," *Fra Nationalmuseets Arbejdsmark*, København (1945), 18-24.

Zinck, L. "Guldkysten og Ashanti," *Fra alle Lande*, København, I (1874), 101-126, 219-247, 279-304, 400-418, 464-486; II (1874), 142-176.

zur-Eich, Hans J. *Africanische Reiszbeschreibung in die Landschaft Fetu*, Zürich, 1677.

Manuscript Collections

RIGSARKIVET, KØBENHAVN

• *Egeskabene* (oak cupboards)

E   Vestindien og den afrikanske handel angående, skrivelse 19/6 1656.

• *Danske kancelli* (DKanc.)

B54   Sjællandske registre XVIII (1624-26), XIX (1632-37), XXIII (1653-55).
B56   Koncepter og Indlæg til Sjællandske registre.
B57   Sjællandske tegnelser XXXII (1651-53), XXXIII (1654-56).
B59   Koncepter og indlæg til Sjællandske tegnelser.
C6   Sjællandske registre XXIX (1673-75).
C8   Sjællandske tegnelser XXXVI (1660-63), XLIII (1681-82).
C24   Vestindiske sager 1671-99.
C25   Koncepter og indlæg til Vestindiske sager.
C61   Henlagte sager 1671-73.
D36   Vestindiske sager 1699-1771.
F71   Kommissionen til at likvidere det forrige oktrojerede guineiske kompagni [1777]-1788.

• *Tyske Kancelli, Indenrigske Afdeling* (TKIA)

A10   Patenten 1655-56, 1657, 1660-64, 1664-65, 1666-67, 1668-69.
A22   Inländische registratur 1648-49.
A24   Inländische 1659, 1661.
A27   Inländische registratur 1664.
A28   Inländische 1667, 1669, 1670.
A93   Indkomne breve.
A171 Diverse akter vedrørende det Ostindiske Kompagni og Guinea 1618-59.
B5   Patenten 1671-72, 1675-77, 1678-80, 1683-84, 1690.
B12   Inländische registratur 1671, 1676-77, 1679, 1686, 1693, Regeringskancelliet i Glückstadt 146; Akter vedrørende Glückstadt by of fæstning 1630-1703.

• *Tyske Kancelli, üdenrigske Afdeling* (TKUA)

Almindelige del: Kopibog Latina 1632-51.
Koncepter til latinske ekspeditioner, som ikke ses at være registrerede 1662-69.

• *Departementet for udenrigske anliggender* (DfuA)

Almindelige korrespondancesager:
Litr. G. Korrespondancesager vedrørende de på kysten af Guinea i året 1775 opkomne stridigheder mellem de danske og hollandske kolonier 1775-1809.
Litr. G. Korrespondancesager vedrørende de danske etablissementer på kysten af Guinea 1804-48.
Litr. S. Korrespondancesager vedrørende slavehandelens undertrykkelse 1792-1848.
Litr. Ø Korrespondancesager vedrørende Ostindien, II, Trankebar 1800-46.

• *Vestindisk-guineisk Rente-og Generaltoldkammer* (V-gRtk.)

Kongelige resolutioner [vedkommende Vestindien og Guinea 1754-58, 1759-60, 1760-63, 1764-68, 1769-71.
Kongelige vestindiske [og guineiske] resolutioner 1771-73, 1773-75, 1776, 1777.

Brevjournal for europæiske og vestindiske samt guineiske breve 1754-60.

Journal over de fra Guinea indkomne breve 1759-68.

Indokmne europæiske og vestindiske [samt guineiske] breve 1755-59, 1760-64, 1764-68.

Indkomne diverse (ujournaliserede) guineiske breve 1746-54, 1755-59.

Vestindisk [og guineisk] journal 1777, 1778, 1781, 1783, 1784, 1785, 1786, 1787, 1788, 1789, 1792, 1793, 1794.

Guineiske sager og aktstykker (ujournaliserede) 1765-1802 (med læg 1756-61).

Guineisk journal 1776-82, 1794-98, 1799-1804, 1804-20.

Dokumenter ved den guineiske journal.

Dokumenter vedkommende kommissionen for negerhandelens bedre indretning og ophævelse, samt efterretninger om negerhandelen og slaveriet i Vestindien 1783-1806.

Udkast og betænkinger angående negerhandelen 1787-89 (med bilag).

Kommissionens forslag og anmærkninger til negerloven med genparter af anordninger og publikationer vedkommende negervæsenet (29/6 1785).

Schimmelmannske papirer vedkommende kommissionerne betræffende Guinea og negerhandelen samt forskellige vestindiske papirer 1778-1809.

Gamle guineiske dokumenter, forterne vedrørende 1765-87.

Det kongelige guvernements arkiv: Brevbøger 1754, 1755, 1756, 1757, 1758.

• *Generaltoldkammer og Kommerce-Kollegiets arkiv* (Gtk.)

Guineisk resolutionsprotokol (Journal for reskripter, resolutioner m.m.) 1816-50.

Guineiske resolutioner 1816-20, 1825-26, 1827-28, 1829-31, 1832-39.

Guineiske journaler 1821-27, 1828-30, 1830-34, 1835-40, 1841-45, 1845-46, 1847-49, 1850.

Dokumenter ved den guineiske journal.

• *Finanskollegiets arkiv.* Diverse sager.

Schimmelmannske papirer vedkommende det østersøisk-guineiske handelskompagni og de danske besiddelser på Guinea-kysten 1765-1802.

Designation med bilag over det østersøisk-guineiske handelsselskabs ejendele i anledning af dets overdragelse til finanskollegiet 1787.

Trækningsprotokol ved finanskollegiet til indløsning af det østersøisk-guineiske handelskompagnis aktier og obligationer af 1787, 1788-1812.

Trækningsprotokol for det østersøisk-guineiske handelskompagnis obligationer 1811.

Regnskab over udbetalt kapital og rente af det østersøisk-guineiske handelsselskabs obligationer, 1797-1807.

• *Overskattedirektionens arkiv.*

Korrespondance A XXXVII (1777).

G. Ekstrakter over udskibede varer til St. Eustace, Guinea og Ostindien 1778-81.

G. Generalbalancer over den islandske, finmarkske, færøske, grønlandske og guineiske handel 1775-81.

G. Subskription på aktier i det østersøisk-guineiske handelsselskab og danske og tyske udkast til oktrojen for det østersøisk-guineiske handelsselskab 1781.

• *Marinens arkiv.*

Skibsjournaler 1680, nr. 4 ("Havmanden") og 1779-80 nr. 531a ("Holsten").

• *Vestindisk-guineisk Kompagnis arkiv.* 1671-1754. (V-gK)

1 Designationen "Guinea wie auch St. Thomas in Westindien."

5   Trykte oktrojer, konventioner, plakater m.m.
6   Participanternes resolutionsprotokol 1671-90.
9   Dokumenter til direktions- og generalforsamlingsprotokol 1725-33.
12-17   Direktionsprotokoller 1671-80, 1682-88, 1697-1734, 1734-40, 1741-52.
21   Kontrakt- og instruksbog 1682-84.
29   Instruktioner for kompagniets embedsmænd i Guinea 1680-1746.
41-45   Brevkopibøger 1671-76, 1676-82, 1682-88, 1688-90, 1690-1713.
77-78   Breve og dokumenter, indgåede og udgåede 1681-82.
120-24   Breve og dokumenter 1697-1705, 1705-16, 1717-32, 1732-45, 1746-54.
136   Dokumenter vedkommende afståelsen af de vestindiske øer og forterne på Guinea-kysten 1753-54.
181   Skibsjournal for "Havmanden" 1682-83 (forhen: Diverse 1671-1750).
189   Frederik P. Svane: En kort, sandfærdog og tydelig omstændelig general declaration og underretning om ti års begivenheder på fortet Christiansborg i Acra på kysten af Guinea i Afrika, 1 juni 1748.
190   Breve og dokumenter vedkommende det guld, som fra Guinea skal sendes til Amsterdam 1738-39.
Uordnede sager 1670-86 (denne pakke er senere opløst og indholdet henført til andre pakker).
Hjemsendt fra Guinea:
880   Sekretrådsprotokol fra Guinea 1723-30.
884   Dagjournaler ført på Christiansborg 1698-1700.
885   Diarie-bøger fra Christiansborg 1744-45, 1746-48.
886   Kopibøger fra Guinea 1703-05, 1723-24, 1725-26, 1727-29, 1729-31.
• Det Konglige Oktroyerede Danske Guineiske Kompagnis arkiv, 1764-78 (KODGKA)
I. Oktroj 1763, koncession 1765, konvention 1766, konfirmation 1766.
Direktionens resolutionsprotokol 1770-77.
Direktionens skrivelser til guvernøren 1765-71, 1772-78.
Indkomne breve 1770-73, 1773-74.
Brevbøger 1766, 1768, 1769, 1770, 1771, 1772, 1773, 1774, 1775.
Kystdokumenter 1767, 1769, 1770, 1771, 1772, 1773, 1774, 1775-78.

DET KONGELIGE BIBLIOTEK, KØBENHAVN
Ny kongelig samling 426 folio (Mariagers historiske efterretninger).

HANDELS- OG SØFARTSMUSEETS ARKIV, KRONBORG, EELSINGØR
J. V. Svedstrups tegninger.

J. G. MOLKTES PRIVATARKIV
C5b Papirer vedkommende det kongelige oktrojerede danske guineiske kompagni 1765-77.

NIELS ROSENKRANTZ' PRIVATARKIV
XIV   Journal du Congres de Vienne 1814-15.

JACOB WULFF BEHRENS PRIVATARKIV
Breve fra W. J. Wulff 1837-42.

PRIVATELY OWNED MANUSCRIPTS IN DENMARK
C. Th. Jørgensen and wife: Letters. Property of Lauritz Jørgensen, Fredensborg.
Personalhistoriske meddelelser om slægten Svanekiær. Property of Edv. E. Th. Svanekiær.

J. V. Svedstrups dagbog. Property of Alexander Svedstrup.
Th. Winther: Fra Guinea. Property of Poul H. Winther.

PUBLIC RECORD OFFICE, LONDON

F.O. 84/142, /158, 474.
F.O. 94/112.
F.O. 211/32, /33, /37, /38.
C.O. 94/112.
C.O. 96/2, /3, /11, /13, /14, /15, /17, /18, /19, /20.
C.O. 267/112, /131, /136, /144, /150, /162, /177.
C.O. 401/1.
C.O. 402/3.

BRITISH MUSEUM, LONDON

Additamenta 28.788. John Barbot: Voyage de Guiné . . . 1678-79.

Appendix

Abbreviations and Translations

akter, aktstykker: documents.

aktier: shares.

alm. korr.s., almindelige korrespondancesager: general correspondence (part of the Danish Foreign Office Archives where parcels are arranged alphabetically by contents).

betr., betræffende: concerning.

bilag: enclosure.

brevbog: letter copybook (containing copies of letters sent).

br. & dok., breve og dokumenter: letters and documents.

C.O.: The Colonial Office Archive in the Public Record Office, London.

DfuA., departementet for udenrigske anliggender: Danish Foreign Office.

designation: list of documents.

diarri-bog: diary.

DKanc., Danske Kancelli: Danish Chancellery (combining the functions of Home Office and ministries of Justice, Church and Education).

direktion: board of directors.

div., diverse: miscellanea.

dok., dokumenter: documents.

Finanskoll., Finanskollegiet: The Finance Collegium (the Danish Finance Ministry).

F.O.: The Foreign Office Archives in the Public Record Office, London.

forordning: decree, ordinance.

G.: Guinea (nearly always refers to the Danish Gold Coast specifically).

guin., guineisk: guinean.

general-balance: general accounts.

g.j., Guineisk Journal: Guinea Journal (letter copybooks containing extracts of letters received by the Guinean Office of the General Customs Department and Commerce Collegium, Copenhagen).

Gtk., Generaltoldkammer og Kommerce-Kollegium: General Customs Office and Commerce Collegium (corresponding to today's Ministry of Trade and to the Customs Department of the Ministry of Finance).

guin. sager og aktstykker: Guinea documents.

handels-direktion: Trade Office.

hollandsk: Dutch.

indk., indkommen: received.

indløsning af aktier og obligationer: repurchase of shares and bonds.

K.B., Kancelliets Brevbøger: letterbooks of the Danish Chancellery (published by the Royal Archives, Copenhagen).

kgl., kongelig: royal.

KODGKA., kgl. octr. da. guin. komp., det Kongelige. Oktroyerede Danske Guineiske Kompagni: the Royal Chartered Danish Guinea Company.

kgl. octr. da. w.i. guin. komp., det Kongelige Octroyerede Danske West Indiske og Guineiske Kompagni: the Royal Chartered Danish West India and Guinea Company.

kommission: committee.

komp., kompagni: company.

koncept: draft.

kopibog: letter copybook.

korr., korrespondance: correspondence.

korr.s., korrespondancesager: correspondence.

kystdokumenter: documents from the (Guinea) coast letter copybook.

Marinen: the Royal Danish Admiralty and Navy.

ny kgl. saml., ny kongelig samling: New Royal Collection (part of the manuscripts held by the Royal Library, Copenhagen).

obligationer: bonds.

octroi, octroy: charter.

Ostindien: the East Indies.

Overskattedirektionen: the Danish Tax Office, Copenhagen.

participanter: participants, shareholders.

plakat: proclamation.

P.R.O.: the Public Record Office, London.

prot., protokol: register.

rds., rigsdaler: rixdollars.

regnskab: accounts.

resol., resolution: assent, order.

R.G.G.A.: Royal Guinea Government Archives (in the Royal Archives, Copenhagen).

Rigsarkiv: the Danish Royal Archives, Copenhagen.

Riksarkiv: the Swedish Royal Archives, Stockholm.

Rtk., Rentekammer: the Danish Agricultural and Taxation Office.

sager: transactions.

sekretråd: secret council, or member of the secret council.

sjæll. reg., sjællandske registre: letter copybooks of the Danish Chancellery (vide K.B.).

sjæll. tegn., sjællandske tegnelser: letter copybooks of the Danish Chancellery (vide K.B.).

skibsjournal: ship journal.

skr., skrivelse: letter.

tidsskrift: review, periodical.

TKIA, Tyske Kancelli, Indenrigske Afdeling: the Home Office of the German Chancellery, Copenhagen, which governed the duchies of Holstein and Slesvig.

TKUA, Tyske Kancelli, Udenrigske Afdeling: the Foreign Department of the Danish government.

trækningsprotokol: register of bonds drawn.

udgåede: outgoing.

udskibede varer: goods exported.

udstedelse af obligationer: the issuance of bonds.

ujournaliseret: uncatalogued.

uordnede sager: miscellanea.

vedk., vedkommende: concerning.

vedr., vedrønende: concerning.

v.j.: vestindiske journal (in V-Gltk. Archiv.).

vestind; vestindisk; V., Vestindien: the West Indies (here often synonymous with the former Danish Virgin Islands).

V-gk., Vestindisk-guineisk Kompagni (1671-1754): the Danish West Indian & Guinea Company.

V-gRtk., Vestindisk-guineisk Rente-og Generaltoldkammer: the Danish West Indian and Guinea Finance and Customs Office.

ø.-g. komp., Østersøisk-guineisk Handelskompagni: the Danish Baltic-Guinea Trading Company.

Index